N SCALE
MODEL RAILROADING

ROBERT SCHLEICHER

Published by

700 E. State Street • Iola, WI 54990-0001
Telephone: 715/445-2214

Please, call or write us for our free catalog of antiques and collectibles publications. To place an
order or receive our free catalog, call 800-258-0929. For editorial comment and further information,
use our regular business telephone at (715) 445-2214

Library of Congress Catalog Number: 00-102690
ISBN: 0-87341-702-X

Printed in the United States of America

Table of Contents

Chapter 1

N Scale Model Railroading

Massive locomotives and mile-long trains are the visions many of us are recreating with our models. The thrill of standing beside the tracks while a trio of locomotives with 18,000 amassed horsepower and a hundred cars, each hauling a hundred tons, thunders by, is an experience you'll never forget—and one you can recreate in miniature. You can recreate that real railroad scene in the smallest possible space by using N scale models.

Selecting A Scale

There is an incredible array of model railroad equipment available in a variety of sizes. I believe that you can buy a model of just about any real railroad locomotive or car. And you can buy a ready-to-run miniature replica of almost any real locomotive that is just 5-inches long as well as a miniature replica of that same prototype locomotive that is 35-inches long. Modelers call these different size models of the same locomotives different "scales." The 5-inch long locomotive would be 1/160 the size of the real thing or, as modelers call it "N scale," while the 35-inch long model would be about 1/20 the size of the real thing or what modelers call "Large-scale" or "G scale." The two most common sizes of railroad models in America, however, are HO scale (1/87 the

size of the real thing) and O scale (approximately 1/48 scale, the size, more-or-less, used for Lionel, K-Line and MTH "toy" trains that run on three-rail track). N scale models, however, account for about one-fourth of the sales of scale model railroad equipment.

All of the models in this book are 1/160 scale or N scale. Krause Publications offers my books on HO scale, *The HO Scale Model Railroading Handbook*, on G scale, *The Large-Scale Model Railroading Handbook*, and on O scale for three-rail track, *Fun With Toy Trains*. Obviously, it takes an entire book to explain how to get the most from each scale, but I can simplify the choice for you. There are two considerations when choosing a scale for your model railroad. First, what exactly is the main appeal that real trains, and hence, models of the same, have for you? Second, how much space do you have available? Generally speaking, the money you will need to spend to fill a given space will be about the same, regardless of which scale you pick. Yes, the larger the scale, the more costly the locomotives and rolling stock, but you'll need fewer of the larger-scale models to fill a given space than with the smaller scale models. Conversely, N scale is about half the size of HO scale, but the prices of locomotives and cars are about two-thirds the cost of HO scale.

Figure 1-1. There's room for long trains and vast scenes in just 6-by-6 feet if you choose N scale for your model railroad equipment.

Figure 1-2. Compare the relative size of these G scale, O scale, HO scale, N scale and Z scale freight cars.

Figure 1-3. This is an example of how much model railroading you can fit into 4-by-6-1/2 feet with O scale three-rail equipment. The layout is the "project" layout in the Fun With Toy Trains *book.*

Figure 1-4. This is what a 6-by-8-foot layout can look like if built with HO scale models. This one is the "project" layout from the HO Model Railroading Handbook.

I would recommend either O scale or large-scale to anyone who wants to capture the sheer mass of real railroading. Get six inches away from a 1/48 or 1/20 scale locomotive and it is easy, indeed, to imagine it is real because you really can feel the earth move and the air being forced aside by the mass of the locomotive. The mass of the larger scale models is much more apparent than the simple numbers would indicate. Of course it has something to do with the fact that the O scale is four-times the nominal size of an N scale boxcar, but there's more to it than that. N scale models are not only shorter, they are lower and narrower than an O scale model because they are three-dimensional objects. So, even though the linear dimensions of an N scale model are only about one-fourth the size of an O scale model, you can fit 64 N scale boxcars in the cubic space of just one O scale boxcar! Your eyes perceive that mass to be 64-times larger than N scale.

I would recommend N scale to anyone whose vision of railroading is long trains snaking through broad curves and stretching out to the horizon. If it's the hundred cars, rather than the hundred tons each car carries, that appeals to you, then N scale is the choice. One of the reasons why HO scale is popular is that it is a reasonable compromise between being able to see and feel the mass (possible, if you get within less than six inches of the locomotive) and having the space for long trains (also possible, but you need at least a 15-by-15-foot space).

N scale models are the smallest practical scale available. There are some model railroad products produced in 1/220 or "Z scale" by Marklin and Micro-Trains, but the selection is limited to just a few locomotives, a passenger train and an assortment of freight cars. There is a wider choice of model locomotives, passenger cars, freight cars, track, buildings, and accessories in N scale than in O scale or large scale. There are about four-times more locomotives, cars and accessories available in HO scale than are available in N scale. There's enough available in N scale, however, for you to be able to create the railroad of your dreams. In fact, the choice of locomotives and rolling stock in N scale is great enough so you can even select a specific era for your layout like 1955 (Figure 1-5) or 1995 (Figure 1-6), with cars and locomotives appropriate to both your favorite prototype railroad and specific eras.

A Direct Comparison of O, HO and N Scale Railroads

Take a close look at the photographs in this chapter that compare O, HO and N scale layouts, all built in about the same 6-by-8-foot space. The locomotives and cars virtually overwhelm any trackwork or scenery on the three-rail O scale layout (Figure 1-3). The rolling hills and distant industrial structures serve as a far more realistic background to the trains on the N scale layout (Figures 1-5 and 1-6). Similarly, the trains on the O scale layout are short, virtually caricatures of real railroad trains, even though the individual cars and locomotives are realistic enough. On the N scale layout, the trains are nearly the length of the prototypes and the individual cars and locomotives are as detailed as their O scale counterparts. The HO scale layout (Figure 1-4) is a compromise between the two extremes, the trains dominate the scene more than on the N scale layout, but there's still room for reasonably large industries and hills. The HO scale trains, however, are also much shorter than the prototypes but, interestingly, the HO locomotives and rolling stock are probably the most realistic of the three scales, with far more free-standing details.

Figure 1-5. Compare this 6-by-6-foot N scale layout with the O and HO scale layouts in Figures 1-3 and 1-4. There's room for longer trains and more scenery with N scale. The equipment in this scene is typical of that used on the real Union Pacific Railroad in 1952.

Figure 1-6. This is the same 6-by-6-foot Union Pacific "project" layout shown in Figures 1-1 and 1-5 and in most chapters of this book. The equipment, however, is that which you would likely see on the real Union Pacific in 1995.

Figure 1-7. The Belmont Shores Model Railroad Club is one of the oldest and largest in the country. The line recreates the scenery and operations along the California coast. Here, a set of Kato PA1, PB1 and PA1 diesels leads a string of Con-Cor passenger cars on the club layout.

Why Choose N Scale?

If you consider yourself to be rather awkward with your hands (be honest, here, only you know the answer), then three-rail O scale is your best choice for a model railroad. Large-scale is about as easy, but it takes a lot of space. There is some excellent ready-to-run track with built-in-ballast in HO scale and a large choice of ready-to-run models. Therefore, it is possible to build an HO scale layout with little manual dexterity. Most dealers, in fact, can suggest someone that will build any kit or even a complete railroad, if you lack that skill.

Frankly, N scale is the most difficult of the popular scales because it requires much more precision in everything from lining up track sections to adjusting couplers. In fact, if you have yet to build a model railroad, I would suggest you consider a "test" layout in three-rail O scale or HO scale just to see if you have the skill and patience to begin to achieve your goals. Nobody has made a thorough survey, but my own experience suggests that there are probably three-times as many abandoned N scale layout projects, than HO, O or Large-scale layout projects that have not been completed, because their builders gave up in frustration.

There are "easier" ways to build an N scale layout, including buying all the locomotives, cars and structures already assembled, opting for Kato Uni-Track, replacing all plastic wheels with metal wheels, and using Digital Command Control (DCC), that I'll describe in later chapters. Even with that knowledge, however, the larger the scale, the easier it is to build a model railroad and, of more importance, the easier it is to keep it running.

How Much Space Do I Need?

Three-rail O scale and Large-scale model railroad track is designed to be rugged enough to operate on the floor. In fact, most large-scale track is rugged enough to be used outdoors. Some of the HO scale track with built-in ballast, like Bachmann E-Z Track, Life-Like Power-Loc track, and Kato Uni-Track is supposed to be rugged enough to be used on the floor. There is, however, no N scale track that I consider rugged enough to be used on the floor. Yes, I understand that many model railroaders in Japan operate their layouts on the floor, using Kato's Uni-Track or the similar, but somewhat more difficult to find, Tomix track by Tomy, but those setups are usually only operated for a single evening or weekend and extreme care is given to having a pristine clean and perfectly level floor. If you are going to build an N scale model railroad, plan on building it on some type of tabletop. If necessary, the tabletop can be laid on the floor or it can be supported on legs. The important thing is to understand that no N scale track is going to retain its alignment closely enough for reliable operation on the floor.

Avoiding Mistakes With Your N Scale Layout

It would seem logical that you could squeeze an N scale (1/160 scale) layout into a space about half the length and width of an HO scale (1/87 scale) layout—if you learn just one thing from reading this book, learn that trying to do that is the one major mistake you can make by choosing N scale. Yes, you can take an HO scale track plan and recreate it in about half the space (actually about 60% of the space) with N scale track and equipment, but it's not going to look as realistic as the HO scale layout and it will not operate as well without a lot more care and maintenance.

It is possible to build a very satisfying HO scale layout in a space as small as 4-by-8 feet. There's a project layout for that size space (plus a 2-by-4-foot "wing") in the *HO Model Railroading Handbook*. Since N scale is roughly half the size of HO scale, you should be able to build a similar layout in N scale in just 2-by-4 feet. You certainly can, but you will miss the major advantage of N scale; the ability to capture the realism of long trains and wide open spaces. You can see dozens of examples of 2-by-4-foot N scale layouts in the books of plans published by Atlas for use with their sectional track. The plans in this book, however, are all for 3-by-6-1/2 feet or larger spaces because that's the minimum size I would recommend for an N scale layout. There are some ways to build test layouts and portions of modular layouts in just 2-by-4 feet, and you'll see them in later chapters.

To me, an N scale train looks far too toy-like when negotiating the 11-inch (maximum size) radius curves that you can squeeze on a two-foot width. There's simply less realism with an N scale train negotiating an 11-inch radius curve, to my eyes, than an HO train negotiating its equivalent 22-inch radius curve. It has something to do with the much smaller three-dimensional mass of the N scale models. You can improve the realism of any model railroad—regardless of the size of the layout, particularly, an N scale layout—if the layout is built on legs or other supports tall enough so the trains are near your eye level. The models look more massive and, hence, more like the prototypes when you are looking at them from the same angle that you generally view the prototype.

I would recommend that you consider 3-by-6-1/2 feet or 4-by-6 feet to be the absolute minimum spaces for an N scale layout. The photographs of the project layout for the *HO Model Railroading Handbook* (Figure 1-4) show how much layout you can get on a 4-by-8-foot tabletop (plus a 1-by-2-foot extension wing) with HO scale models, and the O scale project layout for the *Fun With Toy Trains* book (Figure 1-3) illustrates how much "railroad" you can get in a 4-by-6-1/2-foot space with O scale models. You certainly can build an HO scale layout that looks like the "Union Pacific" 6-by-6-foot N scale layout in this book (Figures 1-5 and 1-6), but it will require at least 11-by-11 feet for the HO scale version. If you want that same layout in O scale, it will require about 20-by-20 feet, or about the space of a two-car garage. Conversely, imagine the empire you could build in N scale if you have that 20-by-20-foot space. If you really must limit your space to 2-by-4 feet, consider building one of the NTRAK modules described in Chapters 2 and 3. The NTRAK layouts allow you to operate your N scale trains in a 20-by-20-foot (or even 200-by-200-foot) space.

A Brief History of N Scale

Model railroading, as a hobby, dates back to the early 1900s, but most models were converted toy trains. Cast-metal locomotive kits and wood and cardboard freight and passenger car kits became common in the forties and fifties. Model railroading took a giant leap in popularity in the sixties, when plastic molding became a viable means of mass producing inexpensive models. Model railroaders have dreamed of a

scale smaller than HO or 1/87 scale since the forties. A cast-metal New York Central 4-6-4 Hudson steam locomotive and some passenger cars to 1/160 scale were available in limited numbers in Sweden during the fifties. They were called HOO and sold under the Micro-Trains label. The first large commercial manufacturer of small scale equipment was Lone Star in England who offered models of British prototype trains in a scale of 2mm equals a foot, or 1/152 scale, which was called OOO scale. The cast-metal Lone Star models were sold as both cast-metal toys and operating electric railroads under the trade name Treble-O, a mnemonic for the OOO scale. The term OOO came from the scale being about half of the most common British scale of 00 (4mm equals a foot or 1/72 scale) which, in turn, was approximately half of the British O scale of 7mm to the foot, which is 1/43 scale—American O scale, however, is 1/48 the size of the prototype. If you're still following all of this, you can guess where HO scale came from: it was exactly half of the British 7mm O scale of the 1930s or 3.5mm equals a foot and, therefore, was called HO scale, which works out to 1/87 the size of the prototype.

N scale, as we know it now, was first produced by Arnold-Rapido in Germany during the early sixties to 2mm scale with a 9-millimeter track gauge. It became known as N scale for the simple reason that 9mm started with the letter N. Trix began making N scale trains about this same time in Germany. Soon, both Arnold-Rapido and Trix responded to the requests from their American importers and began making cars and locomotives patterned after American prototypes. In the mid-sixties, two of the largest hobby manufacturers in America, Revell and Aurora, were both repackaging German N scale sets for the American market. Revell repackaged Arnold-Rapido sets and Aurora repackaged Trix sets and called theirs "Postage Stamp Trains." The marketing and distribution of these products greatly expanded the market for N scale model railroad products.

In the late sixties, the molds from the forties-era Swedish Micro-Trains firm were purchased by Keith and Dale Edwards who jointly owned Kadee (who had pioneered operating magnetic knuckle couples in HO scale). The Edwards brothers divided Kadee into two companies in the late seventies and the now-popular Micro-Trains company was formed to continue to produce true 1/160-scale freight cars, trucks and operating magnetic couples. The N scale hobby evolved through the seventies, and Bachmann began selling trains, first repacked Roco models from Austria and, later, trains made in China by Kader exclusively for Bachmann. Con-Cor commissioned Kato, in Japan, to expand their line of Japanese-prototype N scale trains to include American prototypes and imported Rivarossi N scale models from Italy. Atlas imported both diesels and rolling stock from Roco in Austria in the seventies and began producing N scale track and turnouts in America. By the early eighties, nearly all the American hobby manufacturers and importers were producing or importing N scale trains and N scale had grown to about one-fourth the total market for model railroad products.

Z Scale Trains

Z scale model railroad products are actually smaller than N scale. Z scale was pioneered by Marklin, in Germany, in 1972. Marklin now produces American-prototype diesels, freight and passenger cars as well as track. Z scale is 1/220 scale.

Micro-Trains, in America, also produces a Z scale locomotive as well as finely-detailed freight cars and they custom-make some Z scale steam locomotives on Marklin chassis. The limited choice of locomotives and rolling stock, and the grossly oversize couplers, have limited the popularity of Z scale. It is only about 80-percent the size of N scale, so the amount of extra model railroading you can fit in a given space is not as striking as the comparison of railroad-versus-space between HO and N scale. Less than one-percent of American modelers choose Z scale.

Is N Scale Too Small To Build?

There is no question that it takes more care to assemble an N scale kit or, for that matter, to paint and apply decals to an N scale model than to an HO scale model. In fact, I would strongly recommend that you purchase a magnifying glass or glasses or use a jeweler's eye tool like the Opti-Visor, when assembling an N scale kit or applying decals to an N scale model. Any misalignment error you make on an N scale model will be twice as great (perhaps eight times as great, if the error is three-dimensional) as a similar amount of error on an HO scale model and, yes, it does show. Greater magnification is a real help in getting parts and decals aligned properly. You can, however, build an N scale layout, even the project 6-by-6-foot layout shown in most chapters of this book, without ever painting or decaling a car or locomotive. Further, the structure kits selected for this layout feature nearly all self-aligning parts.

It is much easier to build a layout using two-inch thick slabs of blue Styrofoam insulation board, using the techniques in Chapter 6, for example than the traditional open-grid wood benchwork in Chapter 5. It's also easier to carve the scenery from the same blue Styrofoam than to use plaster, but the plaster-impregnated cloth is just about as simple—both techniques are shown in Chapter 10. Kato Uni-Track provides excellent self-aligning connections, built-in ballast, and hidden switch controls (as shown in Chapter 7) if you don't want to deal with the challenge of aligning sectional or flex track. And the Digital Command Control (DCC) train control systems in Chapter 8 allow you to run two, three, or dozens of trains at the same time without "block" wiring. It can be, then, as easy to build an N scale layout as an HO scale layout, if you choose product over price. I'll illustrate these specific products and techniques that can make it easier to build an N scale layout in the chapters that are appropriate for each segment of the hobby.

It's A Hobby, But Is It Fun?

It would seem strange to ask if you are having fun during your leisure time hours. Strange, because each of us has our own definition of fun. When you look at some of the N scale model railroads in this book you will wonder how anyone could possibly have fun creating such an intricate and precise miniature. If that's your question, you should have another kind of fun with model railroading. I would guess that at least half of all model railroaders are really just toy train watchers. They like to watch the trains roll by or snake through those ess curves. Those model railroaders imagine that the train is rolling through their favorite scene in the real world. I do it myself with three-rail O scale trains running around the legs of a coffee table before disappearing behind the Christmas tree—to my eyes, that train is working its way up Sherman Hill, Wyo-

ming—I don't even notice the coffee table legs or the Christmas tree. To make model railroad watching less of a stretch on your imagination, build tables to raise the trains from the floor, then surround the trains with reasonably realistic scenery and buildings, to make it easier to envision that the train is running through "somewhere" in the real world. Train watching is probably the purest form of "fun" model railroading has to offer. For some model railroaders, however, "fun" is the pleasure derived from creating very realistic scenes, even if it takes more time to research the locomotives, cars, structures and scenery than it does to build them.

There seem to be two types of model railroaders, those who want to play with miniature trains and historians who are using models to recreate specific scenes from the recent or distant past. There are, of course, those who want to do both of these things with their model railroads. I have two model railroads: an O scale three-rail three-train setup I string around the Christmas tree and over half the living room floor during the Christmas holidays, and 2-by-8 feet of an HO scale modular layout (similar to the NTRAK modular layouts in Chapters 2 and 3) that will, someday, be an exact replica of a portion of southeastern Wyoming on the Colorado & Southern division of the Burlington as it was on July 24, 1958. Like most model railroaders modeling specific times and places, I've spent far, far more time researching the prototype for the Colorado & Southern layout than I have spent building it.

Only about ten-percent of the HO scale modelers are recreating specific times and places—most HO scale model railroaders build generically realistic scenes that look like "somewhere" and they operate trains from whatever era appeals to them, through this terrain. If you are part of that majority, N scale is at least as good a choice as HO scale. If, however, you want to recreate history, you should research the available N scale products to determine if the locomotives and cars you need for the era of your historical recreation are available. Only about five percent of the N scale model railroaders are recreating a specific time and place, but their number is growing. The New River group of NTRAK modules, Bill and Wayne Reid, and the Utah-N-Modelers group's Union Pacific modules are some examples of historically-accurate N scale model railroads that appear in this book. "Fun," to the modeler recreating a specific time and place, lies in the research that results in the assurance that his or her recreation really does look exactly like that portion of the real world looked at the given period in history.

Keep It Simple

Today, anyone can practice the art of model railroading. The incredible array of inexpensive products and easy-to-learn techniques gives you a freedom to concentrate on whatever aspect of the hobby you find most pleasing. You can, for example, assemble just a few simple building kits and use ready-built structures in order to have more time to enjoy the actual operation of the set or for adding more details to the scenery. Please do not feel that you must master every technique in this book in order to build a model railroad. Most chapters include enough information so you can "specialize" in that area of the hobby that you find to be the most fun, with just a touch of the techniques from the other chapters applied to those other areas of your miniature railroad. The locomotives, rolling stock, trackwork, wiring, structures, and scenery on the 6-by-6-foot layout in Chapter 3 appear throughout the book, but they are included only as examples. The 6-by-6-foot layout itself is an example that combines all the elements of the hobby into a balanced whole. It should take an experienced model railroader at least two years to build a layout to the state of completion you see in the illustrations; most of us would want to take even more time for such a project. The goal of any model railroader is to have fun first and foremost, and the "old-timers" who have been enjoying the hobby for decades are those who are wise enough to know that their layouts will really never be finished.

Do's and Don'ts for New Model Railroaders

- Do not try to operate any N scale layout on the bare floor. If you do not have the space for a true table, then cover the floor with sheets of 4-by-8 plywood or extruded-poly-styrene Styrofoam insulation board and place the track on the boards.

- Do try different layout designs on your layout boards before deciding on the size and type of tabletop you want.

- Do try all three types of track: sectional track, flex track with cork ballast, and track with built-in ballast, particularly Kato's Uni-Track, Bachmann's E-Z Track, or Life-Like's Power-Loc track, before deciding which track to choose for your model railroad.

- Do tack the track lightly to the tabletop with a few spots of foam insulation cement so you can operate for a month to see if you want to change the track arrangement.

- Do solder each rail joint (except for an expansion joint every five running feet or so of track and any insulated rail joiners) for fewer derailments and less locomotive stalling—after you have decided on a final track plan.

- Do try to build a layout large enough so every train can have two powered locomotives, one to push or pull the other in case either locomotive stalls.

- Do try to imagine that the trains are real and operate them at the relatively slow speeds of real trains. This will increase both the realism of the scene and the illusion of having a larger layout.

- Don't try to operate trains—even passenger trains—as though they were racing cars.

- Do lay the track directly onto the tabletop or roadbed, with no up or down grades for the first layout you build.

- Don't use the over-and-under trestle sets on any model railroad. The steep uphill and downhill grades cause derailments, and the track is both unstable and toy-like.

- Do try the Digital Command Control (DCC) power packs for operating two or more trains before you decide on the seemingly less-expensive and older electrical "block" system described in Chapter 8.

- Do create your own world or copy a real one—duplicate reality or create a fantasy, or combine fantasy and reality. Remind yourself, if you must, that this is fun!

- Don't take model railroading so seriously that it becomes a task or chore with unreasonably high standards of fidelity to prototype or detail.

- Do keep that first layout simple, with no more than six turnouts and no reversing loops or other track configurations that can cause wiring complications.

- Don't try to build the more complex layouts on your first try. Consider that first layout a practice run and just enjoy trying anything.

- Do build any layout with strong enough benchwork or tables so you can add or delete entire sections of track without destroying the remainder of the layout.

- Don't ever consider a layout to be finished or so perfect that you are not willing to change it. Even the real railroads change track alignments and locations as their equipment and traffic patterns change.

Chapter 2
Room For Your Railroad

One of the gems of wisdom I've carried through my life is that I could have anything I wanted; I just couldn't have everything I wanted. There are compromises you must make, even in selecting a scale for your model railroad. The major advantage of N scale is that you can put more railroad and more open space in any given area than with the larger scales.

Now, you have to determine just how much space you can find for your layout. When you translate this to the actual space for a layout, you'll discover that a spare bedroom or guest room as small as 8-by-11 feet is large enough for a very nice N scale layout. There's an example of a layout for just that size space, in fact, in Chapter 3 (Figure 3-11). The 6-by-6-foot peninsula-style layout that's shown in most of the chapters (the plan is in Chapter 3—Figure 3-11) as well as any 4-by-8-foot or 5-by-9-foot layout you might build will also fit conveniently in a small bedroom.

In truth, a spare bedroom is probably the ideal location for an N scale layout because heat and humidity are easier to control than in a garage or basement. Trying to squeeze an HO scale layout into a space as small as a spare bedroom will demand a lot of compromises in curve radii and train length. With N scale, however, you can run 20-car freight trains or 12-car passenger trains in a room as small as 9-by-11-feet.

Traditionally, large model railroads have been built in basements in the Midwest and East and in garages in the Sunbelt. There are, however, far more model railroads that have been built on 4-by-8 plywood panels and about as many have been built on bookshelves than in basements or garages. Clever

model railroaders have even discovered how to make that "bookshelf" railroad a component of 20-by-20-foot or larger layouts using the NTRAK modular system.

N Scale in 2-by-4 Feet

It's the small size of N scale locomotives and rolling stock that usually convinces you that this is the scale you want for your model railroad. That same concept probably extends to space, so you imagine you can squeeze a "vast" N scale model railroad empire into whatever space you can find. The reality of N scale, however, is that 2-by-4 feet is the absolute minimum size for an enjoyable N scale layout. That's small enough to fit on top of a chest of drawers or even to be clamped to one shelf of a bookcase. The 2-by-4-foot layout is also light enough so it can be easily stored, if you must.

The layout in Figures 2-1 and 2-2 is typical of what you can accomplish in N scale in just 2-by-4 feet. Atlas offers dozens of plans for similar layouts in their series of track planning books. This particular layout was made from Atlas sectional track components in the seventies. Atlas no longer produces the right and left curved turnouts on the left, but you can substitute Atlas "Standard" 11-inch curved-route turnouts like those used everywhere else on the layout. It is not really important how all the stub-ended sidings are arranged, all that matters is that there is at least one double-ended siding so the locomotive can "run-around" the train (as described in Chapter 18) to move or "switch" cars in and out of the sidings.

Figure 2-1. This simple oval with a complex industrial switching yard inside was built on a single 2-by-4-foot slab of two-inch thick blue Styrofoam.

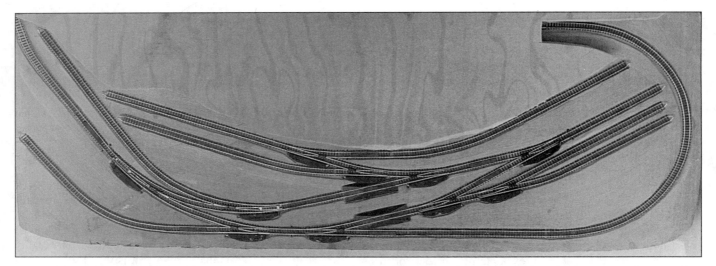

Figure 2-2. An aerial view of the 2-by-4-foot layout in Figure 2-1. There's also a photo of the layout in the color section. It's big enough to allow you to learn basic techniques for building an N scale layout.

If you want to sample some of the model railroad construction techniques, this is a good way to start. This 2-by-4-foot layout was built on a solid slab of 2-inch thick expanded polystyrene insulation board like the blue-colored Styrofoam product described in Chapter 6. The scenery was carved from the same Styrofoam material (as described in Chapter 10). The stream was made as shown in Chapter 11 and the surface textured with ground foam, flocking and real dirt as described in Chapter 12.

You will probably discover that there's just not enough construction or operating challenge in a 2-by-4-foot layout and the N scale locomotives and longer freight and passenger cars will never look as realistic lurching around those 9-3/4-inch or 11-inch radius curves as they would on the 19-inch radius curves used for the 3-by-6-foot and larger plans in Chapters 3 and 4. You certainly can spend countless hours superdetailing not only the cars and locomotives, but the buildings and scenery on a 2-by-4-foot layout. With a compli-

cated switching track plan like the one on the layout in Figure 2-2, you can spend several hours every week switching cars in and out of the sidings as described in Chapters 17 and 18. For many modelers, 2-by-4 feet is just large enough to make it an "attainable" model railroad.

How Anyone Can Find Room for a 20-by-40-foot Layout?

If long trains and lots of them are what you want to see in action on your model railroad, you will want a layout much, much, larger than 2-by-4 feet. There is a way to "build" a 20-by-40-foot model railroad by dividing it into 2-by-4-foot segments. In fact, thousands of N scale modelers have chosen this alternate method of building a layout. It's called "modular" model railroading. Briefly, you build one (or more) 2-by-4-foot portion of a larger railroad. Other modelers build modules that will interface with your module at each end, just as your

Figure 2-3. Ben Davis was one of the pioneers of NTRAK modular model railroading. He built this 2-by-4-foot NTRAK module to interface with other members of the Belmont Shores Model Railroad Club in San Pedro, California. The club is still active.

module interfaces with theirs. This end-to-end interface standard is the basis for NTRAK and its success all over the world. Chances are, you've seen a portable layout that was constructed from NTRAK modules in a shopping mall, particularly near the Christmas season.

The major appeal of N scale is the ability to operate trains that are nearly as long as the real railroads. That, of course, requires a fairly large layout—perhaps 20-by-40 feet or more—even in N scale. Conversely, N scale also has an appeal because it is supposed to require less space than the larger scales. Those conflicting desires led to the creation of the NTRAK modular model railroad system in the late sixties when Jim Fitzgerald and a group of other N scale model railroaders from San Diego, California and from the Belmont Shores Model Railroad Club in Long Beach, California established a set of standards for modular model railroad layouts to be assembled from interchangeable 2-by-4 foot modules with 4-by-4-foot corner modules. There's more information on the basic module construction and wiring standards in Chapter 5. Ben Davis built one of the first 2-by-4-foot NTRAK modules (Figure 2-3) with an oil refinery scratch built from mailing tubes and cardboard. Walthers now has an injection-molded plastic N scale kit for a refinery and oil tanks.

Layouts With NTRAK Modules

The NTRAK modules are designed with standard positions for the three tracks along the forward edge of the module. There are also standard dimensions for the aligning pins and wiring so any NTRAK module, built anywhere in the world, can be assembled or interfaced with an NTRAK module built anywhere else. Sometimes, modelers combine several 2-by-4-foot modules to create 8- to 30-foot long "multi-module sets" that interface with other NTRAK modules only at the extreme ends. There are examples of these multi-module sets in Chapter 4. The *NTRAK Manual* that includes full specifications on 2-by-4-foot standard modules as well as longer modules and both inside and outside corner modules is $1.50 from

NTRAK, 1150 Wine Country Place, Templeton, CA 93465. The *Ntrak Module "How-To" Book* is $10.00. An annual subscription to the *NTRAK Newsletter*, that lists the dozen national get togethers of NTRAK modules is $6.50 a year.

If you've seen an N scale portable model railroad at a shopping mall, it was probably made up of NTRAK modules. The layout in Figure 2-4 was part of the National Model Railroad Association's 1997 Annual Convention, and less than a fourth of the layout is visible in the photograph. The hex-sided center module is unusual and is used only to link hundreds of NTRAK modules together at such large gatherings.

You can use a single NTRAK module as a "layout" at home, supported by its own legs or resting on top of a chest of drawers or clamped to a shelf on a bookcase. There is room enough for a "runaround" siding and stub-ended industrial spurs like those on the 2-by-4-foot layout in Figure 2-2 as well as the three tracks along the edge of even a single 2-by-4-foot NTRAK layout module. You can, then, use a single NTRAK module as a "home" layout. Some modelers even include an NTRAK module in their permanent home layout. Bill and Wayne Reid have an NTRAK module that forms the town of Winchester. Their layout is shown in Chapter 3 and there's a photograph of Winchester in the color section.

NTRAK modules can also be used to build a layout small enough for operation at home. The layout in Figure 2-5 is designed to fit in a 12-by-12-foot or larger room and it includes two standard 2-by-4-foot NTRAK modules, a 2-by-6-foot module, four standard 4-by-4-foot corner modules and two reverse loop modules that are only needed for a home layout. If you build a layout like this, you can load one or more of those standard modules into your minivan or SUV and assemble them with others' modules at a local shopping mall. Some clubs operate in just this manner. One member, who has the space, may operate some of the "key" modules (like those four always-necessary corner modules) at his home, while other members may only have one or two modules. When the members get together every month or so at a shopping mall or gym,

Figure 2-4. NTRAK modular layouts are often seen in shopping malls. Really large NTRAK layouts, however, can be seen at the National Model Railroad Association national conventions, where hundreds of modules from all over the world are joined into layouts large enough to operate four or more 100-car trains at once.

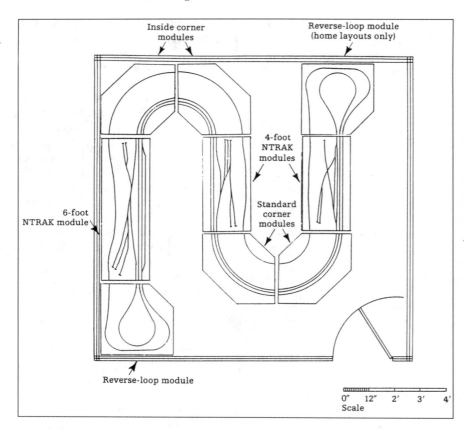

Figure 2-5. NTRAK modules can be combined to create a room-size layout. This walk-in layout occupies a 12-by-12-foot room but the modules can be taken to any NTRAK get-together to be joined with other NTRAK modules.

each member brings his or her modules and the layout is assembled for a day or two of operation. The modules from the layout in Figure 2-5, plus a dozen 2-by-4-foot modules would be enough to assemble an NTRAK modular layout that was 16-by-28 feet, long enough so you really can run hundred-car freight trains. If you want to create your own layout using NTRAK-size modules, you can photocopy this plan, cutout the individual modules and add or subtract and rearrange them to fit your space.

Stand-Up Layout Space

If you have an 8-1/2-by-9-foot space, you have room for the 6-by-6-foot layout (Figure 3-6) shown in Chapter 3. If this space is only available part of the time, you can store this layout in just 1-by-6 feet of floor space by standing it on edge. This layout is built on a four-inch thick base of Styrofoam extruded polystyrene insulation boards as shown in Chapter 6. If you glue-down all the buildings, people and loose scenery textures, the layout can easily be stood on edge as shown in

Figure 2-6. This is the 6-by-6-foot Union Pacific "project" layout that is featured in many of the chapters of this book. It weighs just 30 pounds.

Figure 2-7. The 6-by-6-foot Union Pacific layout can be stored on edge in a corner. The sawhorses fold into their top rails.

Figure 2-7. A pair of folding sawhorses serve as legs and the power pack is supported on a sheet metal shelf. The completely finished layout weighs just 30 pounds so it's easy enough to fit and store. The sawhorses fold into their own crossmembers and they can be stored beneath the "wing" of the 6-by-6-foot layout.

"Zero Space" Layouts

If the layout you desire is too large to store on a bookcase and too large to stand on end, consider suspending it from the ceiling. Rich Romando built his 7-by-11-foot layout from 1-by-4s and 1/2-inch plywood. He made some major modifications to the number N-16 plan in the Atlas' *Nine N Scale Railroads* book to more than double the size of the layout (Figure 2-13). Rich hired professional theatrical stage riggers to devise a cable and electric wench system so he could lift the layout (Figure 8-8) all the way up to the ceiling of his garage to leave room to park a car beneath it. The legs are on hinges with a single bolt and wingnut to hold them in position when the layout is resting on the floor. When the layout is raised to the ceiling, the same bolts and wingnuts keep the legs in their fold-up position (Figure 8-9).

Do not try to duplicate his efforts all by yourself. You don't want 400 pounds or more of layout dropping on your head. You can, however, use his ideas to give a professional an idea of what you want to accomplish and one way it was accomplished. The cables and wench are used ONLY to raise and lower the layout. Angle irons, bolted firmly to the ceiling and to the edges of the layout hold it in place when it is raised. When the layout is in operating position, the legs themselves support it and the cables are disconnected. Rick's crew chose a Dayton 1/2-ton number 5W474 wench (Figure 2-12) mounted firmly to the floor with bolts set in concrete. The wench was purchased from W. W. Granger, an industrial equipment dealer. There are other brands available. The four steel cables to the corners of the layout (leading to the left in Figure 2-11) are 1/8-inch diameter. They are connected to a 1/2-by-2-inch iron "mule" that allows each cable to be adjusted individual for an even lift. The strap iron mule is pulled, through an eye and a hook on a 3/16-inch steel cable (that leads to the right in Figure 2-11), by the wench. Clevis pins and eyebolts (visible in the far left in Figure 2-11) guide the cables to the strap iron mule.

Rich used Micro Engineering turnouts and flex track on cork roadbed. The turnouts are powered by Builders in Scale "Switchmaster" switch machines. The trains are controlled by a Digitrax "Chief" Digital Command Control DCC system. The scenery is made from plaster-soaked paper towels draped over wadded-up newspapers. The rocks are hand-carved plaster of Paris. He used Woodland Scenics ground foam for the earth textures and Woodland Scenics trees and bushes.

Figure 2-8. Rich Romando expanded the N-16 plan in the Atlas Nine N Scale Railroads book to increase the minimum radius of the curves from 9-3/4 inches to 19 inches. His revised version is 7-by-11 feet.

Figure 2-9. Rich Romando's 7-by-11-foot layout can be lifted to the ceiling of his garage by four cables. The cables are only used during the lifting process. The legs are hinged with a single bolt and wingnut to attach them in either their extended or folded positions. The legs are used to support the table—the cables are disconnected and used only for lifting and lowering the layout.

Figure 2-10. Rich Romando's layout is raised to the height of the ceiling. Four heavy cables are connected to hooks in the ceiling so just the cables, not the winch or the rigging, holds the layout to the ceiling. The box is the electric garage door opener.

Figure 2-11. The four 1/8-inch cables from Rich Romando's layout are routed over a series of pulleys and clevis guides to the ceiling of the garage where they are connected to the sheet steel "mule" which, in turn, is connected to the single 3/16-inch cable by a hook and eye. The single cable leads to the corner of the garage, over a pulley, and down to the electric winch on the floor.

Figure 2-12. The Dayton 1/2-ton electric winch is used to raise and lower Rich Romando's layout. The cable leads to a pulley in the ceiling and across the ceiling to the steel bar "mule" where it connects to the four cables that actually attach to the layout.

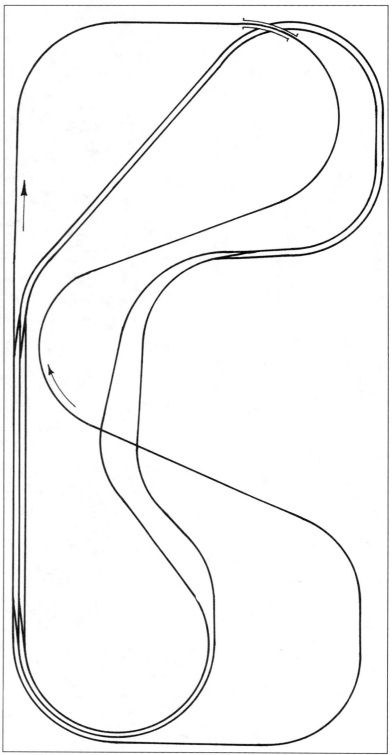

Figure 2-13. A schematic diagram of the trackage on Rich Romando's layout. There are additional photographs of the layout in the color section.

Chapter 3

Your Model Railroad

Study real railroads and you'll discover that they operate a wide variety of trains over an even wider variety of routes. Obviously, there are freight trains and there are passenger trains. What's not so obvious, until you actually examine the real railroads, is that there are a variety of different freight trains and a variety of different passenger trains. Similarly, these trains travel over a variety of different routes and, even on the same route, different trains have differing tasks. You can duplicate virtually anything a real railroad does on your N scale model railroad. Once again, however, you may have to choose specific trains and specific operations to match the space and time you have available.

There's more information on exactly how you can duplicate real railroad operations on your model railroad in Chapters 17 and 18. I would recommend that you read and understand the material in those chapters before you decide on a final plan for your model railroad. In fact, it would be wise to build a temporary model railroad so you can actually test run some of the track planning configurations and the techniques for simulating real railroad operations. You may find, for instance, that you really do not like yard switching operations so you will not want a large yard on your layout. Conversely, you may find you enjoy peddler freight operations using the "Waybill" system in Chapter 17, so you may want to include more industrial sidings. You may also discover you like complicated trackwork that simulates tight industrial areas or you may just want to forget all about switching of any kind and just watch trains run. The design, shape and size of the layout you build will be influenced by the type of operations you desire.

The "Union Pacific" Peddler Freight Layout

The 6-by-6-foot "Union Pacific" layout in Figures 3-4, 3-5 and 3-6 is a perfect semi-portable layout because you can easily store it on end as shown in Chapter 2 (Figure 2-7). If you can have a permanent space for the layout, however, try to negotiate for just a bit more. The 6-by-6-foot layout is virtually a duplicate of the 9-by-9-foot HO scale "Burlington Northern" layout that is featured in the *HO Scale Model Railroading Handbook*, but built in N scale in a 6-by-6-foot area. All of the operations that are possible on that "Burlington Northern" HO scale layout in 9-by-9 feet are possible on this "Union Pacific" N scale layout in just 6-by-6-feet.

Remember, that a 6-by-6-foot layout requires a minimum 8-1/2-by-9-foot space when you leave 2-1/2-foot access aisles along both sides and one end. If you can grab another 2 feet of space for your layout, you can build the "unwrapped" version of the 6-by-6-foot layout in 8-by-11feet as shown in Figure 3-13. All of the operations and the construction techniques shown in this book for the 6-by-6-foot layout can be applied to the 8-by-11-foot version.

Double The Size of Any Layout

The yard in the town of Alliance, on the 6-by-6-foot Union Pacific layout looks twice as large as it really is thanks to a mirror placed along one end of the layout. Alliance is located on a 1-by-2-foot "wing" that extends off the edge of the 4-by-6-foot main layout. The four tracks that end at the one-foot end of that 1-by-2-foot extension are designed to stop at the very edge of the table. There, a 1-by-1-foot mirror is positioned to reflect the image of the entire Alliance end of the layout (Figure 3-2). You can use a conventional mirror, but the reflecting surface is on the

Figure 3-1. The town of Alliance on the 6-by-6-foot Union Pacific layout includes a wye for reversing locomotives (left, center and a runaround tack or passing siding (the two tracks to the left of the station) and a half-dozen industries (left) for interesting switching operations.

Figure 3-2. Alliance is effectively twice the size of the modeled town, thanks to a mirror that is placed across one end. This is the view of Alliance looking from the opposite direction of Figure 3-1.

back of the mirror so there's a fairly obvious 1/8-inch gap between the edge of the table and the reflection. Mirror shops can provide what is called "face front" mirror with the reflecting surface on the front of the mirror. These mirrors eliminate the 1/8-inch gap in the reflection so it looks like the tracks really do continue on into the "reflected world." To mount the mirror on a layout made from blue Styrofoam insulation board like this one, first mount the mirror on a 16-inch high and 12-inch wide piece of 1/8-inch plywood. Mount the plywood-backed mirror to the table with some sturdy angle brackets screwed to a 6-by-12-inch piece of 1/8-inch plywood cemented to the bottom of this Styrofoam table. If you are using conventional plywood tabletop construction for the layout, the plywood-backed mirror can simply be mounted to the layout top with the angle brackets.

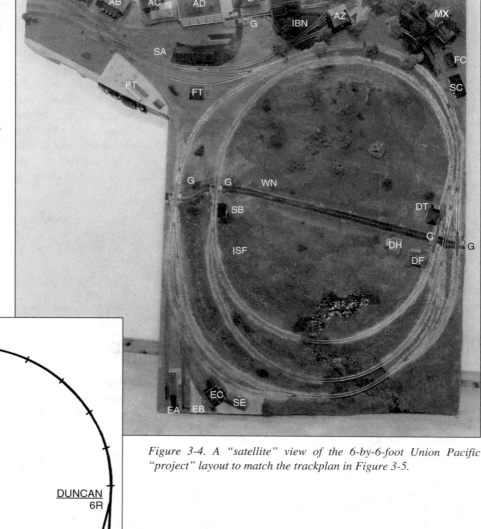

Figure 3-4. A "satellite" view of the 6-by-6-foot Union Pacific "project" layout to match the trackplan in Figure 3-5.

Figure 3-3. The first step in building the 6-by-6-foot Union Pacific layout can be a simple oval. Note, however, that two turnouts have been installed that will be connected to the remainder of the tracks shown in Figure 3-5.

Building Tabletop Layouts in Stages

The Union Pacific "empire" in Figures 3-4, 3-5 and 3-6 has just about everything you could want in a model railroad, from walk-around control to most of the industries served by the real railroads to scenery. The 6-by-6-foot Union Pacific layout has a complex track plan, with passing sidings at Alliance, Bedford, Duncan and Emmett. The sidings at Bedford and Duncan overlap near Duncan. The siding at Bedford can be used either as passing siding or as a switching track to hold cars coming on and off the layout from the Santa Fe Railway that connects with this Union Pacific layout at both Bedford and Duncan. What appear to be two passing sidings at Corning are really a pair of "Loads-In/Empties-Out" industrial sidings described in Chapter 17.

The final plan for the Union Pacific layout will provide just about every type of real railroad operation you could desire, including:

1. Trains can operate in the "orbiting" style so popular in Europe and in toy departments, with two trains circulating endlessly on the inner and outer ovals.

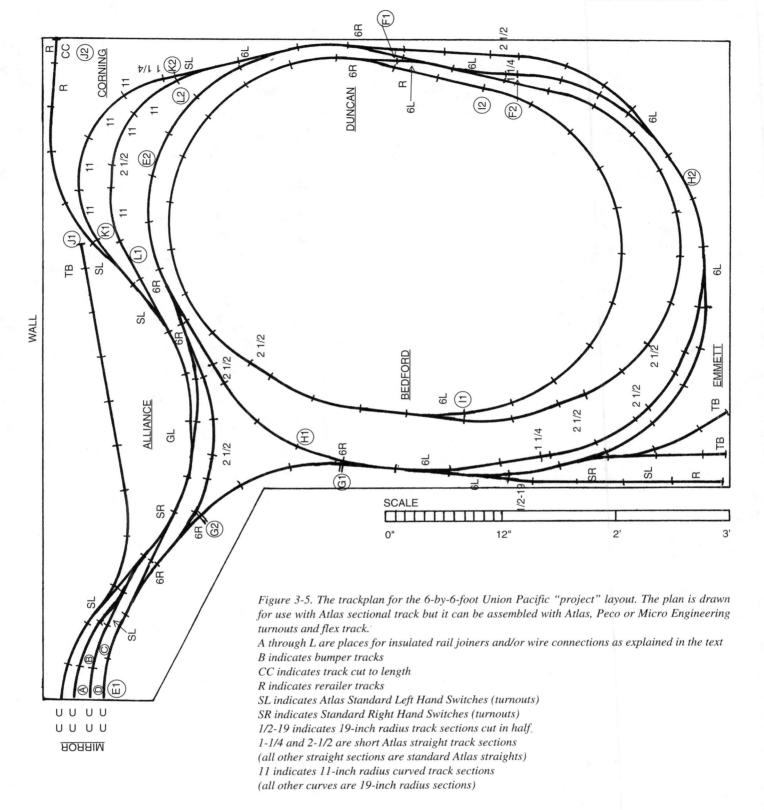

Figure 3-5. The trackplan for the 6-by-6-foot Union Pacific "project" layout. The plan is drawn for use with Atlas sectional track but it can be assembled with Atlas, Peco or Micro Engineering turnouts and flex track.

A through L are places for insulated rail joiners and/or wire connections as explained in the text

B indicates bumper tracks

CC indicates track cut to length

R indicates rerailer tracks

SL indicates Atlas Standard Left Hand Switches (turnouts)

SR indicates Standard Right Hand Switches (turnouts)

1/2-19 indicates 19-inch radius track sections cut in half

1-1/4 and 2-1/2 are short Atlas straight track sections

(all other straight sections are standard Atlas straights)

11 indicates 11-inch radius curved track sections

(all other curves are 19-inch radius sections)

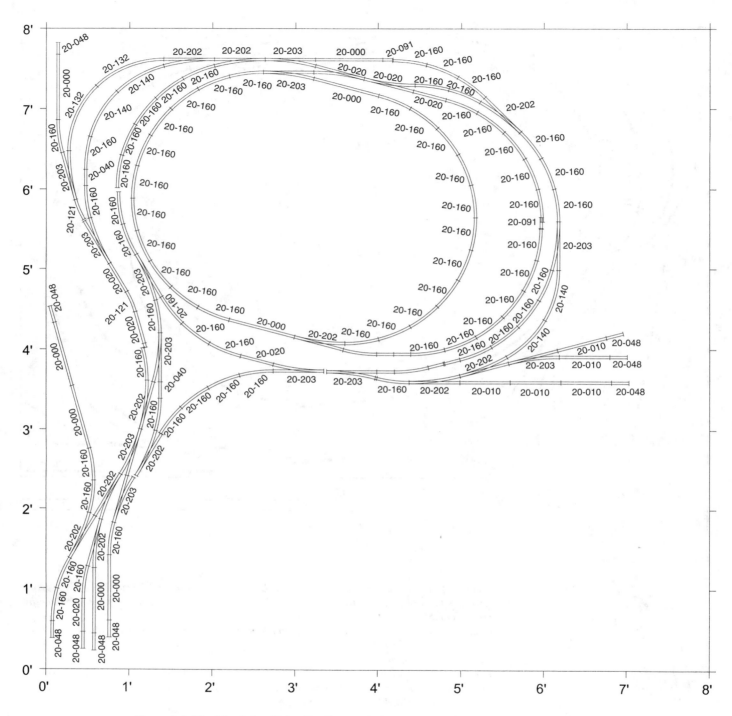

Figure 3-6. The 6-by-6-foot Union Pacific project layout can also be assembled from Kato Uni-Track with built-in ballast. If you are newcomer to the hobby, this track is an excellent choice because it is far easier to lay, it stays in alignment, the rail joints don't work loose, there is no need to apply loose ballast, and the electrical operations for the turnouts are located beneath the turnouts themselves. The numbers are Kato's part numbers for the individual track sections. —Courtesy Kato USA

2. A single train can operate over a rather lengthy route using both the inner and outer oval for a two-lap trip around the layout. That same route can add extra miles to any type of train operation you choose.

3. The railroad can be operated as a point-to-point line (as illustrated in Figure 3-12) to run trains from Alliance to the holding siding "F" called Points East, and back again.

4. The Union Pacific layout can be operated as an out-and-back plan from Alliance to Bedford to Emmett and back to Alliance using the left leg of the Alliance wye.

5. The "Loads-in/Empties-out" trackage can be used through the Corning Mine and the Consolidated Edison Co. on the Union Pacific for switching individual cars, as described in Chapter 17, or for complete unit trains.

6. The hidden siding "J" (the interchange with the Burlington Northern, marked "IBN" on the "satellite" photo Figure 3-4 and the Union Pacific) can be operated as a one-track fiddle yard, where cars and locomotives are hand-carried to and from the layout.

7. The switching operations of the Peddler Freight or Way Freight can be duplicated (with or without the system of waybills in Chapter 17), thanks to numerous industrial sidings.

8. The tracks near the Alliance Station can be used by a locomotive to perform the typical yard switching operations of making up and breaking down trains using tracks A, B, C, and D on Figure 3-5 (as an alternative operating scheme to 9, below). The train being made up can be parked on the siding in front of freight house (SA in Figure 3-4) to await its locomotive.

9. An alternate use for tracks A, B, C, and D on Figure 3-5 near the Alliance Station is to "hold" four locomotives. Each of those track segments must be insulated with a single plastic rail joiner and a wire connection with an on-off switch for each segment (or, all of the locomotives on the layout must be fitted with Digital Command Control (DCC) decoders as described in Chapter 8). Alliance can then be designated as a "crew change" point where fresh locomotives and crews are added to the train.

The Union Pacific, In Stages

The 6-by-6-foot Union Pacific layout was built and detailed for this book, using the techniques you see in chapters 6, 7, 8, 9, 10, 11 and 12. There are a large number of small sections of track because the operating concept of the layout was developed first, and the track was then fitted into that concept. The sectional track, however, does allow you to add just a little bit at a time as your funds allow.

The Union Pacific layout can begin as a simple oval with the "minimum-switch allotment" (Figure 3-3) that I recommend to allow a passing siding or runaround track and both a facing-point and a trailing-point stub-end siding. This layout is designed to operate from three of the outside edges. You can expand outward from the oval in Figure 3-3 in almost any direction, working toward the final plan in Figure 3-5.

What Kind of Track?

The plans in Figures 3-3, 3-5 and 3-13 are drawn using Atlas sectional track. All of the curves are 19-inch radius except for those marked "11" which are 11-inch radius track sections. The designation 1/2-19 indicates that a 19-inch radius curve must be cut in half. All of the straight track sections are standard Atlas straights, except for the shorter sections, which are marked either 1-1/4 or 2-1/2. The letter R indicates a standard-length straight rerailer track section. All of the turnouts are number 6 and are marked right or left as 6R and 6L except for a few leading to industrial sidings where Atlas "Standard Switches" (turnouts) are used and marked SR or SL for right and left. The letters TB indicate an end-of-track bumper section. The letters CC indicate track sections that must be cut to length to end at the edge of the table.

You can also use the plans in Figures 3-5 and 3-13 to build these layouts with Atlas, Peco or Micro Engineering flex track. If you use Micro Engineering turnouts, their number 6-size turnouts will have to be substituted for the Atlas Standard Switches (turnouts) and the resulting sidings will be slightly shorter. If you use Peco turnouts, substitute the Peco number 4 turnouts for the Atlas Standard Switches and use Peco number 6 turnouts in place of the Atlas number 6 turnouts.

The plan in Figure 3-6 is a recreation of the Union Pacific 6-by-6-foot layout adapted for use with Kato Uni-Track with built-in ballast. The part numbers are for the specific Kato track sections needed. The slight misalignments are the result of Kato's own computer drawing; the tracks will align properly if you follow the plan.

Operations on the Union Pacific Layout

The trackage on the 1-by-2-foot "wing" at Alliance (Figure 3-1) is designed so four of the tracks curve to end in a mirror that visually doubles the size of the town. The two middle tracks (designated A, B, C and D in Figure 3-5) can be used to store locomotives or they can be used as a small switching yard. The track nearest the edge of the table is the stub-end of the wye and is used to reverse locomotives or passenger cars as shown in Chapter 17. The fourth track, nearest the wall, is part of the industrial complex at Alliance; six different industries are located along this track (indicated as AA, AB, AC, AD, AE and AX in the "satellite" view Figure 3-4). The short length of the siding at "AE" allows only one car and locomotive which means that only a single car can be switched in or out of this track at a time. This is a design that sometimes happens in the real world and, on a model railroad, it makes switching cars far more complex and interesting. Further, with six different industries, several cars must be moved every time a car is spotted or removed from any one of the industries. There's plenty of conventional switching action available for working cars in and out of the coal dump for Consolidated Edison (tracks K and L in Figure 3-5) and the Burlington Northern interchange ("IBN" in Figure 3-4 and track J in Figure 3-5).

Electrical Wiring

The wiring needed for these track plans on these pages are indicted on Figure 3-5 with the circled letters A, B, C, D, E, F, G, H, I, J, K and L. These wire connections and electrical gaps in the rails are for two-train operation based on the principles of common-rail wiring and blocks for conventional power packs in Chapter 8. A single insulated rail joiner must be installed in the outside rail at both ends of A, B, C, and D and at E1 and E2, F1 and F2, H1 and H2, I1 and I2, J1 and J2, K1 and K2, and L1 and L2. A single wire, must also be connected somewhere within blocks A, B, C, D, E, F, H, I J, K and L and to an on-off switch to allow independent control of two or more trains and or to "park" trains within these electrically-isolated "blocks" as described in Chapter 8. The only wire connections for blocks to allow two-train operations are indicated by the circled letters E, F and H. The blocks marked I, J, K and L are tracks that will be used for "Loads-in/ Empties-out" switching operations (K and L) or for interchange with other railroads (I and J). The block marked G1 and G2 is part of the reversing wye and will need insulated rail joiners in both rails at both G1 and G2. Note that insulated rail joiners for the unwrapped around-the-wall version of this plan are simply marked "RL" for all the two reverse loop connections at "ISF" and "ISB" as well as the wye at Alliance. These reversing "blocks" (G1 and G2 and "RL") require separate wire connections to both rails with a reversing switch as described in Chapter 8.

If you decide to use Digital Command Control (DCC) to operate two or more trains, you will only need the insulated rail joiners and wire connections G1 and G2 (or at the locations marked "RL" in Figure 3-13) at the wye that allows locomotives to be reversed. It would be wise, however, to divide the layout into three electrically-isolated "blocks" E, F and H just to make it easier to trace any electrical short circuits that might occur. The on-off switches to these blocks can be left permanently in the on position unless you are trying to locate a short circuit, then, the blocks can be turned off one at a time to determine where the short is located.

Key to Industries and Features on the Union Pacific Layout (Figure 3-4)

AA   Quality Furniture Co.: lumber (flat cars and boxcars) IN; furniture (boxcars) OUT (reefers) IN; ice (reefers) OUT

AB   Coverall Paints: paint and chemicals (tank cars) IN; boxes and barrels OUT

AC   Jackson Meat Packing: meat (reefers) IN; empties OUT

AD   Harwood Furniture Co.: lumber and hardware (flat cars and boxcars) IN; furniture (boxcars) OUT

AE   Union Pacific Company Coal: coal (hoppers) IN; empties OUT

AX   Consolidated Edison (generating plant): empties (hoppers) IN; cinders OUT

AZ   Consolidated Edison (coal bunkers): coal (hoppers) IN; empties OUT

D   Dwelling or boarding house owned by railroad

DF   Duncan Feed & Fuel: seed and coal (boxcar and hopper) IN; grain (boxcar, hopper, and covered hopper) OUT

DH   Dwelling at Duncan

DT   Duncan Signal Tower for Atchison, Topeka & Santa Fe Railroad interchange

EA   Emmett Feed & Fuel: hardware and feed (boxcars) and Coal (hoppers) IN; Empties (boxcars and hoppers) OUT

EB   Emmett Petroleum Supply: fuel and oil (tank cars) IN; empties (tank cars) OUT

EC   Emmett Packing Co.: Meat (reefers) IN, empties (reefers) OUT

FC   Corning Freight House: lcl merchandise (boxcar) IN and OUT

FT   Alliance Freight House and Team Track: lcl merchandise (boxcar) IN and OUT

G   Grade crossing

IBN   Interchange track with Burlington Northern Railroad (every type of car IN and OUT, empty or loaded)

ISB   (on 8-by-11 layout Fig. 3-13) Interchange track with Seaboard System(every type of car IN and OUT, empty and loaded)

ISF   Interchange track with Atchison, Topeka & Santa Fe Railroad (every type of car IN and OUT,empty or loaded) I

MX   Corning Mining Co.: timber, tools, and empties (flat car, boxcar, and hopper) IN; coal and empties OUT

PT   Trailer Train terminal: lcl merchandise (trailers and containers on intermodal cars and on *flat cars) IN and OUT*

SA   Passenger station at Alliance

SB   Passenger station at Bedford (AT&SF interchange IN and OUT)

SC   Passenger station at Corning

SE   Passenger station at Emmett

W   Water tower (or a diesel fuel oil tank and refueling platform)

WW   Billboard

NOTE: The types of cars in parentheses, near the IN or OUT traffic pattern of each industry, are the types of cars the industry uses to carry the commodities it receives (IN) or ships (OUT).

Alliance to Emmett, "All Aboard!"

You can follow our trip by train from "Alliance" to "Emmett" over an imaginary branchline of the Union Pacific by looking at the illustrations in the color section. A satellite view of the layout is shown in Figure 3-4, a track plan is illustrated in Figures 3-5 and 3-6, and a schematic diagram of the route is shown in Figure 3-12. The three illustrations should provide more than enough reality to allow your imagination to see what real railroading in miniature is all about. Use the schematic diagram in conjunction with the track plan in Figure 3-5 or 3-6 (make a photocopy if you need to) and you will be able to see which direction our train must take at each turnout in order to travel over a two-loop layout as though it were stretched out like a string connecting towns imaginary miles apart. Our train will travel very briefly over the crossed lines on the schematic diagram twice in its journey over the "road"; with the exception of those few feet of track, our flanged wheels will pass over the same rails only once as we travel from Alliance to Emmett on the Union Pacific.

An Imaginary Journey

Imagine the town of Alliance as a place that might have a population of 30,000 people. It could be located in any state. Imagine it in southern Illinois if you wish, but it could be anywhere, with a simple change of railroad names and colors on the locomotives. Alliance is a center of small manufacturing plants and a massive power plant. It is also a collection point for towns from miles around to load and unload trailers from "piggyback" flat cars and other lcl (less than carload) freight at the "Alliance

Freight Station, its "team track," and the intermodal yard. Lumber, chemicals, paint, fuel, coal, and meat are just a few of the commodities that arrive in Alliance by rail. Dozens of carloads of coal are consumed each day by the Consolidated Edison plant. The cars are spotted at a coal-unloading bunker directly from the coalmine at Corning. About a carload a day of cinders is loaded at the Consolidated Edison's generating plant, the residue from all that consumed coal.

An endless string of coal-filled hopper cars are emptied at the electrical power-generating Alliance Company plant on the outside of the town. The Burlington Northern has a connection or interchange with the Union Pacific just far enough away (track "J" or "IBN") from town to keep the Burlington Northern from serving local industry. There is also a coaling dock and water tower (left over from the days of steam) at Alliance to service the locomotives used on the line. The few remaining steam locomotives receive their tender loads of coal by hand shoveling at the coal dock. For a more modern layout, the coal dock could be replaced by a sand-loading facility for the diesels and the water tower by a diesel fuel oil tank and refueling platform. There is also a wye at Alliance to turn locomotives, cabooses, or passenger cars.

"Points East"

Trains are scheduled out of Alliance as rapidly as the line can handle them (see Chapter 17 for Sequence-Timetable operations) for Bedford, Corning, Duncan, Emmett, and Points East. As our freight train leaves Alliance (Figure 3-7) headed for Emmett and Points East, the first stop will be the

Figure 3-7. "All Aboard, Alliance to Emmett!" as a trip over the 6-by-6-foot Union Pacific layout begins when we board our freight in front of the Alliance station. Our train travels through a curve in a deep cut.

Santa Fe Interchange at Bedford, so our train crosses through the turnouts from the outer oval to the inner oval, and rolls right past Duncan and its tiny grain elevator as though it didn't exist (Figure 3-8). There are two cars waiting to be picked up by a Santa Fe freight train waiting on our right for us to clear the joint main line (actually the layout's inner oval) between Bedford and Duncan (Figure 3-9). Our train will continue east through a long, deep cut through the hills and past the Duncan Feed & Fuel grain elevator for the second time, but this trip we cross over from the inner oval to the outer oval (Figure 3-10). The mine at Corning is always switched before dropping off or picking up any cars for Duncan. Our train has one empty hopper car for the Corning Mine and there are two empties waiting to be picked up by the next train. Emmett is our next stop. There's a passing siding at Emmett, so we can keep the mainline clear while we switch cars into the industrial spurs. Our "waybills" tell us

that the boxcar in our train is supposed to be dropped off at the Emmett Feed & Fuel (Figure 3-11). The series of train movements needed to perform those switching operations are illustrated, step by step, in Chapter 18. Finally, the locomotives can be turned to return to Alliance cab-first using the Alliance wye as though it were part of Emmett's trackage (and pretending Alliance itself does not exist). The route our train takes in this point-to-point sequence from Alliance to Emmett (and back to Alliance) is shown in the schematic diagram Figure 3-12. In reality, our train is just making two laps of what is essentially a double-track oval.

If you want to increase the running distance, make a second or third or fourth lap of the outer oval between Alliance and Bedford and another two to four laps of the inner oval between Bedford and Duncan. Or, find another three feet of layout space and build the around-the-wall layout in Figure 3-6 so you really do have some running distance between each of the towns.

Figure 3-8. Our train is routed over the crossover (from the outer oval to the inner oval) in front of the interlocking tower at Duncan (and pretending Duncan doesn't exist as we pass it).

Figure 3-9. Our freight squeals around a broad curve over a small river and heads for the two-story Bedford station.

Figure 3-10. Our train leaves Bedford and runs through another curve in a deep cut to emerge at Duncan. This time, we pass through the crossover (from the inner oval back to the outer oval) and pause to see if the car on the Santa Fe Interchange track ("ISF" in Figure 3-4) is ready to be picked up.

Figure 3-11. The boxcar in our train is assigned to the Emmett Packing Company, so our train stops to spot the car on that industrial siding. Here, we have the choice of (A) simply running the locomotives around the train using the double-ended passing siding at Emmett and heading back, with the diesels' long hood-first, to Alliance or (B) using the Alliance wye (and pretending it is actually part of Emmett) to turn the locomotive before coupling it back onto the train and heading, with the diesels' cabs-first, back to Alliance as shown in the schematic diagram Figure 3-12.

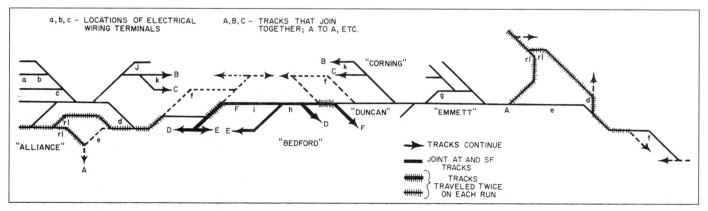

Figure 3-12. The trackage on the Union Pacific layout can be traveled as a point-to-point route that duplicates the actions of a real railroad. Note that the wye at Alliance appears at both the left and right ends of the run.

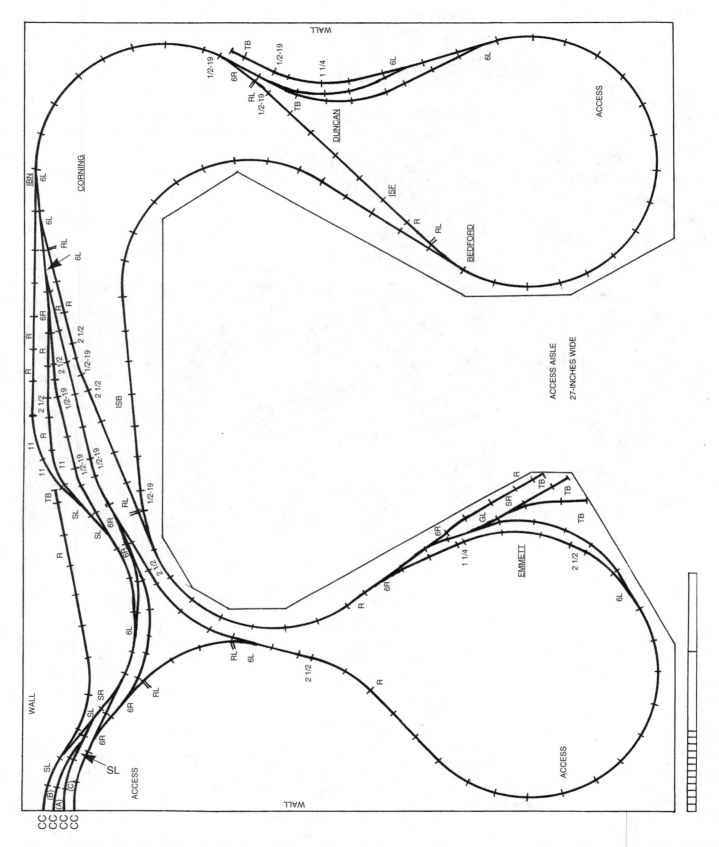

Figure 3-13. The 6-by-6-foot Union Pacific layout in Figure 3-5 can be "unwrapped" to create an around-the-wall layout in just 8-by-11-feet. The letters and numbers are the same as those in Figure 3-5, but the track "ISF" now serves as an optional reverse loop connection to reverse trains traveling clockwise around the layout so they will travel counterclockwise. Track "ISB" has been added to the plan as both an interchange track with the Seaboard System Railroad and to use as a reverse loop connection to reverse trains traveling counterclockwise around the layout so they can travel clockwise.

Meeting the Schedule

The series of "meets" with other trains, the switching operations with cars that carry imaginary loads and with the cars that really are loaded with coal, and the use of waybills to tell our train crew what cars are to be switched are just part of the real railroad action that has been condensed for model railroading. The work of meeting the deadlines of a real railroad timetable has been eliminated by simply scheduling trains as quickly and as often as you can operate them, and the work of making out paperwork for waybills and switch lists has been reduced to just handling some playing cards and plastic envelopes, which is discussed in Chapter 17. The "magic" ways to have loaded freight cars are described in the "Loads-in/Empties-out" section of Chapter 17. All these ideas will help to make even a simple oval with two sidings as much fun to operate as our Union Pacific 6-by-6-foot "branch-line empire."

The Railfan Layout Design

If, like most N scale model railroaders, one of your prime delights is watching trains run, you may want to consider an around-the-wall layout like Figure 3-13. You can walk through the 27-inch wide access aisle and either stand in the middle and watch the trains go by from a distance or get your eyes right up to the edge of the table and walk along beside your train as it travels around the layout. This layout, like just about any other in this book, will appear most realistic if it is built on legs long enough so the trains are with a few inches from your eyes to give eye-level viewing. If you must build it lower, consider buy-ing a roll-around chair so you can operate sitting down and still view the trains at eye level.

This layout is essentially the plan in Figure 3-5 unwrapped. The total length of the mainline on this layout is about 86 feet, compared to the total length of mainline on the 6-by-6-foot layout of just 56 feet. On this larger layout, however, there's a major advantage in that the three major towns of Alliance, Emmett and Duncan are separated from one another by long runs of single-track mainline. In fact, you can use the same industries and structures shown in the satellite view of the 6-by-6-foot version. All of the additional track, in fact, is single-track mainline, so operations on this layout will have far more of the feeling that the trains really are traveling somewhere when they move from one town to another. With the 6-by-6-foot version, it requires a fair stretch of imagination to ignore the fact that the trains pass the same town again and again.

The larger plan also provides another plus: with the 6-by-6 version, the wye is the only place where locomotives or cars can be turned to run in the opposite direction. On this 8-by-11-foot layout, the interchange tracks near Corning (marked ISB) and between Bedford and Duncan (marked ISF) are can be used both for interchange with outside railroads as described in Chapter 17 and as reverse loop connections. You can reverse an entire train traveling in either clockwise or counterclockwise direction on this layout by running it through one or the other of the cutoff tracks marked ISB and ISF. Note that there are additional sets of electrical gaps through both rails, marked "RL" on this layout, that must be cut and the tracks ISB and ISF (and the

Figure 3-14. Al Mack is modeling the Southern Pacific railroad's operations from Mojave to Bakersfield, California. This is his much-reduced recreation of the famous Tehachapi Loop.

Figure 3-15. Most of Al Mack's 14-by-18-foot Southern Pacific layout is visible. The Woodford loop is in the right foreground with the Bakersfield yard to the extreme left and Tehachapi Loop in the upper left.

Figure 3-16. Fontana Iron, on Al Mack's layout, is in the lower right, with the hill in the center of Tehachapi Loop in the upper center.

Figure 3-17. The Mojave yard, on Al Mack's layout. The Woodford loop is in the far upper center in this photo. All of the track on this layout is Kato Uni-Track.

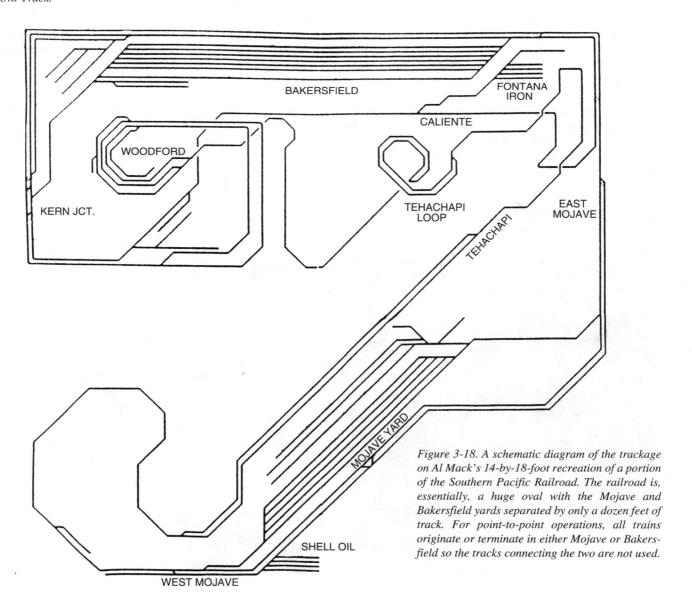

Figure 3-18. A schematic diagram of the trackage on Al Mack's 14-by-18-foot recreation of a portion of the Southern Pacific Railroad. The railroad is, essentially, a huge oval with the Mojave and Bakersfield yards separated by only a dozen feet of track. For point-to-point operations, all trains originate or terminate in either Mojave or Bakersfield so the tracks connecting the two are not used.

curved leg of the wye at Alliance) must be wired with an electrical polarity reversing switch as described in Chapter 8. You can also use the wye, as described in Chapter 18, to turn individual locomotives.

The 6-by-6-foot plan requires access along both sides and one end. The aisle with the 1-by-2-foot wing at Alliance takes some advantage of the wasted space of that side's 2-1/2-foot wide access aisle. With the 2-1/2-foot wide access aisles on one end and both sides, that nominal 4-by-6-foot layout actually requires a minimum of 8-1/2-by-9-feet of space. This around-the-wall plan will require a minimum 8-by-11-feet of space, which, in reality, is just two-more feet than the so-called 6-by-6-foot plan. You will need to provide 2-by-2-foot or larger access openings, as indicated by the words "Access" on the plan, if you cannot reach the end of the Alliance yard and the ends of the loops at Bedford and Emmett. If you can spare another two-feet of space for a 10-by-11-foot area, you can provide two-foot wide access aisles for the ends of the loops at Bedford and Alliance and only the access opening near Alliance will be necessary. This plan utilizes the towns of Alliance, Duncan and Emmett from the 6-by-6-foot plan in this chapter. Emmett, however, is a mirror image on this plan. The "Alliance to Emmett" operating sequence described earlier in this chapter would be virtually the same for this plan as it is for the 6-by-6-foot version.

The Yardmaster Mainline Layout

Al Mack has recreated the Southern Pacific's famous Tehachapi Loop along the railroad's route from Mojave to Bakersfield, California in 14-by-18 feet. The layout has a scale six miles of trackage, all of it constructed from Kato Uni-Track. The layout includes much reduced, but still massive, replicas of the SP's Bakersfield and Mojave yards. Many model railroaders would be satisfied with stub-ended yards, but Al worked out a layout plan that would allow each of the yards to have through sidings with turnouts on both ends like the real railroad. On operating nights a single yardmaster works the Bakersfield yard and another works the Mojave yard in addition to the engineers that operate the mainline and peddler freights and passenger trains. Al uses a schematic diagram (Figure 3-18) to help operators locate specific towns. He has adapted the prototype Southern Pacific timetables to his layout so he can run the actual trains the real railroad operates on their schedules.

If you like yard operations, you could build a 14-foot long oval with a through freight yard similar to either Mojave or Bakersfield along one side of the oval. During the operating session, Al uses both the Bakersfield and Mojave yards to make up and breakdown trains that terminate at those towns. Before the operating session begins, however, the yards are used to prepare the trains that will operate over the layout during that operating session. The concept of having trains ready to roll onto the layout in the sequence shown on the timetable is called "staging" and there's more information on that concept in Chapter 17. You can also make double use of any yards on your own layout, to serve as a place where a switch engine pushes and pulls the cars into trains during the operating session and a place to hand-carry cars and locomotives to make up the trains you will run during your next operating session.

A "Permanent" NTRAK Layout

The members of the Twin Cities Model Railroad Club in Vacaville, California have found an empty warehouse to use for their club layout. Since they did not own the building, this group decided that it was too great a gamble to build a permanent layout. Instead, they opted for a portable N scale layout that is made of NTRAK modules. They decided that they would create continuous scenes on their modules so the layout is, in effect, a portable layout that uses NTRAK standards with several modules forming a "multi-module set" to make it portable. The tracks that run across the joints of each of these multi-module sets are free to wander anywhere across the two-foot width. The tracks swing back into the NTRAK standard three-track alignment only at the extreme ends of these multi-module sets. The design allows a tremendous amount of latitude in layout design, while still allowing the sets of modules to be included in any NTRAK layout.

Figure 3-19. The Twin Cities Model Railroad NTRAK layout, in Vacaville, California, have assembled several multi-module sets that interchange with NTRAK modules at the extreme ends of each multi-module set. This is the "River" multi-module set that is also shown in the color section. Note that the diverging tracks continue on around the curved corner module to the lower right before sweeping back into NTRAK standard three-track alignment.

Figure 3-20. This is another view of the "Canyon" multi-module set in Figure 3-19, but from the opposite end. This set is made up from a 2-by-8-foot module (in the foreground) and a special module (in the distance) that is a 6-by-4-foot corner module. The three diverging tracks sweep back to the NTRAK standard three-track alignment just out of sight to the lower right.

The club's multi-module sets include just two of the standard 2-by-4-foot and two 2-by-8-foot NTRAK modules. The club decided to permanently join each of their four corner modules to one of the side modules so the "Canyon" set of modules (Figures 3-19 and 3-20 and there are photos in the color section) includes a one-piece 4-by-6-foot corner module, and a 2-by-8-foot module. The "Yard" multi-module set (Figure 3-21) is on a one-piece 4-by-8-foot module. The tracks at the extreme ends of the "Yard" module sweep back to the NTRAK standard three-track alignment, as do the tracks on the "Canyon" multi-module set. The "Yard" and "Canyon" multi-module sets are joined, for this particular layout, to make a 22-foot long side, but additional NTRAK standard 2-by-4-foot or longer modules could be inserted between the two to make the layout larger.

The "Green Mountain" multi-module set on the opposite side of the layout (Figure 3-22) is also 22-feet long and is also built on 4-by-6-feet and 4-by-8-feet one-piece corner modules and a single 2-by-8-foot module. There is no NTRAK three-track interface along the "Green Mountain" side of the layout, so its use is fixed at 22 feet. The remaining two sides of the layout are 12-feet long, joining the corners with a single conventional 2-by-4-foot NTRAK module on each side of the layout. Additional modules can be inserted to make the layout even larger or the 2-by-4-foot modules could be removed and the layout would be just 8-by-22 feet. There is space, then, on these sides of the layouts, for members who only have room at home for one or two 2-by-4-foot modules to add their modules to the layout. Since the scenery construction and colors are standardized for the entire layout, these individual modules will fit seamlessly into the overall appearance of the layout.

Jim and Josie Leeds designed and built the original layout and Kip Hartnett, Bob and Carolyn Taylor have finished the scenery and operate the layout. This group usually just sets up their modules with fellow members. If they attend a convention with other NTRAK modelers, they set their layout up as a separate area beside the main NTRAK layout. The advantage of NTRAK, to this club, is that they can enlarge or reduce the size of their layout without having to rebuild the entire layout. And, if a club member must leave the area, he or she can take their

Figure 3-21. This is the "Yard" multi-module set on the Twin Cities Model Railroad Club portable layout. This is designed using the NTRAK standard for 4-by-4-foot corner module and a 2-by-4-foot module but the two are built on a single 4-by-8-foot benchwork that interfaces with other NTRAK module at the extreme ends. In the right, center, the yard tracks converge into the NTRAK standard three-track alignment where they interface with the tracks from the "Canyon" multi-module set in Figures 3-19 and 3-20. The "Yard" and the "Canyon" multi-module sets make up one of the 22-foot sides of the layout.

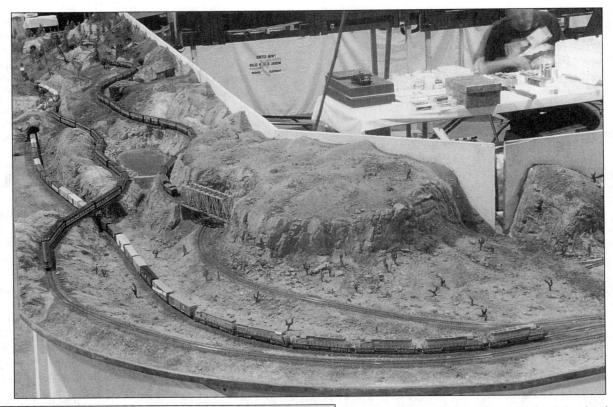

Figure 3-22. The 22-foot "Green Mountain" side of the Twin Cities Model Railroad Club layout that is opposite the "Canyon" and "Yard" side of the layout. The "Green Mountain" side is constructed from a 4-by-8-foot corner module, a 2-by-8-foot module and a 4-by-8-foot module similar to the other 22-foot side of the layout. However, the "Green Mountain" modules have no NTRAK interface along their length. Note that the three wandering tracks do not converge into the NTRAK standard three-track alignment until they are around the corner to the lower right. The three tracks travel a similar path at the other end of this multi-module set as they sweep to the right to align with standard NTRAK modules whose back walls or "skyboards" are visible along the upper edge of the photo.

Figure 3-23. Wayne and Bill Reid have recreated the atmosphere of the Cumberland Valley in Maryland on their 22-foot 8-inch-by-39-foot 6-inch N scale layout. The valley is used by both the Western Maryland and the Pennsylvania Railroads. Here, a pair of Pennsylvania Railroad Class H-9 2-8-0 Consolidations (brass models imported from Korea by Key Imports) cross Rush Run.

modules and operate them with other NTRAK clubs. They are recreating the Northeastern terrain from the Cascades to the Columbia River Basin. With standard scenery, the finished layout has far more overall realism than the random assortment of modules on a typical NTRAK layout. The New River club in Maryland and the Utah-N-Modelers have selected multi-module sets for their club layouts. Examples of their multi-module sets are in Chapter 4.

Creating a Real Railroad in 22-by-40 Feet

Wayne and Bill Reid have created one of the most realistic N scale layouts in the country. Their 22-by-40-foot layout was developed to provide some very complex operating patterns, each based on particular prototype railroads. The layout itself is a recreation of the Cumberland Valley near Hagerstown, Maryland. The specific town sites are imaginary, but they carry names familiar to railfans in the East. The scenery is modeled directly from the Cumberland Valley area. Their layout is credible because they have chosen secondary routes of the real railroads, which are far easier to portray than triple-track mainlines.

Two mainlines traverse the layout, one duplicating the trains and practices of the Western Maryland Railroad and the other the Pennsylvania Railroad. In addition, important connecting railroads are represented with the Reading Railroad's connections with both the Western Maryland and the Pennsylvania, and the Norfolk and Western Railroad's connection with the Pennsylvania Railroad. There are four separate staging yards, one each for the Pennsylvania and the Norfolk and Western and two Western Maryland yards that provide traffic to and from the extreme ends of the system. The concept of staging tracks is explained in Chapter 17. Briefly, it allows you to "feed" entire trains onto the layout in the timetable sequence you have developed, and the staging yard provides a place to accept trains that have traveled "off" the layout. The stub-ended staging yards are the places where trains are made up before the operating session begins.

Figure 3-24. A two-car peddler freight is headed to Greencastle on Wayne and Bill Reid's Cumberland Valley System.

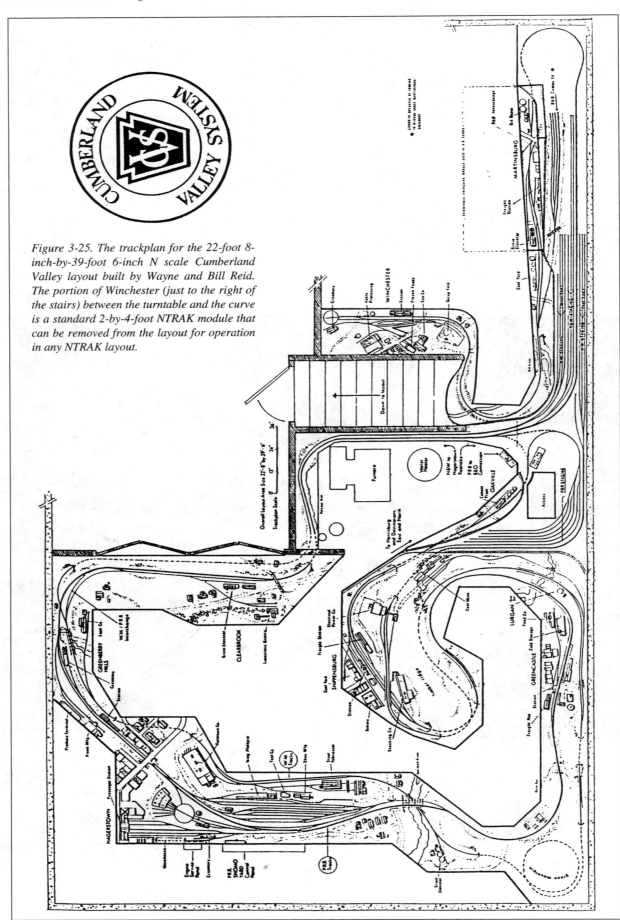

Figure 3-25. The trackplan for the 22-foot 8-inch-by-39-foot 6-inch N scale Cumberland Valley layout built by Wayne and Bill Reid. The portion of Winchester (just to the right of the stairs) between the turntable and the curve is a standard 2-by-4-foot NTRAK module that can be removed from the layout for operation in any NTRAK layout.

Chapter 4

Track Planning

The hobby of model railroading provides almost limitless freedom for expressing your own creativity. For starters, you are the only one you need to please with your model railroad. There are some physical limitations of space and how the track will fit in that space, but you are the only one that determines how that track will flow and how you will operate your trains.

The track plans in this chapter and in other chapters are not meant to be patterns you must follow, but as places to begin. Most of these plans are about as small as is physically possible, but you are free to add track to expand the plans in any direction or even to combine two or more of the plans. You can use some of the finished railroads in this chapter and in Chapters 2 and 3 as inspiration for your layout or create your own. Some model railroaders are perfectly content just to watch the same train run around and around an oval, perhaps adding or subtracting a car or two just to make it a bit more interesting. Many model railroaders prefer to watch two or more trains circulating automatically around the layout, without the need for any more attention than just watching the trains roll by. Other modelers want to duplicate every move that a real railroad makes to pick up a car at a shipping customer, switch it into a mainline train and deliver it to the receiving customer.

Point to Point Operations

I have selected the plans for this book so you can use them to operate trains in a manner that recreates the operations of the prototype railroads. The only difference you might notice between the track plans in this book and the layouts you might see in toy or department stores at Christmas time, is that these layouts seem to have more than their share of turnouts that lead to stub-end sidings. The locations of the other tracks and turnouts have been selected because they can be used to route trains over a track system that is like the real railroads. The purpose of a real railroad is to move goods from one place to another for their customers. In effect, to move a freight or passenger car and its contents from one point to another point. Each of these layouts is designed so that it can be used for point-to-point operations. The model trains that move over these tracks, like the real trains, will be bound for some distant town, rather than just running in circles. These miniatures will be running from one point to another; hence the term point-to-point. The layouts in this chapter may look like only double-track ovals and figure eights with a few extra switches and sidings. These layouts, however, have a purpose like the prototypes, thanks to careful track planning.

Figure 4-1. The "Loads-in/Empties-out" operations are described in Chapter 17. They require just two parallel passing sidings like those on the layouts in Figures 3-5, 3-6 and 3-13, and they can be added to almost any track plan. This is the mine end of the pair of industries on the 6-by-6-foot Union Pacific layout.

A Matter of Space

Two conflicting desires are present in most model railroaders' minds. Each of us wants to build our railroad as much like the real ones as possible—and to operate it that way. Each of us also wants to see trains run and run and run. It's okay to watch a switch engine or a peddler freight move cars in and out of sidings, but at least half the trains should still be running, or at least appear to be. You'll have to balance your list of priorities with the amount of space you have available. Most of the ready-to-run track sections and turnouts (switches) are inexpensive enough, so it will be space, rather than money, that will probably be the limiting factor. Remember, you can often select a rather complex track plan that can be started with just a simple oval or figure eight and extended with turnouts and track as quickly as your budget allows. If you happen to have the almost limitless space of an empty basement, a complete spare room, or a garage, you'll have to restrain yourself and build a smaller first-time layout before attempting to fill the larger space with benchwork, track, and scenery.

I suggest that you consider the following priorities before you create or select the track plan for your first layout.

1. Try to have at least four turnouts so you can include a passing siding as well as a "facing-point" and a "trailing-point" stub-end siding, such as those described in Chapter 18.

2. Do not feel you have to have enough length of storage tracks to hold every one of your cars and locomotives. Only 40 percent of the length of all the passing sidings and stub-end sidings should be "filled" with cars and locomotives. You need the "empty" factor in order to give the trains enough room to maneuver so they can switch. Keep any extra cars or locomotives on shelves beneath the layout.

3. Try to include at least one stub-end siding near the edge of the table. This can serve as a fiddle yard so that you can maintain a 40-percent "full" rate by hand-carrying cars and locomotives from storage shelves or drawers (rather than from storage tracks) to and from the layout. You may want to include a two, three, or four-track fiddle or staging yard (such as the ones on Bill and Wayne Reid's layout in Chapter 3, Figure 3-22) inside an existing or specially built cabinet. The extensive fiddle yard trackage will allow you to have complete trains that appear and disappear from the scene during operating sessions (as they leave and arrive at those hidden fiddle yard tracks). The contents of those trains can be fiddled by hand before each operating session in order to arrange whatever variety of freight or passenger trains you might want to schedule on the layout.

4. I recommend that you arrange the layout so that there will be at least one possible route that is an oval or a figure eight. This will allow continuous operation of the trains. Obviously, real railroads don't run around in circles; they have hundreds of miles of space.

5. You should arrange some of the sidings to allow point-to-point operation like the real railroads.

A Minimum Radius for Curves

I would strongly recommend you consider 19 inches as the minimum radius for your N scale layout. Ironically, this is about the same as the 18-inch minimum radius used in most HO scale train sets or the 16-inch minimum radius used in three-rail O scale train sets, but it allows N scale trains to both look and operate at their very best. The comparison of N, HO and O scale layouts in Chapter 1 will give you an idea of how much more realistic N scale looks when built in the same space as the minimum for an HO or three-rail O scale layout. All of the plans in this book utilize 19-inch radius curved track sections except for some industrial sidings. I would also recommend that you consider a number 6, the sharpest-radius turnout for your N scale layout. Again, all of the plans include number 6 turnouts except for industrial sidings and the "starter" plans (Figures 4-2, 4-3 and 4-4) in this chapter, which use Atlas "Standard Switches" (turnouts) which have a 19-inch radius curve.

The tight-radius 9-3/4-inch and 11-inch curves are not only far too sharp to look anything like the prototype curves, but they force the trains to lurch into the curves like trolleys or toy trains. Atlas publishes several track plan books and the majority of the layouts in those books use a single piece of 19-inch radius curved track leading into the 9-3/4 or 11-inch curves. The 19-inch radius curve, in these examples, serves as a "transition" or spiral easement to ease the trains into the tighter curves. If you can spare the space, however, why not use 19-inch radius for the entire curve?

The Figure-Eight Plan

The figure eight is one of the most interesting of all the possible model-railroad track plans because it gives the effect of many trains crossing at a single point. The effect is somewhat more credible and more realistic than watching a train work its way around and around an oval. If you follow the layout geometry design rule for any of these sectional track systems, you must add track to the opposite sides of the two curves of the figure eight to compensate for the extra length of the 30-degree crossing and the straight track sections leading in and out of the crossing. The Atlas track system is designed so this particular crossing matches the lengths of the curve track sections that are replaced. The advantage of the Atlas "Standard Switch" is that the curved route is an exact match for their 19-inch radius curved track sections, so you can replace a curve track with one of these turnouts and not effect the geometry or alignment of the layout. The turnouts in this plan, can, then, be located anywhere on the curves. You can also add additional turnouts. This particular plan requires a minimum of 40-by-92-inches.

The Double-Track Main Line

The track plan in Figure 4-2 shows how to make a double-track main line layout in a minimum 44-by-90-inch space. The inner oval on this plan includes a diagonal cutoff track that makes a reverse loop for turning whole trains. That inner oval is also the minimum size layout to include a reverse loop, 42-by-86-inches. The letters "RL" on the plan indicate where insulating rail joiners must be installed to avoid electrical short circuits on the reverse loop. Additional insulated rail joiners and feeder wires to on-off switches would have to be located at each of the crossovers between the inner and outer ovals ("D" and "E") with an insulated gap and feeder to an on-off switch about midway around the upper, right ends of both the inner and outer oval ("C" and "F") to allow two-train operations with conventional power packs. The use and installation of these rail joiners is explained in Chapter 8. If you want to avoid using these gaps, do not include the diagonal track across the oval. To avoid the need for the other two insulating gaps (at each crossover), use one of the DCC systems described in Chapter 8, or simply do

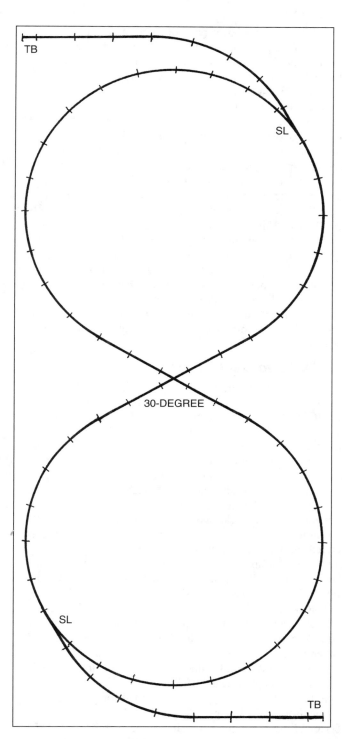

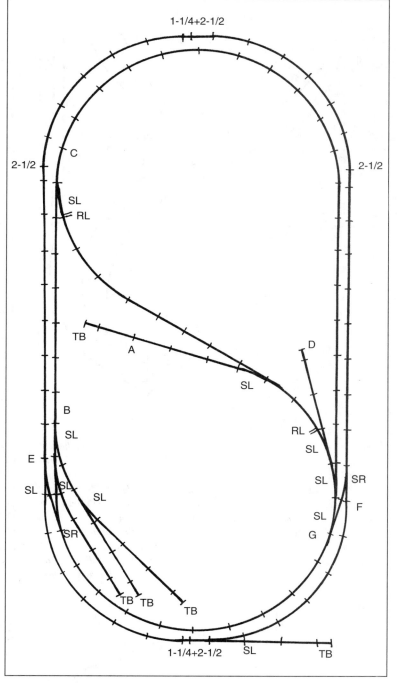

Figure 4-2. This figure 8 plan is designed with Atlas 19-inch radius curves, standard-length straights and bumper tracks, Standard Switches (turnouts) and a 30-degree crossing. It will fit in a 40-by-92-inch space.

Figure 4-3. This Double-Track Mainline layout requires just 44-by-90-inches of space. It is designed with Atlas 19-inch radius curves, standard-length straights and bumper tracks (TB), Standard Switches (SL and SR) (turnouts) and a 30-degree crossing. The 1-1/4 and 2-1/2 markings indicate the shorter Atlas straight track sections. The letters A through G indicate one possible point-to-point route for trains as described in the text. Note that the inner oval is the minimum size to include a reverse loop (42-by-86-inches) when using 19-inch radius curves. The letters "RL" on the plan indicate where insulating rail joiners must be installed to avoid electrical short circuits on the reverse loop.

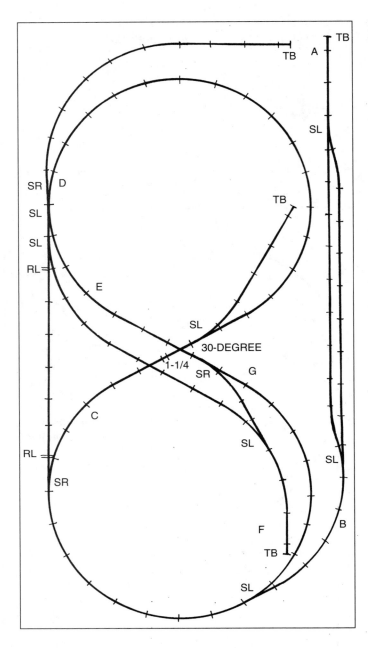

Figure 4-4. This Out-And-Back plan requires 46-by-90-inches of space. It is designed with Atlas 19-inch radius curves, standard-length straights and bumper tracks (TB), Standard Switches (SL and SR) (turnouts) and a 30-degree crossing. The 1-1/4 and 2-1/2 markings indicate the shorter Atlas straight track sections. The letters A through G indicate one possible point-to-point route for trains as described in the text. The letters "RL" on the plan indicate where insulating rail joiners must be installed to avoid electrical short circuits on the reverse loop. It is designed for point-to-point operation (A to F), but you can run trains continuously on the figure 8 portion of the layout.

not install the two crossover pairs of right and left turnouts on the far left of the plan so you have two concentric ovals with no rail connections between each other. You can then use two separate transformers, one for the outer oval and one for the inner oval, each controlling its own train.

This plan is designed so either one or two trains can be operated at the same time. One train can be circulating on the outer oval while the second runs on the inner oval and switches the sidings. For realistic operation, however, the layout can be used as a point-to-point run for a single train: beginning at siding "A" and traveling (in this example) clockwise to B, C, D and G to crossover to the outer oval at E. The train would then travel through F and crossover back to the inner oval at D and on to B and C. It would then back into A to complete its run. If you wanted to reverse the direction of the train, allow it to continue backing through A, D and G. It could then head forward, now in a counterclockwise direction, to C or F. Additional Atlas "Standard Switch" turnouts could be added in at least two of the corners to provide other "towns" and industrial-switching possibilities along the way. Several turnouts could be added at "A" and "E" for locomotive "holding" tracks and additional industries.

The "Out and Back" Plan

The layout plan in Figure 4-3 is one of the best I have seen using conventional sectional track in a minimum amount of space, 46-by-90 inches. This layout is small enough to fit easily on a 4-by-8-foot board. The only drawback to this layout, however, is that you cannot see two trains in motion and sit back and watch them run like you can with the layout in Figure 4-2. You can set the turnouts so a train will follow just the figure 8 path and watch that one train operate. A second train could be switching cars on the siding at "A." The layout is drawn with just enough terminal tracks and gaps for operating one train (the gaps on the reversing section are there just for that feature, as described in Chapter 8) with a conventional power pack. There's room for an additional stub-ended siding on each side of the tracks at "A" if you want more switching action. The long siding "A" to "B," as well as the siding "F," could become a separate "block," (for a conventional power pack) so you could operate one train switching in either of those areas while a second train circulated around the figure eight. If you use a Digital Command Control (DCC) system, you can keep at least two trains busy on this layout without the need for any electrical gaps or wires except those at "RL."

This layout (Figure 4-4) is also designed for point-to-point operation from "A" through "B," "C," "D," and "E" (in that order) to "F." A run-around or passing siding at both "A" and "F" allows the train to operate engine-first on the return trip to "A," and to be rearranged or switched for an engine-first trip back to "F." If you want to add some "mileage" on the route from "A" to "F," circulate the train around the figure eight (just as you would circulate around either or both ovals in Figures 5 and 3-6) until you're "scheduled" to have it arrive at "A" or "F." The advantage of this layout, as compared to many others, is that it includes a reversing-loop section so you can turn complete trains around "hands-off." The reversing loop would allow you to operate to and from "A," with "F" as a town along the way. The route would begin at "A" and proceed through "B," "C," "D," and "E" to "G," and from "G" on back to "B," around into the reversing-loop section through "E," "D," and "C," before going back to "B" and into "A." This type of operation is called "out and back," and its advantage is that most of the switching operations, including placing the locomotive at the front of the train, are only done in one "large" yard (at "A" on this layout).

A Mainline Layout for Kato Uni-Track

This 6-by-6-foot layout (Figure 4-5) is designed to fit the same tabletop as the layouts in Chapter 3 (Figures 3-5 and 3-6), but it utilizes Kato's Uni-Track with built-in ballast. If you prefer to avoid the wye and the yard on the 1-by-2-foot extension "wing" you can build the layout in just 4-by-6 feet. The plan was designed by Kato on their computer and it will work perfectly, the slight misalignments that are visible are the result of small errors in the computer program. The numbers are those used for Kato's track sections. The layout is a more conventional alternative to the plan in Figure 3-6, but it can be operated in about the same manner, with trains starting at the yard and making a trip around the outer, then the inner oval to finish their runs at the town in the lower left. The five-track yard on this plan, is, however, more useful as a yard than the tracks on the plan in Figure 3-6. It would also be somewhat easier to apply a scenic treatment to this layout because the tracks occupy less of the available space.

Designing Layouts with Track Sections

If you are using sectional track, you can use the track itself to design the layout. This is the best way to design a complex layout because, frankly, the actual track sections are not precisely the size and angle suggested by their numbers. Atlas and Kato each have geometric systems that their track sections are designed to fit for perfect alignment. Both are based on 15-degree segments of a circle but there is some difference in the length of the turnouts and the radii of the curves. Pick one or the other or, if you'd prefer, draw the trackplan and use flexible track as shown in Chapter 7.

If you lay the track on a perfectly smooth table and align the joints so both rails firmly abut both rails of each adjacent track section, you will actually have far better track alignment than if you attempt to draw the plan and fit the track to the plan. I know because I tried both systems. To double-check the alignment, lay the side of your head on the table so you can sight down the track. Any misalignment at any track joint will be quite visible. This same technique works better than a ruler to align a series of straight track sections.

The Atlas system is based on their "Standard Switch" which has a 19-inch radius curved route. The turnout is packaged with a piece of 19-inch curved track so you can make an ess bend to create a passing siding. If you decide to use the more realistic number 6 turnouts, however, the angle is somewhat less than with the "Standard Switch" (turnout). To make an ess bend into a passing siding with a number 6 turnout you must cut the rails for the length of 10 of the plastic ties (about 1-3/4 inches) from one end of a piece of 19-inch radius track (Figure 4-6). The parallel tracks on this siding were made with a number 6 turnout so the parallel tracks were spaced 1-1/4 inches apart. You will also need to use a piece of the Atlas 1-1/4-inch straight track between the number 6 turnout and the shortened (by that 1-3/4-inch) piece of 19-inch radius curved track to complete one end of this siding. If you want to make a crossover from two right

hand (or two left hand) number 6 turnouts, you'll need a piece of the Atlas 5/8-inch straight track between the two turnouts to produce a 1-1/2-inch center-to-center spacing between the two parallel tracks.

I wanted a wye for the layout in Figure 3-5 using number 6 turnouts and 19-inch radius curves and I wanted it to fit the least possible space. I discovered that only one leg of the wye could be curved, the one that passes by the intermodal terminal (marked "PT" in Figure 3-4, and even it required a piece of 1-1/4-inch straight. The other two legs need a standard length of straight track plus a 2-1/2-inch piece of straight track, but the 2-1/2-inch section needed to be inserted between two curve sections. The finished product is shown in Figure 4-8 and the plan in Figure 3-5 and you can use it as a track planning "segment" to fit a wye into other layouts. The process would have been vastly simpler if I had been willing to use the Atlas "Standard Switch" because it simply replaces a 19-inch curve.

If you are going to use passing sidings on your layout, assemble the sidings with all the track and turnouts as a multi-section segment of the layout. You can then shift the entire siding around to align it with the curves of the remainder of the layout. That's how the plan in Figure 3-5 was designed.

When I designed the layout in Figure 3-5, I started with an oval made from 19-inch radius curves and standard straight track sections (Figure 4-9). Next, I fitted the wye and the passing siding segments I had developed through trail-and-error (Figure 4-10) around the edge of the table. Finally, I connected the inner oval to the outer oval (Figure 4-11) and, because the number 6 turnouts have a bit of straight track, I had to insert a piece of 2-1/2-inch straight track into the oval to compensate for one of the number 6 turnouts. Finally, I added the "Loads-in/Empties-out" sidings in the upper right of the plan (Figure 4-12), using some Atlas Standard Switches and 11-inch radius curves to squeeze the two sidings into the tight area.

Do-It-Yourself Track Planning

You can create your own track plans by taking advantage of the simple slide-together feature of most brands of N scale sectional track. Each section of track is part of a geometric system based on five-inch pieces of straight track (or fractions thereof) and on 15-degree and 30-degree segments or sections of a 360-degree circle of track. If you use a 30-60-90-degree plastic triangle to help plan your trackwork, you'll be far more likely to get those critical track alignments right. Atlas has a set of full-size track planning templates you can use and Kato offers a plastic template you can use to trace plans onto paper (Figure 4-13). Atlas also offers a computer software track planning program called Right Track© software so you can use a PC (the program is not available for Macs) to design both the trackplan and scenery.

Reduce to Scale

All the plans in this book are reduced to a scale of 1 inch to the foot, which means that each foot on the layout is just 1 inch on the plan, and each inch on the layout is but 1/16 inch on the plan. A draftsman's triangular ruler has one side marked in one-inch scale, or you can use the 1/4-inch marks on any ruler for measuring 3-inch increments on these plans. Use the drafting triangle or ruler to pencil in the outline of the available area you have for your layout.

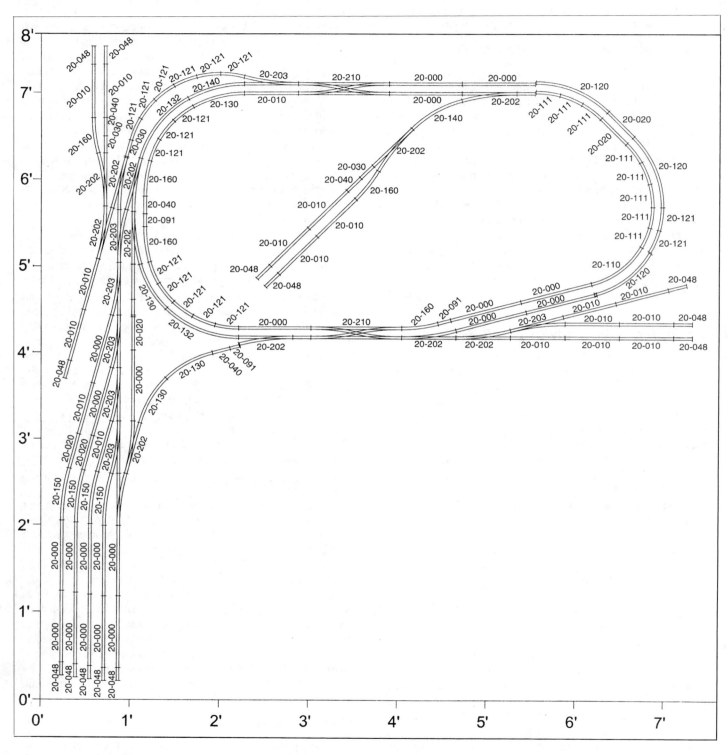

Figure 4-5. This double-track mainline layout with a yard can be squeezed into just 4-by-6-feet, but you'll need an access aisle along both sides, so the 1-by-2-foot yard on the upper left really doesn't take up any extra space. It is designed for use with Kato Uni-Track sections with built-in ballast. The part numbers identify the specific Uni-Track sections needed. --Courtesy Kato USA

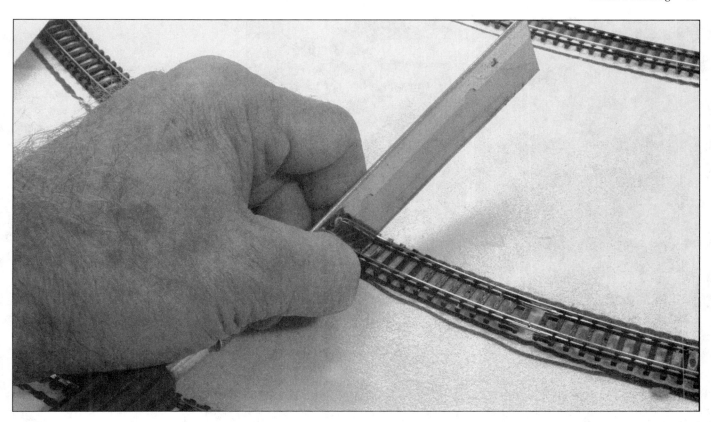

Use an X-Acto razor saw to cut through the 19-inch radius curved track sections to make the shorter-sections needed for some of these plans. There's more information on modifying track sections in Chapter 7.

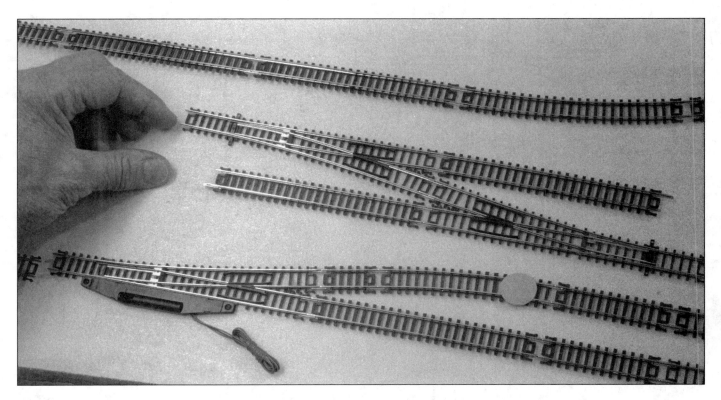

Figure 4-7. A pair of Atlas Standard Switches (turnouts-center) or a Standard Switch with a piece of 19-inch radius curved track, produce parallel tracks spaced 1-5/16-inches apart. To match that dimension with a number 6 turnout, you'll need to cut a piece of 19-inch radius curve (the section with the dot) and insert a piece of 1-1/4-inch straight between the turnout and the curve (bottom). Assemble some of these turnout combinations and use them when planning your own layout.

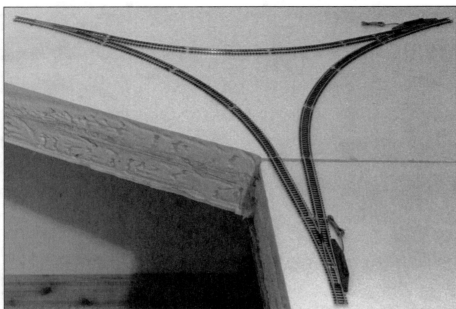

Figure 4-8. The smallest-size wye I could assemble using number 6 turnouts and 19-inch radius curves appears on the layout in Figure 3-5. If you want a wye, assemble one and move it around the table to align it with the rest of the trackwork.

Figure 4-9. You can begin any layout in this book with a simple oval. The next step, in designing the trackplan for the 6-by-6-foot layout in Figure 3-5, was to install two turnouts in this inner oval to connect it with the outer oval.

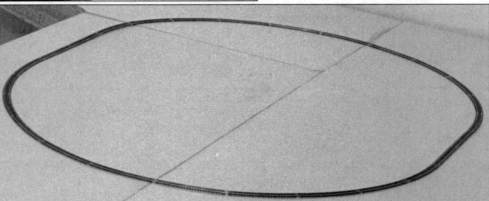

Figure 4-10. To design the trackplan in Figure 3-5, I fitted the wye and the passing siding segments I had developed through trial-and-error around the edge of the table.

Figure 4-11. I connected the inner oval to the outer oval and to complete the mainline trackage for the layout in Figure 3-5 and, because the number 6 turnouts have a bit of straight track, I had to insert a piece of 2-1/2-inch straight track into the oval to compensate for one of the number 6 turnouts. Finally, I added the "Loads-in/Empties-out" sidings in the upper left of the plan.

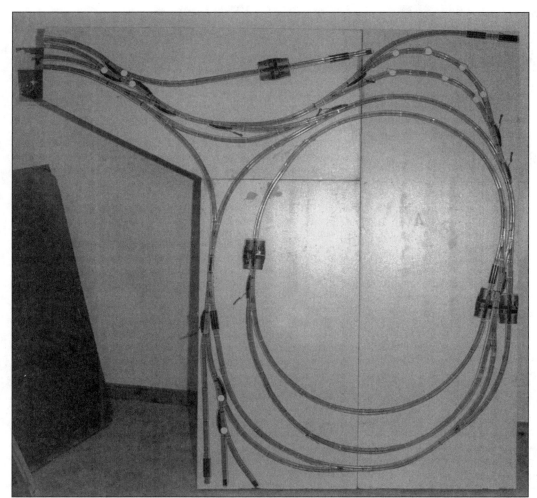

Figure 4-12. A "satellite" view of the completed track plan, designed on the tabletop, for the layout in Figure 3-5.

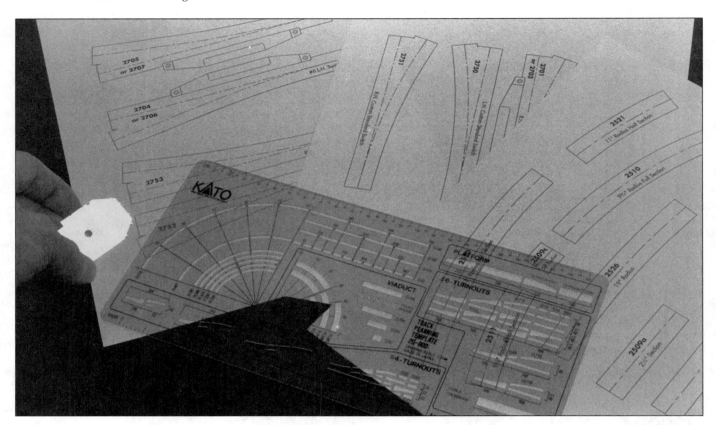

Figure 4-13. Atlas has a set of full-size track planning templates shown here that you can use on the layout itself and they offer a computer program so you can design your own layout with Atlas track on a PC. Kato offers this plastic template you can use to trace plans for layout to be made with Kato's Uni-Track onto paper. The metal piece is an NMRA Standards Gauge to check track and clearances.

Clearance

It's best to check very tight track-planning situations with actual pieces of track and, if necessary, with structures you might want to include. You don't need to build the entire layout, just temporarily install the buildings and simulate any cuts or tunnels with scraps of wood or cardboard in the area where you expect to have tight clearance problems. Always try to leave room at the end of any passing siding for at least one locomotive, and, if switching must be done through turnouts with facing points toward that end, allow room for a locomotive and your longest car. The far upper left corner in the town of "Alliance" on the track plan in Figure 3-5 is an example of a confined area where a minimum car-and-locomotive length is needed. You can often gain a few extra inches in such tight areas by using conventional track rather than bumper tracks at the end of the stub-end siding. You can just glue-on some plastic ties cut from old track sections. The real railroads often use a method to stop cars from rolling off the ends of tracks.

Planning Uphill and Downhill Grades

Uphill and downhill grades are more trouble than they're worth in terms of realism. You can make the edge of the table slope up or down like it does for the river crossing (Figure 10-20) on the 6-by-6-foot Union Pacific layout, so the tracks appear to be going upgrade or downgrade. It's hard enough to keep the tracks level without trying to build in a slope. The most difficult problems to overcome are those that result from too sudden a change at the top or the bottom of any hill. The diagram in Figure 4-14 shows the percentage of grade that is needed for the bridge and trestle kits in the train sets to elevate the tracks about 1-3/4 inches above one another at the crossing. If you are using a 1/2-inch plywood roadbed (see Chapter 5) at a bridge, you will need to have at least 2-1/4 inches of clearance between the tops of the upper track's rails and the tops of the lower track's rails to leave room for the plywood at the bridge. That 1.2-percent to 1.7-percent grade is almost as gentle as the grades on most prototype railroads, thanks to the relatively broad 19-inch radius curves and the distance around such curves. If you decide to use 9-inch or 11-inch radius curves, the grade will be more like a very steep 5-percent or 6-percent, steep enough to limit trains to three or four cars. The real trains seldom exceed 1 percent on their climbs. That grade percentage is figured on so many units per hundred, so a 2.5-percent grade would be a rise of 2.5 units for every 100 units of track.

It is extremely difficult to apply scenery to the simple plastic trestle supports, except on a short industrial trestle. If you do use grades on your layout, then you should be capable of doing the carpentry work to build the open-grid type of benchwork shown in Chapter 5. Alternately, you can use the lightweight blue Styrofoam insulation construction methods with Woodland Scenic's "SubTerrain" system of 2-percent or 4-percent grades made with flexible "Inclines" supports shown in Chapter 6. Use the chart in Figure 4-15 to determine how steep any of the grades on your layout must be. The figures above 3.0 percent are there only for interest. You would be lucky to get just a locomotive alone up a hill as steep as 10.0 percent.

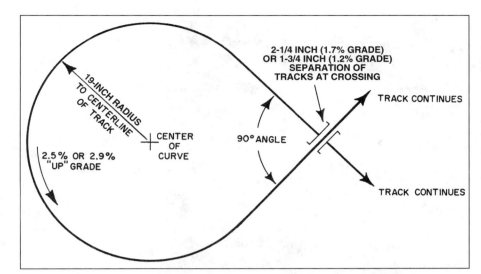

Figure 4-14. The shortest route to create an overpass for N scale layouts using 19-inch radius curves.

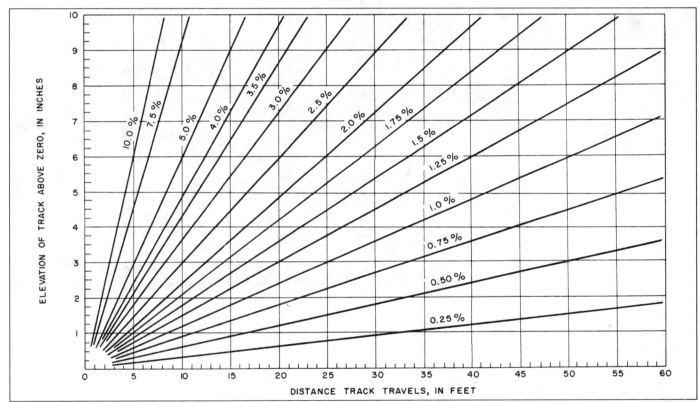

Figure 4-15. Chart of grade percentages.

Track Planning With NTRAK Modules

The NTRAK modular system allows you to build a model railroad at home, in as little as 2-by-4-feet, and connect that module to others so you can run 100-car trains over your own module. Robert Mohr built a city on a single 2-by-4-foot module and used another 2-by-4-foot module on each end to bring the city's seven-track passenger train yard tracks back to the NTRAK three-track mainline (Figure 4-16). The NTRAK Standards are illustrated in Chapter 5, but, briefly, they demand that there be three parallel tracks at each of the module, spaced 4-, 5-1/2- and 7-inches in from the edge of the table and parallel to the edge of the table for at least 4 inches. Once they are four inches in from the ends, the tracks can wander anywhere.

The NTRAK module can be 2-by-4-, 2-by-6- or 2-by-8-feet and it can even have a 6-inch wide extension at the front or the rear to be as deep as 36 inches. The important standards apply to the three tracks and at the ends, benchwork height and strength, and standard wiring. In fact, the number of modules between each interface end can be virtually unlimited. There are also NTRAK standards for 4-by-4-foot and 6-by-6-foot corner modules. But the three tracks must remain parallel through the corners. Gene Burtnett built a 6-by-6-foot city scene corner module for the Orlando NTRAK Club and used a mirror on the diagonal skyboard panel to effectively double the size of the city (Figure 4-17). You can use these NTRAK modules as part

Figure 4-16. Robert Mohr's city is built on a single 2-by-4-foot module with additional 2-by-4-foot module on each end to bring the city's seven-track passenger train yard tracks back to the NTRAK three-track mainline.

Figure 4-17. A mirror on the diagonal skyboard on Gene Burtnett's 4-by-4-foot city scene corner module for the Orlando NTRAK Club effectively doubles the size of the city.

of a club layout like those in this chapter and in Chapter 2 (Figure 2-4) and Chapter 3 (Figures 3-19, 3-20, 3-21 and 3-22). NTRAK modules can also be combined to build a home layout in as little as 12-by-12 feet as shown in Chapter 2 (Figure 2-5).

Model Railroads Built From Modules

Some of the finest N scale model railroads in the country are constructed from modules that, at the ends, can be interfaced into any NTRAK layout. The Utah-N-Modelers, for example, have a 21-by-33-foot portable layout that is made up of a combination of standard 2-by-6 and 6-by-6 modules and a series of modules that are just as portable as NTRAK but do not interface with NTRAK modules except at the extreme ends (Figures 4-18, and 4-19). There are photographs of Kelley Newton's recreation of the Weber Canyon, Utah, and Bob Gilmore's superb modeling of the Union Pacific's route through Utah's high desert in the color section.

The New River Subdivision layout is a recreation of some spectacular scenes along the Chesapeake and Ohio Railroad in and near the New River in West Virginia. Individual members have created their own multi-module sets that interface both NTRAK modules at the extreme ends of

the sets. What sets this group of modules apart is that, like the Utah-N-Modelers and the Great Northern Modelers shown in Chapter 3 (Figures 3-19, 3-20, 3-21 and 3-22), the New River club members have selected standard materials and colors for the scenery so the modules blend together in to one harmonious scene. There are photos of this large array of multi-module sets in the color section.

The group of New River Subdivision multi-module sets in Figure 4-20 is about 16-by-34 feet. This string of modules includes Paul Fulk's 2-by-8-foot multi-module recreation of Thurmond, West Virginia, Bernard Kempinski's 6-by-6-foot multi-module set that recreates Quinnimont, West Virginia and John Plant's 6-by-16-foot multi-module set that duplicates the Chesapeake and Ohio Railroad's yard and operations at Hinton, West Virginia. Carl Schaeffer has recreated the Chesapeake and Ohio Railroad's route along the New River near Hawk's Nest, Carl and Steve Zutter have duplicated the atmosphere at Prince, and Art Frankfurter has modeled a simple scene at CW Cabin, West Virginia. Any of these New River multi-module sets will interface with any other. Most of these modules are also used as part of home layouts when they are not assembled into NTRAK layouts.

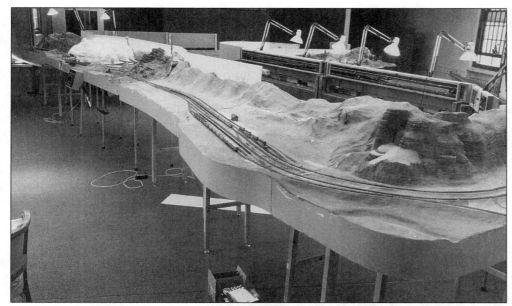

Figure 4-18. The Utah-N-Railers 21-by-33-foot portable layout is made up of a combination of standard 2-by-6 and 6-by-6 NTRAK modules and a series of multi-module sets so the entire layout is portable.

Figure 4-19. Kelley Newton's recreation of the Weber Canyon, Utah, on the Utah-N-Railers portable layout.

Figure 4-20. John Plant's 6-by-16-foot multi-module set duplicates the operations at Hinton, West Virginia. The other modules in the New River Sub-division club (also shown in the color section) stretch out in the distance in the upper left.

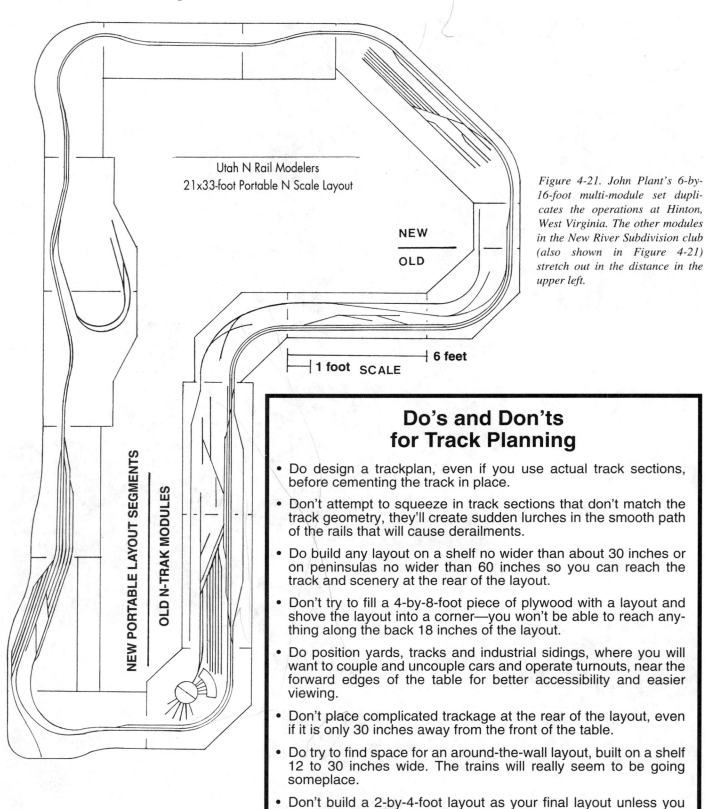

Utah N Rail Modelers
21x33-foot Portable N Scale Layout

NEW

OLD

| 1 foot SCALE   6 feet |

NEW PORTABLE LAYOUT SEGMENTS

OLD N-TRAK MODULES

Figure 4-21. John Plant's 6-by-16-foot multi-module set duplicates the operations at Hinton, West Virginia. The other modules in the New River Subdivision club (also shown in Figure 4-21) stretch out in the distance in the upper left.

Do's and Don'ts
for Track Planning

- Do design a trackplan, even if you use actual track sections, before cementing the track in place.

- Don't attempt to squeeze in track sections that don't match the track geometry, they'll create sudden lurches in the smooth path of the rails that will cause derailments.

- Do build any layout on a shelf no wider than about 30 inches or on peninsulas no wider than 60 inches so you can reach the track and scenery at the rear of the layout.

- Don't try to fill a 4-by-8-foot piece of plywood with a layout and shove the layout into a corner—you won't be able to reach anything along the back 18 inches of the layout.

- Do position yards, tracks and industrial sidings, where you will want to couple and uncouple cars and operate turnouts, near the forward edges of the table for better accessibility and easier viewing.

- Don't place complicated trackage at the rear of the layout, even if it is only 30 inches away from the front of the table.

- Do try to find space for an around-the-wall layout, built on a shelf 12 to 30 inches wide. The trains will really seem to be going someplace.

- Don't build a 2-by-4-foot layout as your final layout unless you really are limited to that small an area.

- Do keep most of the tracks at least 6 inches away from the forward edge of the table to leave room for some foreground scenery on at least half of the layout.

- Don't try to cram track into every square inch of tabletop. There won't be room for credible scenery or structures.

Chapter 5

Benchwork

Any model railroad is more realistic if viewed from track level than from the altitude of an airplane. Yes, there is a fascination in looking down to see the trains snake through ess curves, with each car mysteriously following the next in a perfect pattern. That's one of the fun aspects of model railroading and it is certainly a sight that is worth recreating. Your models will look much more like the real trains, though, if you look at them down near track level.

There are several ways of getting your eyes to the level of the trains: you can operate the trains on the floor and lie down to see them at a realistic viewpoint, you can elevate the tracks to about waist high and sit in a chair or kneel beside the table to bring your eyes down to the level of the trains, or you can elevate the tracks to about the level of your shoulders. If you want to see the waist-high trains from the altitude of an airplane, just stand up. If you want to view the chest-level trains from a higher altitude buy a one- or two-step stool and stand on it to gain the altitude you wish.

Tables & Benchwork

For purposes of building a model railroad, the "benchwork" is whatever it takes to support the tracks above the floor and to support the legs that will elevate the tracks to the level you choose. For decades, model railroaders have built benchwork with no tabletop, just an open grid of 1-by-4 or 1-by-3 lumber that looks something like an egg crate. Model railroaders refer to this style benchwork as "open-grid." The tracks are usually supported by a strip of 1/2-inch plywood about 2-inches wide for single-track and about 3-inches wide for double track or passing sidings. The plywood is cut to the same shape as the trackplan. Usually, the plywood is elevated at least 4 inches above the edges of the open grid benchwork on 1-by-2 or 1-by-4 risers (Figure 5-11).

With open-grid benchwork the track itself is then supported on roadbed cut from 1/2-inch thick Homasote (a building board

Figure 5-1. Paul Biermann built this portion of Baltimore, Maryland on a 2-by-4-foot NTRAK module with a 6-inch extension at the front to support the edge of the harbor.

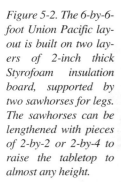

Figure 5-2. The 6-by-6-foot Union Pacific layout is built on two layers of 2-inch thick Styrofoam insulation board, supported by two sawhorses for legs. The sawhorses can be lengthened with pieces of 2-by-2 or 2-by-4 to raise the tabletop to almost any height.

similar to thick grey cardboard), Upsom board (a similar material about 1/8-inch thick) or on cork roadbed or one of the similar commercial roadbeds like Woodland Scenics' Track-Bed or the clay-like AMI "Instant Roadbed." You may simply hang your layout off the wall on shelf brackets, build it across the tops of a few bookcases, or build a special table from wood or from panels of extruded-polystyrene blue Styrofoam insulation board as shown in Chapter 6. Yes, you can even slap the track down on a 1/2-inch thick piece of 4-by-8-foot plywood and support it on sawhorses (Figures 5-3 and 5-4).

Figure 5-3. Lightweight steel sawhorses with folding legs can be used to support a plywood tabletop-style layout. If you choose conventional wood sawhorses, the legs can be cut to any length you desire to elevate the height of the layout.

Figure 5-4. A single sheet of 1/2-inch plywood can be used for a tabletop layout. The tabletop can support cork roadbed or the Woodland Scenic's "SubTerrain" system of roadbed and scenery-supports from Chapter 6 (Figure 6-13).

Two Choices for Benchwork

There are two different types of benchwork in this book: the conventional wood open-grid-style benchwork described above, with wood supports for the roadbed benchwork and the blue Dow-Corning extruded-Styrofoam insulation board benchwork in Chapter 6. The open-grid style has been traditional with model railroaders for over 50 years. The blue extruded-Styrofoam is a relatively new development that provides somewhat lighter construction and provides for valleys and water-crossings below the layout. Look at both methods and decide which one you like best.

Table Height

To decide on the height of the top of the table (or the top edges of the open-grid benchwork), decide how high you want the tracks to be and deduct at least four-inches from that to provide space for rivers, streams and roads beneath the tracks and to allow construction of the embankments of "fills" that are such a common sight on real railroads. The embankments are used, in part, to provide water drainage. However, most often, they are required to keep the track level while the earth undulates up and down. Too often, model railroaders only provide the cuts through hills or, if the hill is high enough, a tunnel, and they ignore the real railroads' right-of-way that is elevated above the earth on embankments.

About 1/2 of all real railroad tracks are supported on embankments. About 1/4 of the railroad rights-of-way cut through hills or bore through tunnels, which leaves only about 1/4 of the real railroads' tracks resting on more-or-less level ground. The embankments may only be a few feet high and part of that height may come from drainage ditches as illustrated in Chapter 6 (figure 6-1). You will, in any case, want the tracks to be elevated high enough so you can model the drainage ditches that are part of most real railroads right-of-way even on level ground.

Just how high a tabletop should be is a matter of individual opinion. Personally, I like the trains to be at about shoulder level. I'm five-eleven and that puts the highest rails at about 56 inches from the ground. Others prefer them waist-high or somewhere in between. You may, of course, want to place the trains at the shoulder level of the shortest member of your family so no one has to stand on a box to view the trains in action. It's your choice.

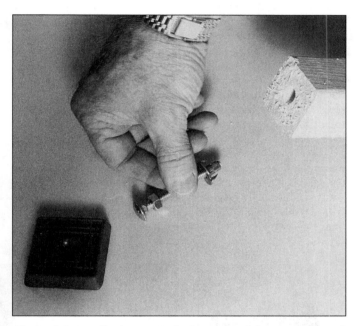

Figure 5-6. Install adjusters in the base of each leg using a 2-inch long 1/4-inch stovebolt, and nut with a tee-nut to secure the bolt to the leg. A square carpet pad (left) can be used to keep the carriage bolt from digging into the linoleum or carpet.

Tabletop Layouts

The 1/2-inch plywood tabletop is stiff enough to be supported by legs as long as the legs are spaced no further than two-feet apart. If you are only building a 4-by-6-foot layout, four legs, spaced about a foot in from the ends and six-inches in from the sides, will be ample. Or, you can opt to simply support the sheet of plywood on a pair of sawhorses.

I do not recommend that you build your model railroad, however, on a flat plywood tabletop unless you are modeling only a freight yard or industrial area. The flat tabletop makes it very difficult to provide drainage ditches and embankments that lead down from track level and to provide a place for any kind of stream or other water course that will be bridged by the tracks. You can, of course, cut through the plywood tabletop to provide a cavity or hollow for a lake. However, at best, it looks contrived and unrealistic.

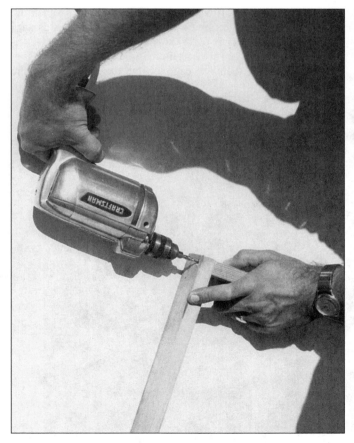

Figure 5-5. Use an electric drill with a number 8-by-1-1/4-inch pilot bit to prepare holes for number 8-by-1-1/2 inch woodscrews at each joint of the 1-by-3 or 1-by-4 boards of the open-grid benchwork.

Open-Grid Benchwork

Open-grid-style benchwork is similar to the framework for your house, and it's made of many of the same materials. Open-grid benchwork is often selected for model railroads where the builder wants to have upgrades or downgrades. It is relatively simple to move the vertical risers that support the subroadbed beneath the track up or down before fastening them to the benchwork, to produce uphill or downhill grades. The open-grid benchwork will eventually be hidden by scenery on the top and by Masonite or plywood panels along the sides so that only the legs will show.

Use only the best grades of 1-by-3 fir or pine with no knots for your benchwork. You don't want warped wood and other track-distorting problems, and quality wood will help to avoid them. Use well-braced 2-by-2s or 2-by-4s for the legs. Divide your layout into subassemblies or modules that are no more than 30-by-60 inches. A 4-by-8-foot area can, for example, be divided conveniently into four 2-by-4-foot subassemblies. Make a box with overall dimensions to match each of these subassemblies, with the 1-by-3s placed on edge. Add enough cross braces so there is no open area wider than 18 inches (for example, two cross braces are needed for each 2-by-4-foot subassembly). Secure each of the joints with two No. 8-by-1-1/2 inch wood screws. Drill a pilot hole for each of these screws with an electric drill and a No. 8-by-1-1/2-inch pilot bit, which you can buy in any hardware store.

You can make quick work of driving the screws by buying or renting either a Yankee screwdriver, where you just push the handle down to drive the screw, or a screwdriver attachment for an electric drill with variable speed. Touch each of the screws with a dab of soap to make it even easier. Bolt the subassemblies together with 2-by-1/4-inch stove bolts, washers, and nuts (Figure 5-7).

Legs For Open-Grid Benchwork

Attach the legs with two 2-1/2-inch-long-by-1/4-inch stove bolts or hex-head bolts with flat washers and nuts. Attach one leg to the table with a single screw, and clamp the others with C-clamps or vise-grip clamps while you adjust the legs to see that the benchwork top surface is level. Don't trust the floor to be level: use one of the carpenter's spirit or bubble levels to determine where to move the benchwork or open-grid so the top surface is level. When the legs are in the correct position, drill them and attach each leg with two of the 2-1/2-inch stove bolts. It is wise, too, to put levelers into the base of each leg. Drill a 5/16-inch hole into the end of each leg, insert a tee-nut for a 1/4-inch bolt, then thread-in a 2-inch carriage bolt with a nut on the bolt (Figure 5-6). The end of the carriage bolt can be protected with one of the furniture-leg pads. Turn the bolt in or out to raise or lower the height of the leg and use the nut to lock it in place. This completes the "open-grid" portion of the benchwork.

The top of the benchwork should be 1/2-inch plywood (inexpensive C-C grade is fine) with 1/2-inch Homasote or 1/8-inch Upsom board wallboard or cork roadbed between the plywood and the track. If you are using Kato's Uni-Track, Bachmann's E-Z Track or Life-Like's Power-Loc track, you will not need the Homasote, Upsom board or cork roadbed. The Homasote or Upsom board are some of the best materials to support sectional track with just rails and ties or flexible track because it is soft enough to make it relatively easy to carve ballast shoulders with a utility knife and soft enough to be sound-deadening, yet firm enough to hold track nails or spikes. It must, however, be supported by plywood or it will sag. There is no known substitute for the Homasote or Upsom board, so call the lumberyards until you find one willing to order as many 4-by-8-foot sheets as you'll need. When you are certain the track plan you are using is perfect for you, then you can cut both the plywood and the

Figure 5-7. Two 2-by-4-foot open-grid benchwork units being clamped together so they can be joined with 2-inch carriage bolts, nuts and washers. The legs are 2-by-2s braced with 1-by-2s.

Figure 5-8. Open-grid benchwork can be free flowing like that for Ron Burkhart's HO scale layout. His layout is actually being built on two levels or decks, one at about 48-inches and the other at about 66-inches from floor to track.

Homasote or Upsom board about an inch on each side of the track's centerline. You can use a utility knife, guided by a steel ruler, to cut the Homasote. Most tool supply firms also sell knife blades for saber saws like the Sears' Craftsman 2873 or the Vermont American 30022 that can be used to cut the Homasote quickly and easily and with nearly no mess.

The plywood supports for the Homasote, Upsom board, or cork roadbed can then be elevated about three or four inches above the top of the 1-by-3 benchwork, with short lengths of 1-by-3s placed vertically and attached to the plywood and the benchwork with number 8-by-1-1/2-inch wood screws (Figure 5-8). You can also extend the rear legs of the benchwork to support a sky backdrop like that on Ron Burkhardt's HO scale layout in Figure 5-8. The sky backdrop can be made from three-foot wide linoleum hall runners or aluminum rain gutter flashing, painted sky blue.

You can finish off the edges of the benchwork with a fascia or profile boards of 1/8-inch tempered Masonite or plywood cut to match the proposed hills and valleys. I suggest you delay cutting the fascia until you have mocked up the shape of the hills with wadded-up newspapers, as described in Chapter 12. A lot of construction time is needed between the completion of the benchwork and the initial scenery work; all the tracklaying and wiring should be completed and the structure sites selected (even if the structures themselves have not been purchased) before scenery is started.

Most modelers hide the benchwork's legs and the other under-the-table debris with drapes made from inexpensive

materials. If you do decide on drapes, avoid the mistake of selecting those bright railroad-style patterns; they are a major distraction from what is on top of the table. A nice dark green or blue or brown, which will make the underside of the benchwork seem to disappear, is the shade to select.

NTRAK Modular Layout Benchwork

The NTRAK system of modular layouts allows you to build and operate a portion of a very large model railroad in just 2-by-4 feet. Your NTRAK module can be connected to other NTRAK modules from anywhere in the world to create truly massive layouts like those in Chapter 2 (Figure 2-4) and Chapter 3 (Figures 3-19, 3-20, 3-21 and 3-22), or you can assemble your own home layout for a series of NTRAK modules like the layout in Chapter 2 (Figure 2-3) or simply include one or more NTRAK modules in conventional around-the-wall layout like the town of Winchester on Wayne and Bill Reid's layout in the color section and in Chapter 3 (Figure 3-25).

The NTRAK modular layout system is based on a standard design for the size, height, end construction, track positions and electrical wiring of each module. These standards allow your module to interface with any other module from anywhere in the world. NTRAK does not demand specific materials for the construction of the module, but the basic grid can be made from either 1-by-3s or from 3/4-inch plywood cut into 3-inch wide strips. The layout must be supported on legs to elevate the tracks to 40 inches, with adjusters on the bottom of each leg that allow plus or minus one-inch of adjustment. NTRAK also prefers that

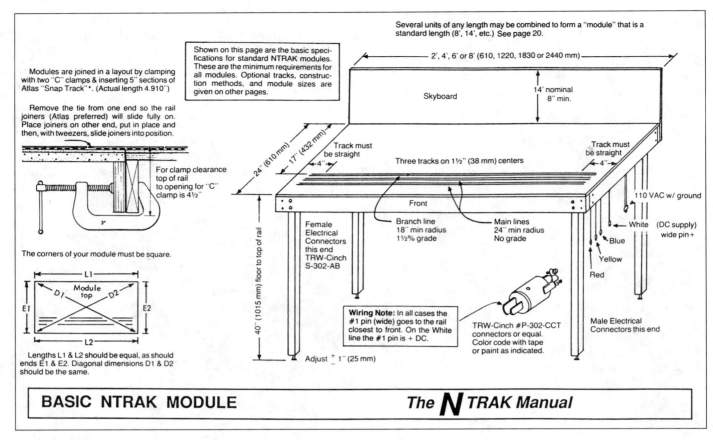

Figure 5-9. The basic NTRAK module specifications from the NTRAK Manual. –Courtesy NTRAK, Inc.

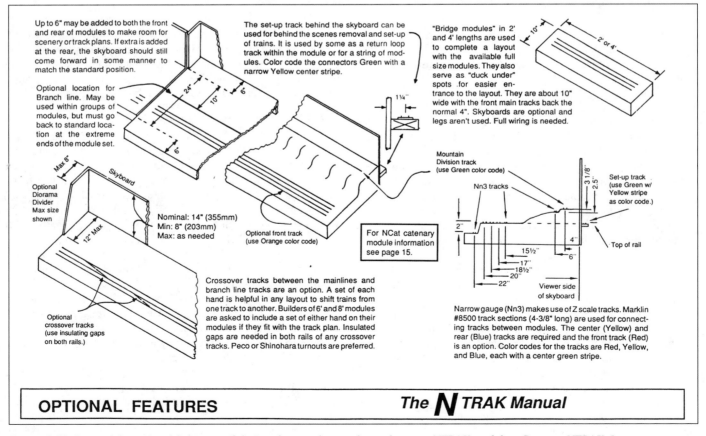

Figure 5-10. Some of the optional features and design changes that can be made to any NTRAK module. –Courtesy NTRAK, Inc.

you have a back wall or "skyboard" that extends between 8 and 14-inches above the tabletop. The basic specifications for an NTRAK module are shown in Figure 5-9.

It is critical that the three tracks be spaced 4, 5-1/2 and 7 inches from the front of the module (17, 18-1/2 and 20 inches from the rear of the module). The three tracks can wander around on the module as long as the two outer tracks have no up or downgrades and a minimum 24-inch radius. The inner track can climb up or down 1-1/2-percent and include curves can be as tight as 18-inch radius. The three tracks must, however, be parallel and straight 4 inches in from each end of the module. There is a reasonable amount of latitude in the NTRAK Standards, including the option of 2, 4, 6, or 8-foot modules and extending the rear of the module 6 inches and the front 6 inches. Some of the options are illustrated in Figure 5-10. If you are going to build an NTRAK module, I would recommend that you purchase the $1.50, 16-page *NTRAK Manual of Module Specifications* and the $10.00, 100-page *NTRAK Module "How-To" Book* from NTRAK, Incorporated, 1150 Wine Country Place, Templeton, CA 93645.

Do's and Don'ts for Benchwork

- Do consider building the benchwork so the track is at about the level of your chest or shoulders so you can view the model trains from the same angle you view the real trains.

- Don't build a layout at waist or hip level unless you want it to be visible or accessible for very small children—from that high viewing angle even the most realistic models look like toys.

- Do use screws to assemble every joint in the benchwork and install those screws from below the table so they will be accessible even when the layout is completed. You will be able, then, to alter or move the track without destroying the entire layout.

- Don't use nails or glue to assemble the benchwork. If you do want to make any changes later, the terrific force needed to separate the joints will destroy most of the layout.

- Do use only well seasoned or aged wood that has been stored in the same area as the layout for a year, if possible, to avoid any radical changes in the benchwork caused by the lumber warping and bending. For this same reason, it's also wise to seal all wood with at least one coat of paint.

- Don't use green, freshly-cut wood for benchwork. It's better, in most cases, to find old used wood (that has already warped or bent as much as it is likely to) before it becomes part of your model railroad.

- Do build the benchwork in modules or sections no larger than 30-by-60 inches and bolt the sections together so you can unbolt them if you ever need to move the layout. The 30-by-60-inch sections will fit through most standard doorways.

- Don't build a room-filling layout with 8 foot or longer boards that can only be moved by tearing the layout completely apart.

- Do raise the roadbed and track (or lower some of those segments of the benchwork) so the track can be elevated above the earth on embankments or fills and to provide spaces, below track level, for rivers and streams.

- Don't build the entire layout on a flat piece of plywood unless you are creating just an industrial yard or city scene.

Chapter 6

Lightweight Benchwork

Model railroaders have developed a layout and scenery-construction technique that utilizes extruded polystyrene insulation board like Dow-Corning's blue-colored Styrofoam. The material can be used to replace much of the conventional wood benchwork that is shown in Chapter 5 and it can also be used to carve hills and valleys as shown in Chapter 10. It is not necessary, however, to use the Styrofoam for both benchwork and scenery. You can use the Styrofoam for benchwork simply to build a sturdy, level tabletop, like that on the 2-by-4-foot layout in Chapter 2 (Figures 2-1 and 2-2) or the 6-by-6-foot Union Pacific layout that is shown in most chapters of this book. You then have the option of building scenery using conventional plaster and paper towels, plaster-soaked gauze or carving the scenery from Styrofoam.

Dow-Corning makes their extruded Styrofoam insulation board with a blue color. Other brands use other colors, but be sure the insulation board is extruded polyfoam. The white insulation boards (sometimes called "beadboard") are expanded polystyrene and are much too soft and fragile for this application. Also, do not use the urethane boards because they are brittle and far more difficult to work with for this type of project.

Styrofoam Benchwork

The simplest form of model railroad benchwork is two or more two-inch thick sheets of extruded polystyrene insulation board like the blue-colored Dow-Corning Styrofoam product. This material is strong enough to be self-supporting, so legs are only needed every two to three feet. If your model railroad is a shelf-style layout, you can even support a two-foot wide "shelf" of two layers of extruded polystyrene insulation board on common shelf brackets with a piece of 1-by-2 mounted on top of the brackets to enlarge the mounting area so the shelf brackets do not dig into the foam.

The Styrofoam is very strong, especially when two or more layers of the 2-inch thick material are cemented together. The entire 6-by-6-foot Union Pacific layout is one bonded-together stack of two layers of 2-inch thick Styrofoam. It weighs just 30 pounds without legs. A sheet of 1/2-inch plywood cut to the same size and shape weighs 26 pounds, but almost any scenery technique would add 30 to 80 pounds to that. At 30-pounds, the 6-by-6-foot layout can be considered portable enough to be stored upright against a wall as shown in Chapter 2 (Figure 2-7), if you do not have room for permanent layout.

Figure 6-1. The three curves on one end of the 6-by-6-foot Union Pacific layout are on embankments or "fills" cut into the 4-inch thick Styrofoam tabletop.

The only real drawbacks to the use of Styrofoam is that it is not strong enough, by itself, to support legs and the edges are quite fragile. You can get around the leg problem by simply supporting the layout on two sawhorses as shown in Chapter 5 (5-3 and 5-4). The problem with sawhorses is that they are only about 28-inch high and, unless you are building the layout exclusively for small children, you will probably want the track to be elevated to about twice that height. You can, of course, raise the height of the sawhorses by replacing the 28-inch legs with longer 2-by-4 legs to raise the benchwork to as much as 56-inches. The all-steel sawhorses' legs are just wide enough to accept a 2-by-2 or 2-by-4, so even those can be elevated to any height you wish. You can also provide 2-foot triangles of 1/2-inch plywood underneath each corner of the blue Styrofoam to support the legs, and protect the edges of the Styrofoam with 1/8-inch plywood —those techniques are described, step-by-step, in the *HO Scale Model Railroading Handbook*. Perhaps the simplest method of supporting and protecting the Styrofoam is to build an open-grid benchwork of 1-by-3 boards to match the outer dimensions of the Styrofoam tabletop. The 1-by-3 boards, placed on edge, provide ample anchor for the 2-by-2 or 2-by-4 legs. You can either bolt the legs inside the corners of the 1-by-3s or assemble separate 2-by-2 legs, with 1-by-2-inch diagonal braces as shown in Chapter 5 (Figure 5-7). You can then nail fascia or profile boards of 3/32-inch plywood veneer to the sides of the 1-by-3s, extending a foot or so above the Styrofoam. The fascia will protect the soft edges of the Styrofoam and it can be cut to match the shape of the hills and valleys with a saber saw when the scenery shaping is complete.

The Styrofoam Tabletop

The blue extruded Styrofoam seems to be the most readily available material of its type. This is a dense extruded polystyrene material, far stronger than the white expanded-foam beadboard that is also available at lumber dealers. Woodland Scenics offers small sheets of the white expanded foam for their "Sub-

Terrain" system shown later in this chapter. I used that material for the road surfaces and building bases, but it lacks the strength for a layout surface. There are other brands of extruded-polystyrene insulation, offered in other colors, so check with your local lumberyard. The blue extruded Styrofoam seems to be commonly available in 2-by-8-foot sheets, two inches thick. The 8-foot edges have a tongue-and-groove design to interlock the panels. You can cut the "tongue" from the exterior edges with a hacksaw blade (Figure 6-2) or hot wire cutter and use the piece to fill in the "groove" on the opposite edge of the tabletop. Use latex cement to attach the Styrofoam to itself and to the plywood. Liquid Nails makes a latex-based compound for a caulking gun called "Projects and Foamboard" cement and Chem Rex makes a special PL300 "Foam Board Adhesive" that is designed especially for use with Styrofoam. There may be other brands of latex-based cements designed for bonding two layers

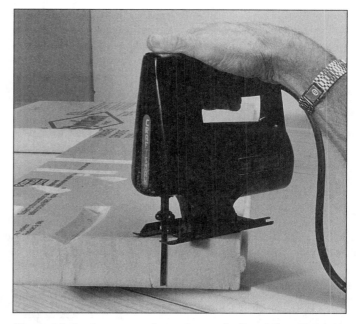

Figure 6-3. A saber saw can be used to cut the Styrofoam with a knife blade like the Sears' Craftsman 2873 or the Vermont American 30022.

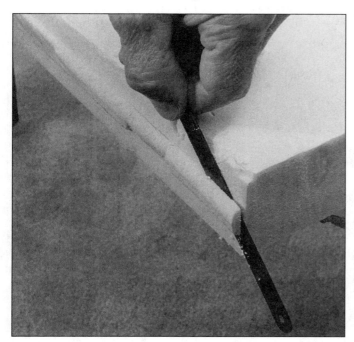

Figure 6-2. The "tongue" on the tongue-and-groove Styrofoam insulation panel can be easily removed with a hacksaw blade.

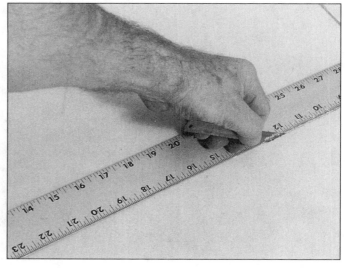

Figure 6-4. Use a ruler to guide the hacksaw blade (shown), saber saw or hot wire cutter to be sure the cut is straight.

of Styrofoam. I used the PL300 to assemble the two layers of 2-inch thick Styrofoam as well as the hills for the scenery. I also used it to hold-down the track, to attach the Atlas electrical switches to the side of the layout and to attach the duct tape that serves as a fascia or "profile board" to protect the sides of the layout. Test any cement on the Styrofoam, because some will dissolve the Styrofoam.

You can cut the Styrofoam with a variety of tools including a hacksaw blade, saber saw, serrated kitchen knife or special hot wire cutters. Knife blades are available for saber saws, including Sears' Craftsman 2873 or the Vermont American 30022, that work well cutting Styrofoam (Figure 6-3). The hacksaw blade and knife produce a dust and shavings that are difficult to clean up. The saber saw with a knife blade and the hot wire produces fumes that can be toxic, especially to anyone with allergies. If you use a saber saw with a knife blade or hot wire cutter, then, work outdoors. Always use a ruler to guide the blade or hot wire to produce a perfectly straight cut. If you use a hacksaw blade, you can hold it in your hand (Figure 6-4) or buy one of the holders that allow about half of the length of the blade to protrude. I would recommend a serrated knife only for smaller cuts and for shaping finished scenery.

Cutting Styrofoam With A Hot Wire

The quickest and least messy way to cut foam is to use a hot wire cutter. I used a hot wire cutter made by Avalon Concepts to cut the foam for the 6-by-6-foot Union Pacific layout. It is a relatively expensive tool but it works quickly, and the only mess, even when sculpting scenery shapes as shown in Chapter 10, are potato-chip-size flakes. The Avalon Concepts hot wire "Foam Sculpting Detail Station" set includes a transformer to reduce the 110-volt current to a usable level and a "Detail Wand" handle (Figure 6-5). The heated wire is still potentially dangerous, however, because it is very hot —it can become as hot as an electric stove —and the melted plastic that can dripoff the wire is hotter than melted candle wax, so burns are possible. I'd suggest you wear cloth gloves and long sleeves so no skin is

exposed. The fumes that the melted Styrofoam produces can also be harmful, so always work outdoors when using any type of hot wire cutter on any type of Styrofoam. Caution: **Do not** try to use a hot wire cutter with the urethane foams because the fumes produced can be toxic.

I bent a piece of Avalon Concepts wire to form a 2-1/2-inch long-by-1/2-inch wide U-shape with 90-degree bends (Figure 6-6), to be clamped into Avalon Concept's "Detail Wand" that is included in the "Foam Sculpting Detail Station" set so the tool can be laid flat on the Styrofoam (Figure 6-7) and it will automatically produce a clean 90-degree cut. Experiment with the edge of

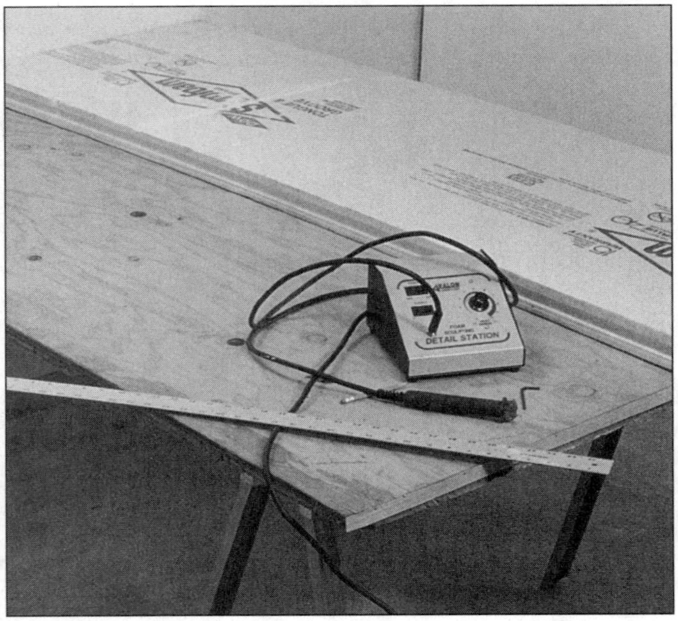

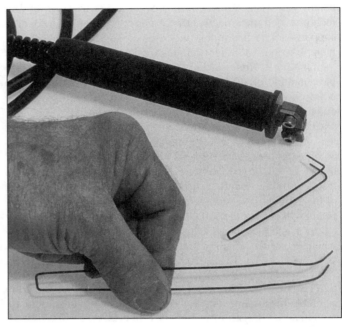

Figure 6-6. Bend the Avalon Concepts wire into two U-shapes, one about 4-inches long to use in carving scenery, and another about 2-1/2-inches long (top) to use for cutting Styrofoam panels to size.

Figure 6-7. Clamp the 2-1/2-inch U-shaped wire into the Avalon Concepts "Detail Wand" and use a steel ruler to guide the tool when cutting Styrofoam panels.

Figure 6-5. The Avalon Concepts "Detail Station" includes a power supply and the black-handled "Detail Wand" hot wire cutter.

one of the pieces of blue Styrofoam to be sure the cutter really is producing that right angle cut and make any bending adjustments that are needed to the wire. Use a ruler to guide the tool for perfectly straight cuts while the 90-degree bend in the hot wire helps make the cut a right angle. Follow Avalon Concept's instructions and clamp the wire securely with at least a half-inch between the wires so, even when hot, the wires won't touch one another. If they do, it forms red-hot wire sections that can blow the fuse in the Avalon Concepts' Detail Station transformer.

Adjust the controls on the Avalon Concepts "Detail Station" so the wire is just hot enough to cut about as fast as you can saw through l/4-inch plywood with a hand-held jigsaw. You'll hear a popping sound as the hot wire breaks the countless air bubbles that are trapped in the Styrofoam and wisps of white smoke will emit from the cut. The blade should float through the material with little or no drag. Do not force the wire through the cut or you'll bend the wires, which will make the cut uneven and can force the two wires together. If you are producing lots of hair-like wisps of plastic, you are pushing the hot wire too rapidly through the Styrofoam.

Avalon Concepts also makes a jigsaw-like hot wire "Shaper." You can use it to make relatively shallow cuts for slicing off the tongue from the Styrofoam. Use a ruler to guide the hot wire for a straight cut. Woodland Scenics makes a similar hot wire cutter called a "Foam Cutter." These jigsaw-like tools are fine for cutting strips, but they cannot reach down into the Styrofoam like the Detail Wand hot wire cutter or even a hacksaw blade.

Building the 6-by-6-Foot Union Pacific Layout

I assembled the two layers of 2-inch thick Styrofoam for the 6-by-6-foot Union Pacific layout on a sheet of 1/2-inch plywood, but you could do the work just as easily on a flat garage or patio floor. There is no need to cement the Styrofoam to the plywood (or, for that matter, to the floor). First, I cut two 6-foot long pieces from 2-by-8-foot Styrofoam panels (Figure 6-8). I wanted the finished 6-by-6-foot layout to be self-supporting with no open-grid benchwork, so I overlapped the two layers so the joints between the panels on one layer did not overlap the joints between the panels on the second layer. I started with a 2-by-6-foot piece along the back of the layout that extends off the

4-by-6-foot plywood (to form the wing where the "Alliance" yard will be built) and a 2-by-4-foot piece along one edge, then I cemented a 2-by-4-foot piece to finish the two layers in the "Alliance" yard area (Figure 6-9). Next, I filled-in the gap on the first layer of foam with another 2-by-4-foot piece and spread the PL300 adhesive over it and the original 2-by-4-foot piece. I then installed a second 2-by-6-foot piece of Styrofoam along the side to finish that portion of the second layer (Figure 6-10). Finally, I added another 2-by-4-foot piece to complete the two layers. It is best to test-fit each piece before you actually make the cuts because some may need to be fraction of an inch longer or shorter than that nominal "4-feet" or "6-feet" to fit precisely. Also, push the pieces firmly together while you are fitting them. When everything fits perfectly, cement the pieces together.

Figure 6-9. The beginning of the two layers of 2-inch thick Styrofoam for the 6-by-6-foot Union Pacific layout. A 2-by-6-foot panel rests against the wall, with a 2-by-4-foot panel on top of it and a second 2-by-4-foot panel along the right edge of the layout.

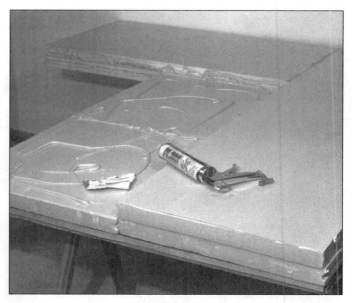

Figure 6-10. A second 2-by-6-foot panel has been attached along the right edge and a third 2-by-4-foot panel has been added to complete the first layer. The cement is spread for the installation of a fourth 2-by-4-foot panel to complete the two 2-inch thick layers of the 6-by-6-foot layout.

Figure 6-8. Two of the 2-by-8-foot Styrofoam panels cut to fit a 4-by-6-foot area with the "tongue" removed from one outer edge and cemented to the "groove" on the opposite outer edge.

Figure 6-11. The 2-by-2-foot "wing" on the upper left of the 6-by-6-foot Union Pacific layout is cut so the far left end is just one-foot wide. A hacksaw blade, guided by a ruler, is used to make the cut through both 2-inch layers of Styrofoam.

Figure 6-12. A single 2-by-2 wood leg is used to support the 2-by-2-foot "wing". The metal leg-mounting bracket is cemented to the bottom of the Styrofoam and a bolt is threaded into the 2-by-2 leg to fit the bracket. The round pads are furniture pads to keep the 2-by-2 leg from damaging the linoleum floor or carpet.

The trackplan for the 6-by-6-foot layout indicated that the "wing" extension from the 4-by-6-foot main layout could be smaller than 2-by-2 feet. After the adhesive dried for a few days, I used a hacksaw to trim the piece at an angle starting at the two-foot wide intersection with the main layout and sloping back to a one-foot end at the far right (Figure 6-11). I cut a single 2-by-2 board for a leg to support the wing. I fitted a leg-attaching bracket to one end and a round furniture pad to the other. Cement the leg-mounting bracket to the bottom of the Styrofoam and attach the leg with a combination wood screw and 1/4-inch bolt. Protect the linoleum or carpet from the bottom of the leg with a round furniture pad (Figure 6-12).

The Woodland Scenics Lightweight Sub Terrain System

Woodland Scenics is producing white expanded-Styrofoam components, with a redesigned foam that is somewhat stronger than conventional white Styrofoam, for an alternate method of lightweight layout construction. Their system begins with a plywood or blue Styrofoam flat tabletop. The track is elevated on 2-inch flexible risers (Figure 6-13) placed beneath the track all around the layout. This elevation provides space for rivers and streams below track level. If you want deeper riverbeds, Woodland Scenics offers a 4-inch flexible riser. Woodland Scenics also makes "Inclines" that match the risers. The Inclines start at a zero level, so you can begin grades right from the tabletop (Figure 6-14), but it's best to start with at least 2-inches of riser to leave space for rivers and roads to cross beneath the tracks and for embankments beside the track as described in Chapter 5. The Risers and Inclines are two-inches wide, so they can be used for double track or for passing sidings. For single-track, the edges

Figure 6-13. The Woodland Scenics "Risers" and "Inclines" can be attached to either a plywood tabletop or a Styrofoam tabletop. Tee pins can be used to position the "Risers" or "Inclines" until the track is alignedt, then Liquid Nails "Projects and Foamboard" cement or Chem Rex PL300 "Foam Board Adhesive" is used to attach the riser permanently to the layout and to each other.

Figure 6-14. The Woodland Scenics "Inclines" start with a zero elevation so they can be used to bring track upgrade from a level tabletop as shown.

Figure 6-15. The corners of the "Risers" or "Inclines" should be carved away with a hacksaw blade or serrated knife for single-track support. Sectional track can be supported on cork roadbed or Woodland Scenics Track-Bed, or you can use track a with built-in ballast like Kato Uni-Track, Life-Like Power-Loc track or Bachmann E-Z Track (shown).

should be cut at any embankments or approaches to bridges (Figure 6-15). Woodland Scenics also has a "Low Temp Foam Gun" that can be used to attach their Risers and Inclines to the tabletop and to one another. The glue is cool enough so it can be used with the blue Styrofoam as well. Or, you can use the Liquid Nails "Projects and Foamboard" cement or Chem Rex PL300 "Foam Board Adhesive" to assemble the SubTerrain components.

Woodland sells 12-by-24-inch sheets of white expanded Styrofoam in 1/4-inch and 1/2-inch thicknesses to allow you to build lightweight "building sites" and towns and roads at track level. Woodland Scenics also sells 12-by-24-inch sheets of white expanded-Styrofoam in 1-inch, 2-inch, 3-inch and 4-inch thicknesses you can use if you want to support buildings or roads on solid blocks of Styrofoam.

Building Roadbed Upgrades

The major drawback to the use of the blue extruded-Styrofoam tabletop construction is that there is no simple way of providing for upgrades, short of tilting the Styrofoam itself. You can, however, combine the blue extruded-Styrofoam system with the Woodland Scenics SubTerrain "Incline" system. Woodland Scenics has white Styrofoam flexible "Inclines" to create either 2-percent or 4-percent grades. The "Inclines" come in sets that elevate the track in 2-inch increments—just the thickness of the blue extruded Styrofoam—so you can use stair steps of the 2-inch thick material for up or down grades (Figure 6-16). The 2 inches is enough height so one track can pass over the other, even if the lower track is mounted on cork roadbed. If you want an upper level, then, it can simply be mounted on a second 2-inch layer of blue Styrofoam. Frankly, I do not recom-

Figure 6-16. The "upper" level in the distance is a piece of 2-inch thick blue Styrofoam placed on top of the Styrofoam tabletop. A set of Woodland Scenics' "Inclines" brings the track from the lower tabletop to the upper. The grade can continue upward on the second 2-inch layer of Styrofoam.

mend using grades on layouts as small as 4-by-8 or 6-by-6 feet because there just isn't enough room to gain elevation and maintain realism. You can achieve the same effect by cutting away the edges of the table as was done on the Union Pacific layout that is visible in overall views of the layout in the color section and in Chapter 1 (Figures 1-5 and 1-6).

Finishing The Fascia

The outer edge of a lightweight layout should be protected. The extruded polystyrene can chip easily and the expanded polystyrene beadboard is even softer. You can add a fascia to surround the entire layout. The fascia gives the layout a finished look and protects the foam. I used green duct tape to protect the edges of the 6-by-6-foot Union Pacific layout. The edges of the Styrofoam are too porous, however, to provide a surface to grip the duct tape. The duct tape must, then, be cemented to the Styrofoam with Liquid Nails "Projects and Foamboard", Chem Rex PL300 "Foam Board Adhesive" or a similar latex-based cement that will not attack the Styrofoam. You can use the same

cement to attach a fascia made from 3/32-inch plywood veneer. When the cement dries, cut the duct tape with scissors (and the plywood with a saber saw —Figure 6-17) to match the contours of the scenery at the edge of the table.

The control panels can also be mounted above or below the fascia. The Digitrax system for the 6-by-6-foot Union Pacific layout was mounted in cavities cut into the 1-by-2-foot wing area at Alliance as shown in Chapter 8 (Figures 8-18 and 8-19). Computer supply stores and some larger office supply stores carry slide-out panels for computer keyboards. These can be mounted beneath the Styrofoam tabletop. It's best to attach the slide-out brackets to pieces of 1/4-inch plywood for a greater contact area with the Styrofoam and cement the plywood to the Styrofoam with Liquid Nails "Projects and Foamboard", Chem Rex PL300 "Foam Board Adhesive" or a similar latex-based cement that will not attack the Styrofoam. The slide-out panel (Figure 6-18) can then serve as a shelf to hold a power pack and walk-around hand-held throttle or a DCC system like the MRC Command 2000 shown in Chapter 8 (Figure 8-16).

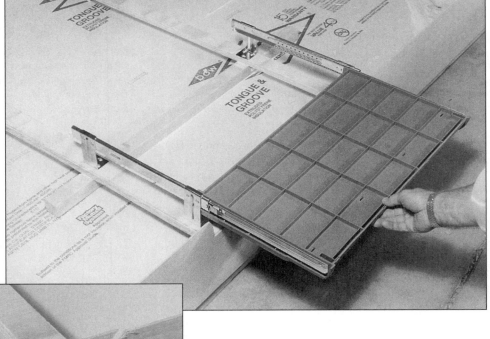

Figure 6-18. A slide-out computer keyboard shelf makes a perfect place to support a power pack on the side of the layout. Here, the layout is upside down. The shelf is attached to plywood with screws and the plywood is cemented to the bottom of the Styrofoam.

Figure 6-17. Protect the edges of the Styrofoam with duct tape or 3/32-inch plywood veneer. The plywood can be cut to match the scenery contours with a saber saw.

Chapter 7

Trackwork

Track is the most important component of any model railroad. Smooth trackwork will allow smooth-running trains that seldom derail. Smooth trackwork will also allow trains to sweep gently into curves, rather than lurching into them, and allow trains to track dead straight down the tangents without wobbling. For most model railroaders, however, track is just a necessary evil; an aspect of the hobby, like scenery, that's just a backdrop for the locomotives and rolling stock. If you are using the track merely to support the trains in a static diorama that's true. If, however, you want those trains to display the same life-like movements that the real ones do, the track has to be nearly perfect. Laying smooth trackwork can, however, be one of the most difficult skills to learn when building an N scale layout.

Smooth track always starts with a firm and flat roadbed. Use a file, a Surform plane or sandpaper to smooth any joints between the different pieces of plywood, Homasote or extruded polystyrene (like Styrofoam) that you have used, as described in Chapters 5 and 6, to support the track or roadbed. I cannot say it often enough; the base beneath the track is the most important factor in smooth trackwork.

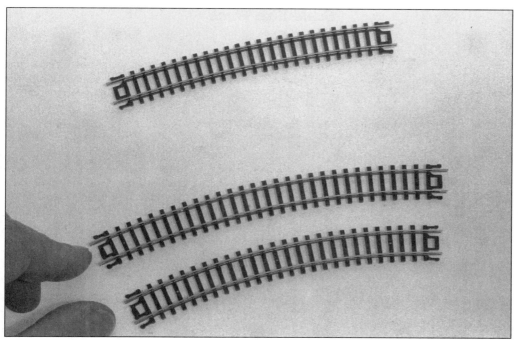

Figure 7-1. The 6-by-6-foot Union Pacific layout was made with the largest radius sectional track Atlas offers, the 19-inch (top) radius sections. Most of the plans in the Atlas plan books utilize the 9-3/4-inch and 11-inch radius curve track sections (bottom).

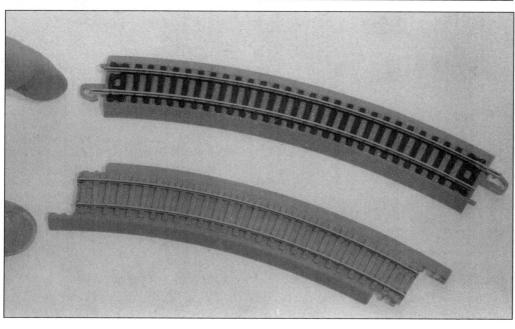

Figure 7-2. Bachmann offers E-Z Track (top) and Life-Like offers Power-Loc (bottom) with built-in plastic ballast and clips that lock the track together so the fragile metal joiners only carry electrical current. Bachmann offers 11-inch radius and Life-Like has 9-3/4-inch radius curves. The two brands are not interchangeable, however.

Three N Scale Track Systems

Some N scale train sets are supplied with track sections that are joined with a pair of rail joiners. This sectional track is most definitely not designed for operation on the floor. The simple operation of trains over the track is enough to loosen any of the joints, which results in stalled trains and derailments. If you try to shift or move a completed layout, the rail joiners will bend easily and must be carefully retightened by squeezing each side with a pair of pliers. To use the track supplied with the train sets, it must be glued or nailed to a tabletop. If you want ballast shoulders, you must use either cork roadbed or, if you are building a layout with a blue Styrofoam tabletop as shown in Chapter 6, you can cut the shoulders into the tabletop with a knife or hot wire tool.

The second type of N scale track has built-in plastic roadbed and ballast that snap the track sections firmly together. Bachmann's E-Z Trac, Life-Like's Power-Loc track and Kato's Uni-Track are the most common N scale sectional track systems with built-in ballast. Tomy's Tomix track is similar to Kato's Uni-Track, but it is somewhat more difficult to locate. Bachmann's E-Z Track and Life-Like's Power-Loc track are included with most of the train sets sold by those firms. This track locks together much better than the older sectional track but, because N scale is so small, I cannot recommend that you use any of this track on the bare floor or carpet. Replacement sections of Bachmann's E-Z Track are available only in 9-3/4-inch radius curves and standard straight track sections and Life-Like's Power-Loc is currently only available in 11-inch radius curve sections, standard straight track sections and turnouts with 11-inch radius curved routes. The two brands are not interchangeable unless you are willing to use a razor saw to slice off the interlocking tabs and rely on just the rail joiners to connect the two different brands.

If you are a newcomer to the hobby, the Kato Uni-Track is an excellent choice because it is far easier to lay than flex track, it stays in alignment better than conventional sectional track, the rail joints don't work loose, there is a wide choice of track curve radii and turnout sizes, there is no need to apply loose ballast, and the electrical operations for the turnouts are located beneath the turnouts themselves. The disadvantages of Kato Uni-Track are that it is much more expensive than any other track and it can sometimes be difficult to locate all the pieces you require.

The third most common N scale track is called flex-track. It utilizes the same turnouts (switches) as the sectional track, but the remainder of the layout is made from three-foot lengths of track. These three-foot lengths of track can be used as-is for straight sections or cut to length with a razor saw or flush-cut diagonal cutters. These three-foot lengths of track have ties designed so the track can be curved to any radii in any direction. When you force the flex-track into a curve, the inner rail will eventually protrude farther than the outer rail. The ends of the rails can be cut, after you have shaped the flex track to perfectly match the plan, with diagonal cutters. If you want ballast shoulders for the flex track, like the sectional track, you must use either cork roadbed or cut the shoulders into the tabletop with a knife or hot wire tool.

Scale-Size Track

One of the advantages of using flex track is that you can choose track that has more closely-spaced ties and smaller rail, that is far more realistic reproduction of the prototype track than any brand of sectional track. Most sectional track and the track with built-in ballast is fitted with rail that is approximately .070-inches high or, as modelers refer to it, "code 70" rail. Peco and Micro-Engineering offer both turnouts and flex track with code 55 rail that is a near-perfect match for most mainline rail. Peco offers number 4, number 6 and number 8 turnouts, wye turnouts and double-slip switches (a combination of a 12-degree crossing and four turnouts in the space of a single turnout). For those modeling industrial tracks laid with lighter rail, Micro Engineering also offers flex track with code 40 rail but, be cautioned, many of the car and locomotive wheel flanges will hit the spikes on track with this tiny rail.

For whatever reason lost to some obscure toolmaker, the ties are also far too large and far too far apart on nearly all brands of N scale track. You can disguise the out-of-scale ties with weathering and bury them in ballast, but the effect is still disturbing. Micro Engineering is the only firm I know of that offers both code 70 and code 55 flex track and number 6 turnouts in either rail size with scale-size ties and tie spacing, although Shinohara offers similar track and turnouts but with code 70 rail.

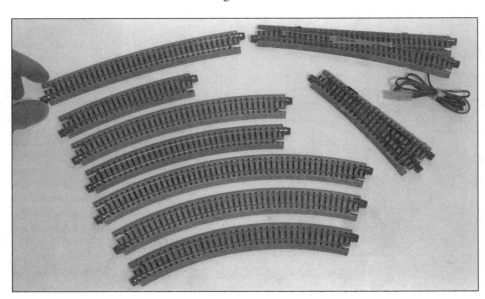

Figure 7-3. Kato Uni-Track has built-in ballast with snap-together alignment that does not rely on the rail joiners to hold the track together. They offer 7 different curve radii in a variety of lengths of straight track as well as both number 4 and number 6 turnouts with either manual or remote control (upper right).

Figure 7-4. Virtually all of the sectional track and flex track, including the track with built-in ballast like E-Z Track, Power-Loc Track and Uni-Track, have oversize ties spaced about twice as far apart as the prototype and oversize code 70 rail (top). Micro Engineering flex track with code 55 rail (bottom) has the tie size and spacing that matches most prototypes and rail that is also correct for most mainline railroads.

What Kind of Track?

The plans in Chapter 3 (Figures 3-3, 3-5 and 3-13) and Chapter 4 (Figures 4-2, 4-3 and 4-4) are drawn using Atlas sectional track with number 6 turnouts and 19-inch radius curves except for a few Atlas "Standard Switches" (turnouts) and 11-inch radius curves. You can also use the plans to build layouts with Atlas, Peco, Micro Engineering or Shinohara flex track. If you use Micro Engineering or Shinohara turnouts, their number 6-size turnouts will have to be substituted for the Atlas Standard Switches (turnouts) and the resulting sidings will be slightly shorter. If you use Peco turnouts, substitute the Peco number 4 turnouts for the Atlas Standard Switches and use Peco number 6 turnouts in place of the Atlas number 6 turnouts.

Selecting the Right Turnouts

Model railroaders refer to the piece of track that allows the trains to take a diverging route as a "turnout," not a "switch." The moving parts of the turnout that actually change the train's route are called "switch points." I opted for Atlas turnouts and sectional track for the 6-by-6-foot Union Pacific project layout. Atlas offers four different turnouts: "Standard Switches" (turnouts) in both manual and remote-control versions, with a 19-inch radius curved route and a 4-7/8-inch long straight route. These turnouts can be used in place of 19-inch curved sections or standard straight sections with no modifications in the plan. Atlas also offers number 6 turnouts that have the more-gently curve route that matches the prototype but you must custom-cut some curves to use these turnouts as described in Chapter 4 (Figure 4-7), they are also offered both as manual and remote controlled.

Turnout Positioning

There are good and bad places to put turnouts. In some places, you should use remote-controlled turnouts, and in other places it's better to use manual turnouts. The track plans

in Chapter 3 (Figures 3-5, 3-6 and 3-13) and Chapter 4 (Figures 4-2, 4-3, 4-4 and 4-5) show some examples of where curves and turnouts can and cannot be mixed in order to minimize the chances for track misalignment and the resulting derailments. In brief, the standard straight/curve turnouts should be used only in place of straight track sections or at the beginning of curves. The curved/curved switches should be used only in place of a piece of curved track.

If a turnout is placed more than 2-1/2 feet from the edge of the table or in a tunnel, it should definitely be a remote-control turnout. Try to avoid placing turnouts in tunnels, and, if you must, make a portion of the mountain above the turnout removable so you can work on the turnout or rerail any wrecks. Turnouts that are within 2-1/2 feet of your control panels might just as well be the manual type, which are thrown by moving the pin directly at the turnout. The remote-control turnouts add three more wires for each turnout to what may already be complicated wiring. The fewer turnouts you can use, the easier your layout will be to maintain. If you have to walk up to the control panel to work a remote-control button or turnout lever for a turnout that's as easy to reach as the panel itself, you are adding unnecessary complication to the layout. The remote-control turnouts can still be operated by moving the pin beside the turnout, however.

Vanishing Switch Machines

The switch machines on the E-Z Track and Uni-Track turnouts are hidden beneath the roadbed, with just a small pin visible to manually control the turnout. Most other brands, however, and all the Atlas and Model Power sectional track, have bulky switch machines beside the turnout. Nothing on a real railroad even resembles the switch machine beside the Atlas or Model Power turnouts. You'll increase the realism of your layout considerably, then, by hiding those switch machines. Do not try to cover up the switch machines with the plaster scenery. There is no room for the added thickness of scenery on the rail side of the switch machine. The best trick is

Figure 7-5. Some of the N scale turnouts include (left to right): Atlas "Standard Switch" and number 6 turnout, Micro Engineering number 6 turnout, Shinohara number 6 and number 4 turnouts, and Peco number 6 and number 8 turnouts.

to paint the switch machine with the basic brown earth color. When you mask the switch points during the ballasting, keep the switch machine clear so that it will receive some of the wash of flat black and earth colors used to weather the rest of the track. Do, however, completely seal the slot where the manual-operating pin is located so no fluid can get inside the turnout's control mechanism. You'll be amazed at how well the switch machines blend into the layout when their colors match the scenery. It's not so obvious in the photographs because the switch machines' shape is still visible, but the camouflage-with-paint technique does work.

You can go a step further, with some of your switch machines, and hide the portion that is away from the track with bits of ground foam-rubber leaves to simulate weeds and bushes. A few scraps of balsa wood or some old brass rail can be cut and piled on the backside of switch machines where there are no adjacent tracks. The switch machine will then become just part of the pile of wood or rail. Be careful, when working with glue around the switch machine, that no glue finds its way inside the switch machine or anywhere near the switch points.

The Atlas Standard Switch turnouts for remote-control operation have the switch machine located in a rectangular box mounted beside the turnout with two screws (Figure 7-6). There's an electrical solenoid inside that box that can be actuated by a remote-control push button or slide switch on the control panel. There is also a pin beside each turnout that can be used to operate the turnout manually, in addition to the electric remote-control feature. The Atlas Standard Switch

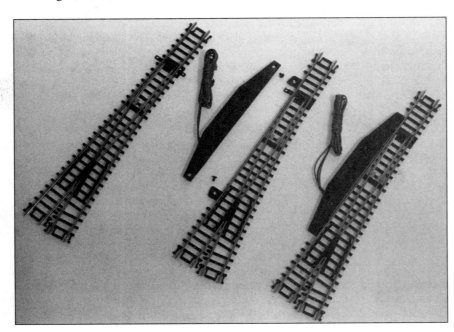

Figure 7-6. The Atlas "manual" number 6 turnouts (left) have no provision for mounting a switch machine or for holding the points in either position. The remote-control number 6 turnouts, however, have a removable control box that includes the electrical solenoid's and a small pin that can be used to move the turnout points by hand.

Figure 7-7. The Atlas switch machines are much less noticeable if mounted upside down. Remove the switch machine and hook the plastic throw-bar onto the wire in the switch machine as shown.

Figure 7-8. The Atlas Standard Switch with the control box in the conventional position (left) and mounted upside down (right) so it is level with the tops of the ties.

manually-operated turnouts have this same box, but with no internal electrical parts. However, the pin can be used to move the switch points. The Atlas number 6 turnouts are different, however, in that the "manual" version has no control box, nor lugs to mount the control box. In fact, there is no way to hold the moving points in position unless you install some kind of remote-controlled switch machine or at-the-turnout control lever. (The Shinohara turnouts also lack any means of operating the points.) The Atlas remote control number 6 turnouts have the same electric control box (including the small turnout-actuating lever) as the Standard Turnouts. If you want to have manual operation of the Atlas number 6 turnouts, you might consider buying the remote control version, cut-off the wires and use the small pin on the control box for at-the-turn-

out manual operation. If you need to replace the control box, you can remove it by simply removing the screws.

The rectangular boxes on the Atlas turnouts can be mounted upside down so the bulk of the mechanism is level with the tops of the ties. Remove the two screws that retain the control box. Turn the box upside down and hook the wire that moves the switch points to the small black plastic hook inside the box (Figure 7-7). Use five-minute epoxy to hold the hex nuts inside the tabs on the sides of the turnout. Use the original mounting screws to mount the control box upside down (Figure 7-8). Carefully adjust the box and, if necessary, bend the wire that moves the switch points, until the turnout operates flawlessly. If you need to replace a burned-out control box, you must pry up the entire turnout, however.

Figure 7-9. This Rix switch machine has coils that move the bar from side to side. It is designed to be mounted below the table so it can be linked to the turnout points with a wire or through levers.

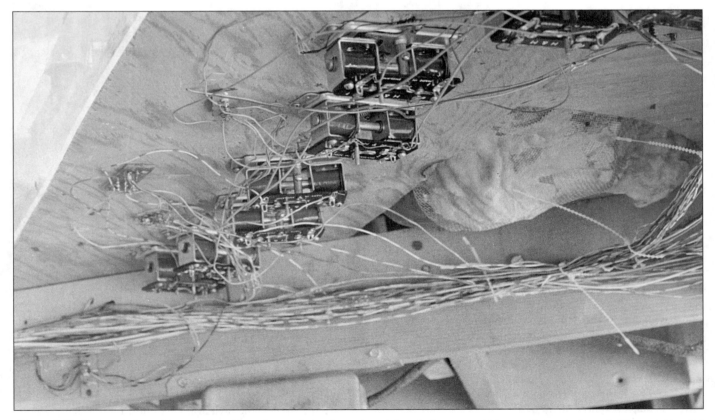

Figure 7-10. Each switch machine requires three wires so it can be activated from buttons or switches on the control panel. These eight switch machines are mounted beneath a six-track freight yard with a passing siding.

Beneath-The-Table Switch Machines

Most experienced model railroad builders use a heavy-duty type of electric machine when they want remote-control operations of turnouts. These turnout-actuating devices are usually called "switch machines." Peco offers a reliable double-solenoid switch machine that is designed to fit their turnouts, but it also can be adapted to many other brands. Atlas, NJ International, Precision Scale and Rix also offer solenoid-style switch machines. Switchmaster division of Builders in Scale and Circuitron's Tortoise offer smooth-running and silent electric motor-driven switch machines. You can use any of these machines with a layout built using 1/2-inch plywood supports for the cork roadbed. Most firms offer linkages that allow the switch machine to be mounted directly beneath the turnout on the underside of the tabletop (Figure 7-9). If you have a number of turnouts, the array of switch machines can be rather intimidating, but each is wired with the same three-wire system. The array of switch machines in Figure 7-10 is an example of what a 6-track freight yard and passing siding can look like from beneath the layout.

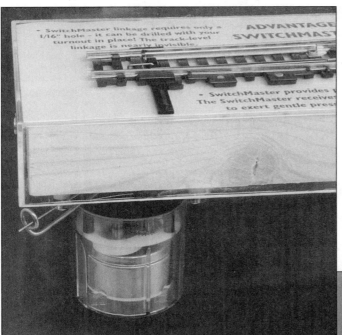

Switch Machines for Styrofoam Layouts

If you decide to build your layout from 2-inch thick slabs of extruded polystyrene insulation board, like the blue Styrofoam products shown in Chapter 6, the tabletop may be four-inches thick. It is difficult to use a lever-type switch machine linkage with such a thick tabletop. The motor-style switch machines like the Switchmaster (Figure 7-11) and Circuitron's Tortoise can be used because their linkage is a simple twisting action. You can also use the linkage from Earl Eshleman (Ye Olde Huff n Puff) as shown in Figure 7-12. To install the link, simply drill a 1/8-inch hole through the table beside the turnout throwbar as described in the instructions furnished with the linkage. When the linkage is installed, only the short bar is visible beside the track (Figure 7-13). Below the table, the linkage can be connected to virtually any type of electric switch machine including Peco, Atlas, NJ International, Precision Scale, Rix, Switchmaster and Circuitron. If you prefer to have remote-control manual operation, you can connect the Eshleman link to an automobile choke cable as shown in Figure 7-14. The knob on the cable can be mounted in a 1/4-inch hole drilled in a piece of Masonite or 1/8-inch plywood on the edge of the layout.

Figure 7-11. The Switchmaster switch machine by Builders in Scale is a small electric motor that moves the switch points through a rotating lever. It is also designed to be mounted below the table and to be activated by a switch on the control panel. It can be used with either conventional plywood tabletop construction or with layouts that have four-inches of Styrofoam insulation board for the tabletop.

Figure 7-12. The Earl Eshleman turnout linkage is shown laying beside the turnout. To install the linkage, drill a 1/8-inch hole beside the switch points as described in the instructions.

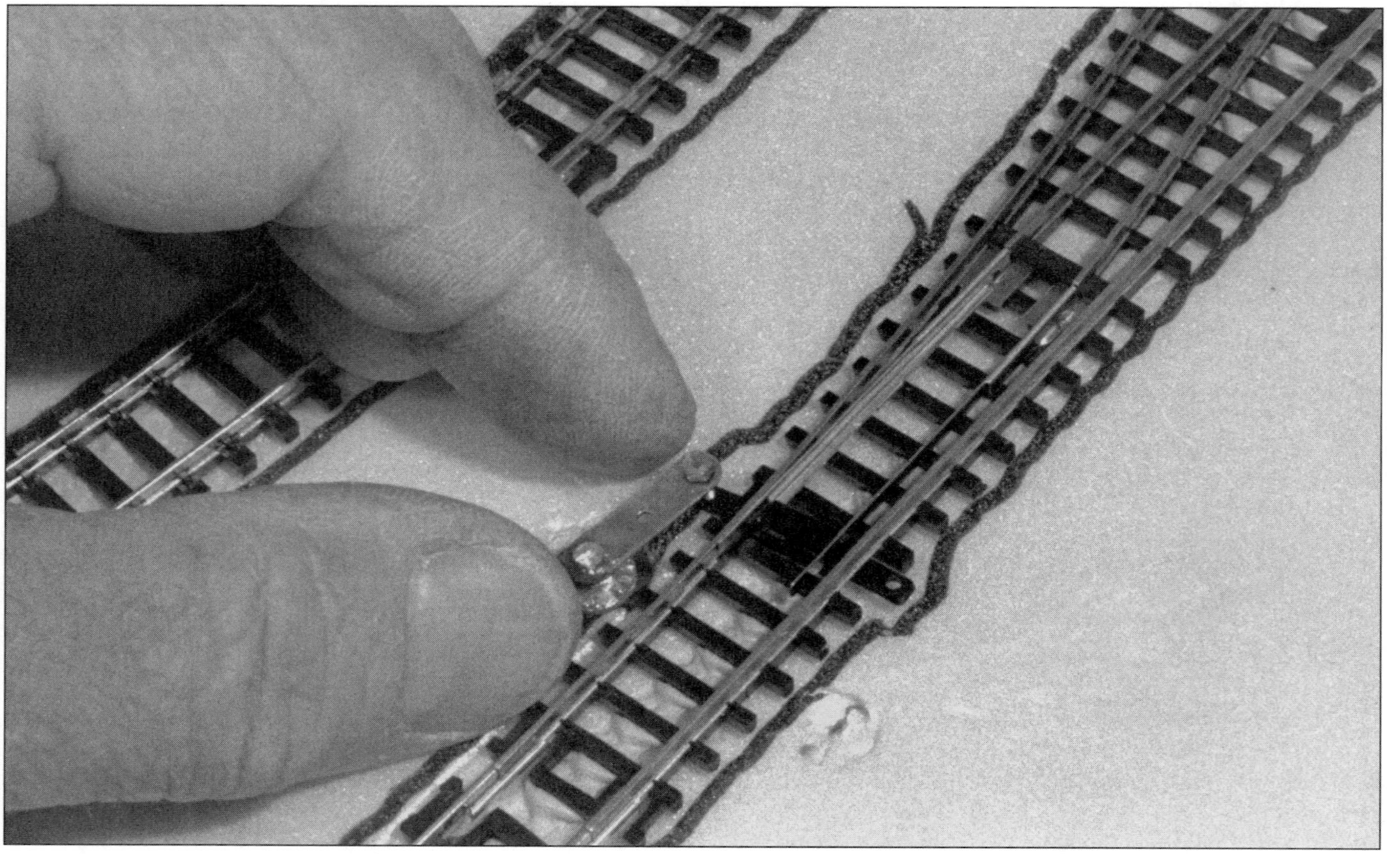

Figure 7-13. The Earl Eshleman link has a small brass lever that pivots right and left beside the turnout to push and pull the turnout points.

Figure 7-14. The bottom of the Earl Eshleman turnout linkage installed beneath a plywood tabletop. Here, the linkage is being actuated by an automobile choke cable rather than an electric switch machine. The knob on the choke cable is mounted on the edge of the table to provide manual-style remote control of the turnout.

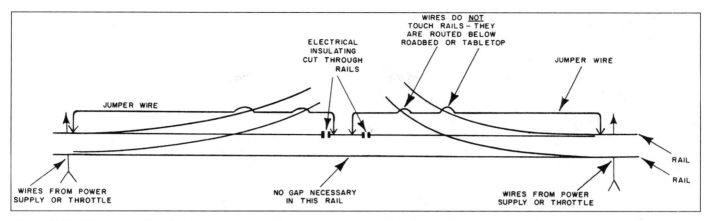

Figure 7-15. When using "live frog" turnouts from Micro Engineering or Shinohara, additional electrical gaps and jumper wires must be installed between any two facing turnouts.

Turnout Wiring Fundamentals

Working with the wires from a remote-control turnout may very well be the first bit of "complicated" wiring you will have to do on your layout. The actual track wiring is seldom complicated by the addition of a turnout because most of the N scale turnouts, including Atlas, Bachmann, Kato, Life-Like and Peco, have a system of routing electrical power through the turnout regardless of which direction it is thrown. The only time you must add additional track wiring is when the addition of a turnout creates a wye or a reversing loop as part of the track plan. Wiring for wyes and loops are shown in Chapter 8; the loops in two of the figure-eight plans in Chapter 3; and wyes in the 6-by-6-foot, 8-by-11-foot plans in Chapters 2 and 4. The Micro Engineering and Shinohara turnouts have a different design that requires electrical power connections only at the point ends of the turnouts and electrical insulation gaps in the rails whenever a right and left pair of turnouts are mounted with the frog ends facing on another (Figure 7-15).

Each of the remote-controlled turnouts has three wires leading from the switch machine, and these must be connected to the turnout controller on your control panel and to the "AC" terminals on your power pack. Circuitron and NJ International offer momentary-contact lever-style switches for the control panel that work well with switch machines and Atlas has a momentary-contact slide switch (called a 150-56 "Switch Control Box") that is included with their remote control turnouts. The momentary-contact switches are necessary with the solenoid-style switch machines. The Circuitron Tortoise and Switchmaster switch machines have electric motors with built-in off circuits so a conventional on-off switch can be used with these switch machines. On a complicated layout, which might have dozens of turnouts, it's a good idea to purchase a separate power pack for the turnouts and use another one to operate the accessories. The use of a turnout or an accessory can affect the speed of a train at a critical moment. For most first-time layouts, a single power pack for all three (trains, turnouts, and accessories) is sufficient.

Beside-The-Turnout Operations

I would suggest you consider using controls for the turnouts that are located right beside the turnout. Remote controlled turnouts are an interesting action item, but the maintenance can be a nightmare. You can use the control boxes supplied with the Atlas turnouts, as described earlier, to actuate these turnouts manually with the sliding lever beside the switch points.

The Peco turnouts (Figure 7-16) have a trigger-style spring that holds the switch points against the outside rail. To throw these turnouts manually, you need only move the switch points with the tip of your finger and they will snap tightly in the direction you move them. Micro Engineering has a similar feature on their turnouts. If you want to actuate an Atlas turnout without using the unsightly Atlas control box, you can

Figure 7-16. The Peco turnouts (shown) and Micro Engineering turnouts have a built-in lever that automatically snaps and holds the switch points to one of the outside rails. You can actuate these turnouts by merely flicking the points to the proper path with your fingertip.

Figure 7-17. The Caboose Industries "Ground Throw" lever can be used to manually operate Atlas or Shinohara turnouts. The lever's arm is moved with your fingertip from laying horizontal to the right, to lying horizontal to the left as it moves the switch points from one direction to the other.

purchase one of the "ground throw" levers made by Caboose Industries (Figure 7-17). These tiny levers are somewhat less obtrusive than the Atlas control boxes but they must be mounted firmly to the layout. They can be operated with a fingernail to flip the switch lever over to move the switch points at the turnout. You can use these same levers to operate the Atlas manual number 6 turnouts and the Shinohara turnouts.

Railroad Grades

I cannot recommend upgrades or downgrades for anything but industrial sidings. If you're an experienced carpenter and like to build benchwork, you may not have too much trouble. The plastic supports for "over-and-under" figure-eight-shaped layouts are nice toys, but they are neither substantial enough, nor realistic enough for a model railroad. The transitions between the level and the bottom and the tops of any grade are very difficult to make. An abrupt change isn't that much of a problem when you're just pushing a single car or two into a siding on a hill. Pulling or pushing long trains up or down-grade, however, will cause derailments, and that can take a lot of the pleasure out of the hobby.

Try it this way: When you've built a layout as complete as the 6-by-6-foot empires in Chapter 3 (Figures 3-4, 3-5 and 3-6) and you have smooth operation with few derailments, then you can advance to your "third" layout and experiment with all kinds of up and downgrades. (The charts for figuring grades appear in Chapter 3 (Figure 3-14 and 4-15 are for advanced modelers.) Spend your track-laying time on that first layout or two, and get the track to align properly in the two dimensions of a level layout before complicating things with the third dimension of up or downgrades.

Laying Sectional Track

The sectional track, with only ties and rail, slides together easily with rail joiners. In fact, it's almost too easy; the slide-together feature of the individual track sections makes it seem that that's all there is to laying track. But if you've operated a

train set on the floor before, you know that it's not quite that simple. The tracks do slide together easily, but they slide apart even easier. And sharp dips and bends in the track are the rule rather than the exception. The primary method of ending the battle with track joints is to attach the track to a roadbed or ballast board with cement. In this way, the track will be secure and won't move about. The trap here, however, is that you won't solve all the track-caused derailments and train stallings by simply gluing the track down, particularly if you haven't been extremely careful. With some care and the application of the experience of other model railroaders, though, you can virtually eliminate derailments and other track problems.

The Surveyor's Task

No brand of sectional model railroad track is self-aligning except, of course, even the track with built-in ballast like E-Z Track, Power-Loc Track or Uni-Track. Even if you manage to get every single rail joint to fit tightly, other problems can occur. Slight variations in the length of the individual pieces of rail, slight warpage in a few plastic ties, and a few other minor misalignment problems can add to one another to create a major problem. In fact, just bumping against the side of the table can disturb the track alignment. Once you do get sectional track aligned, so the joints are perfect fits, use push-pins to hold it temporarily to the tabletop. When it is aligned, then squeeze the track joiners tight with needle-nose pliers.

Track Alignment

I suggest that you purchase a three-foot-long steel or aluminum ruler or, at least, a perfectly straight two- or three-foot 1-by-4 board. The board will keep the straight track sections truly straight when two or more of them are pushed together. An extra piece of curved track can be used as an alignment gauge for curve-to-curve joints, but it's best to make a compass or trammel to draw a perfect radius right on the tabletop or roadbed to check the curve alignment. Make a compass or trammel from a wooden yardstick. Drive a nail at the one-inch

Figure 7-18. Make a trammel from a yardstick so you can mark the exact radius of any curve. This is one way to double-check that sectional track is in alignment. The trammel is more useful, however, to mark the centerline of the track when you are using cork roadbed with flex-track.

mark, and then drill 1/4-inch holes to match the radii you have used for your layout. If you are using the plans from this book, you will need only 11-inch and 19-inch radii, so drill the holes at the 12 and 20-inch marks. Hold the nail in the center of the circle and push a pencil through the appropriate hole. Use the pencil to move the trammel around the curve (Figure 7-18).

That leaves only one problem—the places where a curved section joins a straight section must be aligned so the geometry will be almost perfect. Any sudden lurch to the left or right at the beginning of a curve is too toy-like, and, worse, it can be the cause of unpredictable derailments. Use a pair of right and left turnouts to help you eyeball that curve-to-straight alignment. The turnouts are "perfect" combinations of straights and curves. By placing the turnout upside down over the curve-to-straight transition, you can see that the curved rails are all in alignment. The transition from curve-to-straight is more gentle through a number 6 turnout than through the Atlas Standard Switch or other turnouts, so use a number 6 right and a number 6 left to check those straight-to-curve transitions when you are using flex-track.

The Basic Tools

The tools that are the most important are the ones that are necessary to lay the track, assemble plastic building kits, and perform any necessary maintenance or adjustments on the rolling stock, locomotives, and track. You may already have many of the tools around the house, but it would be better to get a specific set for the exclusive use of building and maintaining your model railroad. You can make some minor substitutions for the tools I suggest in terms of sizes; a five-inch pair of needle-nose pliers will do just as well as a seven-inch pair. However, do not try to second-guess the list. Don't, for instance, substitute common pliers for needle-nose pliers or a pocketknife for an X-Acto hobby knife.

One final bit of experience garnered from more than thirty years of similar mistakes; spend the extra few dollars to get the very best tools at a hobby or hardware store rather than picking up "dollar" bargains. The better tools will probably last a lifetime, so their cost on a per-year basis is only pennies:

Basic Model Railroading Tools

- Pointed tweezers
- Small standard screwdriver
- Small Phillips-head screwdriver
- Flush-cut diagonal cutters (small)
- Flush-cut diagonal cutters (to cut rail optional)
- Small needle-nose pliers
- Scissors
- Micro-Trains Number 1055 coupler-height gauge
- X-Acto Number 1 hobbyknife handle with extra Number 11 blades
- X-Acto Number 5 hobbyknife handle with Number 235 razor-saw blade

The use and purpose for most of these tools will be obvious to anyone who has assembled a train set. Some of them, though, are intended for rather obscure purposes. The flush-cut diagonal cutters are sold by many hobby, hardware and electronics supply stores. Like most diagonal cutters, they are designed to cut wire by virtually squeezing through it to produce a cut that has a 45-degree bevel on both sides. The "flush-cut" diagonal cutters have angled cutting surfaces on their jaws, so that the angle is on just one side of the cut; one side produces a perfectly flush or vertical cut. Do not attempt to use them for cutting the track rails. This will dull the cutting surfaces. Some hobby shops also sell larger flush-cut diagonal cutters that are designed to cut brass or nickel silver rail. The small flush-cut diagonal cutters are intended to cut wires with a minimum of pulling and damage to the individual wire threads. Their most important use, for a model railroader, will

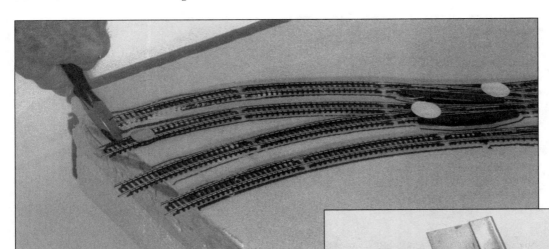

Figure 7-19. Use flush-cut diagonal cutters or "Rail Nippers" to cut special lengths of track or, as shown here, to cut-off the ends of tracks flush with the edges of the table.

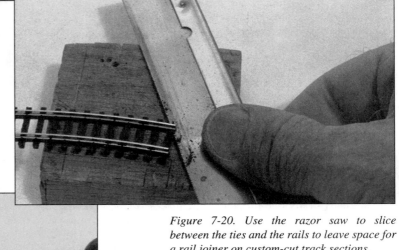

Figure 7-20. Use the razor saw to slice between the ties and the rails to leave space for a rail joiner on custom-cut track sections.

Figure 7-21. These Life-Like crossing gates were cut so two of them could be used side-by-side on a passing siding at Duncan on the 6-by-6-foot Union Pacific layout.

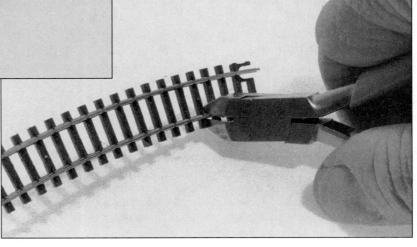

Figure 7-22. The flush-cut diagonal cutters can be used to custom-fit track sections. Hold the cutters so the flush-cut side faces the part of the track you want to use.

be to cut the windows and other plastic parts for structure kits from the molding sprues, or "trees," of scrap plastic. If you cannot find flush-cut diagonal cutters, buy regular diagonal cutters and use them for cutting wire.

The X-Acto Number 1 hobby knife handle and Number 11 blades can be used to cut these structure parts from their sprues. Hobby shops also sell "Sprue Cutters," that are smaller versions of the flush-cut diagonal cutters, for cutting plastic parts from their sprues. Do not attempt to pull or break the plastic parts away from their sprues; there's a good chance you'll break the part rather than the sprue! The Micro-Trains Number 1055 coupler-height gauge is absolutely essential for adjusting the height of the knuckle couplers on rolling stock or locomotives shown in Chapter 16.

The X-Acto Number 5 hobby knife handle and the Number 235 razor-saw blade are the tools you need to cut the rails for custom-fitting snap-together track on some layouts as shown in Chapter 4 (Figure 4-6) or for cutting the track so it extends all the way to the edge of the table (Figure 7-19). The razor saw will also be useful for slicing between the ties and the rails on any track sections you have cut (Figure 7-20) so the rail joiners can be pushed into place. The razor saw can also be used to cut through other plastic surfaces like the edges of the road surfaces when you want a crossing to fit in a tight area (Figure 7-21), if you do not wish to purchase the second pair of large flush-cut diagonal cutters.

Custom-fit track sections are necessary with some track plans, and a cut-to-fit end-of-track piece for a siding can often mean the difference between the siding holding one car or two. You can save money and have a smoother flow of track on your second model railroad layout by substituting 3-foot lengths of flexible track for long stretches of sectional track. The flexible track will seldom fit in any layout without at least one of the rails being cut to fit. It's somewhat tricky to get the flexible track shaped into smooth curves, so I suggest that you build at least one layout with the track with built-in ballast, like Kato's Uni-Track, Bachmann's E-Z Track or Life-Like's Power-Loc track, before using sectional track or flexible track.

You will probably use the razor saw most for cutting plastic walls and other structure parts for building "conversions" such as some of those discussed in Chapter 9.

The larger flush-cut diagonal cutters are useful for cutting rail to custom-fit sectional track or to trim the rails to length when using flex-track (Figure 7-22). Model railroad shops sell special cutters called "Rail Nippers" for this purpose. The cutters make a clean cut on one side that can be lightly scraped with a hobby knife or a jeweler's file to remove any trace of burrs.

There are some additional tools you may want to purchase to use when assembling structure kits or rolling stock kits that are described in Chapter 9.

Mounting Sectional Track On the Tabletop

I would suggest you use some type of glue or caulking compound, not nails or brads, to secure N scale track sections. If you are gluing the track directly to the Styrofoam, you'll need something that will not attack either the plastic ties or the Styrofoam. Liquid Nails for "Projects and Foam board" or Chem Rex PL300 are two brands intended for use with Styrofoam and other expanded or extruded polystyrene materials.

Before you cement the track in place, be certain that the sectional track is precisely where you want it and that every single joint is perfectly tight with the ends of both rails touching and no sudden jogs or angles in any rail anywhere. You won't get an easy second chance, so get the alignment perfect now.

Next, I strongly recommend that you solder every rail joint except those where you are using an insulated plastic rail joiner. If you heat the rails while you are touching the tip of the wire solder to the joint, as shown in Figure 7-23, the soldering gun can be removed the instant the solder flows. The solder will flow into the rail joiner area and the plastic ties will stay put. If you are concerned about melting the ties (and/or the molded-in plastic spikes near the joint) keep a cup of cold water and an eye dropper handy so you can douse the joint with water the instant after the solder flows. I find that 60/40 tin/lead solder with a flux core works best. Ersin is one brand, but there are others avail-

Figure 7-23. If you are using sectional track I would recommend that you solder virtually all of the rail joiners. The flimsy metal joiners are far too soft to hold the track in place even long enough to get the track cemented to the tabletop.

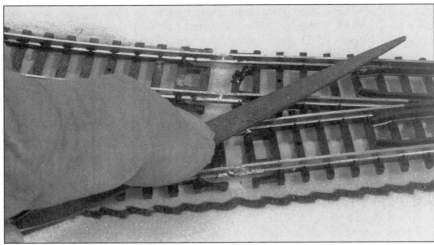

Figure 7-24. If you accidentally get too much solder on the joint, slice any major amounts away
with a hobby knife and file the tops and sides of the
railhead smooth with a jewelers file.

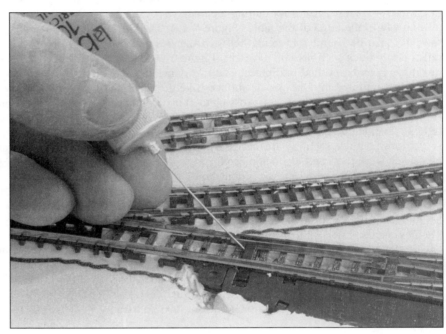

Figure 7-25. Apply a few drops of plastic-compatible oil to the bottom of the moving switch points
so they cannot accidentally be glued-down when
you glue the track to the tabletop.

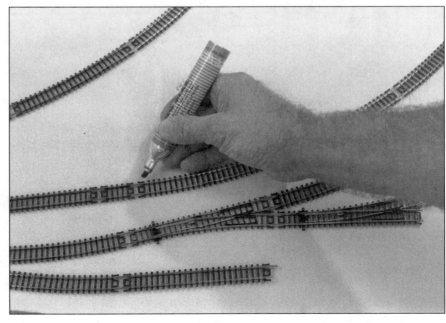

Figure 7-26. Mark both edges of the track with a
felt-tipped pen. Solder the rail joiners together,
then move the track aside in 2 x 4-foot sections
while you apply cement between the lines you
marked with the felt-tip pen.

able from electronics hobby stores like Radio Shack. If you do get a bit too much solder, you can slice away extreme excess amounts with a hobby knife, then file the tops and sides of the railhead smooth with a jewelers file (Figure 7-24). Leave a few joints loose, for now, so you can disassemble the layout into sections about 2-by-4 feet so you can move the track aside while you apply cement or caulking compound to hold the track permanently in place. Finally, apply a bead of plastic-compatible oil beneath the switch points and moving mechanism of all the turnouts so the working parts will not be cemented to the tabletop (Figure 7-25).

Use a medium-size felt tip marker to mark both sides of the ties all around the layout (Figure 7-26). Move the track aside, but leave it on the tabletop so it will be supported. If you do have to move it off the tabletop, have a 2-by-4-foot piece of 1/8-inch or thicker plywood ready to receive the track as you slide it off the table. Apply a thin bead of the PL300 or Projects and Foamboard caulking along one edge of the marked lines (Figure 7-27). Experiment with some leftover track and scrap wood or Styrofoam board to see just how much cement to apply. You want just enough so the ties will be buried to about half their depth in the cement.

If you get too much it will squeeze up between the ties and will look very strange. If you get just enough it will hold the ties firmly but be easy enough to pry loose later if you do have to relocate some of the track or remove a turnout for maintenance. If you get too much, you can scrape some up or spread it a bit thinner with a steel spatula. You will need to master the application of the caulking compound. It dries quite rapidly, so you will only have a minute or so to get the track back into position between the marked lines. Use firm finger pressure to push the track down firmly into the layer of cement. It is best to only apply cement to 2-by-4-feet or less of the track at a time. I divided the 6-by-6-foot layout into four segments. Remember to get each and every rail joiner in place as you add the second or third segments of the track. I would suggest that you merely tighten those rail joiners with pliers, but do not solder those final joints. You will want to leave a few places, besides the plastic insulated joiners, where the rails can expand and contract as they get hotter and colder during different times of the year. As soon as all the track is in place, try each turnout to be sure it still functions. If the moving switch points are cemented to the tabletop, you can free them by running a steel spatula between the ties and the tabletop (Figure-28).

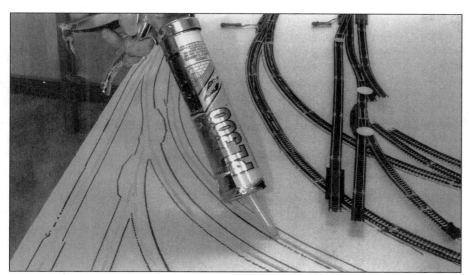

Figure 7-27. I used Chem Rex PL300 to hold the track to the Styrofoam tabletop on the 6-by-6-foot Union Pacific layout. Experiment to find out how small a bead of cement is necessary to avoid oozing over the tops of the ties. Spread the cement flat with a spatula, then push the track into the still-wet cement.

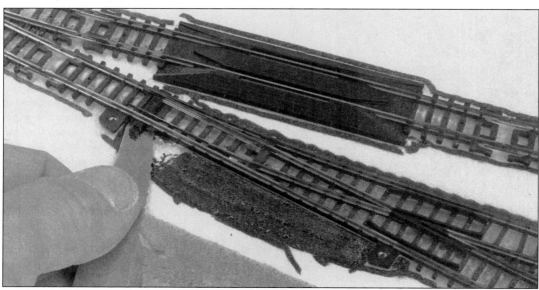

Figure 7-28. Check each turnout to be sure the switch points still move freely and, if not, pry them loose with a spatula before the cement dries completely.

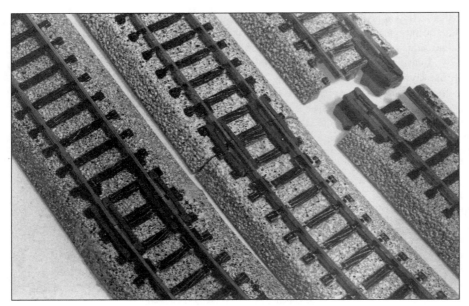

Figure 7-29. Kato Uni-Track has built-in ballast. Slide the two pieces (top) together until they click. Apply a pin-size bead of the Chem Rex PL300 or grey automobile body putty to each of the seams in the ballast and spread it evenly with screwdriver blade to disguise the joints between the Uni-Track sections (bottom).

Laying Kato Uni-Track

You can use the same caulking cement suggested for sectional track to hold Kato Uni-Track in place. The self-locking design of the Uni-Track will hold in alignment, so you only need a dab of caulking every foot or so to 'tack' the track to the tabletop. To ballast the Uni-Track, simply apply a trace of the grey Chem Rex PL300 Foam Board Adhesive, or common grey automobile body putty, to each joint and smear the cement or putty across the joint as shown in Figure 7-29. The newest Kato Uni-Track has a two-color ballast that is far more realistic than the single color of their earlier track or the colors of Bachmann's E-Z Track or Life-Like's Power-Loc Track. You can improve the realism of these single-color ballasted tracks by painting the entire track section with a wash of about five-parts water and one-part black acrylic paint. Experiment with how much paint to apply; you want just enough so the black paint fills-in around the simulated grains of ballast so the grey shows through as individual scale-size rocks.

Laying Flexible Track

You may want to consider using the three-foot sections of flexible track (flex-track) in place of several shorter pieces of sectional track. The flexible track can make the transition from curve to straight even gentler because the transition point can extend for an inch or two into the curve. Flexible track is also useful when there are three-foot and longer stretches of just straight track because the flexible track comes in straight pieces. You must bend the flexible track into a curve by carefully working apart ties on the outside of the curve as shown in Figure 7-30.

If you are going to use cork roadbed beneath the flex-track, it is the cork roadbed that will determine the alignment and flow of the track, so the cork roadbed must be installed perfectly and precisely. If you are laying the track directly onto a Homasote, Upsom board or Styrofoam tabletop, you have the "luxury" of being able to align the track rather than the cork roadbed. Carefully mark the centerline of the track with a

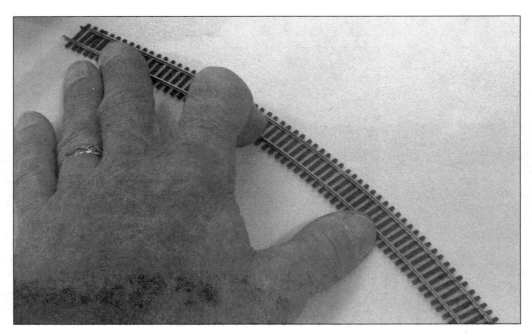

Figure 7-30. To bend flex-track, use your fingertips to gently work the ties apart on the outside of the curve. Check the alignment of the curve against the pencil line you have drawn with a trammel to be sure the curve is smooth and even.

compass for the curves and a straightedge to guide your pencil line for the straights. Make a trammel so you can mark the centerline of the curves as described under the section on laying the sectional track (Figure 7-18). When you align the straight sections with the curves cheat just a little bit and let the straight be 1/2 inch away from the OUTSIDE (away from the pivot point of the trammel) of the pencil-marked curve line. That will give you a chance to position the cork roadbed and, later, the flex-track, into a slight spiral or easement into the main curve.

Use the turnouts themselves as their own templates for marking the centerline. Be sure to keep a section of curved track to use as a guide for the radius of any curves you may bend with flexible track. This way you're sure to have a smooth radius all the way through the curve.

The secret to perfect trackwork with flexible track is to see that the cork roadbed for the entire layout is in perfect alignment before you install any track or permanently secure the track with cement. The artist's Matte Medium that will be used to secure the ballast will also secure the track.

Laying Cork Roadbed

If you choose flex-track or sectional track without built-in roadbed, you really should support the tracks on some kind of separate roadbed, if only to match the appearance of the prototype track. Cork roadbed has been a traditional choice for supporting model railroad track for almost 50 years. The cork provides a dampening boundary between the track and the tabletop or subroadbed so the trains sound more realistic. The techniques used to install cork roadbed are similar to those used to install the similar commercial roadbeds like Woodland Scenics' Track-Bed or the clay-like AMI "Instant Roadbed."

You can use cork roadbed with sectional track but you must be as careful aligning the roadbed as you were with the track. If you are using cork, you can use the ends of the ties you marked with a felt tip pen to also position the cork (7-26).

I cannot, however, recommend using cork with sectional track because it is so difficult to get the cork and the track to both be in perfect alignment. If you are using sectional track, I would recommend that you lay it directly on the tabletop. If you are using conventional wood benchwork, the tabletop beneath the track (the roadbed) can be one of the grey cardboard-like wallboards like 1/2-inch Homasote or 1/8-inch Upsom board. You can use a craft knife or a framing matt-cutter (Figures 7-34 and 7-35) to cut ballast shoulders and drainage ditches into the Homasote or Upsom board. If you are using extruded polystyrene insulation board like Styrofoam, you can also lay the track directly onto the tabletop and use the same technique to cut ballast shoulders and drainage ditches, but the Styrofoam is far, far easier to cut. Obviously, you can use these same materials and techniques with flex-track if you'd prefer to avoid using cork roadbed or a similar product.

If you are using flex-track, you must carefully and precisely mark the centerlines of all the track and turnouts with a pencil. Use a hobby knife or craft knife to finish the pre-cut slice between the two halves of the cork roadbed (Figure 7-31). You can use the Liquid Nails for "Projects and Foam board" or Chem Rex PL300 to cement the cork to plywood or Styrofoam. Run a thin bead of the cement along one side of the pencil line and push half of the cork into the cement with the square edge (the center of the roadbed) positioned exactly along the pencil line (Figure 7-32). Complete the outside of about half the layout, cementing only the outer half of the roadbed in place. Next, apply the cement to the tabletop beside the already-installed half of the cork roadbed. Then push the

Figure 7-31. Use a hobby knife to slit the pre-cut cork roadbed into its two halves.

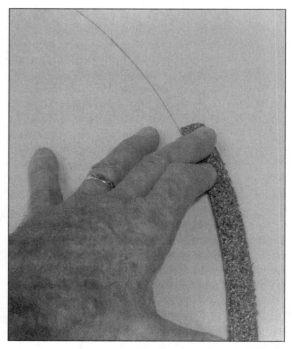

Figure 7-32. Cement one half of the cork roadbed to the tabletop so the vertical center edge of the roadbed aligns precisely with the pencil lines you drew indicating the center of the track.

other half of the cork roadbed into place, forcing it firmly against the first half (Figure 7-33). You can work the half-width cork roadbed around the outside of any turnouts, then cut wedges of the cork to fill-in the gaps.

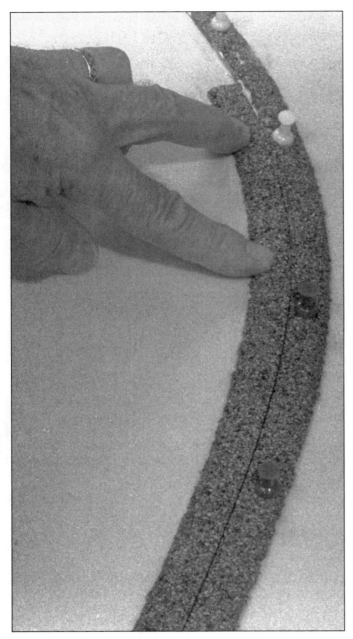

Figure 7-33. Cement the second half of the cork roadbed snugly against the first half. Work around the outside of any turnouts, then cut vee-shaped pieces of cork to fill-in the gaps.

Laying Track On Cork Roadbed

Begin laying the actual track starting with the turnouts, then connect them with pieces of flex-track cut to fit. Hold all the track to the cork with push-pins until you have applied the ballast and the artist's Matte Medium that will hold ooth track and ballast in place. When you have moved any flexible track into a curve, you'll find that the outer rail will be longer than the inner rail. Cut that longer rail with a razor saw and trim

away any burrs with a hobby knife. The sections of flexible track must be pre-fitted and the rail joiners installed, just like any other piece of track, before installing the pushpins to hold the track in place. When you are completely satisfied that all the track is in perfect alignment, solder each of the rail joints as described for sectional track. The pushpins must stay in place until the track is completely ballasted and the artists Matte Medium that secures both ballast and track has dried. If you are using conventional wood and Homasote benchwork, you can secure the track with a few nails, driven so the heads are 1/16-inch or so above the ties (for easy removal) to help hold the track you have already aligned in place. Check the alignment of each rail-to-rail joint. If there is a sudden bend at the joint, reshape the rails with needle-nose pliers so the rails, not just the rail joiners, are in alignment with each other.

The Train that Never Derails

There will never be such a thing as a train, real or model, that never derails. However, you can come very close if you pay careful attention to the alignment of your track and to the operation of your turnouts.

The ends of the turnout's moving switch points are just sharp enough to sometimes cause derailments. The flanges of the cars and locomotives tend to pick at the sharp corners of the switch points and derail. If you have a turnout that causes persistent derailments, you may want to trim just 1/32-inch of the corner of the turnout points. Do not trim any more than that or you'll make the point-picking problem even worse. Don't tempt the fates either; if your other turnouts are working without causing derailments, then leave them and their points alone!

Many model railroaders place a hatpin or a map pin into the layout at every place a derailment has occurred. The pin reminds them where to look for trouble (see the Derailment Troubleshooting Chart in Figure 7-43) when it comes time for an evening of maintenance. Cars or locomotives that are persistent derailers are placed on a shelf for attention at the same time. If you follow this kind of maintenance, you will soon locate and eliminate all of the troublesome spots on your layout.

Cutting Roadbed and Ditches

I would recommend building the tabletop for an N scale railroad from extruded polystyrene like Styrofoam as described in Chapter 6. If you prefer conventional wood lay-out construction, or if you're building NTRAK modules, the tabletop can be plywood. You should not even try to mount track directly onto plywood. Ordinary plywood is too hard; you'll snap plastic ties (and your temper) trying to get the track laid and the trains will sound like toys when you're done. Homasote or Upsom board can be laid on top of the plywood to support N scale track. Other types of wallboard, such as Celotex, are too soft, and plasterboard is too brittle and crumbly. The Homasote can be cut with a hardware store's carton-cutting knife, and then you can shape the edges into ballast shoulders with any hobby knife. The Homasote is just hard enough to hold the track nails securely, but it's soft enough so you can drive the nails into place with a pair of needle-nose pliers. Be sure to support the Homasote or Upsom board with at least 1/2-inch thick plywood.

Real railroad tracks have both ballast shoulders and drainage ditches as shown in Figure 7-35. Few model railroads have both ballast shoulders and these drainage ditches, but they lend an incredible degree of realism. Also, the drainage ditches will help to ensure that you do not place any cuts, tunnels or buildings so close to the tracks that they interfere with the passing trains. Real railroads bank the tracks slightly in curves as do most Interstate highways. The banking is so slight, however, that it is really not worth recreating in N scale.

You will want to cut both the ballast shoulder and the drainage ditch. You can make a single slice into the surface with a craft knife or for the ballast shoulder, then fill in part of the resulting "ditch" with ground foam to create the second shoulder and drainage ditch. The picture-framing matt-cutter (Figures 7-36 and 7-37) can be used to cut the ballast shoulder 5/8-inch from the centerline of the track. Make the cut about 1/4-inch deep. Repeat the process with the cutter entering the surface about one-inch from the previous cut. Adjust the blade so it

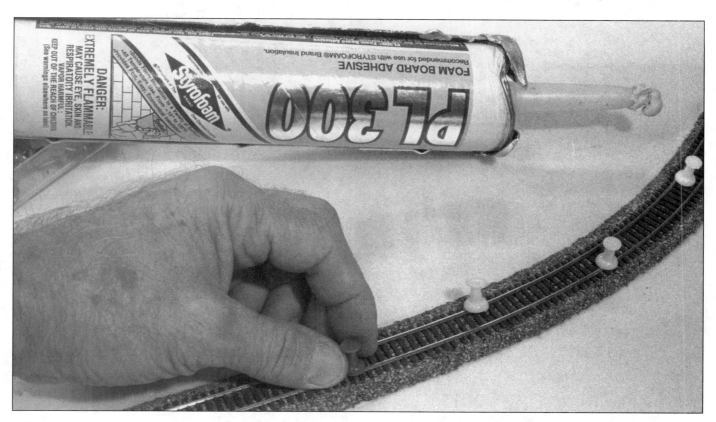

Figure 7-34. Hold the flex track and turnouts in place on the cork roadbed with push pins until you have applied the ballast as described in Chapter 12. The artist's Matte Medium that holds the ballast will also hold the track.

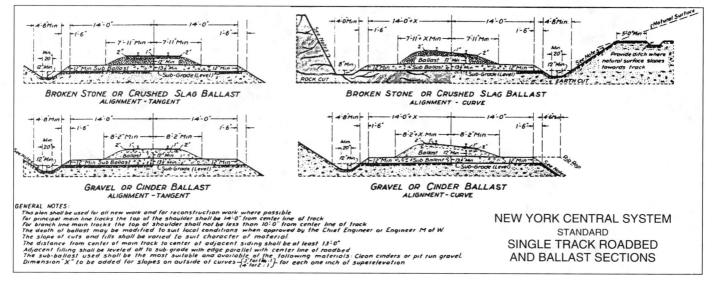

Figure 7-35. The New York Central Railroad's Standards for ballast and drainage ditches. You will want to duplicate both the ballast shoulder and the drainage ditch on your model railroad.

cuts the areas deep enough so they meet in the bottom and you can remove a vee-shaped piece of Homasote, Upsom board or Styrofoam from the "ditch" (Figure 7-38). You can do the job with a craft knife, but it is difficult to control both the angle and the depth, as well as guiding the path of the knife. The picture-framing matt-cutter allows you to concentrate on just guiding the knife.

If you are using extruded polystyrene insulation board like Styrofoam, for the tabletop, you can make the cuts far easier and more accurately with a hot wire cutter. Avalon Concepts makes a variety of hot wire cutters including a "Detail Wand" and "Sculpting Station". The components are described in Chapter 6. Bend a wire for the Detail Wand so the wire has a square-cornered U-shape that will fit across the tops of the rails

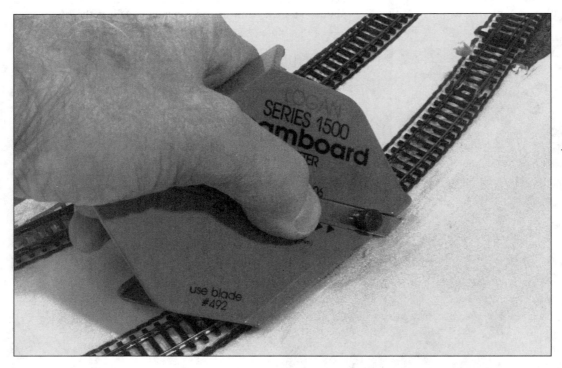

Figure 7-36. Use a picture-framing matte-cutter to slice the ballast shoulders into the Homasote or Styrofoam tabletop. Make the cut about one-inch from the center of the track and work carefully to maintain that spacing.

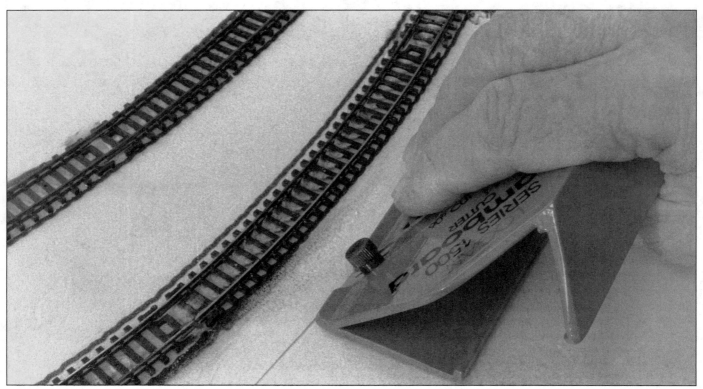

Figure 7-37. Make a second cut about two-inches out from the first to create the opposite side of the drainage ditch. The bottom of the ditch will be filled-in with sifted dirt and ground foam to simulate the prototype railroad's drainage ditch slope, shape, and size.

with the wire forming both the ballast shoulder and the drainage ditch on just ONE side of the track. Make the bends so the wire does not touch either the plastic spike heads or the ends of the ties, but rests solely on the tops and sides of the rails. It will take some practice and you may make three or four before you get it exactly right, so the wire just clears the outside of the rails (Figure 7-39 and 7-40). It's almost impossible to make a really tight bend here, so make one about 1/4-inch-by-3/4-inch as shown

and bend it 45-degrees sideways after the wire is mounted in the Detail Wand to make the U-shape shallow enough so it just clears the molded-in spike heads of the track. Make the other angle bends to match the wire in Figures 7-39 and 7-40.

To use the hot wire "ditcher," simply pull it along the track so that both sides cut equally wide ditches in the blue Styrofoam. It is, of course, essential that the track be located precisely where you want it so it will be centered over these two ditches. I would

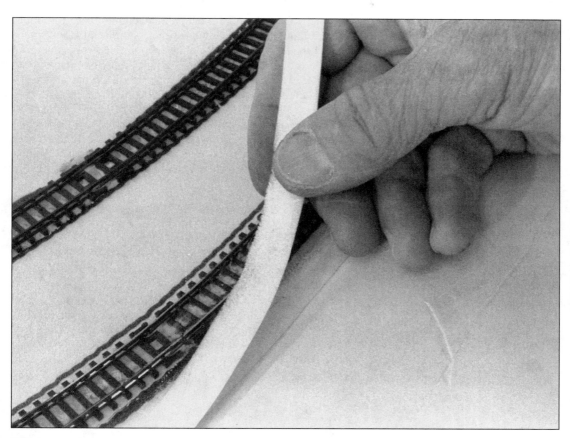

Figure 7-38. Remove the vee-shaped strip you just cut with the two passes of the matte-cutter. You can use a common utility knife but it is much more difficult to maintain a smooth and even cut.

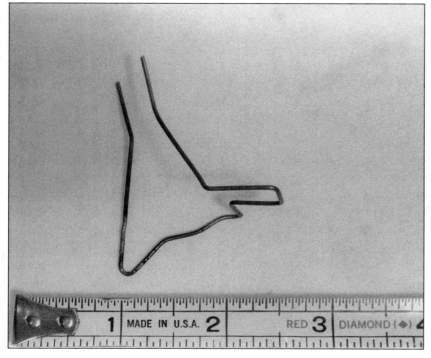

Figure 7-39. Bend the wire for the Avalon Concepts hot-wire Detail Wand so it will cut one of the ballast shoulder and one of the drainage ditches. Use the dimensions in Figure 7-34, but adjust the bends so the wire will ride along the tops of the rails without touching the plastic spikes or the ends of the ties.

advise waiting until you are confident enough to glue the track down before cutting the drainage ditches. Adjust the controls on the Avalon Concepts "Detail Station" so the wire is just hot enough to cut as described in Chapter 6. If you used the hot wire to cut the blue Styrofoam panels for the layout, you should already be familiar with the technique. Rest the wire on the tops of the rails and pull the tool along using the rails as a guide to cut the ditch along one side of the track. Repeat the process to cut the ditch along the other side of the track.

Practice cutting the ditches, however, on the bottom side of some of the leftover blue Styrofoam panels to get the feel of using this cutter. You will find that the hot wire changes shape slightly after it gets hot and you may need to bend a new one with extra lengths in between some of the bends to compensate for the way the wire bends when heated and pulled through the Styrofoam. I did not bother to try to cut a ballast shoulder between double tracks. I also did not cut ditches in the areas with industrial tracks. The single layer of ballast is enough to produce the effect of a ballast shoulder in N scale. The process goes quite fast once you've bent the hot wire to the shape that works. I was able to trace all the tracks on the Union Pacific layout in about three hours.

Caution, This Track is Fragile!

The major disadvantage of N scale is directly related to its advantage: size. A pine needle on the track can easily derail an N scale train and it is possible it could derail even an HO train if it were lodged in the right place. But an O scale train will either snap the pine needle or shove it aside. That pine needle is the size and, probably, the weight of a 10-foot long, six-inch diameter log (but as strong as a piece of iron) compared to the size of an N scale locomotive. The same pine needle is about the size and weight of a twig compared to an HO scale locomotive and the pine needle is but a stalk of wheat compared to an O scale locomotive. Clearly, tiny problems like dust, dirt and even layers of oxidized metal on the rails, have a far greater effect on N scale locomotives and wheels than they do on HO or O scale locomotives or wheels. It is most important to get N scale track installed perfectly, and then to clean it regularly.

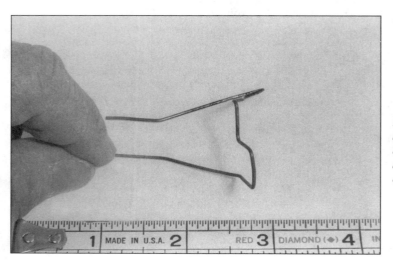

Figure 7-40. A side view of the wire used to cut the ballast shoulders and drainage ditches for the 6-by-6-foot Union Pacific layout. You will have to try the hot wire to see if it produces the size and shape you want and, if not, rebend it or bend a new one. This one was my fourth try and it may not work for you.

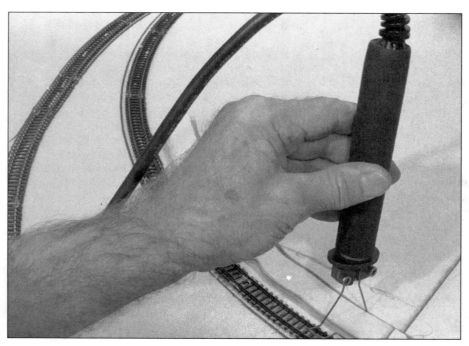

Figure 7-41. Use the rails to guide the ballast shoulder and drainage ditch cutter. The hot wire dissolves the plastic air bubbles in the Styrofoam as described in Chapter 6.

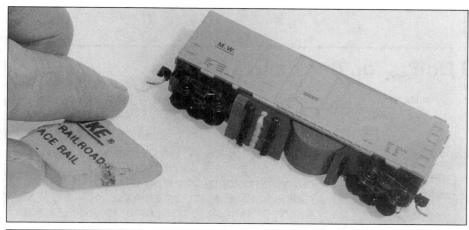

Figure 7-42. Use a hard rubber eraser intended for track cleaning like Life-Like's left. Aztec and others make special track cleaning cars that include hard rubber erasers, scrub brushes and a pad that can be moistened with track cleaner.

Derailment Troubleshooting Chart

Trouble	Probable Cause of Trouble	Solution
Train derails frequently at one particular place.	1. Offset rails at joiners.	1. Align rails and rail joiners with steel ruler and needlenose pliers.
	2. Excess plastic "flash" or wisps from ties on inside edges of the rails.	2. Trim "flash" with a hobby knife.
	3. Plaster, glue, or some foreign object stuck to track.	3. Remove it.
	4. Ends of rails burred or rough.	4. Smooth the tops and inside edges of the rails with number 400 sandpaper.
Train derails at turnout.	1. Switch points not throwing far enough to make firm contact with "through" rails.	1. Remove any foreign matter from area around points and check the action of switch lever inside the switch machine.
	2. Turnout twisted or bent, so all rails do not align in both "main" and "siding" turnout positions.	2. Bend the turnout into perfect alignment.
	3. Coupler pins hitting switch rails or frog.	3. Cut pins to proper length
	4. Any of four problem areas for "regular" track.	4. Correct, as outlined above.
Train derails everywhere.	1. Running the train too fast.	1. Run it slower.
Turnouts do not throw.	1. Turnout buttons on remote-control unit wired incorrectly.	1. Be sure wires are connected exactly as shown on the turnout's package and to "AC" terminals on the power pack.
	2. Button on turnout control not depressed when it is moved into position.	2. Simple operator error. Remember to *both* slide and push the button to actuate remote-control turnouts.
	3. "AC" portion of power pack not functioning.	3. Touch the wires from an r-t-r street light (test light) to just the "AC" terminals of the power pack. If light does not glow, have your dealer check the power pack.
	4. Turnout control is faulty, or contacts inside are dirty.	4. Touch the street-light wires to screws number 1 and 2 (the center screw) while you move the switch lever to the left and to the right and press it down. The light should glow. Touch the street-light wires to screws number 2 and 3 while you slide the switch lever to the right and push it down. The light should glow. If the light does not glow with the button to the right *or* left and depressed, replace the switch controller.
	5. Mechanical portion of the turnout and switch points may be bent or clogged.	5. Remove any debris from points and from switch machine and align switch parts.
	6. Hair-size wire inside remote-control switch machine broken.	6. Have wire soldered together at an electronics store.

Figure 7-43. Derailment Troubleshooting Chart

Do's and Don'ts for Track and Turnouts

• Do cut track sections to fit precisely into any odd-length gaps so the track and rails flow smoothly with no kinks.

• Don't try to bend the track to fill any gaps.

• Do squeeze each rail joiner with pliers, along the base or web of the rail, to be certain it fits tightly.

• Don't rely on the fit of rail joiners as they are furnished by the factory.

• Do be certain the track is in perfect alignment across each rail joint, then glue the track in place.

• Don't rely on the rail joiners to hold or push the track into alignment.

• Do place at least one 5-inch section of straight track between any ess bend so the trains will not lurch from left to right as they travel through the ess bend. The lurch is not realistic and it can cause derailments.

• Don't connect any radius right curve to a left curve without that "transition" section of straight track.

• Do try to place a larger-radius "transition" curve at the beginning and end of every curve. Use, for example, one length of 19-inch radius track at each extreme end of every 9-3/4-inch or 11-inch radius curve.

• Don't join any tight curves (9-3/4-inch or 11-inch radius) directly to straight track sections except in yards or industrial areas. Use a single piece of 19-inch radius track as an "easement" or spiral between the straight track (or a curve in the opposite direction) and the curved track.

• Do use only a hard rubber eraser like those sold by Life-Like, Model Power and Bright Boy to clean the tops of all rails.

• Don't use a file, emery paper or sandpaper to clean the rails. The surface of the rail will be scratched and the scratches will make it easier for dirt to collect and oxides to re-form.

Chapter 8
Control Panels and Wiring

All of the N scale locomotives are powered by electric motors that receive their current through the wheels or drivers of the locomotive and, in turn, through the rails of the track. The current enters the locomotive and the motor from one rail and returns through the opposite rail. The rails, then, are part of the "wiring" of any N scale model railroad. The flexible wire connections to the track are what modelers refer to when they talk about "wiring" a model railroad.

It's really quite simple to connect two wires to the track and run a train. Wiring becomes more complicated, however, when you provide places in the track plan like wyes and reversing loops to turn the trains around. The wiring can become even more complex when you want to operate two or more trains on the same track. There are three "easy" methods of keeping the wiring as simple as possible. First, you can avoid including any reversing loops or wyes in the track plan. Second, if you want to run two or more trains buy two power packs and construct a layout with two separate routes, like a double-track oval, with no track connections between the inner oval and the outer oval. Third, buy turnouts that require no additional wiring. The Micro Engineering and Shinohara turnouts will require the additional wiring to carry the power across the frog area , but all of the other popular brands of N scale turnouts, including, Atlas, Bachmann, Life-Like, Kato, and Peco, are designed so the electrical current is routed through the turnout, so no additional wires are necessary.

If you do want to run two or more trains on the same track, I would recommend that you consider using one of the Digital Command Control (DCC) systems described later in this chapter because only two wires need be connected to the track with the DCC systems. If you prefer to use conventional power packs to control two trains, then the common rail wiring system described later in the chapter (Figure 8-14), for two-train operation is another wiring shortcut that allows you to use an additional power pack for each train, but with just one additional wire (and one rail gap) for each electrically isolated block. You can decide how complex you want the wiring for your railroad in miniature by a thoughtful selection of the track plan and train control system.

Walk-Around Control

Walk-around control can make your entire railroad seem more realistic, with little expense or labor. Walk-around control is available from most manufacturers of model railroad power supplies. The walk-around control is a box about the size of television remote control that includes the throttle (speed control and reversing switch) on a tether or extension cord so you can walk around your layout to follow your train (Figure 8-1). It was developed about twenty years ago for large shelf-style around-the-room layouts, such as the 8-by-11-foot track plan in Chapter 3 (Figure 3-13). With it the operator has the ability to run the railroad from a single control panel in the manner of a real railroad dispatcher or towerman, but it also offers the chance to be an "engineer" and follow along beside the train.

Walk-around control will have a far greater effect on your attitude toward your models than you could imagine. Even a simple model will seem to be many times more true to life when you are moving along beside it with the throttle and reversing control in your hands. The controls for the turnouts and the blocks (for two-train operation) are still located on control panels, but those panels can be located near the yards or towns or other concentrations of complex trackwork. On basement-filling layouts, the turnout and block controls are strung out all along the edge of the benchwork just in front of the tracks they control.

Each brand of walk-around throttle has its own specific wiring instructions, but most can be connected with four long (10- to 20-foot) wires to the four terminals on the back of most power packs. Those four wires are the "tether" cable for the walk-around throttle. Some of the walk-around controls, like MRC's Tech IV (Figure 8-1), are simply plugged into a telephone-style jack on the back of the power pack. You will be able to walk along beside your train for the length of that cable. Position the power pack near the center of the edge of the layout. The best places to have a connection of the tether of a walk-around control would be on the end of the 6-by-6-foot Union Pacific layout near "Emmett" (Figure 3-5 in Chapter 3) or near the track marked "ISB" in the center access aisle on the "Around-The-Wall" layout (Figure 3-13). If you use a 12-foot long tether cable, you will be able to have just a single connection for the walk-around throttle's tether cable. The 12-foot tether cable will allow you to walk beside the train anywhere on those two layouts.

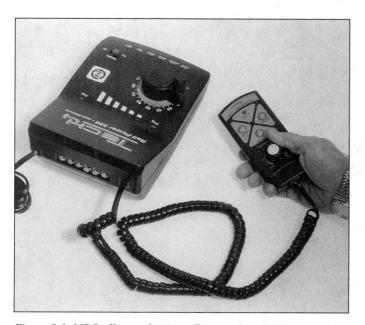

Figure 8-1. MRC offers a plug-in walk-around controller on a tether cable for their Tech IV power pack. The hand-held controller allows you to walk beside your train as it proceeds around the layout.

On really large layouts, you will probably want to provide jacks or sockets, located around the edges of the layout about every 20 linear feet. Some of the walk-around throttles use a standard telephone jack and they are pre-wired to their own plug, so you need only install the telephone-style jack on the edge of the layout.

All of the walk-around throttles are designed to be held in one hand with the throttle knob or switch operated by a thumb or forefinger of that same hand. That leaves your second hand free to operate the block switches or to uncouple the cars from the train as shown in Chapter 16. Your dealer can order MRC, Aristo-Craft, PSI, and other brands of walk-around throttles for you. The least expensive ones will have only the throttle and reversing switch, but some may also have a "pulse" control on-off switch for better slow-speed control or momentum so the train feels like it really weighs thousands of tons.

Two-Rail Wiring Basics

It's to the credit of the engineering efforts of the model railroad manufacturers that they have managed to make the "electrical system" of their trains look so much like the tracks of the real railroads. The rails of the tracks on your model railroad lead a double life. They guide and support the flanged wheels of the locomotives and rolling stock just like real railroad rails. The rails of a model railroad, however, also function as exposed "wires," which are part of the electrical circuit that carries the power to the electric motor in the locomotive. One of the rails is "positive" and the other "negative," and these carry the current to and from the locomotive. If the positive rail ever touches the negative rail, it will cause a short circuit. The plus and minus rails would appear to cross at every turnout or every 30-degree or 90-degree crossing track (Figure 8-2). The Atlas, Bachmann, Kato, Life-Like and Peco turnouts and crossings, however, are designed so that the "plus" rail passes beneath the "minus" rail at the frog (the plastic center of the turnout where the rails cross). A thin piece of plastic molded into that plastic frog insulates the two rails. An insulating gap has

been placed between the turnout's moving switch points and the rest of the rail, so no short circuit can occur there.

"Frog" Systems

The majority of N scale turnouts, including Atlas, Bachmann, Kato, Life-Like and Peco, have what is called the "insulated frog" system, and its greatest advantage is that it allows you to connect the track wiring on either side of the turnout and to mix in any quantity of turnouts and still have power (but no short circuits) anywhere on the track system. You must, of course, still provide insulating gaps and extra wiring at reversing loops and wyes. If you decide to use another brand of turnout that has a "live frog" design (like those from Micro Engineering or Shinohara) with an insulated frog turnout, you may create a short circuit in your layout. The "live frog" turnouts must receive electrical power from the "point" (or single-track) side of the turnout as shown in Chapter 7 (Figure 7-15). If you want to mix Micro Engineering or Shinohara turnouts with other brands, you can avoid the special wiring by placing the Micro Engineering or Shinohara turnouts so they lead to stub-ended industrial sidings or yards. In these places, the turnout can be at the end of the track.

Wyes and Reversing Loops

The N scale turnout and crossing design contains one problem that can't be eliminated. A short circuit is created whenever the track is arranged to form a reversing loop or a wye, such as those in this chapter. The reversing loop or wye is designed to allow you to turn a train around without removing it from the tracks. If you think about the logic of reversing a complete train or even a single locomotive, you'll realize (the diagrams will help) that the "positive" rail must touch the "negative" rail and vice versa. You may accidentally include a reversing loop or wye in a free-lance track plan; a diagonal track across an oval layout, with turnouts on both ends of the diagonal, will create a reversing loop like that in Figures 8-2 and 8-3 and on the track plan in Chapter 4 (Figure 4-3). A similar, but less obvious, reversing loop is part of the figure-eight track plans in Chapter 4

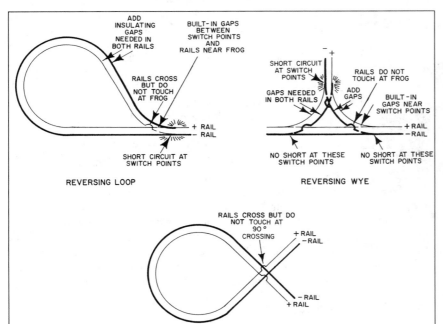

Figure 8-2. Short circuits will occur at wyes and reversing loops unless gaps are cut through both rails.

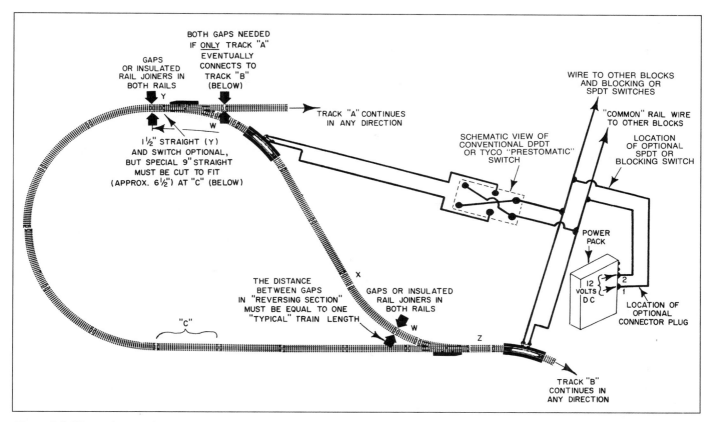

Figure 8-3. Wiring diagram for reversing loop trackage.

(Figure 4-4). Reverse loop connections are also located at "ISB" and "ISF" in the 8-by-11-foot track plan in Figure 3-13. Wyes are included in the 6-by-6-foot and 8-by-11-foot track plans in Chapter 3 (Figures 3-5, 3-6 and 3-13). Generally, you will want to include a wye or reversing loop on the layout just to add the variety of clockwise and counterclockwise operation without hand-carrying the trains.

A wye or reversing loop must have a section of track that is used for the actual reversing action. The diagonal track on the typical reversing loop and, sometimes, the stub end of a wye (as in Figure 8-4 and the track plan in Figure 3-5) are the obvious portions of the track that will be used mostly just during the time when the train is being reversed. A connection between a main line and a branch line, such as that in Figure 8-5, is a third example of where a reversing section might be located—this is the type of wiring that would be used with the wyes in Figures 3-5, 3-6 and 3-13. In every case, the reversing section must be isolated electrically from the rest of the layout by cutting right through both rails on both ends of the reversing section.

You can substitute the insulated plastic rail joiners for metal rail joiners (Figure 8-6), rather than cutting the rails if you wish. The rail joint created with plastic rail joiners is not quite as rigid as that done with metal rail joiners, so I recommend that you actually cut the rails whenever there is room. Cut the gap with a razor saw and apply a dab of five-minute epoxy or household cement (but not plastic cement) into the gap. This will prevent the rails from moving back in contact with one another. Sometimes it may be necessary to place an insulating gap between turnouts where there is space for only an insulated rail joiner.

The "reversing section" must be fed with electrical power, but an electrical reversing switch must be placed in the circuit between the wires from the power pack and the connections at the track (Figures 8-3, 8-4 and 8-5). Use a toggle or slide-type DPDT switch as a reversing switch by crossing the wires on the back as shown in (Figures 8-3, 8-4 and 8-5 and 8-7). Atlas makes a set of two pre-wired DPDT slide-type switches in one plastic housing called the "Controller" (far right in Figure 8-8). Either of the two can be used to control the operation of trains through the "reversing sections" of the track. When the train enters the reversing section, it will either stop or proceed, depending on how the reversing switch on the power pack is set in relation to the DPDT switch that controls the reversing section. If the train stops, then you must flip the DPDT switch that controls the reversing section until the train is just about to exit the reversing section. While the train is in that reversing section, the direction switch on the power pack must be flipped to the opposite direction. When the train leaves the reversing section, it will proceed onto the mainline. You must, of course, change the turnouts to route the train so it won't derail as it moves through the reversing loop or wye to reverse direction.

If the train proceeds through the reversing section, then you do not have to flip the switch. The DPDT (direction or reversing) switch on the power pack must, however, be flipped each time the train leaves the reversing section.

The short length of the "reversing section" may not allow you to use one of the terminal track sections to connect the wires to the track. In that case, I would suggest you solder the wires to the outside of the rails as shown in Figure 8-12.

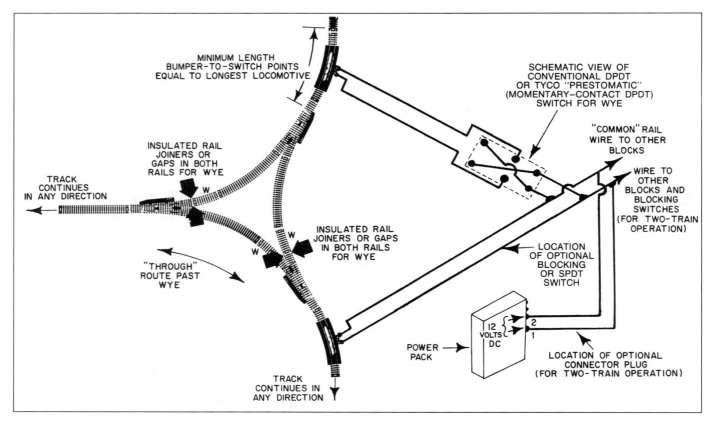

Figure 8-4. Wiring diagram for stub-ended reversing-wye trackage.

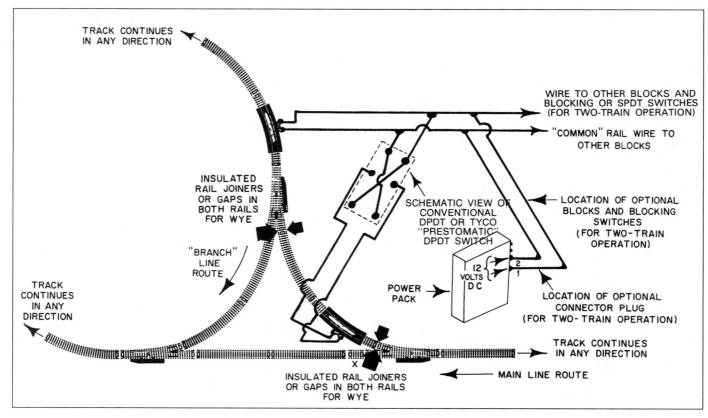

Figure 8-5. Wiring diagram for the mainline/branchline "through" reversing-wye trackage.

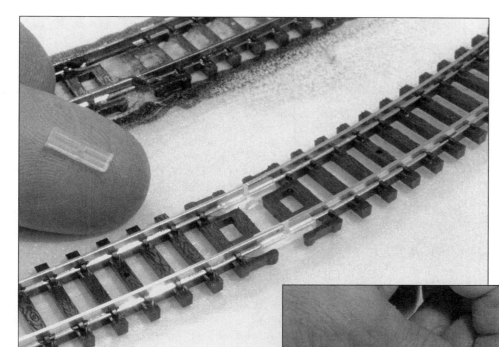

Figure 8-6. Insulated rail joiners are needed in both rails, and at both ends, of a reversing section in a wye or reversing loop.

Figure 8-7. Electronics hobby stores like Radio Shack or Allied Radio, carry these switches: SPDT toggle-type switch (left), push-button SPST (center)—a simple on-off switch, and slide-type DPDT switches (right). You must solder the wires to them as shown before mounting them in holes bored into the control panel face like those shown in Figures 8-20 and 8-21).

Figure 8-8. The Atlas switches can be mounted on a sheet of Evergreen .015-inch thick clear styrene plastic painted black, using caulking compound. This small panel includes two turnout control switches (left), a block "selector" for up to four blocks and the Atlas "Controller" (right) that has two reversing switches for use at wye or reversing loops.

Wiring Fundamentals

It is usually not necessary to solder any of the connections on your model railroad. You can buy rail joiners with wires soldered to them, but I do not recommend them because the N scale rail joiners are just not strong enough to make a reliable electrical connection with the rails. You can, however, purchase terminal track sections with screw attachments for the wires.

However, there are right and wrong ways to perform that seemingly simple task. I suggest that you use a sharp hobby knife to cut through the insulation on the wires, rather than using a conventional wire stripper. You can feel the point when you reach the wire with the hobby knife, so you can avoid even nicking the delicate hair-like strands of wire. It takes some practice to get the feel of cutting just the insulation and not the wire, but it's a technique that will always work once you learn it.

You'll need to remove only about 1/4-inch of insulation. If you remove much more, you'll have an excess of wire, and it might touch a nearby terminal screw and cause a short circuit. If you remove too little insulation, it will be difficult to get the terminal screw to grip the wire. When the insulation is off, twist the wire strands together immediately by rolling the exposed end of the wire between your fingers. Watch those ends carefully until you get each terminal screw tightened; retwist the wire if the individual strands start to wander about.

Each of the wire strands must be captured under the head of the terminal screws. If you leave a few of the hair-like strands free, they'll eventually find their way to the next terminal screw for that hard-to-locate short circuit. The twisted ends of the wires must be bent in a backward question-mark shape, with the loop just 1/32-inch or so larger than the diameter of the screw threads and about that much smaller than the diameter of the screw head. The reverse question mark shape loops the wire, so the action of the tightening screw head will tend to pull the wire around the screw for an even tighter joint. Any other bend or even straight-in installation of the wire on the screw terminal will result in several of those individual wire strands popping out from beneath the screw head. This may all sound like a lot

of bother, but, really, it's just as easy to do it the right way once you learn how.

There will undoubtedly be times when you need a wire longer than that supplied with the turnouts. Save any leftover wires for just that purpose, or buy some additional hook-up wire from an electronics hobby store. Do try to match the color of the two wires you splice so you can trace any short circuits or loose connections by wire color.

It is not necessary, incidentally, to solder simple wire-to-wire connections if you carefully twist both the individual wire strands and the ends of the two wires together (Figure 8-9). Be sure to twist both of the wires so you will not have just one straight wire with the other curled around it. Bend the twisted ends back over the insulated part of the wire and wrap the joint with about an inch of plastic electrical tape. Bend the last 1/8-inch of the tape back onto itself (sticky side to sticky side) to form a tab. The tab looks sloppy but you'll be glad to have it when it comes time to unwrap the tape to make a wiring change or repair.

Each of the remote-control turnouts, and most accessories, also have screws to attach the wires that power the switch machines that move the turnout points or control the accessory, but these wires do not supply electrical power to the tracks themselves.

Connecting the Wires to the Track

If you are using a plywood tabletop, drill 1/8-inch or larger holes through the plywood so you can route the wires beneath the tabletop. If you are using the blue Styrofoam insulation board for the layout, as described in Chapter 6, you can simply punch holes through the Styrofoam with an awl (Figure 8-10) then tuck the wires into the holes (Figure 8-11). Be sure you have at least three

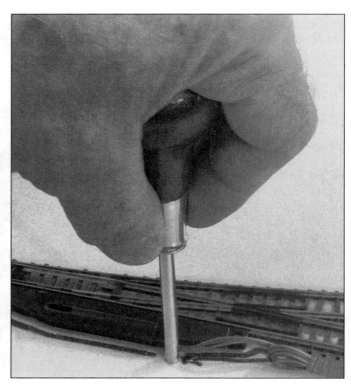

Figure 8-10. If you are using a Styrofoam for the layout tabletop, you can punch holes for the wires with an awl.

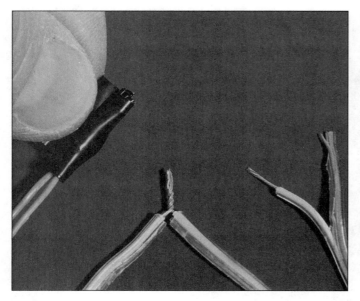

Figure 8-9. Twist the wires to be joined together (right), bend the ends back (center) and wrap them with plastic electrical tape to leave a tab (left).

inches of "slack" in the wire between the turnout and the switch controller and/or the power pack. You might have to lift the turnout slightly to adjust or relocate it or move the turnout controller. The extra length of wire will give you enough "room" to make such changes. The extra length may also be needed, someday, if you build a master control panel and need to splice in extra wire length to reach the new control panel.

If you are going to build an N scale using sectional track, I would suggest you learn to solder. The only way to have reliable electrical contact between track sections, with the flimsy N scale rail joiners, is to solder the rail joiners to the rails as shown in Chapter 7 (Figures 7-22 and 7-23). I would also recommend that you solder the wire connections to the sides of the rails so you do not have to use a terminal track section, or rely on a wired rail joiner. Purchase a soldering gun and some 60/40 tin/lead solder with an acid core from an electronics hobby store. I prefer Ersin "Multicore" solder, but there are similar products from other firms. To solder a wire to the rail, simply strip the insulation from about 1/4-inch of the wire and bend the wire at about a 90-degree angle so you can use the insulated portion of the wire to help force the bare wire against the outside of the rail. Hold the tip of the solder against the wire to help push the wire against the rail (Figure 8-12). Heat the rail with the soldering gun until the solder just flows, then instantly remove the soldering gun. If you apply the wires to the outside of the rail, there is less chance that any solder will reach the top or inside of the rail to cause derailments. If the solder does flow onto these areas, you can slice it away with a hobby knife and smooth the area with a jeweler's file. Practice the soldering operation on a scrap section of track so you can judge just how quickly to remove the soldering gun so you do not melt the plastic ties.

Troubleshooting

For your first layout, I suggest a relatively simple track plan with no more than six or eight turnouts and a single train and a single power pack. Try as many aspects of the hobby that you feel might interest you, from track laying to "waybill" operations. Once you've completed the wide range of projects possi-

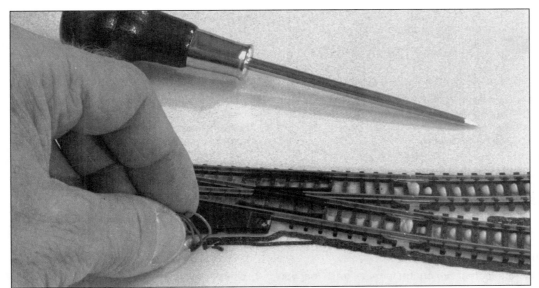

Figure 8-11. Push the wires through the hole in the Styrofoam and make the connections to the control switches by routing the wires beneath the tabletop.

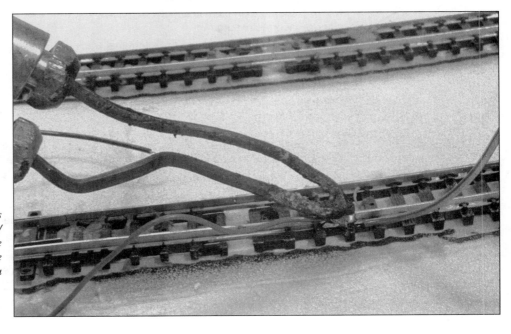

Figure 8-12. To solder the power wires to the rails, strip the insulation from 1/4-inch of the wire, then push the wire against the outside of the rail with the tip of a strip of wire solder, while you heat the rail with a soldering gun.

Locomotive and Electrical Troubleshooting Chart

Trouble	Probable Cause of Trouble	Solution
Locomotive does not run (and headlight does not glow).	1. Power pack not plugged in, or the outlet is faulty.	1. Plug in the power pack or check an appliance in the outlet.
	2. Track wires may be attached to the "AC" terminals of the power pack.	2. Connect the track wires to the two "DC" terminals.
	3. Wires may be improperly connected to the track terminals.	3. Check the "rules" and diagrams in this chapter
	4. Insulated rail joiners may not be in correct positions.	4. Check the "rules" and diagrams in this chapter.
	5. Locomotive may be off the track.	5. Rerail the locomotive.
	6. Wheels or track rails may be dirty.	6. Clean the tracks.
	7. Nails, wires, tinsel, or other metals may be causing a short circuit by laying on the track.	7. Remove the material.
	8. Locomotive may be sitting on the plastic frog of a switch or crossing; on an insulated rail joiner; on a track with an operating-signal man or operating crossing gates.	8. Move the locomotive.
Locomotive does not run (but headlight does glow).	1. Check all of the above probable causes. Number 2 is the most likely.	1. Be sure to turn the power pack off immediately while you search for and correct the problem.
Locomotive does not run, and none of the above 8 checks solves the problem.	1. Use an operating light or 12-volt lamp bulb as a "test light." Touch the two wires to the "DC" terminals of the power pack with the "throttle" on. If the light glows, the pack is fine.	1. If the light does not glow with the power pack plugged into a working outlet and with the throttle full on, have the pack checked by your dealer's service department.
	2. Touch the test-light wires to the terminals on each of the terminal tracks with the throttle full on and the "Blocking Switch" (if any) for each block turned on. If the light glows, the problem is likely in the locomotive. If the light does not glow, there is a break in one or both of the wires from the power pack to the terminal.	2. Replace the wires.
	3. Place the locomotive on the terminal track that you just checked and found to be working. If the locomotive runs, then the problem is a loose or missing rail joiner or incorrect wiring.	3. Check every track joint and see that any complex wiring is correct according to the "rules" and diagrams in Chapter 7.
	4. If the locomotive does not run on a terminal track you know is getting power, and you have performed every other troubleshooting check, the problem is likely to be the locomotive. Try another locomotive as a double-check; if it does run, the fault lies in the first locomotive.	4. Have locomotive checked by your dealer's service department.
Locomotive runs but in a series of jerks and stops.	1. Dirty track or locomotive wheels, or, on some steam locomotives, dirty truck-pivot area.	1. Check everything as outlined in chapter 13.
	2. Loose wire connections or loose rail joiners.	2. Check EVERY one in the areas behind and in front of places where the locomotive stalls, and check the terminal track and the power pack wires.
	3. Lack of lubrication on the locomotive (but this is highly unlikely).	3. Lubricate as outlined in this chapter.
	4. Worn motor brushes.	4. Replace motor.

Figure 8-13.

ble, you'll know if you want to attempt the more complicated wiring required for two-train operations and other more advanced model railroading possibilities.

Even with a simple layout, however, there is the chance for operating problems. "Locomotive and Electrical Troubleshooting" (Figure 8-13) includes several solutions to problems that can be related to track wiring. You can use one of the 12-volt bulbs (with built-in wires) sold by hobby stores to illuminate buildings or passenger cars as a "test light." Touch the bare wire ends from the bulb to the rails, and the bulb should glow if the power pack, throttle and on-off switches are all turned on. The same bulb can be used to see if the power is reaching the terminals of the walk-around throttle and the terminals on the power pack.

Two-Train Control With Two-Wires

The least expensive method of controlling two trains is to use two power packs and to divide the layout into electrically-isolated "blocks" as shown later in this chapter. You can, however, avoid the need for all those blocks and for a second power pack by purchasing one of the Digital Command Control (DCC) systems and a second locomotive equipped with a decoder. Most of these DCC systems allow you to run any one of your non-DCC-equipped locomotives on the same track with that second locomotive that is equipped with the DCC decoder.

The DCC systems truly do provide two-train control and, like a real railroad, you can have head-on or tail-end collisions. It's also far more realistic to skip the need to turn a toggle switch on or off every time you want your train to move a few feet around the layout. Once you've operated a layout with two or more trains running at the same time under DCC control, you'll never want to go back to the conventional "block" system (Figure 8-14) again. Remember, though, you will still need to have the electrically-isolated blocks for reverse loops and wyes (Figures 8-3, 8-4 and 8-5). If you have a really large layout, say twice the size of anything in this book, you may want to divide the layout into four or more blocks to make it easier to isolate any short circuits that might occur. Also, even with these smaller layouts, it's wise to connect additional "booster" wires so that there is a connection for about every 30 feet of mainline track. I'd suggest connecting booster wires to both the inner and outer ovals of the track plans in this book. You may want to electrically isolate the inner and outer ovals on the track plans in Figures 3-5 and 3-6 and divide the track in Figure 3-13 into two blocks to make it easier to find any short circuits.

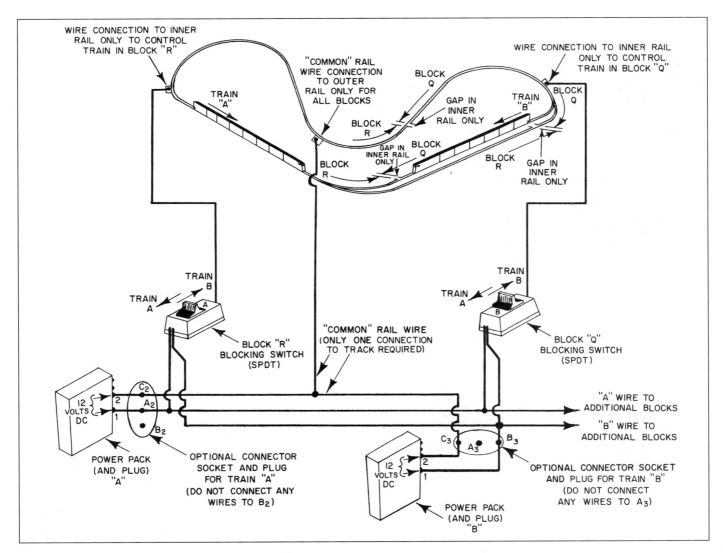

Figure 8-14. Wiring Diagram for true two-train control.

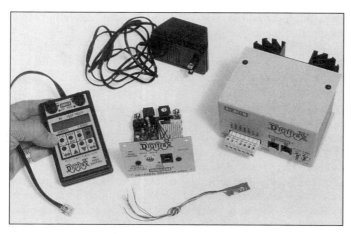

Figure 8-15. Digitrax is one manufacturer of Digital Command Control equipment. Their "Chief" unit (left) includes a 12-volt converter (top), and a walk-around controller (left). Digitrax also offers a variety of plug-in decoders or receivers for locomotives as shown in Chapter 7, as well as a dime-size wire-in decoder (bottom). They also offer the option of wireless remote control throttle units with the "Loconet" unit (center).

Figure 8-16. The MRC Command 2000 DCC system offers the option of a central control panel with three throttle controls and a sockets for an additional walk-around (hand-held) throttle controller. The control panel unit can be mounted on top of the table or on a slide-out computer keyboard shelf like that shown here and in Chapter 6 (Figure 6-18).

You can purchase the less expensive DCC systems, like Digitrax (Figure 8-15) or MRC's Command 2000 (Figure 8-16) for about the price of three or four medium-priced locomotives. The systems need a 13- to 22-volt AC power supply with a minimum 5 amps and an overload protection up to a maximum of five amps, but you may already have that available with your train set's power pack. If you find you do need a power supply, both Digitrax and MRC sell them as add-ons to their DCC systems. The DCC systems include a push-button set of encoding commands that are explained in the instructions. For about the price of another locomotive, you can purchase the MRC Walkaround 2000 controller for the MRC Command 2000 system (a walk-around controller is included with the Digitrax "Chief") to have both walk-around control and DCC. In addition, Digitrax offers WDCC (Wireless Digital Command Control—Figure 8-15) which uses infrared signals to carry the commands from your hand-held throttle to the receiver on the layout. Digitrax also offers true radio control if you prefer that system. With this type of system you can eliminate the tether cable to the layout and use a hand-held controller much like a television remote control. Wangrow, Lenz, PSI and others offer systems similar to those sold by Digitrax, and the decoders or receivers from any of these firms that are fitted to the locomotives will respond to the Digitrax, MRC, Wangrow, Lenz or PSI commands.

The MRC Command 2000 system has three controls at a stationary panel so you can have independent control for three locomotives. MRC offers a plug-in Walkaround 2000 add-on that has controls for two more locomotives. The Digitrax Chief system has a separate hand-held walk-around controller for each locomotive. If you want to run more than two locomotives, you simply add more walk-around controls. You can set two locomotives in operation and both will continue at that speed while you operate a third or fourth with the two throttles.

The MRC Command 2000 has sockets to allow you to plug in their Walkaround 2000 hand-held controllers and that controller has levers to operate up to two locomotives at a time, so with the locomotives being controlled by the three throttle levers built into the Command 2000 unit, plus the controls on the Walkaround 2000, you can operate up to five locomotives at a time, each under completely independent control. MRC has an accessory unit that will allow you to operate another 117 locomotives. With the Digitrax Chief, you add walk-around throttles and sockets, placed around the layout, so you can run as many trains as you have throttles, up to 120 and, again, each under completely independent control. As you add more than two or more trains to the layout, however, you will also have to provide enough amps of power to run the motors in the locomotives, so additional power supplies or boosters may be needed as the number of trains being run at once is increased.

The second, third, fourth and other additional locomotives must be fitted with decoders for any DCC system. You can buy additional locomotives from Atlas with decoders installed or buy the Digitrax or Lenz plug-in decoder boards for most locomotives as described in Chapter 13. Each decoder installed in a locomotive can be assigned its own address by the DCC system you use. The MRC Command 2000 can assign 10 locomotive addresses and MRC offers an accessory that allows you to expand that to an additional 117 addresses. Digitrax and most other DCC systems allow you to set up addresses for over 9,000 locomotives. You might only want to run two trains at a time, but the remainder of your locomotives can have addresses assigned to their decoders so those locomotives can rest anywhere on the layout awaiting their call to operate. Each locomotive will have its own "code" and the MRC Command 2000 system allows you to encode five more, for a total of ten locomotives. Digitrax and most other systems allow you to encode as many as 120 locomotives and throttles.

There's a memory function, so you can set up to five of those locomotives running and use the same throttles for independent control of five more with the MRC Command 2000 system and up to 120 with the Digitrax system. You can also use the DCC system to double-head two or more locomotives, with each one's decoder adjusted so it runs at approximately the same speed as every other locomotive.

Remember, you can get started in this DCC system with any conventional locomotive and just the one DCC decoder-equipped locomotive. You can then expand to control as many additional locomotives as you wish to equip with DCC decoders. You can also park any locomotive not fitted with a DCC decoder, on special insulated sections of track I call "holding tracks", using the insulation gaps and push-buttons described later in this chapter, while you operate just one other non-equipped locomotive plus any more decoder-equipped locomotives you may want to run with the Digitrax or MRC Command 2000 DCC systems. If all of your locomotives are equipped with DCC decoders, you will not need any of those electrically-isolated holding tracks, because you can park a DCC-equipped locomotive anywhere while you operate other locomotives on the same track.

There are many DCC systems and a host of accessories for all of them, including Digitrax and MRC. You may opt for a basic system just to run a few locomotives or you may want to run dozens of locomotives, control sounds, or even control turnouts and signals. Most systems are expandable to allow you to add these features if you wish. Your hobby dealer should be able to suggest systems that are popular in your area or you can consult the ads in the model railroad magazines to find different brands of DCC systems. Most of these systems use the same decoder technology, so you can operate your locomotives that are equipped with most brands of decoders on another model railroad with another DCC system and the locomotives from that layout can operate on your system.

Conventional Two-Train Control

Two trains can be operated on the same layout by simply dividing the track into three or more blocks in a manner similar to that used for reversing loops or wyes. The two-train wiring and rail-gapping is much simpler, though, than that required for reversing sections if you use the common rail wiring system. Most model railroad books and magazines suggest the use of a single power pack with two throttles for two-train operation. That system dates back to the days when a power pack cost as much as $50 or more. Today, it's just about as inexpensive to buy two complete power packs as it is to buy or add on that second throttle. You'll save countless hours of wiring and even more time troubleshooting any short circuits with the double power pack "common rail" wiring system shown here.

"Common Rail" Wiring Systems

With the "common rail" wiring system (Figure 8-14) you designate one rail as the common and connect a single wire to that rail through the usual terminal track. The only secret to the application of the system is to be absolutely and positively certain always to remember which rail is common regardless of how the track twists or turns. If you have a complex layout, I suggest that you tear off some short skips of masking tape and place them temporarily on top of the common rail every few feet until all of the wiring is complete and the layout is operating with no short circuits.

Notice that most power packs with two throttles will NOT work as the only power pack for common rail wiring. You must purchase an additional power pack for operating that second train with this system.

"Blocking" the Track

You will need to cut insulating gaps in the rail opposite the one you have designated as common to divide the track into "blocks" for independent control of two trains. Cutting gaps in just one rail means that just one wire need be connected to supply power to each of the "blocks" of track between the gaps. Even on a medium-size layout, that can mean almost a fifty-percent savings in wire and in complexity. Each of those blocks needs to receive power; the SPDT or "Blocking Switch," wired as shown in Figures 8-7 and 8-14, will do the job. The Atlas "Connector" switch (Figure 8-8, right) has three SPDT slide switches in one box. The Atlas "Selector" (Figure 8-8, center) has four SPDT slide switches, each with a center-off position. Similar SPDT slide switches are available from Model Power, Peco and Roco. Electronics stores, such as Radio Shack, sell SPDT and DPDT switches (Figure 8-7). Atlas offers additional panel-mount slide switches including the momentary-contact switches supplied with their remote control turnouts (Figure 8-8, left).

Blocking Switches

There's somewhat more logic in having the "Blocking Switch" decide which train, rather than which track block, you will operate. If you reverse the wiring direction of the switch, so the one wire connects to the block, one each of the two wires can connect to the two power packs. This is the system used in Figure 8-14. You will need almost twice as many SPDT or blocking switches, but the layout wiring will actually be simpler this way once you add a third, fourth, or fifth block. This system also avoids any possible chance of your trying to "switch" both power packs into the same track, because the blocking switch can only be turned to one power pack at a time. All of the wiring connections you'll see in this book are based on the possible use of both this type of block-selection system and on "common rail" wiring.

The wiring diagram in Figure 8-14 is somewhat more complex than it needs to be for just two power packs and two blocks because it includes the wires you'll want for any number of additional blocks; for example, "A" and "B" connect to future blocks "S," "T," "U," and so forth exactly the same way the two wires from either "Q" or "R" blocking switches connect. The diagram also includes the locations for wiring the optional connector plugs and sockets for plug-in power pack connections to make walk-around control easier. You can use telephone cables and jacks or larger plug and sockets available for electronics supply stores. Notice that block "A" must have a different connection to socket "A" than the connection to block and socket "B." The plugs, which connect to those sockets, are attached to the walk-around throttles through 8- to 20-foot-long tether wires. Those plugs are wired in the same way so that either walk-around throttle can be plugged into either socket "A" or socket "B." The wiring to the sockets makes "A" different from "B." You can add additional pairs of "A" and "B" sockets along the layout (so you don't have to have such long tether wires on the throttles) by extending all three wires ("A," "B," and "C") on and around the edges of the layout to sockets. You can install any number of additional pairs of sockets or any number of additional blocks with the use of these wiring diagrams. Note that these wiring diagrams are only for conventional power packs and blocking systems; the DCC systems will have different connections for their walk-around throttles that are in their instructions.

Reversing Sections

The "reversing sections" of the reversing loop or wye track arrangements should have both an SPDT blocking switch (to allow use by either train or throttle A or B) and the DPDT (reversing) switch. The arrows in the wiring diagrams in Figures 8-3, 8-4 and 8-5 show where the SPDT (blocking) switches should be installed. Briefly, another C (common-rail) wire connection is needed for each reversing section. The two end wires

on a slide-type DPDT switch (Fig. 8-7, right) will connect to the C wire and to the "block" wire from the blocking (SPDT) switch; the two upper wires will connect to the two terminals (track rails) on the track.

If you find the whole concept of wiring the reversing wyes or reversing loops too complicated to understand at this point, just cut the gaps in the rails (there's no way around that!) and buy another power pack to operate only the electrically isolated reversing section of your layout. You would simply turn control of any train ("A" or "B") over to the reversing section power pack during that portion of the train-reversing moves. This second power pack system for reverse loop wiring will only work if you are using conventional power packs, not the DCC systems. Most of the manufacturers of DCC systems do, however, offer automatic reverse loop control systems so you can avoid the need for the DPDT switch, but not the need for additional wire connections to the reverse loop or wye.

Control Panels

The more complicated your layout becomes with additional turnouts, electrical block switches for two-train control, and animated accessories, the more you'll need a control panel. It's best to include a control panel in the layout design from the very beginning. If you make the control panel large enough, you'll have a ready place to mount the switches to actuate remote-control turnout controls when you add additional turnouts. If, however, you make the wiring simple

Figure 8-17. The Digitrax "Chief" (left) and "Loconet" for wireless infrared remote control of the walk-around throttle are mounted in cavities cut through the 4-inch Styrofoam table of the 6-by-6-foot Union Pacific layout.

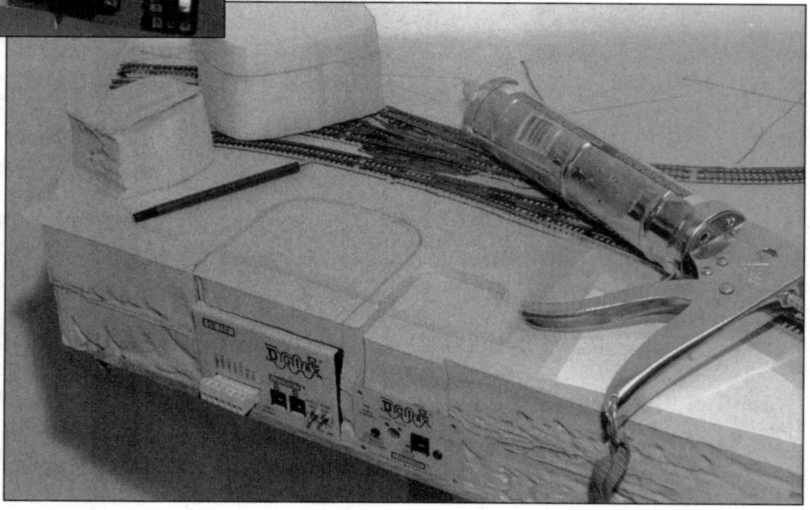

Figure 8-18. The Digitrax components rest on a metal shelf supported by one of the 2-by-2-inch table legs. The Styrofoam cut from the cavities was reduced in height and cemented back in place to "bury" the Digitrax components. The same system could be used, of course, with any conventional power pack.

enough, by using a DCC control system and operating the turnouts manually, you may only need a walk-around controller and a slide-out computer keyboard shelf (Figure 8-16) to hold the DCC power pack. The slide-out shelf is also a handy place to hold the boxes and cards for the "Waybill" operating system shown in Chapter 17.

The control panel for the 6-by-6-foot Union Pacific layout was made by cutting notches in the edges of the table with a hacksaw

blade (Figure 8-17). The Digitrax DCC control boxes were then inserted in the cavities and the Styrofoam was cut to cover the tops of the Digitrax units. A piece of steel was placed beneath the layout, supported by one of the 2-by-2 legs, to support the Digitrax equipment. (Figure 8-18). The edge of the layout was finished with green duct tape, cemented to the Styrofoam, and the Atlas controls for the wye and some of the remote control turnouts were mounted on their plastic panel (Figure 8-19).

Figure 8-19. The edge of the layout was finished and a 4-by-6-inch piece of plastic cemented to the edge of the table to hold the Atlas switch controls, the Atlas "Selector" block controls and the Atlas "Controller" reversing switch for the wye to the left of the Digitrax DCC components.

Figure 8-20. A typical control panel with the track plan for the immediate area copied with tape lines. The long levers are on-off block switches and the push buttons are for operating remote-control turnouts.

Figure 8-21. The backside of the control panel in Figure 8-20 shows just how complex the wiring can be for conventional two-train "block" wiring systems and remote-control turnout actuation.

If you want to build a conventional control panel, I suggest you make a frame for the control panel from 1-by-2 lumber and the face from 1/8- or 1/4-inch plywood. You'll need so little material that it might actually be cheaper to have a cabinet shop make your control panel (or control panels) than to do it yourself. Of course, you will have to drill the holes for the wires and screws that will connect the controls to the face of the panel. Paint the face of the panel flat black. Leave the top half of the panel clear so you can use draftsman's 1/8-inch-wide striping tape (or colored plastic hardware tape cut into 1-inch skips) to put a schematic diagram of your layout on the panel. Use decal or dry-transfer numbers and letters (available at most artists' supply stores) to designate the blocks and the track switches. Put matching letters and numbers right on the electrical switches themselves. You might also want to get some decal or dry-transfer arrows or other symbols to mark the panel and the electrical switches.

The control panel shown in Figures 8-20 and 8-21 is typical of that for a layout with conventional block control and remote-control turnouts. If you use a DCC system rather than conventional block control and operate the turnouts manually, the three pairs of wires to a reversing switch for the wye, and two block switches for the inner and outer oval, are all that would be required for the 6-by-6-foot Union Pacific layout.

Holding Tracks

The wiring system described here has no provision for shutting the power off in any block. It only turns off the power pack itself. This is fine if you have only two locomotives and the two power packs to run them. When you add a third locomotive, however, you need some place to park it when the other two are in operation. The blocks A, B, C, and D in the engine terminal of the 6-by-6-foot Union Pacific layout in Chapter 3 (Figure 3-5) are there to hold locomotives; blocks I, J, K and L are long enough to hold a locomotive and a few cars. A SPST push-button style switch (Figure 8-7, center) is inserted into the wire leading from the blocking switch for those blocks to the track. The button will then be used to control the flow of power to that isolated block so that the locomotive runs only while the button is being pressed. Install an insulated rail joiner in the rail opposite the "common rail" (Fig. 8-14) to isolate each of these locomotive-holding blocks to be controlled by the push-button SPST switch. With this system, you can park a locomotive in one of these electrically isolated blocks and forget about it until you want it; the locomotive will only leave that block when you hold down the button controlling that block. Again, you will not need these wires or gaps if all of your locomotives are equipped with DCC decoders.

Do's and Don'ts for Wiring and Control

- Do use extreme care in cutting the insulation from wires so that the delicate individual wire strands are not broken. Twist the strands together as soon as the insulation is pulled free.

- Don't attempt to squeeze the wire tight enough to break through the insulation or to simply slit the length of the wire to pull back the insulation.

- Do purchase a separate power pack to control switch (turnout) machines and lighting as well as a separate power pack for each additional train (when you want to operate two or more trains at once) or purchase a DCC system for operating two or more trains.

- Don't attempt to use one power pack for more than one function. Some of the power packs, however, do have provision for separate control of two trains. A third power pack will still be needed for switch machines and lighting.

- Do at least consider the advantages of a separate throttle for walk-around control so you can walk along beside your train with its controls in your hand.

- Don't attempt to make your own walk-around control. The available units are simple enough to attach with four wires to the back of most power packs, using the wiring diagram supplied with the walk-around control.

- Do drill holes in the tabletop or roadbed so all wiring can be routed beneath the table so it will be accessible even after all the scenery is in place.

- Don't run wires on top of the table or beside the tracks.

- Do consider purchasing one of the DCC systems for operating two or more trains at once, rather than wiring with blocks for two or more convention power packs.

- Don't attempt to run two trains with two conventional power packs without making at least three electrically-isolated blocks so you can park one train while the second goes to the next available block.

Chapter 9

Structures

Figure 9-1. Two of the most common stations on any N scale layout are Bachmann's plastic ready-built 45907 "Freight Station" (left) a replica of the Plains, Georgia station and the replicas of the Rico, Colorado station (right) sold as plastic kits by Model Power and Pola.

In the real world, scenery appeared long before any structures. On your N scale layout, however, you will want to be sure you have room for the structures to fit comfortably into the scenery, so the structures come before the scenery. It is wise to plan for every structure you will ever want on your layout, even if you do not have the exact model you want to put there.

You can estimate the space you will need for your proposed structures by comparing the size of the proposed structure to that of similar kits. You may decide, later, on a different style structure, but you will at least have the space available. The Walthers catalogs and the catalogs of some of the kit makers provide dimensions for buildings so you can prepare a site for a structure even if you have not yet purchased the model.

You will need to provide plenty of level space for each building, as well as some space on at least one side for a small parking space for trucks or automobiles, before you begin constructing hills and valleys. Once you've positioned at least the dimensions of the base or "footprint" of the structures on their proposed sites, you may discover you do not have anywhere near the amount of room you want for scenery, so you

may have to remove a structure or a few to leave space for the "natural" scenery.

Structures as Essential "Scenery"

Structures can certainly be considered part of the "scenery" in the sense that they duplicate a large portion of the real world environment you are trying to recreate. The structures also provide an element of credibility because they imply, at least, that there are people living and working within sight of the railroad.

Each real life structure is a bit different from the next, just as one tree or one hill is different from another. Railroads sometimes standardize on station designs and designs for small buildings, and you may see rows of similar houses, but structures are seldom the same. There are, however, only a limited number of scale model plastic and laser-cut wood structures, so you most certainly will see duplicates of your structures on other railroads. You can customize every structure with at least one color change or, better, modify it by removing part of it and combining it with other structures. You'll see examples of both in this chapter.

Figure 9-2. Only the station and the industrial portion of alliance have been modeled on the 6-by-6-foot Union Pacific layout.

Special Plastic-Working Tools

Most plastic kits can be assembled with just a hobby knife and a file, but you may want some additional tools so you can custom-build or kit-convert structures. The X-Acto razor saw is the basic cutting tool for these custom-built models, and the Number 1 knife and Number 11 blade can be used for final trimming and finishing. The pointed tweezers and tube-type as well as liquid cement for plastics that are needed to assemble box-stock kits will work just as well for any "conversions" involving the use of two or more models. The secret to success in making conversion models, however, lies in seeing that your modified parts fit at least as well as the stock-kit components, and that means you'll need a few more tools.

Plastic-Working Tools

X-Acto Number 1 knife with Number 11 blades
Medium-size sprue cutters
Small-size sprue cutters
12-inch-long steel ruler or straightedge
Draftsman's plastic triangle
Medium-cut large flat-mill file or cabinetmaker's file
File card or brass-bristled suede shoe brush
Bench vise (with adjustable head), such as a PanaVise
Liquid and tube-type cement for plastics
Tube of patching or spot automobile body putty

Larger hobby shops can supply two different sizes of sprue cutters. The "sprues" are the round plastic runners or strips that are attached to the smaller parts like windows and doors in structure kits. The sprues are cut into the metal molds that are used to create the plastic parts. The sprues are necessary for the still-molten plastic to reach the cavities that will form the windows and doors. Testors offers a medium-size tool they call a "sprue cutter" that is a miniature version of a pair of flush-cut

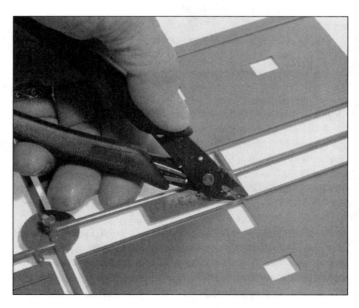

Figure 9-3. Use flush-cut diagonal cutters or Testors Sprue Cutters to remove the plastic parts from the molding sprue.

diagonal cutters. Other tool companies offer similar tools. These are fine for trimming windows, doors and other medium-size parts from their molding sprues. If you are going to assemble some of the highly detailed plastic freight car kits, like those from Red Caboose, DeLuxe Innovations, InterMountain and Dimi-Trains, you will want the small sprue cutters. These small sprue cutters look like tweezers but with the tips bent at a 90-degree angle. The tips are sharpened to form a pair of cutting edges. These small sprue cutters are available from P-B-L, InterMountain and others. The small sprue cutters will also make it quicker and easier to remove windows and doors from their molding sprues. With practice, you can make the cuts precise enough so no filing is necessary. Still, it is a good idea to make a quick swipe with the fine-tooth side of the mill file or cabinetmaker's file on any edges that have been cut from the molding sprues.

The steel straightedge or ruler and plastic triangle are necessary in order to guarantee that all of your cuts are straight and true. The mill file will help keep the surfaces true as well, but it's most useful for filing 45-degree bevels on the mating corners of walls cut to length so they can be assembled in the same manner as those in a stock kit. The best type of file for working with plastics is one sold by hardware and cabinetmaker's shops that sell cabinetmaker's files. These files are about 12-inches long with perfectly straight and parallel sides and edges. The cabinetmaker's file has medium-cut teeth on one wide side, smooth-cut teeth on one wide and one narrow side, and no teeth on the other narrow side. The smooth narrow side allows you to file into corners without cutting both faces of the corner. The medium-cut teeth make it quick and easy to remove as much as 1/8 inch from the edge of a part, while the smooth teeth and flat faces of the file make it easier to obtain perfectly straight edges on the parts you are filing.

If you are going to work with structure-conversion projects, where you need to cut plastic parts, I recommend that you consider purchasing one of the bench vises with an adjustable head, such as the PanaVise. You can also use the vise for making more precise and safer cuts to shorten and fit track sections. The vise should not be used to actually clamp the plastic pieces but, rather, to clamp a 3-inch long scrap of 1-by-3 or 1-by-4 wood. The wood serves as a firm and stable backing for the part you are cutting, while your fingers serve as clamps to hold the plastic against the wood by squeezing the plastic part and the wood backing together. The vise keeps the wood stable and secure, and the adjustable (or swivel-style) head allows you to position the block comfortably both for clamping by hand and for cutting or filing. You can use the same technique with a conventional bench vise, but you'll have to contort your body into some rather uncomfortable positions to clamp the parts to the vise with one hand while cutting or filing with the other.

Assembling Plastic Structure Kits

Virtually all of the plastic structure kits have parts that fit together properly. The plastic parts are supplied still attached to the sprues that are used to help the molten plastic flow into the molds that created the parts. The parts must be cut from the sprues with either a hobby knife, medium-size sprue cutters or small flush-cut diagonal cutters (Figure 9-3). Do not try to break the parts from the sprue or you may leave a large chunk of the part behind.

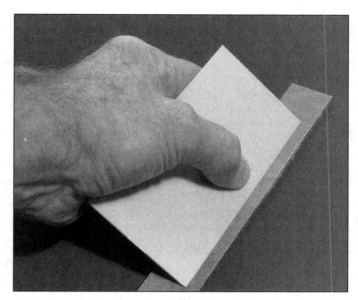

Figure 9-4. Use a cabinet-maker's file to smooth the joining edges of any plastic structures kit.

Test-fit every joint to be sure it fits. There are often tiny lumps or bends right on the seams that must be removed with a file. I would suggest that you file each joining surface just to remove the shiny surface for a quicker and better bond (Figure 9-4). For most plastic buildings in kits, I would recommend the thick-liquid cements like Testors Model Master "Liquid Cement for Plastic Models". Model Power and Kibri offer similar cements. These cements are packaged in bottles with a needle-type applicator that makes it easy to spread a pin-size bead of cement along a joint. They are just thick enough to provide a bit of stickiness to help hold the parts. You can increase the stickiness by firmly rubbing the two parts together so you literally rub the cement into the joining surfaces. The cements dissolve the plastic and the rubbing action helps speed-up that process. The manufacturing processes for molding plastic can, however result in slightly warped parts, so you occasionally need to push two parts together firmly and hold them there until the cement dries. You can hold the parts in place by wrapping the outside of the joint with masking tape. Remove the tape when the cement has dried overnight.

Painting

The prelude to any assembly should be painting, even though the parts are almost always supplied in two or three or more colors. Unpainted plastic has a certain transparency that is visible and immediately identifiable to even a casual visitor. However, if you paint the plastic before the final assembly process, an expert model builder won't be able to tell if its plastic or wood, or even real brick or stone or concrete.

Testors is just one firm that makes a subdued rainbow of "flat" colors in their series of Model Master paints, and these are perfect for painting the structures on a model railroad. Floquil has a similar series of flat model railroad paints in aerosol cans. The bottled Model Master paints are intended for military figures, but the flat-finish dark greens, beiges, browns, grays, and blues are precisely the colors you want for your model railroad structures as are the flat model railroad paints from Floquil.

Most of the Floquil paints are offered only in bottles, but they're easy enough to apply with a brush because one coat is usually enough to cover the plastic. Testors also has flat black, flat white, and flat red in spray cans, and some of the primers (which don't "eat" plastics) come in light and dark gray and brown. You can find most of the colors you'll need in spray cans. All of these paints are solvent-based so spray outdoors and hold the parts with disposable rubber gloves.

Floquil makes an acrylic-based line of model railroad paints as the Polly Scale series and similar colors are available in water-based paints in Badger's Modelflex series. These paints can be applied with a brush or you can use an airbrush. Spray or brush-paint the windows and doors for the structures while they're still attached to the molding sprues or trees. The easiest way to paint most buildings is to assemble all the outer walls without the windows. The roof panels can be painted as separate pieces.

Plastic cement will not hold two painted surfaces, so the windows, details, and roof will have to be installed with one of the cyanoacrylate cements, such as Aron-Alpha, Hot Stuff, Zap or Super Glue, or with five-minute epoxy. If you feel you must use plastic cement, then scrape the paint away from the areas that will be joined and glue the parts in place by installing them and holding them there with a knife blade while you brush on some of the liquid cement for plastics. Use the plain white glue, Testors Model Master cement for clear plastic, or epoxy to glue the clear-plastic window "glass" in place. The plastic cements (either tube-type or liquid) and the cyanoacrylate cements will frost or craze the clear styrene plastic used in most model kits. Weather the building, as described in Chapter 15, after the building is assembled, complete with windows—but before installing the clear window glazing.

More Realistic N Scale Structures

The most glaring giveaway that almost any N scale plastic structure is a model are the windows. The plastic kit manufacturers mold overly thick window mullions that are often a scale 6-inches thick. Some of the plastic kits from England, like the Ratio kits imported by F & H Enterprises, have etched-brass

Figure 9-6. To replace the windows with the clear plastic Signs Galore pieces, apply a drop of white glue to each inside corner of the walls, then drop each window carefully into place.

windows with scale-size mullions. The Grandt Line series plastic windows also have scale-size mullions, but they will not fit any plastic kit—they're most useful if you are willing to scratch-build your own structures from sheet styrene plastic. The mullions in the laser-cut wood kits, like those from American Model Builders and Northeastern Scale Models, are also very near scale thickness. You can often improve the realism of an N scale structure by cutting out all the window mullions and just leaving clear plastic. Or, you can use a drafting pen or draftsman tape to apply your own mullions to the clear window material supplied with most kits.

Signs Galore offers pre-printed windows for a number of the Walthers kits. The windows in the Harwood Furniture Company are typical of the over-thick mullions in nearly all the plastic kits (Figure 9-5). It is easiest, for me, to assemble the walls and roof and add the windows last. If you are going to "weather" the building, it is best to do it before you install the clear windows. Cut

Figure 9-5. The Walthers "Harwood Furniture" kit has windows with the overly-thick mullions that are common to nearly all N scale plastic kits.

Figure 9-7. The Walthers "Harwood Furniture" with the Signs Galore windows no longer looks like a N scale kit, it looks far more like a real structure.

each individual window from the Signs Galore sheet. Work with only one wall at a time. Apply a dot of white glue or Testors Model Master Clear Parts Cement to each corner of each window opening on the inside wall, then carefully position each of the clear plastic windows so you do not smudge the glue (Figure 9-6). Let that wall dry for two or three hours and repeat the process on the second wall, the third and the fourth. The finished building has the light and airy look of the prototype (Figure 9-7). In fact, you can see through it too easily, I would recommend that you cut some partitions for the interior from old cardboard or from sheet styrene so it is not possible to see through the structure from any direction. You might also want to add some paper cut-out profiles of machinery or stacks of boxes against the interior walls.

Assembling Laser-Cut Wood Kits

Many modelers would prefer to work with wood rather than plastic. There are dozens of wood kits with the parts completely pre-cut with lasers (Figure 9-8). American Model Builders has dozens of models, including the four stations used on the 6-by-6-foot Union Pacific layout (Figure 9-9), and there are others including Northeastern Scale Models and many other brands. Blair Line offers a simple loading platform that is a good kit to use to learn how to assemble a laser-cut wood kit (Figure 9-10). American Model Builders number 603 "Miners Cabin" is another good kit to pick to learn how to work with laser-cut kits. Do not try to break the pre-cut parts from the sheets. Use a sharp hobby knife to slice along the seams so the knife both cuts and pries the parts apart from one another.

The hobby-type cyanoacrylate cements like Super "T" or "Hot Stuff" make almost instant wood-to-wood joints, so the assembly goes almost as fast as you can align the pats. American Model Builders provides aligning tabs to make even that part simpler. Just be sure the parts are perfectly square when you join them because the cement won't give you a second chance. Many of the parts, like the multiple layers for the doors and shingles for the roof have a self-adhesive backing, so no

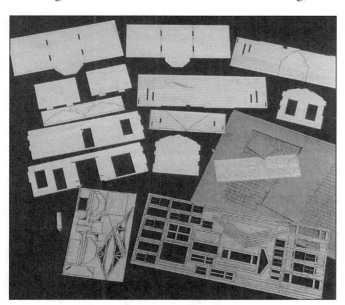

Figure 9-8. American Model Builders is one firm that produces laser-cut wood kits. The AMB kits include tabs to make it easier to align the parts and self-adhesive window frames and shingles for easier assembly. This is the AMB number 638 "Springfield Depot."

Figure 9-9. All four of the passenger stations on the 6-by-6-foot Union Pacific layout are American Model Builders 627 laser-cut wood kits, including (clockwise from upper right): 627 "UP Style One-Story Depot" at Alliance, the 638 "Springfield Depot" at Emmett, the 609 "Yard Office" at Bedford, and the 612 "Two-Story Depot with Square Bay Window" at Corning (with the station sign for "Duncan"). The station signs are cut from the names in Figure 9-26.

Figure 9-10. Learn how easy it is to assemble a laser-cut wood kit by starting with something simple like the American Model Builders "Miner's Cabin" or this Blair Line 074 "Loading Ramp. Slice the pre-cut parts apart with a sharp hobby knife.

Figure 9-11. The Blair Line 074 "Loading Ramp" can be used either beside the tracks or at the stub end of siding to unload wheeled vehicles from flat cars. –Blair Line photo

glue is necessary. If you would rather use white glue, I would suggest a needle applicator or buy Testors "Clear Parts Cement" which is very much like white glue and comes in a bottle with a needle applicator. The assembly will be somewhat slower, but the aligning tabs usually hold the parts in place so you can build most of the structure in an evening, even using white glue.

Structure Conversions

You can produce custom-built buildings for your layout by modifying kits. Modelers call the technique "kit-conversion," or "kit-bashing." The fundamental principle of structure conver-

Figure 9-12. The Consolidated Edison power plant (left) and coal bunker (right) at Alliance on the 6-by-6-foot Union Pacific layout.

Figure 9-13. Use a razor saw to remove about 2-inches from the tops of the smoke stacks from Walthers "Superior Paper Company" so the structure is not so visible from the "Corning" side of the layout.

Figure 9-14. The Walthers "Superior Paper Company" with the modified smoke stacks. The triangular-shaped piece on the right will be used to rest one end of the conveyor from the coal bunker.

sions is that the finished product should look unlike anything you can buy. The actual conversion could be as simple as adding a new roof to the Bachmann 35156 assembled "Rural Freight Station". Kit-conversions can also be as complex as the Consolidated Edison industry at Alliance and the Corning Mining Company at Corning on the 6-by-6-foot Union Pacific layout (Figure 9-12). The coal bunker at Alliance and the mine at Corning were both made from a single Walthers 3241 "Glacier Gravel Co." kit. The generating plant for the Consolidated Edison Company at Alliance is a Walthers 3237 "Superior Paper Co." with the doors enlarged to fit a freight car or locomotive and the stacks shortened by about 2-inches (Figures 9-13 and 9-14), using a razor saw to cut the assembled stacks after they were cemented together.

Checking Buildings for Clearances

The Consolidated Edition generating plant at Alliance, on the 6-by-6-foot Union Pacific layout has a siding that passes right through the building, so it is essential to check that there is clearance for the longest car or locomotive to clear the exterior and the interior of the building. The openings must be enlarged to 1-1/4-inch wide and 1-3/4-inches high. The mine at Corning has a similar through-the-building siding, but it is located on a curve (Figure 9-21 and 9-24) where the side-to-side clearance must be great enough to clear the longest car or locomotive you might ever want to operate. I used a Con-Cor auto rack car and a Kato streamlined passenger car to check the clearance on both the inside and outside of the curve (Figure 9-21).

To enlarge the doors on the Walthers 3237 "Superior Paper Company," use a razor saw to make the vertical cuts (Figure 9-15). Make the horizontal cuts between the two razor saw cuts with a hobby knife. Make several cuts with the hobby knife, guided by a steel ruler (Figure 9-16), then snap-out the parts. Use a flat cabinetmaker's file to smooth the edges of the cuts (Figure 9-17).

All of the structures should also be checked with a NMRA Standards Gauge to be sure they clear the cars and that their loading ramps are near the right height. If the structure is located on a curve, it must be moved far enough away from the track so the longest car or locomotive does not sideswipe the building.

Buying Structures

There are a wide variety of structure types on the 6-by-6-foot Union Pacific layout, including ready-built plastic buildings, ready-built cast-resin buildings, plastic kits and laser-cut wood kits. In addition three of the industrial structures are kit-conversions. Bachmann and Model Power offer completely assembled buildings that usually include a few figures and other details. Model Power offers the same buildings as kits (with a different part number) and nearly identical buildings are available from other firms. If you compare these brands of kits, you'll often find the same kit with, perhaps, a different front or color or with a change in the arrangement of multiple-building kits. In some cases, the simulated material of the walls of the kit are different.

The Period Miniatures models on this layout are one-piece cast-resin buildings. The freight station at Alliance is the Period Miniatures' "Weston's Warehouse" and includes a piece of white styrene plastic that must be cut to size, cemented to the roof, posts added and the building painted. The stations at Alliance, Bedford, Corning and Emmett are all laser-cut wood kits from American Model Builders. Most of the remaining structures are plastic kits. The names and brands of the plastic kits change quite often, so it's nearly impossible to provide a number-by-number interchange, but you can spot the shapes of the models if you look carefully.

I recommend that you purchase a Walthers catalog from a hobby shop. With the catalog, you can get a better idea of what the box-stock buildings look like. Refer to the current catalog to find out what is available. Most of these structures have been

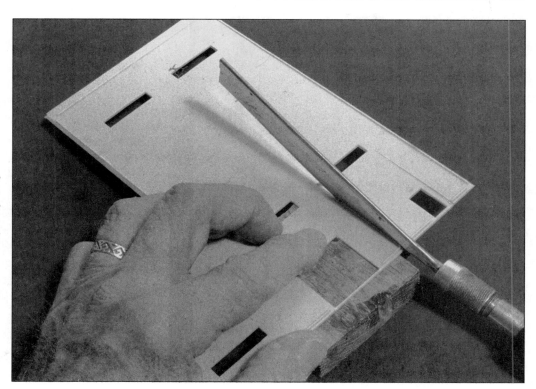

Figure 9-15. Enlarge the doors to 1-1/4-inch wide on the Consolidated Edison generating plant so railroad cars can enter the building. Use a razor saw to make the vertical cuts.

Figure 9-16. Increase the height of the doors to 1-3/4-inch to clear railroad cars. Use a hobby knife to make several cuts across the top of the door opening.

offered by at least four different model companies under a half-dozen different titles. I have listed the current structures by model company, part number and title in this chapter, but look for the overall shape because the "titles" and even the brands change every year or so.

Figure 9-17. Use a cabinetmaker's file to smooth the cut edges of the opening.

The Buildings on the Union Pacific Layout

The buildings on the 6-by-6-foot Union Pacific layout shown in the "satellite view" in Chapter 3 (Figure 3-4) include ready-built plastic buildings, plastic kits, laser-cut wood kits, cast-resin kits, and two plastic kits that have been modified or kit-converted into structures much different from the stock kits. The buildings are identified by two letters in Figure 3-4 and identified by the type of structure. Here, the manufacturer of the kit, its part number, and the description of the kit are listed. Please, do not consider this an order blank for structures for your layout. First, not all of these models or kits are available at any given time; they are often cycled in and out of production. More importantly, you'll want your layout to reflect your interests, not mine. Finally, there are some excellent substitutes for every single one of these buildings. There are several brands of mines and conveyors that can be used, too, for the much-modified Walthers "Sand and Gravel" that serves as both the "Corning Mine" (MX) and as the coal bunker and conveyor at Consolidated Edison (AZ). Use the list as a rough guide to gather your own selection of structures for your layout.

List of Structures on the Union Pacific Layout

(The letters are identified in Chapter 3, Figure 3-4)

AA   Quality Furniture Co.: Heljan 672 plastic "Furniture Factory"

AB   Coverall Paints: Model Power 2589 assembled plastic "Coverall Paints"

AC   Jackson Meat Packing: Model Power 2593 assembled plastic "Jackson Meat Packing"

AD   Harwood Furniture Co.: Walthers 3232 plastic kit "Harwood Furniture Company"

AE   Union Pacific Company Coal: Arnold, out of production (can substitute Kibri 7434 plastic kit "Coaling Point with Water Tower" or Vollmer 7542 "Trackside Details")

AX   Consolidated Edison (generating plant): Walthers 3237 plastic kit "Superior Paper Co."

AZ   Consolidated Edison (coal bunker and storage): Walthers 3241 plastic kit "Glacier Gravel Co." (modified for this and for Corning Mine at Corning)

D   Dwelling or boarding house: AHM, out of production (can substitute Model Power plastic kit 2560 "Jordan's House")

DF   Duncan Feed & Fuel: Heljan 673 plastic kit "Meat Packing Plant" (can substitute Walthers 3238 plastic kit "Farmer's Co-op Rural Grain Elevator")

DH   Dwelling at Duncan: Bachmann 45812 assembled plastic "Farm House with Figures"

The 6-by-6-foot Union Pacific layout is the "project" layout for this book. It is built from two layers of two-inch thick Styrofoam insulation boards. The cars and locomotives in this scene are typical of those that would appear in 1995.

The easiest method of building an N scale railroad is to use extruded polystyrene insulation board like this blue-colored Styrofoam product. Two, 2-inch thick layers of the material provide enough strength to serve as both benchwork and self-supporting scenery as described in Chapter 6. Position all of the tracks (Chapter 3) and the structures (Chapter 9) precisely where you want them before beginning work on the scenery.

Use a hacksaw blade or a heated wire tool like Avalon Concepts "Detail Wand" to cut the shape of the roadbed and drainage ditches (Chapter 7), the valleys and the hills (Chapter 10) on the 6-by-6-foot layout. Cut the Styrofoam from below the tracks where the valleys or riverbeds cross beneath the tracks (Chapter 11). The highways and parking lots are covered with masking tape before scenery colors and textures are applied.

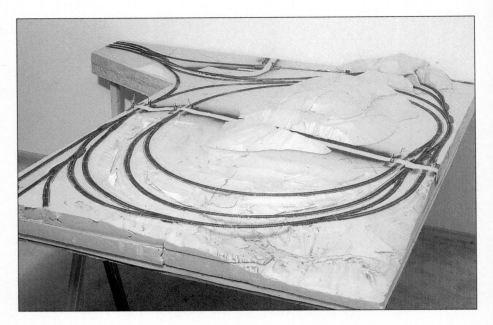

Paint the tracks (Chapter 7) and apply ballast and ground cover (Chapter 12) to the 6-by-6-foot Union Pacific "Project" layout. Paint and weather the structures (Chapter 15), install them, then surround them with dirt or weed textures.

Add the 'water' to the river and lake beds using artist's Matte Medium (Chapter 11), then place the bushes and trees (Chapter 12) on the layout.

The industrial area at Alliance, on the 6-by-6-foot Union Pacific layout, is being worked by a Life-Like SW9 Conrail diesel switcher pushing a pair of well cars into the intermodal terminal track. The Amtrak passenger train, powered by a Life-Like F40PH with Con-Cor cars, is waiting at the station while a high-priority intermodal train rolls by on the mainline.

The town of Emmett, on the Union Pacific 6-by-6 layout is in the foreground and the Duncan tower and grain elevator are visible in the distance. The freight and passenger trains are made up from equipment that would have been common in 1952.

The station, freight station and coal mine at Corning. A Life-Like SD9 is pushing empty hoppers into the "empty" track at the mine and is about to pickup a hopper loaded with coal from the "loaded" siding. The system of always leaving empties and picking up loaded cars at the mine is described in the "Loads-In/Empties-Out" section of Chapter 17.

Use artist's Gloss Gel to shape the rapids and waterfalls. Dab the putty-like material into the wavy shapes and let it dry for a few days. Have a few small stones ready to push into the still-wet fluid in the steeper areas of the "rapids" as described in Chapter 11.

The finished lake and stream. Add the fiber mesh and ground foam willows and bushes along the edges of the water.

The Utah-N-Railers layout includes several multi-module sets that interface with NTRAK modules at the extreme ends. This is part of the incredible Weber Canyon scene created from hand-carved plaster of Paris by Kelley Newton.

The NTRAK modelers from the Twin Cities Model Railroad in Vacavillle, California have created a layout with multi-module sets that interface with standard NTRAK module. The club operates two complete sets of trains, one set in the 1955 era as shown and the other set in the 1990 era. There are more photographs of their layout in Chapter 4.

Bob Gilmore is modeling the Utah's high desert on his multi-module set that is part of the Utah-N-Railers layout. There's more information on the layout in Chapter 4.

This 2-by-4-foot layout is one easy way to try N scale modeling techniques in a limited space. The layout is built on a single 2-inch slab of blue Styrofoam insulation. There are more photos in Chapter 2.

There are intermodal cars, containers, trailers, and unloading equipment available so you can duplicate the most modern intermodal terminals. All of these models are from Walthers. (Photo courtesy Wm, K. Walthers, Inc.)

Buzz Lenander assembled this oil refinery from several Walthers plastic kits. It is part of a 2-by-8-foot NTRAK module. The farm combine is a GHQ Models cast metal kit. The crop is clumps of cut fiber twine.

DT   Duncan Signal Tower: Con-Cor, out of production (can substitute Atlas 2840 plastic kit "Signal Tower")

EA   Emmett Feed & Fuel: Period Miniatures 443 assembled resin "Maple Valley Coal & Ice"

EB   Emmett Petroleum Supply: Model Power 2501 assembled plastic "Tank Filling Station"

EC   Emmett Packing Co.: Model Power Bachmann 45902 assembled plastic "Factory with Accessories"

FC   Corning Freight House: Bachmann 35156 assembled plastic "Rural Freight Station"

FT   Alliance Freight House: Period Miniatures 442 assembled resin "Weston's Warehouse"

G   Crossing gates: Life-Like 7209 Crossing Gates

MX   Corning Mining Co.: Walthers 3241 plastic kit "Glacier Gravel Co." (modified for this and for Consolidated Edison coal bunker and storage at Alliance)

PT   Trailer Train terminal: Arnold, out of production (can substitute Micro Engineering 60149 plastic kit "Section House" or Period Miniatures 406 resin kit "Trackside Shanties" or American Model Builders 603 laser-cut wood kit "Miners Cabin")

SA   Passenger station at Alliance: American Model Builders 627 laser-cut wood kit "UP Style One-Story Depot" (can substitute Walthers 3240 "Clarkesville Depot")

SB   Passenger station at Bedford: American Model Builders 609 laser-cut wood kit "Yard Office"

SC   Passenger station at Corning: American Model Builders 612 laser-cut wood kit "Two-Story Depot with Square Bay Window"

SE   Passenger station at Emmett: American Model Builders 638 "Springfield Depot"

W   Water tower (or a diesel fuel oil tank and refueling platform): Arnold (out of production), can substitute Bachmann 45810 assembled plastic "Water Tower" or Walthers 3205 plastic kit "Shady Junction Structures", "Loads-In/Empties-Out" Buildings.

Figure 9-18. The railroad siding goes right through the Consolidated Edison generating plant so cars can be loaded with cinders leftover from the coal-burning process.

Coal is the major commodity shipped and received by the two major industries on the 6-by-6-foot Union Pacific layout. Coal is mined at the Corning Mining Company and shipped (over hundreds of imagined miles) to the coal receiving bunkers at the Consolidated Edison in Alliance. These two industries are intended to be operated as coal-shipping and receiving pairs as described in Chapter 17. The coal receiving bins at the power plant are on a curve and the two tracks beneath those bins (track "K" and "L" on Figure 3-5 in Chapter 3) are supposed to end at the foot of the hill behind the power plant. In reality, both tracks continue through the hill to the other side of the layout to emerge beneath the coal mine at Corning. The Consolidated Edison generating plant also ships out cinders leftover from burning coal, but that is a separate siding and switching operation from the "Loads-in/Empties-out" coal shipping/receiving pair of tracks.

The Walthers 3241 "Glacier Gravel Co." kit (Figure 9-19) was used to make both the coal bunker at Alliance and the mine at Corning. The taller concrete bunker was used on the coal

bunker at Alliance. The center pillars were cut away to clear the curve and the leftover partition angled on one side to help disguise the curve (Figure 9-20). The structure was not tall enough to clear a car, so a piece of Evergreen .080-by-.100 inch styrene was cemented to the bottom of both sides with pieces of .125-by-.125 cemented to the bottom of each of those to form a T-shaped support for each of the side walls (Figure 9-21). This concrete bunker and the shorter foundation for the mine at Corning were both painted with Testors Model Master Flat Gull Grey to simulate concrete.

The kit was assembled into four major components: the short and tall concrete foundations and the upper and lower buildings, plus the conveyors and conveyor supports (Figure 9-22). The upper building was moved from the tall concrete foundation to the short concrete foundation and used for the Corning Mine, and the lower building was mounted on the tall concrete foundation and used for the coal bunker at Alliance (Figure 9-23). The steel bunker and the upper building with the lower foundation were used at Corning with two conveyors cut to fit (Figure 9-24). The lower building and modified tall concrete foundation

Figure 9-19. Walthers "Glacier Sand and Gravel" is a plastic kit to build this replica of a prototype gravel bunker and conveyor complex. Courtesy Wm. K. Walthers, Inc.

Figure 9-20. The tall concrete bunker from the Glacier Sand and Gravel will be used for the coal bunker at the Consolidated Edison in Alliance. Add styrene strips at the bottom to provide clearance for cars and locomotives. The center wall is moved to one side to help disguise the fact that the curved track disappears beneath a hill.

Figure 9-21. It is always important to check that the longest cars and locomotives clear structures or scenery. This auto rack car and passenger car overhang the tracks on curves both near the center of the cars and at both ends.

Figure 9-22. The Glacier Sand and Gravel buildings have been assembled as components so they can be rearranged to provide the coal bunker at Alliance and the mine at Corning.

Figure 9-23. The corrugated buildings have been cemented to each other's simulated concrete bunkers (far left and right). The center wall in the tall bunker (far right) will be removed as shown in Figure 9-20.

Figure 9-24. The steel bunker is placed sideways above the tracks and the modified corrugated building with its coal chutes is placed beside the tracks to create the Corning Mining Co. complex.

Figure 9-25. The Consolidated Edison generating plant and coal bunker (left) at Alliance and the mine at Corning (right) are a pair of "Loads-in/Empties-out" industries.

were placed at Alliance and linked to the Consolidated Edison generating plant with two of the conveyors cemented together end-to-end (Figure 9-25).

The hills and the forest that separate Alliance from Corning also disguise the fact that the two tracks extend through the scenery so that empty hopper cars can be continually pushed into the Corning Mining Company (Figure 17-7 in Chapter 17) and, later picked up as empties from the power plant at Alliance (Figure 9-8). The hoppers loaded with coal are picked up from beneath the tipple at the Corning Mining Company and delivered to the siding beneath the coal bins at the Consolidated Edison power plant (to be picked up later as loaded cars at the Corning Mine).

The overhead conveyors at both the mine tipple and the power plant help distract the eye from the fact that the siding holds more than just the three or four cars it would apparently accommodate. If you intend to operate complete unit trains of coal through these structures, as described in Chapter 19, be sure that the largest locomotive, not just the cars, will clear the structures.

Structures that Speak

The weathering steps in Chapter 15 will help bring those painted plastic buildings into the realm of reality. You will want to carry it a step further, however, to make those buildings come to life. Populating the buildings with people and vehicles will help add that breath of life. And the final touch will be added when the various signs of the buildings and industries are in place. These include the railroad station signs, a few advertising posters, and perhaps a billboard or two. Make a photocopy of the signs in Figure 9-26. Then you can cut out the various signs to supplement those supplied with the majority of the buildings.

You can piece together the names of all the towns and industries on the 6-by-6-foot Union Pacific layout and hundreds of others from the words on that page. Cut the words out and paste them to pieces of a file card or postcard with rubber cement. If you want a color, add it with a felt tip pen. Spray the signs with a light coat of Testors DullCote, and, when they dry, attach them to your buildings with five-minute epoxy. When the waybill tells your Peddler Freight's switching crew to spot a car at Consolidated Edison Co., all the crew needs to do is find the right car and look for the industry's sign. Your "empire" is now a part of the real world.

The "Live-There" Look

The structures on your layout should be surrounded with "dirt" so they look like their foundations really are embedded in the earth. If you are using plaster for the surface of your scenery, brush or trowel the brown-colored plaster (see Chapter 10) around the plywood, Styrofoam or Homasote tabletop before the building is installed, and push the structure into the still-wet plaster. About 1/16-inch of the plaster is deep enough. Be sure the building is level when you sink it into the plaster. If you are using Styrofoam for the tabletop, as shown in Chapter 6, you can coat the building site with a thick layer of artists Matte Medium, then sprinkle real dirt through a tea strainer onto the still-wet Matte Medium and spray the area with a mixture of three-parts water and one-part Matte Medium. Finally, push the building into the still-wet dirt to "bury" its foundation. You can then use the same

dirt and grass effects that you select for the rest of the scenery to blend the area around the building into the rest of the world (or to blend the rest of the world into the building area if you installed the building before the rest of the scenery). If you want to "bury" the structure in simulated concrete, trace the outline of the building, then slice about 1/16-inch into the Styrofoam with a hobby knife (Figure 9-27). Use a screwdriver or putty knife to pry out the Styrofoam, then set the structure down into its new foundation hole (Figure 9-28). You can fill in the gaps with concrete-colored plaster or the grey Chem Rex PL300 Styrofoam cement.

Highways and Parking Lots

Highways and parking lots would seem to fall under the "scenery" category but, for your model railroad, they are part of the structure-placing process. Also, highway and parking lots are usually flat, as are the sites for any buildings. You can finish the building sites, highways and parking lots before starting construction on the actual scenery. In fact, I would strongly suggest that you do just that and operate the layout for a few months to be absolutely certain that the structures are in the places you want them before you begin to construct the scenery. You may decide that the structures are too large or too small, or

Station/Industry Names for Signs

ALLIANCE	BUILDERS
ARLEE	CHEMICAL
BEDFORD	COAL
CORNING	COKE
DUNCAN	CONCRETE
EMMETT	DAIRY
FALLS	FARMING
GURNSEY	FEED
HASTINGS	FUEL
ISLAND	FURNITURE
JUNCTION	GROCERY
KIMBALTON	HARDWARE
LAKE	ICE
MASON	IRON
NEW	LUMBER
ONEIDA	MINE
PADUCAH	MINING
SPRING	OIL
TIMBER	PACKING
TREES	STEEL
UDELL	STORAGE
VALLEY	STOVES
WOODWARD	SUPPLY
YOUNGSTOWN	WHOLESALE
	WINERY

Figure 9-26.

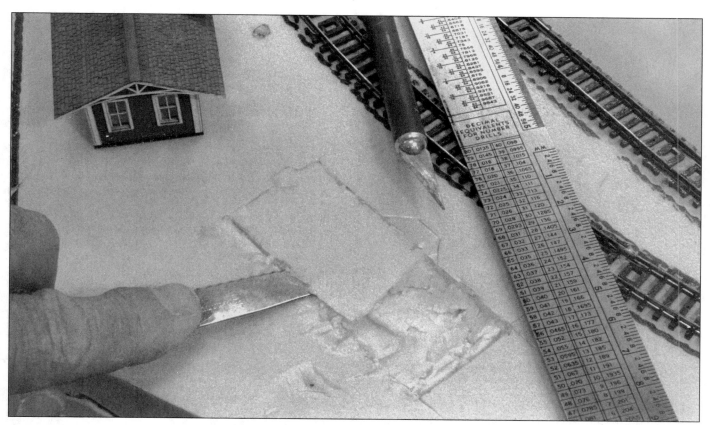

Figure 9-27. To lower the Emmett station into the "concrete", slice into the Styrofoam tabletop around the edges of the station and pry-up the Styrofoam with a knife or spatula.

Figure 9-28. The Emmett station is now nestled into the "concrete". Fill-in the gaps around the edges with grey automobile body putty or the Chem Rex PL300 cement used to assemble the Styrofoam as shown in Chapter 6.

Figure 9-29. The structures are all in their final positions on the 6-by-6-foot Union Pacific layout and the parking lots and highways are masked to prepare the layout for the scenery-construction steps in Chapters 10, 11, and 12.

that there are too many or not enough, and it is easy to make changes when you are still working with a flat tabletop. That is precisely what I did when building the 6-by-6-foot Union Pacific layout. Once the structures were in positions that seemed best after operating the layout, the parking lots and highways were completed. These areas were simply masked-off during the scenery construction stages (Figure 9-29). If you need an uphill road you might want to include that and, especially, the level site for the structures that road might serve, at this stage of construction. You can then insert the road and site into the hills as you create them as shown in Chapter 10.

The bare Styrofoam surface works just fine to simulate either blacktop (tar and gravel) roads and parking lots or concrete parking lots. Mask-off the edges of the road or the parking lots. The blacktop road on the 6-by-6 Union Pacific layout is 1-3/16-inches wide, which is about 16 N scale feet (Figure 9-30). Spray the road flat black. Use two or three very light coats so the paint does not attack the Styrofoam. That 16-foot width is common only to very narrow country roads, but it matches the width of the road on the Life-Like 7209 Crossing Gates I selected for the five road crossings (marked "G" on Figure 3-4 in Chapter 3). My favorite era is the fifties, so I was willing to settle for such a narrow blacktop road. If you are modeling a more modern era, I would suggest that you use two Life-Like Crossing Gates for each road/rail crossing, cutting each one to provide twice the 1-3/16-inch road width for a total width of 2-3/8 inches which is much closer to the prototype. You should also double the length of the pivoting arms by splicing-on the last inch or so of the arms leftover from the

second Crossing Gate. I would also recommend that you disconnect the operating mechanism and cement the simulated wood planks between the ties. When the paint dries, draw the centerline down the highway with a Testors or similar fine-tip paint pen (Figure 9-31).

To simulate concrete, mask off the edges of the area and spray the parking lot or highway a light greenish grey; I used Testors

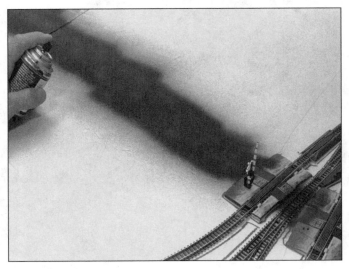

Figure 9-30. Use a pencil to mark the edges of the roads and parking lots. For blacktop roads, spray that area with two or three very light coats of flat black.

Model Master Light Gull Grey. When the paint is dry, use a fine-point felt-tip pen to mark the expansion joints every 8 to 12 N scale feet (5/8 inch to 7/8 inch) and add a few zigzag lines to indicate cracks. Dampen a piece of facial tissue with water and touch the felt-tip pen to it, then smear the ink along the center of the concrete roadway or parking lot to simulate oil-drippings. Practice on a scrap of paper to learn the technique. If you get too much, you can always spray the area grey and start over.

You can also finish any dirt road or parking lots and the areas around all the structures before starting on the hills and valley. These flat areas can be textured by coating them with artist's Matte Medium, then sprinkling on real dirt sifted through a tea strainer as described in Chapter 11. Add any weeds or bushes you will want at this time. Let the Matte Medium dry for a day. To simulate used dirt roads, rub a track-cleaning eraser over the surface to scuff and pulverize the dirt. The process also produces a somewhat lighter color that is most realistic. When all the paved and dirt roads are complete (Figure 9-32), it's time to begin construction of any hills or valleys.

Intermodal Yards and Team Tracks

Real railroads have always provided special sidings and parking lots where freight can be transferred directly from trains to trucks. If its boxcars, flat cars, gondolas, reefers, or even covered hoppers or tank cars that are being unloaded, these areas are usually referred to as "team tracks". There is usually a freight platform the height of the bottom of the freight cars with a ramp so fork lifts or trucks can drive onto the ramp. Sometimes, a ramp is provided at the stub end of siding so vehicles can be driven off flat cars. Some larger team tracks provide

Figure 9-31. Use a yellow fine-tip paint pen, guided by a small steel ruler, to draw the center-lines down the paved roads.

Figure 9-32. The intermodal yard (lower left) and freight station team track area and the station parking lot are all simulated concrete at Alliance.

Figure 9-33. Monroe Stewart has created a rail-to-ship intermodal terminal for his N scale layout.

heavy overhead cranes so machinery and other loads can be lifted from gondolas or flat cars. Many modern railroads provide bins beneath the track and a conveyor so covered hoppers can be dumped and reloaded into trucks. Some also provide pipes, flexible hoses and pumps so tank cars can be unloaded into tank trucks.

On modern railroads, the truck/railroad interface is provided at similar sidings with large expanses of paved parking that are called "intermodal yards". In the fifties, an intermodal yard was only used to unload trailers from flat cars, so ramps were provided at the end of each stub-end siding so the trailers could be hitched to a tractor and pulled to the ground or, reversing the process, loaded. When containers became popular, in the seventies, the intermodal yards were equipped with at least one loading machine that would pick up the containers and place them onto the flat car or "well" car. Some of these intermodal sites were places where the containers were transferred from the railroad (and from trucks) to ships. Monroe Stewart searched through hobby shops that sell marine supplies to find a ship hull large enough for N scale, then built the deck details to match photographs of a prototype container ship. He used Plastruct H-beams and I-beams to build a container transfer hoist, again copying photographs of the prototype (Figure 9-33). Most highway-to-railroad intermodal yards have either an overhead crane or a side-lift crane like the Showcase Miniatures cast-metal kit of the

Kalmar Container Loader shown in the intermodal yard on Gene Burtnett's layout (Figure 9-34). Gene also has a more conventional freight warehouse adjacent to his intermodal yard, a practice quite common on the prototype, especially in the sixties and seventies. GHQ offers a superbly-detailed cast-metal and etched-metal kit to recreate the Mi-Jack Translift Straddle Crane (Figure 9-35).

Automobiles and Trucks

The selection of ready-built plastic N scale vehicles is relatively limited. Atlas offers a nineties-era Ford F150 pickup with

Figure 9-34. Gene Burtnett has combined the modern era freight house (the flat-roof building) with small intermodal yard. The container lift truck was built from a Showcase Miniatures kit.

a choice of standard or flared sides (Figure 9-36) and a 1984 Ford LNT9000 Front Runner highway tractor. Busch has a VW Passat, VW minibus and Mercedes. Con-Cor offers a Kenworth tractor. Kato has a Toyota "sedan." Noch has an Audi A4. Wiking has a nineties-era Audi A6, Mercedes E230, VW Golf and VW Passat, a seventies-era Volkswagen 411, Ford Capri, Audi 100 and Porsche 911 and a fifties-era VW. Plastruct has an eighties-era Ford Mustang and Falcon and a "generic" four-door sedan and station wagon and four buses as well as a series of trucks. If you are willing to assemble and paint a cast-metal kit, there are far more choices, including excellent products from C in C (Figure 9-37), GHQ, Showcase Miniatures, Period Miniatures, Gloor Craft, Alloy Forms and Detail Associates.

N Scale People

The assembled buildings from Bachmann and Model Power are an inexpensive source of scale-model people for all parts of your railroad. Remove the people by applying about six coats of liquid cement for plastics to dissolve the factory-glue joints. Let the glue soak in for about an hour (but no more) and then gently pull and pry away the parts you want.

Finely-painted N scale people and animals are available from Preiser, but they are relatively expensive. Model Power, Noch, Kibri, and Plastruct also offer a large selection of less expensive painted figures. If you are willing to paint your own, Preiser has several inexpensive sets of unpainted figures, and LaBelle, Plastruct and NJ International offer unpainted figures.

Figure 9-35. The GHQ N scale replica of the Mijack container straddle crane is a highly-detailed cast- and etched-metal kit. —GHQ photo

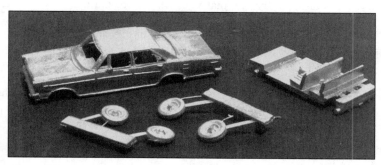

Figure 9-37. C in C produces a number of highly-detailed replicas of late-model automobiles and trucks as cast-metal kits.

Figure 9-36. Atlas offers ready-to-run replicas of the nineties era Ford F150 pickup trucks with either flare sides (right) or standard sides.

Do's and Don'ts for Model Buildings

- Do use cement for plastics to assemble even the snap-together building kits.
- Don't rely on just a few plastic tabs or pegs to hold a plastic building together.
- Do paint every building on your layout so each looks like solid material rather than translucent plastic.
- Don't use buildings just as they come from the box. Paint the building and or the trim a different color.
- Do modify all the buildings, before you assemble them, so they are at least a bit different from the stock kit and, thus, unique to your model railroad.
- Don't use buildings exactly as found in the kits; they will look like the buildings on every other model railroad. With freight cars, that's realistic because freight cars travel from town to town. Buildings, however, are unique to specific areas.
- Do apply enough dirt around the base of any building so the building appears to be resting in the earth.
- Don't drop buildings on top of the layout so they look like oversize children's building blocks sitting on carpet.
- Do arrange buildings in small groups to match the style of industrial, downtown or residential areas with open areas of scenery between clusters of buildings.
- Don't spread houses, stores and industries at random around the layout.

Chapter 10

Lightweight Scenery

Scenery is often considered to be just a backdrop for the trains. In fact, on some model railroads, scenery is left to the imagination. Only about one model railroad in ten is ever completed to the stage where the scenery is finished. Never forget, it is your railroad and if you want to leave scenery as an imaginary part of the railroad—no more present than the distant cities where your trains are headed—by all means, forget about scenery. I would hope, though, that you will understand that it is really quite easy to build scenery. Modelers have developed shortcuts over half a century of searching, trying, and redoing their scenery to discover some really quick and simple means of making scenery that is far more realistic than the oil-painted pictures done by most professional artists.

Simple Scenery, Step-By-Step

Scenery is just another form of model making. It's a step-by-step process that has a definite beginning and definite goal. For this book, I have divided the process into three general categories: the simplest steps to build the basic shapes of the mountains and hills, and the cliffs and valleys are in this chapter. The proven techniques to provide the textures for the scenery shapes, as well as bushes and tress are in Chapter 11, and the proven techniques for installing bridges and making streams, rivers, ponds, and lakes are in Chapter 12.

Four Scenery-Shaping Processes

There are, essentially, four different processes that you can use to create the hills and valleys for your model railroad. The time-proven technique for building scenery is to use plaster of Paris troweled over a door screen that is supported by wood forms. That is also the most difficult process and it produces a very heavy layout when you're finished. The second method is a better choice; shape the mountains with wads of paper towels and the valleys with nets woven from masking tape, then cover those shapes with industrial paper towels soaked in a special super-hard plaster called Hydrocal. An alternative to the paper towels and Hydrocal is to use the plaster (it's also Hydrocal)-soaked gauze designed for casts and splints for broken arms and legs. Hydrocal and plaster-impregnated gauze are both available at most hobby shops; Woodland Scenics offers Hydrocal and what they call "Plaster Cloth" and Activa offers plaster-impregnated gauze called "Rigid Wrap". I prefer the plaster-impregnated gauze because it is less messy than the Hydrocal-soaked paper towels method. You simply dip the plaster-impregnated gauze in a tray of water and avoid mixing any powdered plaster. A third method is to use Woodland Scenics selection of expanded-polystyrene white beadboard-type panels and track supports that they call their "SubTerrain" system. The SubTerrain system provides support for both the tracks and the hills and valleys which are then covered with plaster-soaked gauze (or, you can substitute the industrial-grade paper towels soaked in Hydrocal). The fourth method of building scenery shapes is to carve them from stacks of extruded polystyrene insulation board like the blue-colored Styrofoam described in Chapter 6.

This is the method used for building scenery on the 6-by-6-foot Union Pacific layout (Figure 10-20).

If you cannot pick a favorite, try them all by building a few square feet of the layout with each method. The door screen and plaster and the Hydrocal-soaked paper towels or plaster-impregnated gauze methods are easier to use with the open-grid style benchwork described in Chapter 5. Most modelers now seem to prefer the lightweight carved-Styrofoam or plaster cloth methods, so that's what you'll find in the book. If you want more information on the traditional wire screen or plaster-soaked paper towels methods, those techniques are described in the *HO Scale Model Railroading Handbook* and in the *Scenery For Model Railroads, Dioramas And Miniatures* book; both published by Krause Publications. None of these scenery construction methods are permanent so you can rip up the surface

Figure 10-1. Kelley Newton carved gypsum plaster for the rocks on his N scale recreation of the Union Pacific Railroad's route through Weber Canyon, Utah.

textures and cut a valley or remove the trees and add hills years later. That's one of the many joys of model railroading, there's no "construction schedule" so you can build and finish any part or all of the layout on your own timetable.

Any of the four scenery-shaping techniques can, however, be used with open-grid or plywood tabletop types of benchwork. I would suggest you build your railroad with the track elevated above the tabletop by at least two-inches using risers from an open-grid-style benchwork, Woodland Scenics' SubTerrain system of "Risers" and "Inclines" if you have a plywood tabletop, or build the layout from at least a 4-inch thick stack of extruded-polystyrene like the blue Styrofoam panels that were used for the 6-by-6-foot Union Pacific layout that is shown in most chapters.

The Field Trip

Try to select geography that is either near your home or that you can visit at least once a year. Take some photographs and make some plan-type sketches to show the scene in the photographs. Let those photographs encompass the terrain for a quarter-mile or so on either side of the tracks, and take some close-ups of just the cuts and fills and bridges next to the tracks. It's a good idea to even take some samples of the soil, both for color and to actually use on your layout.

Pay particular attention to the way cuts (through mountains or hills) and fills (over valleys or streams or hollows) begin and how they blend in with the edge of the track and with the surrounding terrain. These are the most difficult-to-capture aspects of real scenery. It's relatively simple to use latex rubber molds to cast rocks or to spread plaster around a hillside. However, the abrupt change from almost vertical sections of scenery to the gentler slopes and the edges of the railroad right-of-way are not so easy to capture on a model railroad. If you have a color photograph, some samples of the rocks and soil in the area, a bird's-eye-view sketch of the area, and a few notes to tie it all together, then you're prepared to make a model of the area.

I recommend that you try to include at least three or four of these real-world vignettes in your scenery. Finish them before you complete the rest of the scenery so you'll learn the feeling of creating scenery. The rest of the layout's scenery can then be "freelanced," drawing on the experience you have with those proven-to-be-genuine scenes from the real world. Please do not try to duplicate any of the scenery you see on other model railroads; you'll be translating only what someone else has interpreted to be "real," and you'll lose much of the realism in the process.

Go directly from your research in the real world to the methods and techniques that other modelers have developed. You don't have to invent new ways to make scenery. What you do have to do is to try to capture the shape and color and texture of the part of the real world that you have selected as your prototype. You will need to make several trips back to that "source" for information you forgot to get the first time and, perhaps, to collect more dirt and rocks for the layout. While you're on those field trips, you can also collect rocks to be used as molds (this will be discussed later in this chapter) and a variety of weeds and twigs to be used for tree trunks and bushes on your layout.

The Hydrocal Plaster and Gauze System

Plaster-impregnated gauze scenery is created in almost the exact same way as the traditional Hydrocal-soaked paper towel method that has been one of the traditional systems model railroaders have used to make scenery. The plaster-impregnated gauze is available from hobby stores as Woodland Scenics "Plaster Cloth", Activa's "Rigid Warp" and others, or you may find it at hospital supply firms. The plaster-impregnated cloth can be somewhat lighter than Hydrocal-soaked paper towels because the cloth is stronger than paper and, therefore, only two layers will be needed. Also, the plaster is sprayed evenly through the cloth so there is less of the heavy material. With Hydrocal plaster-soaked paper towels, you will have about twice as much plaster and, therefore, about twice as much weight.

Hydrocal is a special building plaster that becomes virtually as hard as rock after it sets; in fact, it becomes a type of alabaster. Some building-supply firms will order it in 100-pound bags if you ask them. Hydrocal is almost self-supporting; no chicken wire or screening is necessary as with other systems. Woodland Scenics sells smaller packages of Hydrocal through model railroad dealers. If you cannot find Hydrocal, then settle for the best grade of regular gypsum plaster you can find. You'll also need gypsum plaster if you wish to cast your own rocks as described later in this chapter; the finished Hydrocal is too hard to carve into rocks and erosion gullies.

The Full-Size Mock-Up

This scenery system only requires piles of wadded-up newspapers to create the shapes of the hills and mountains and valleys (Figure 10-2). You will need some sort of 1-inch or thicker Masonite or plywood "profile" boards to match the shape of mountains and valleys where they meet the edge of the table. Alternately, you can use 1-inch thick white extruded-Styrofoam from a lumberyard for the "Profile" boards or use the ribbed white expanded-Styrofoam "Profile" boards from Woodland Scenics SubTerrain system. You will also need a few vertical

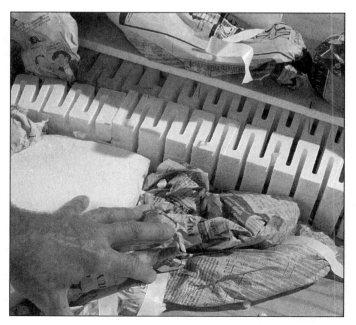

Figure 10-2. Use wadded-up newspapers to shape the hills and valleys. Here, the track will be elevated two-inches above the plywood tabletop with the zig-zag-shaped Woodland Scenics "Risers".

braces to support the tops of the hills or mountains in the center of the layout. The system allows you to actually mold the shapes of the hills and valleys with old newspapers before you apply any plaster. The profile boards can be cut to match the profiles you've made with the paper towels.

The basic humps and lumps that are the future hills and valleys are wadded-up newspapers. The almost-final surfaces of the hills and valleys are then shaped by draping wet newspapers over the wads of newspapers. If you see that a hill is too high or a cut is too close to the tracks, all you have to do is shove the newspapers aside. Strips of masking tape will help to hold the wads of newspapers down, and strips of tape can be used to make a netlike support to carry the newspaper wads over any large gaps or access holes in the benchwork. When you think you're satisfied with the shapes, drape the layout with a single layer of wet brown industrial paper towels. The brown paper towels will give you a much better idea of the shapes than the camouflage effect produced by the pictures, ads, and headlines in the newspaper.

Be sure to push the highest boxcar and the longest locomotive or passenger car you have over the railroad while the scenery is still in the mock-up stage. This will allow you to determine whether there is enough clearance through all the cuts and tunnels. Often an overhanging pilot on a diesel locomotive or the skirt on a passenger car will hit scenery placed too close to the track.

Tunnels

Most model railroads can benefit from the use of tunnels because they help disguise the fact that the trains really don't travel as far as they should and that they really don't connect with the outside world. Here, again, you'll find yourself working in the opposite direction of the real railroads, which try to avoid the expense of a tunnel whenever possible. Very few model railroads are large enough to have a mountain that's

Figure 10-3. Mask-off all the roads and parking lots, then cover all the other surfaces that are to remain flat with plastic bags.

gigantic enough to warrant a tunnel; the real railroads would have used cuts in almost every example you see on a model railroad. If you expect those "mole hills" to look like mountains large enough for a tunnel or two, you'll have to be careful to apply the practices the real railroads use, although in somewhat smaller than true N scale proportions.

You'll see that there are several smaller buildings in the "Alliance" area of the 6-by-6-foot Union Pacific layout because the "clutter" of a dozen buildings is far more realistic than the three or four structures that would fill that size area if everything were in exact scale. The windows and doors are precise N scale, and the proportions are correct for 1/160 scale people, but most of those buildings are closer to the size of a two-car garage than to that of the gigantic factories they represent. That same principle must be used for the hills and valleys on your model railroad. Use several smaller hills rather than one large mountain, for example. Copy the dirt or rock cuts through the earth that lead to every real railroad tunnel (including the rather deep cut leading to the top of each tunnel portal), but don't make the mountain above the tunnel as large. You can disguise the size of the mountain, to some extent, by "planting" smaller trees on its upper slopes to give the illusion of distance.

Tunnel Portals

Each tunnel must have some type of tunnel portal. A few tunnels are blasted through solid rock, so the rock itself forms the shape of the portal. Most tunnels, however, have wood, concrete, brick, or stone portals and linings through the length of the tunnel. When you build the portal, don't forget to extend the material far enough into the tunnel to give the illusion that the tunnel is lined through its entire length. Real mountains aren't hollow like those on a model railroad, and that mass is what you are trying to duplicate.

Model railroad shops sell a large selection of simulated wood, cut stone and rock tunnel portals, or you can make your own. The 1/4-inch thick white expanded-Styrofoam sold by Woodland Scenics makes a fine material to use for tunnel portals. Carve the foam with a common kitchen steak knife to create the graceful arch over the top of the tunnel portal, and make the arch at least 1-1/4-inches high and the vertical walls at least 1-3/16-inches wide (as wide as 2 inches if the tunnel is on a curve). The portal can be covered with the same plaster you use for your scenery. Smooth on the plaster to simulate a concrete tunnel portal and lining, or rough it up to simulate a tunnel carved through solid stone.

Plaster Mountains

When you're satisfied with your newspaper mock-up scenery, cover all of the roads and parking lots (Figure 10-3) and every inch of the tracks with wide masking tape. You can tape plastic trash bags over large flat areas, such as the "Alliance" yard and around any bridges. You will want to apply some plaster near the tracks on most flat areas to simulate hills and cuts, so use just the masking tape over the track in most places. The plaster-impregnated gauze will remain self-supporting. Use the wadded-up newspaper mock-ups, regardless of whether you opt for plaster-impregnated gauze or use the Hydrocal-soaked industrial-grade paper towels, to help you to decide on the shape for the upper edges of the 8-inch high plywood or Masonite profile panels that should be nailed and glued to the sides of the benchwork. There is no way to color the Plaster Cloth or Rigid Wrap as effectively as you can color raw plaster, except to apply paint as described later in this chapter or simply cover the finished plaster surface with felt using the "Grass-That-Grows" system from Chapter 11.

Use a Pyrex-type glass pan about 12-inches long and at least 2-inches deep to hold the water for soaking the plaster-impregnated gauze. You can impart some color into the white plaster if you pre-color the water with the powdered pigment sold for coloring concrete. You can buy the pigment at most construction supply firms. Mix the pigment into the water in about three-times the concentration suggested on the instructions. It is not possible to get as strong a color in

Figure 10-4. Dip the plaster-impregnated gauze in water, and then drape it over the wadded-up newspapers.

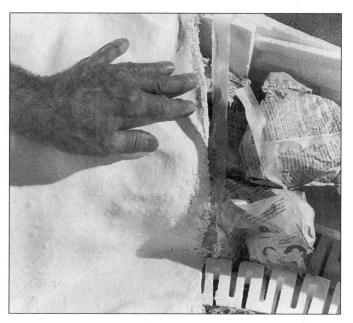

Figure 10-5. Use your fingers to roughen the surface of the almost-set plaster.

the finished plaster as you would using this same method to pre-color the water for the Hydrocal with the industrial-grade paper towels soaked in Hydrocal technique. Pre-coloring the water will, however, take away some of the harsh white when the plaster-impregnated cloth sets.

The plaster-impregnated gauze is supplied on a roll, so you must use scissors to cut it into sheets about 12-by-12 inches. I'd suggest cutting at least two dozen sheets at a time. Dip the entire piece of plaster-soaked gauze into the pre-colored water. The dried plaster on the gauze will soak-up the water. Drop the gauze into the water, folding it accordion pleat-style until the entire piece is submerged, then shake it lightly and remove it immediately so the plaster is not washed from the gauze.

The wetted gauze and plaster can now be draped over the hills and valleys you have prepared (Figure 10-4). I would suggest starting at the edge of the tracks and working your way out to the profile boards on the edge of the table. Fold the cloth over itself at the edges of the track and at the edges of the profile boards. The plaster itself should make a strong enough bond. If it won't stick, use some plastic-headed push pins (like those used to hold down the cork roadbed in Chapter 7 (Figure 7-33). In some places, you may need to use caulking cement to hold the dried plaster and gauze to the profile boards after the plaster dries. Overlap each additional piece of plaster-soaked gauze about halfway across the area of the first one. This interweaving technique will give you the two layers you need for strength. Continue to add plaster-soaked gauze pieces around the layout until the scenery shapes are complete. The new plaster will stick nicely to the old if you continue the work on the same day.

If the job takes more than a day, be sure to spray some water on the places where you will add new plaster to the old so that the two will bond together nicely. I suggest that you rub the surface of the last layer of plaster-soaked gauze with your hand during the last few minutes of the hardening or setting stage to roughen the surface (Figure 10-5). When you do this, the particles of just-hardened plaster will act like very rough sandpaper to roughen the rest of the surface. It's a bit hard on your hands, so apply some hand cream or salve to replace the natural body oils the plaster leaches out. The roughened surface can be used as is for just about everything, but for those almost vertical walls and cliffs, you'll want to carve or cast rock or erosion marks into the plaster.

Woodland Scenics' SubTerrain System

Woodland Scenics has some grooved sheets of 1/2-inch white Styrofoam called "Profile Boards" that interlock to form the edges of the layout and supports for the profiles of the scenery. These can be cut with a hacksaw blade, a serrated kitchen knife, or a hot wire as shown in this chapter. Shape the scenery with wadded-up newspapers as described earlier. When you are satisfied with the shapes, cut the Woodland Scenics white beadboard "Profile" board around the edges of the layout to match the shapes of the edges of the hills and valleys, then drape Hydrocal-soaked paper towels or plaster-soaked gauze over the newspaper and onto the edges of the profile boards. The stages of scenery construction with this system are shown in Figure 10-6.

This layout was built on a piece of 1/2-inch plywood, but it could just as easily be built on one or two layers of 2-inch thick extruded polystyrene, like the blue Styrofoam insulation board. This extruded-polystyrene material is much, much stronger and

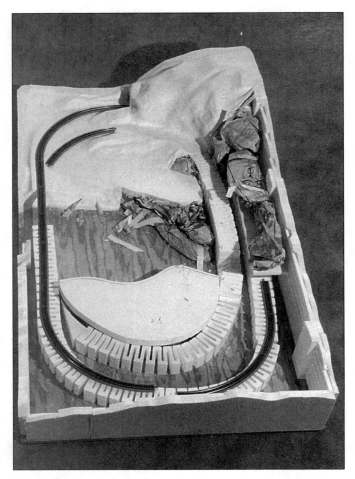

Figure 10-6. This 2-by-4-foot demonstration layout is being constructed with the Woodland Scenics SubTerrain system of Risers to support the tracks, Profile boards around the edges, bead board for structures sites and other flat areas, wadded-up newspapers for shaping hills and valleys and scenery shaped with Plaster Cloth.

Figure 10-7. To use real rocks or pieces of coal for molds, first coat the rock with mold release or cooking pan non-stick fluid like Pam.

denser than the expanded-polystyrene used with the Woodland Scenics "SubTerrain" system—the white beadboard is not strong enough to be used as benchwork. The track is elevated 2-inches above the plywood on Woodland Scenics "Risers" to leave room for streams and roads to cross below the tracks and to provide paled for embankments leading down from the tracks. The "Profile" boards are in place on all four sides of the layout, but the board on the left is cut down nearly to the tabletop to provide a place for a stream and valley. One-inch thick white beadboard is used to provide level areas for structures that lie inside the curve.

The track on this particular example is Bachmann's E-Z Track with built-in ballast, but any of the track and roadbed systems in Chapter 7 could be used. You can choose to remove the track before applying the plaster-soaked gauze or paper towels, or simply push the plaster material up to the edge of the roadbed. Woodland Scenics recommends that you remove the track so the plaster-soaked gauze can better bond to their Risers and Inclines and to the Profile Boards and the plywood or blue extruded-Styrofoam baseboard for greater strength. If you opt to remove the track, you must smooth the surface of the hardening plaster with sandpaper to provide a perfectly-level sub base for the cork roadbed or for the Kato Uni-Track, E-Z Track, Power-Loc track or similar plastic roadbed. There will be a bit more noise from the trains with the plaster sub-roadbed technique than there will be if you mount the roadbed directly to the Styrofoam or Riser or Inclines. Finish the layout using the surface texturing techniques in Chapter 11.

Real Rocks

It's possible to carve simple rock structures like the layers of sandstone and the erosion marks that water makes on smooth earth cuts and fills. That's the technique Kelley Newton used to create the spectacular canyon in Figure 10-1 and in the color section. He used photos of the prototype Weber Canyon in Utah and made a half-dozen attempts, however, before he was able to achieve these results. More complex rock structures are best duplicated with latex rubber molds taken from real rocks. Chunks of coal can often provide rock-like strata that is even more realistic than genuine rocks when applied to a model railroad. Spray or brush the portion of the rock or the piece of coal you want to duplicate with silicone spray or with one of the non-stick cooking sprays, such as Pam (Figure 10-7).

Liquid latex can be purchased in cans from many craft-supply stores. If you cannot find the liquid latex, you can substitute artists Matte Medium, but the resulting mold won't last for more than one or two castings. Brush a thick layer of the latex or white glue over the rock, apply a layer of gauze or cheesecloth to act as reinforcement (Figure 10-8), and brush on another layer of latex or white glue over the gauze or cheesecloth. Repeat the process until you have a total of three layers of liquid latex and two layers of gauze or cheesecloth. Allow the mixture 24 hours to dry before gently peeling it away from the rock. You now have a mold of the rock, which can be duplicated in plaster.

Use gypsum plaster or plaster of Paris for the rock castings so that you can carve the edges to help them blend into the surrounding scenery. Mix the plaster for soaking the industrial paper towels in flexible plastic pans that you can throw away or purchase a large Pyrex glass mixing bowl. The Pyrex can be washed clean much more easily than regular glass, and it is somewhat stronger.

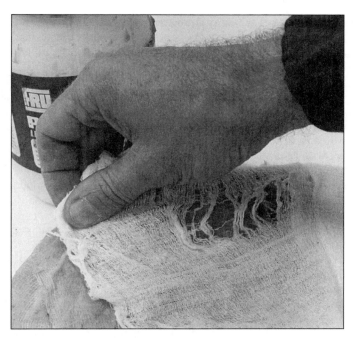

Figure 10-8. Apply a single layer of gauze over the rock or coal, then brush-on a thick layer of liquid latex.

Purchase some dark-brown powdered pigment for concrete from a building-supply dealer (who might also have Hydrocal or gypsum plaster). Buy enough to give a light-brown color to all the plaster you purchase. The powdered pigment should have instructions to tell you how much is needed for that particular brand, or you can ask the dealer.

Pour about four cups of water into your mixing bowl and slowly sprinkle in about an equal amount of plaster while you stir. Always add the dry plaster to the water, not the water to the plaster. The exact ratio of plaster to water can vary considerably, so keep stirring while you add the plaster. You want a mix about the consistency of thick cream. When the consistency is right, stir in the proper amount of the dry pigment. With practice, you'll learn how much plaster is about right, and then you can stir in both the plaster and the pigment at the same time. You might want to use a shade of gray or beige dry-color pigment for the rocks rather than brown. Use only about half as much of the pigment as you did to simulate dirt on the rest of the scenery so the rocks will be a pastel shade, rather than solid brown or beige. Mix the plaster until it is just a bit thicker than before (but it should still be pourable).

Pre-wet the area where the rock casting will be placed with a spray bottle or plant atomizer. Pour the wet plaster into the mold and immediately slap the mold and the plaster against the place where you want the rock. Hold it there until you can feel the plaster harden (it will take only a minute or two) and immediately peel the mold away before the plaster is completely hard. You can add as many applications of rocks made from the same mold as are needed to give the cliff the "face" you want. Overlap each casting slightly, and tilt each one a few degrees to give a slightly different appearance to each segment (Figure 10-9).

You can, of course, use many different rock-casting molds on various parts of the layout or even on a single cliff face. Remember that the rocks must match the texture of the rocks in the cuts and cliffs you see in the geographic area you have selected as the prototype for your layout. Crumpled aluminum foil can be used in place of the latex-and-gauze molds to duplicate one specific type of rock texture with this same casting pro-

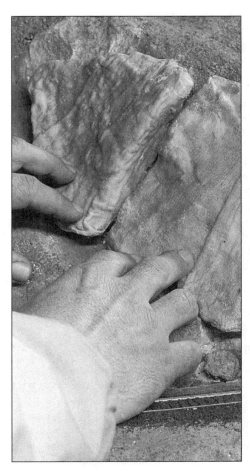

Figure 10-9. Apply the plaster-filled rock mold directly to the scenery. For larger areas, refill the mold and apply the plaster a second time, overlapping the first "rock".

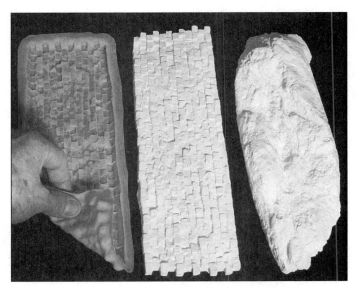

Figure 10-10. If you want to work with separate rock or stone wall molds, let the plaster dry before peeling away the latex mold.

cedure. You can use this same mold-in place technique with the carved-Styrofoam system described later in this chapter, or you can cast the rocks as separate pieces (Figure 10-10) and cement them to the surface with Liquid Nails "Projects and Foamboard", Chem Rex PL300 "Foam Board Adhesive" or a similar latex-based cement that will not attack the Styrofoam.

The Flat Earth Alternative

It is not absolutely necessary to carve valleys or build hills. Remember, most of the real world is relatively flat. If you elevate the track on roadbed (an automatic process if you use track with built-in roadbed like Uni-Track, E-Z Track, Power-Loc track or True Track), add building sites and roads as shown in Chapter 6, you can simply texture the surface and use trees to provide view block between scenes.

Carving Styrofoam Mountains

The plaster-impregnated gauze or Hydrocal-soaked paper towel scenery construction methods allow you to mock-up the hills and valleys with wadded-up newspapers covered with brown paper towels. You really cannot do that with the blue Styrofoam system. I would suggest that you make a scale model of the scene shapes you hope to achieve. Use a block of child's modeling clay and carve the valleys with the end of a paper clip. I used this technique to see if it were possible to produce both the valley at one end and the mountains in the middle of a 4-by-6-foot layout and still retain relatively gentle slopes.

It is possible to use these techniques to create mountains and valleys from the white expanded-Styrofoam of "beadboard" but I would not recommend that for a model railroad, because it is just too weak. The white Styrofoam material can be carved for dioramas or small scenes and it works well for roads and for the basics of Woodland Scenics "SubTerrain" system shown earlier

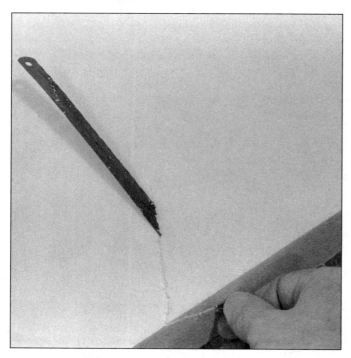

Figure 10-11. If you have built the tabletop from at least a 2-inch thick layer of Styrofoam, you have space to cut valleys below the tracks. Use a hacksaw blade (shown) or hot wire cutter to shape the hills.

in this Chapter. The blue Styrofoam is the material used to build the lightweight benchwork in Chapter 6. If you have planned on having rivers and valleys, you have included 4 to 8-inches of the blue Styrofoam beneath the track as shown in that chapter. Use the same material to make the mountains.

The blue Styrofoam can be carved with a hacksaw blade (Figure 10-11) or a serrated kitchen knife. These tools will produce some nearly weightless dust that can be readily removed with a vacuum cleaner. An alternative method is to use a special hot wire cutter that produces only a few drips of melted plastic foam and wisps of white smoke. The hot wire softens the microscopic air bubbles that are trapped in the Styrofoam to produce a cut. The hot wire produces fumes that can be toxic, especially to anyone with allergies, so always work outdoors.

I used Avalon Concepts "Foam Sculpting Detail Station" set to cut the Styrofoam benchwork for the 6-by-6-foot Union Pacific layout in Chapter 6 (Figures 6-5, 6-6 and 6-7). It is relatively expensive but it is one of the few hot wire tools that can be used to cut into the center of a 2-by-2-foot or larger panel. The Avalon Concepts set includes a transformer to reduce the 110-volt current to a usable level, the Detail Wand and a single short hot wire blade. You will want to purchase at least two of the Avalon Concepts "Wand Wire" packs that include three 9-inch pieces of wire that can be bent into any shape. I used the jigsaw-shaped Avalon Concepts "Shaper Tool" (Figure 10-16) to carve the Styrofoam hills because it works faster than the Detail Wand. Woodland Scenics, Plastruct and others make similar jigsaw-shaped hot wire cutters.

The wire can become as hot as an electric stove and the melted plastic that can drip off the wire is hotter than melted candle wax, so burns are possible. Wear cloth gloves and long sleeves so no skin is exposed. Caution: do not try to use a hot wire cutter with the urethane foams because the fumes produced can be toxic.

I bent three different cutting wires for the Detail Wand Bend as shown in Chapter 6 (Figure 6-6). The 4-inch long U-shaped piece that is clamped in the Detail Wand was used for carving the valleys and mountains. Be sure the parallel wires are at least 1/2-inch apart so there's less chance they can accidentally touch if you push the heated wire through the blue Styrofoam with too much force. Bend a similar hot wire cutter, but with only a 2-1/2-inch deep U-shape and bend the ends at a 90-degree angle to make a cutter that will make right-angle cuts in 2-inch thick sheets of blue Styrofoam as shown in Chapter 6 (Figure 6-7). I also bent a multiple Z-shaped piece with the full 9-inch wire to make cuts for the drainage ditches on the sides of the railroad roadbed (Figures 7-39, 7-40, and 7-41).

Carving Out the Valleys

Carve the blue Styrofoam with a hacksaw blade (Figure 10-11), or serrated kitchen knife or one of the hot wire cutters. I used the U-shaped 4-inch long wire to shape all the valleys and hills on the 6-by-6-foot Union Pacific layout. One of the detriments to realism that is common to many model railroads is the sight of nearly-vertical slopes on the mountains and cuts. In the real world, only rock cuts are that steep. I wanted the Union Pacific layout to represent the gentle slopes that are common to most of North America. Most real railroad cuts through the earth and earthen fills or embankments are no steeper than 30-degrees, so I used a 30-60-90 triangle to guide the cutter when

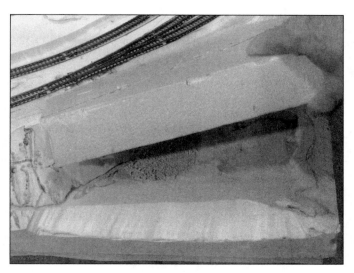

Figure 10-12. You may need to make additional cuts to free the piece of Styrofoam so it can be removed from the layout.

making those cuts. The hot wire is only long enough to make a cut at 30-degrees through a single 2-inch layer of blue Styrofoam. If you are making shallower cuts, make the first shallow-cut pass, then use the cutter vertically to remove the material and make a second pass. When the cut is complete, lift the layer of blue Styrofoam (Figure 10-12) away and resume cutting through the second layer.

One of the secrets of working with blue Styrofoam for scenery is that you can replace or add material as well as remove it. If, for example, you discover that you have made any portion of the valley too deep, find the chunk of blue Styrofoam you removed and slice off the bottom of it to fill in the bottom of the valley.

Preparing for Bridges

This scenery construction system allows you to make decisions about bridges and tunnels after you see that there would be a need for such features. The long, curved embankment on the Union Pacific layout crosses a shallow valley that would, logically, have been the course of a small stream. That was the place where the real railroad would have installed a bridge. A real railroad probably would have installed a small culvert down near the level of the stream. I postulated, however, that the stream flooded frequently, so a steel viaduct was needed to span most of the valley. I used a Micro Engineering 518 "Tall Steel Viaduct" for this span. The short girder bridges that fit below the tracks were also used for the shorter bridge. The abutments are simply 1-1/2-inch long pieces of Evergreen .125-by-.125-inch styrene.

Determine the length of the bridge and wiggle a serrated knife between the roadbed and the blue Styrofoam to free the track from the Styrofoam. Remember that the embankments beneath the bridge should be no steeper than 30-degrees, and make the cuts through the embankment with the hacksaw blade or hot wire. The embankment can then be removed from beneath the track and roadbed. The shapes of the valley sides and floor can be sculpted by trimming off potato-chip-size pieces of the blue Styrofoam with either a hot wire or a hacksaw blade or, for smaller, cuts, a serrated knife.

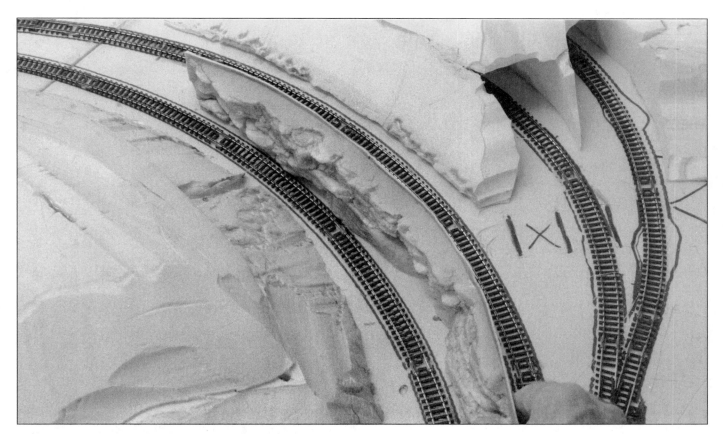

Figure 10-13. Mountains-in-Minutes flexible "Flexrock" can be used to create rockfaces for cuts and tunnels through the hills.

Carving the Mountains and Hills

The hills are carved with a process that is almost the reverse of that used for carving valleys. Leftover pieces cut for the valleys can be turned upside down and used for small hills (Figure 10-14). To make larger hills, begin by laying a fresh sheet of 2-inch thick blue extruded-Styrofoam over the portion of the layout that will be occupied by the future hill or mountain. Use a marker to indicate where the building sides are located. Use spare pieces of track to duplicate the pattern of tracks beneath the Styrofoam and mark the locations of the edges of the drainage ditches beside the track (Figure 10-15). Use the hot wire cutter or hacksaw blade at a gentle angle (Figure 10-16) to cut around the Styrofoam to the edges of the buildings or the drainage ditches. I made some of the cuts to the track at a 60-degree angle because I knew these steeper cuts would be hidden by trees and buildings.

When the hill is completely cut, notice if there is still a flat top. If so, you can pin another piece of blue Styrofoam to the cut piece with 4-inch long concrete nails. Turn the two pieces upside down and use the slopes from the original piece as a guide for the hacksaw blade or hot wire to cut into the new piece. When the cuts are completed, turn the two pieces over and position them beside the tracks and hold them to the tabletop with 4-inch long concrete nails. When you are satisfied with the position and shape of the mountains and hills, double-check the side-to-side clearances by pushing the longest passenger or freight car through the tracks. If everything is acceptable, cement the layers together with Liquid Nails "Projects and Foamboard", Chem Rex PL300 "Foam Board Adhesive" or a similar latex-based cement that will not attack the Styrofoam.

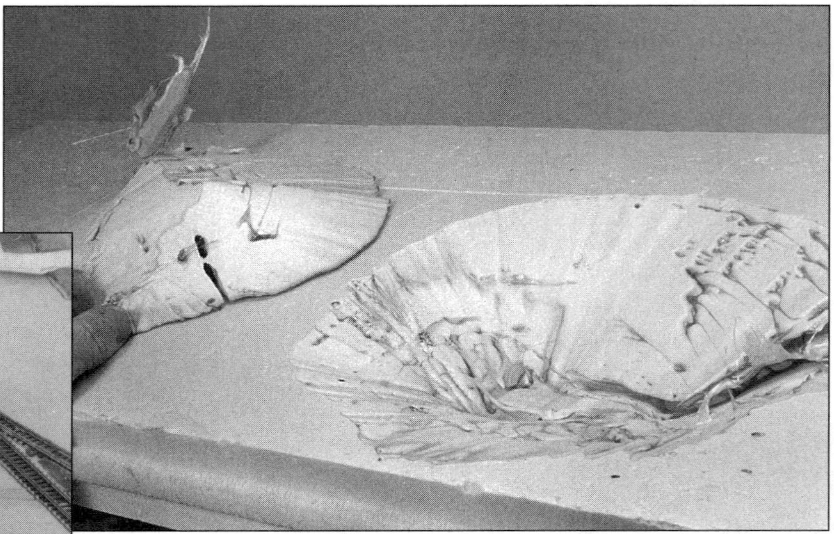

Figure 10-14. You can cut a valley into the Styrofoam (right) and use the piece you removed to make a small hill (left).

Figure 10-15. Cut a two-inch thick piece of Styrofoam large enough to cover the base of any hill and lay it over the tracks. Mark the positions of the tracks and the edges of the drainage ditches on the Styrofoam.

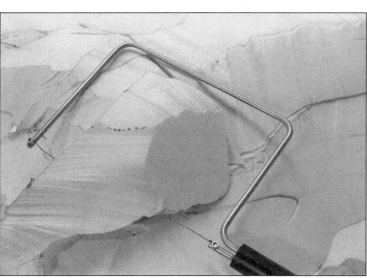

Figure 10-16. Use a hacksaw blade or a hot wire cutter (shown) to cut through the two-inch Styrofoam that will become the mountain.

Boring Tunnels

If you find that a two-inch thick layer of carved Styrofoam still allows a flat top, you may have a place where a tunnel can be used (Figure 10-17). Repeat the process used for carving the hills to carve the top of the tunnel (Figure 10-18). Finish shaping the hills with the hot wire cutter or hacksaw blade (Figure 10-19).

If there are areas where you simply must have steep scenery beside the tracks, you can use the Mountains-In-Minutes pre-painted urethane foam rock (Figure 10-13). Do not, ever, attempt to cut these products with a hot wire because the resulting fumes are toxic. The urethane foam is, however, easily cut with a hacksaw blade. The tops of the rock cuts can be finished off with small pieces of blue Styrofoam.

When the scenery is complete, check all the tracks again for adequate side clearances by pushing the longest passenger or freight car you will operate around all the tracks as shown in Chapter 9 (Figure 9-20). Mark the outlines of all the buildings. Remove buildings. The scenery—now looking very much like ice blue surfaces of the Arctic (see the color section)—is ready for final texturing (Figure 10-20). If you cover the surface with plaster, paper towels dipped in plaster or Plaster Cloth, you will be adding unnecessary weight to the layout. I would recommend that you use the "Grass-That-Grows" system of treated felt in Chapter 11 for as much of the surface as possible because it adds only ounces of weight. I painted the bare Styrofoam with latex paint and sprinkled on fine-ground foam, real dirt and flocking (in that order) for the surfaces of the scenery on the Union Pacific layout.

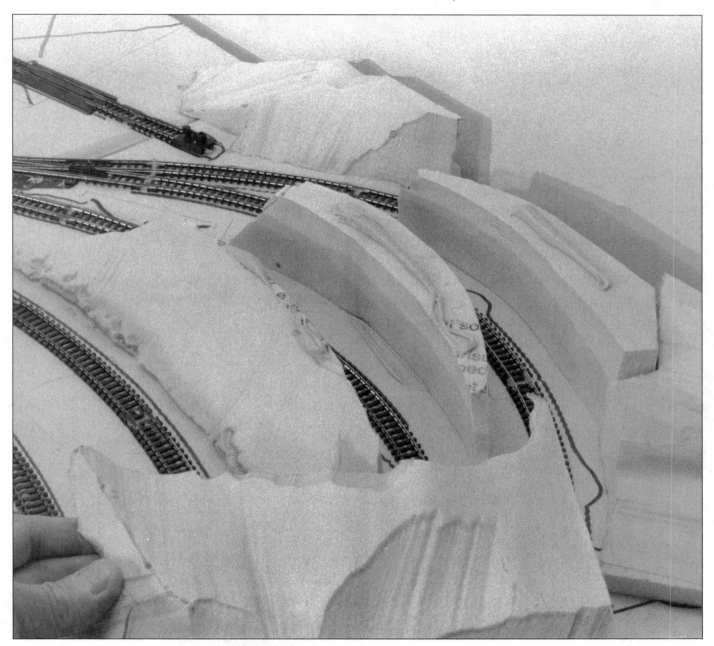

Figure 10-17. Cut separate pieces of Styrofoam to fit between the tracks, The vertical walls will become the sides of tunnels, and the gentler slopes up from the tracks will be visible open cuts through the mountain.

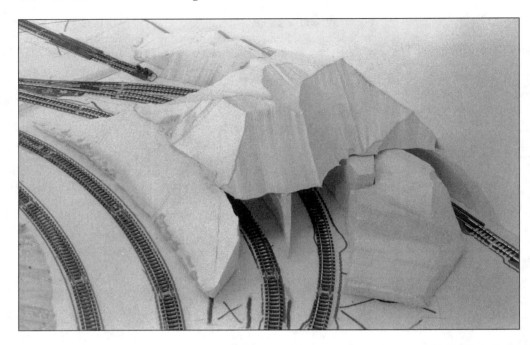

Figure 10-18. The mountain is just high enough to provide a tunnel over the two tracks (the "Loads-in/Empties-out" tracks described in Chapter 17 (Figures 17-2 and 17-3).

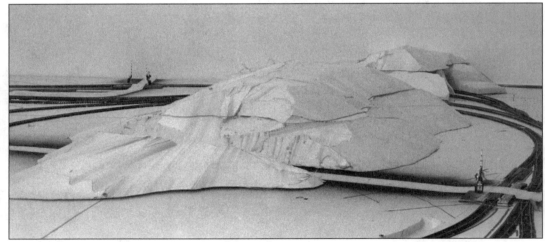

Figure 10-19. Carefully blend the bottoms of the hills with the tops of adjacent valleys using a hacksaw blade or hot wire cutter.

Figure 10-21. The backdrop buildings and hills were cut from their paper sheets to be mounted on the sky blue-painted aluminum backdrop with rubber cement.

Finishing the Surface

Most model railroaders select one of two methods for finishing the surface of the scenery: the first method requires a plaster surface, which can come from Hydrocal-soaked paper towels or plaster cloth. You can also use plaster to cover the carved Styrofoam. The plaster should be pre-colored with powdered paint pigments sold for use with concrete. Construction supply firms usually have the pigments under the Rainbow brand or others. The pre-colored plaster will not be so difficult to cover completely with earth-colored paint as white plaster and, if the plaster chips, the chipped areas are not so evident. The plaster surface is then painted with latex paint and real dirt and ground foam or flocking is added to model grass and weeds. Those are the methods used for the 6-by-6-foot Union Pacific layout. An alternate method is the "Grass-That-Grows" method shown in Chapter 11. This method can be used with either plaster-covered contours or with the bare blue extruded -Styrofoam shapes.

Mix-and-Match Techniques

There are two methods of making the basic scenery shapes in this book and two methods of finishing the surface for earth and grass effects. You can mix-and-match all of them or build part of the layout with one system and part with another. Each has its advantages: the paper towel method is the least expensive and it allows you to pre-color the plaster so chips and areas you miss with paint will not be so visible, but it is the messiest and the heaviest. If you substitute Plaster Cloth, you avoid most of the mess of dipping paper towels in Hydrocal plaster and it's just as quick, but is still fairly heavy and it is more expensive. However, the Plaster Cloth method can be about as light as carved blue extruded-Styrofoam if you also use the Woodland Scenics "SubTerrain" system for supporting the roadbed and use the techniques shown in Chapter 6 for building a tabletop from blue extruded-Styrofoam. The carved-blue extruded-Styrofoam method is the lightest (especially if the surfaces are textured with the felt "Grass-That-Grows" techniques),

and it is the least messy, but it takes some practice to learn to carve out the contours and it is slightly more expensive. Confused? Just pick the methods that seem the most fun to you.

Sky Backdrops

Like it or not, your model railroad world ends at the edge of the table. You can soften the shock of that sight by finishing the edge of the table in an earthy brown or green that blends with the scenery. The area where the layout backs up to the wall, however, can be used more effectively to provide a seemingly more-distant horizon to your modeled world. The 6-by-6-foot Union Pacific layout was finished with a sky blue backdrop painted on a 6-foot long piece of 2-foot wide aluminum roof gutter flashing. The aluminum can be attached to the wall with double-sided foam "poster stickers" (from a stationery store), nails or contact cement. I elected to expand the "horizon" on the layout by adding more of the buildings of the town of Alliance. I simply cut away the sky from one of the Detail Associates HO scale 7503 and 7506 "Background Scenes" (Figure 10-21) and cemented the hills from the scene to the backdrop with rubber cement (from a stationery store). The Walthers 711 "Instant Horizons" painted backdrops can also be used. The buildings and people in the foreground are HO scale, but, with the fences and doors hidden by the modeled buildings, what's left is close enough to N scale. I also used one of the Faller 515 photomural scenes of rolling hills, with the sky cut off with scissors.

If you are using photomurals, the colors will be far brighter than on your layout. To make them appear to be more distant and more like extensions of the "modeled world" spray the photomurals with a very thin coat of light grey to soften and blend the colors and make them appear more distant. The Faller 514, 515, 516 and 517 photomurals are excellent and typical of many areas of North America. The Vollmer 6113 is also a good choice for rolling hills and woods. Additional choices of photomurals can be found at some hardware stores. Paint the sky with Sherwin Williams SW17832 "Bold Blue" or an equivalent sky blue color from another paint maker.

Do's and Don'ts for Creating Scenery

- Do have color photographs, postcards or magazine illustrations of the general area you wish to model beside the layout so you can match colors, shapes and plant/earth textures with model materials.

- Don't attempt to create scenery by using only the packaged model scenery materials arrayed by whim.

- Do use real dirt sifted through a fine wire screen to simulate dirt.

- Don't use dyed sawdust or ground foam to simulate dirt.

- Do check the clearances beside and above the tracks, at tunnels, and cuts through the hills by running the longest locomotives and the longest cars over the layout.

- Don't build rock walls or cliffs so close to the tracks that long locomotives or cars will sideswipe the scenery and derail.

- Do spray any of the too-bright greens with a fine mist of light beige wash (a mix of about nine-parts water to one-part beige acrylic paint plus a drop of dishwashing detergent) to blend the colors of the layout and avoid too much contrast between earth and leaves or grass under the relatively dim indoor lighting.

- Don't settle for bright greens and deep browns as the only scenery colors.

- Do apply ballast to any mainline tracks (and dirt to industrial sidings) but keep the ballast well away from the moving parts (the switch points) of all the turnouts. Glue the ballast in place with a mixture of nine-parts water to one-part artist's Matte Medium with a drop of dish washing detergent.

- Don't use loose ballast and do not allow any glue or ballast around the points of any turnout.

Chapter 11

Earth, Weeds, Bushes, and Trees

Scenery begins at the ground. Far too many modelers skip right ahead to bushes and trees and wonder why their layouts look like deserts with trees on them. The basic scenery shapes and any exposed rocks should already be in place as described in Chapter 10. To finish the scenery, you will need to add earth, weeds, bushes and trees (and, perhaps, water as illustrated in Chapter 12).

I suggest that you complete the scenery on just a few square feet of the layout to this stage so you can apply your lessons to the rest of the railroad after you have learned them through practice. There's no real reason why you cannot create scenery in just one small corner of the layout, from the plaster or carved-Styrofoam stage right through water and foliage. When you feel like making more scenery, begin another section and gradually work your way around. You can also use this period to experiment with other techniques like using the "Grass-That-Grows" method of providing both earth and grass effects shown later in this chapter. If you decide to use plaster, I suggest that you place that pre-colored plaster just about everywhere in order to get the messy part over and done with. If you find later that you need to change a mountain or add a river, it's easy enough to break through the plaster to mock-up a change in the scenery and recover it with plaster. Apply the final touches of foliage to only those areas where you're pleased with the rest of the scenery. Those finished areas will include the tracks and their immediate surroundings.

Ground Color

If you were able to pre-color the plaster, you won't need to paint the surface. If, however, you cannot locate powdered colors or if you use Plaster Cloth or Rigid Wrap, or if you carved the scenery shapes from extruded-polystyrene-like Styrofoam, you must paint the scenery surface. First, however, mask all of the track and the highways and parking lots so you won't have

to worry about dripping paint (Figure 11-2). The tape should remain in place until the final step in the scenery-texturing process, adding ballast to the track. Paint every square inch of the plaster or Styrofoam surfaces with latex wall paint to match the color of earth you will be using (Figure 11-3). Use a floodlight to help accent any of the bare white plaster or blue Styrofoam that might show through the paint.

Rocks can be colored by simply spraying on a wash of 95 parts water and 5 parts dark-brown or dark-gray acrylic paint. The wash will collect in the crevices and hollows of the rock castings and the almost white plaster will show through as highlights for some incredibly realistic rock effects.

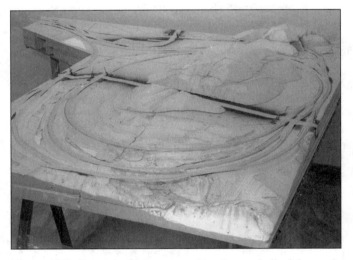

Figure 11-2. Cover the highways, parking lots and all of the tracks with masking tape while you texture the scenery surfaces.

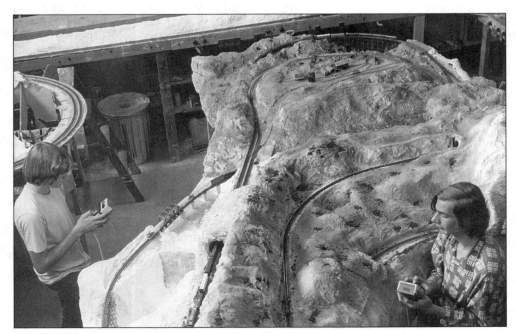

Figure 11-1. The N scale layout of the East Valley Lines club in California has the track elevated to realistic viewing position near eye level and the members have tethered walk-around controllers. The scenery on this layout was built with conventional door screen and plaster construction (lower left).

Figure 11-3. Paint the shaped Styrofoam (or plaster) surfaces with a thick coat of earth-color latex wall paint.

Real Dirt

On a model railroad, as in the real world, scenery begins with the base rocks and dirt. I suggest that you use at least two different kinds of ground cover in addition to real dirt: ground (chopped) foam rubber dyed green and the flocking sold by Woodland Scenics, Scenic Express, Noch, Vollmer and others. The real dirt and the ground foam can be held in place on the layout with artist's Matte Medium.

You can find real dirt anywhere. I would suggest, however, that you bring along a magnet to be sure the dirt does not contain some iron oxide that is magnetic enough to be pulled into the motors of your locomotives. Sift the dirt through a fine-mesh tea strainer and save only the dirt that passes through the strainer. It is just possible that some micro-organisms are living in the dirt, so it's a good idea to bake the dirt in an oven at 400-degrees for an hour to kill anything that might be in there. Cover the areas of the scenery that are not occupied with buildings, track, or cliffs with real dirt. Brush full strength artist's Matte Medium over any scenery shapes not covered with rock castings or retaining walls and use a strainer or flour sifter to sprinkle real dirt on those areas. Add dirt to the horizontal surfaces of the rocks using the same technique. Cover only about a square foot at a time so the Matte Medium does not dry before you can apply the textures.

After you have applied the loose dirt, ground foam and flocking, the materials can be cemented firmly to the layout by spraying them with a mixture of three-parts water to one-part artist's Matte Medium with a drop of dishwashing detergent to break

the surface tension of the fluids or you can use Woodland Scenic's Scenic Cement or Champ Decal Company's Resibond Spray. When the spray dries, the material will look loose and powdery but will be held firm enough so you can even stand the layout on end for storage.

When all the dirt is in place, you can remove the masking tape from the track and highways to add whatever matching or contrasting shades of dirt you have selected for track ballast. Part of the earth and even some of the track sidings should be covered with grass and weeds.

The ground foam rubber is available in a variety of "grinds" (sizes of the foam pieces) and colors to match summer foliage, as well as spring and fall colors, and the bright hues of flowers. The foam is even available in earth or dirt colors and it makes a surprisingly realistic substitute for sifted real dirt. Hobby shops carry the foam under the AMSI, Bachmann, Life-Like, Plastruct, Scenic Express, and Woodland Scenics labels. The foam can simply be sprinkled on trees, shrubs or ground for now.

Weeds and Grass

Polypropylene twine is available from macramé shops and craft departments. The twine must be cut into 1/8-inch lengths. Polypropylene is the only material that will retain the individual strands after it is cut this short. You can do this with other synthetic macramé or knitting twines, but they'll bunch together to form clumps very similar to tumbleweeds. Polypropylene, on the other hand, will simulate grass, hay, wheat, and similarly textured weeds. Buy dark green, light green, and avocado colors if you can. Faller, Kibri, Noch, Preiser, Vintage, and Woodland Scenics (available to dealers from Walthers), and Scenic Express sell similar materials, already cut.

A squeeze-bottle applicator is the best tool to use to apply the 1/8-inch strands because the squeezing action creates some static electricity on the strands, which makes them stand up like a crew cut when they come in contact with the glue. Use Woodland Scenic's "Scenic Sifter" or you may be able to find a flexible plastic container with a half-dozen 8-inch holes in the lid. A container from bathroom cleanser or table salt will do, or you can make your own from a plastic baby-powder bottle. Drill 1/8-inch holes in the lid, using a second drill bit to keep the two layers of the lid from rotating. When the lid is snapped back onto the bottle, each of the little sawtooth tabs must be positioned so they fit inside the neck of the bottle. Just squeeze the bottle to "spray" the simulated grass onto the glue-dampened "earth."

The "Grass-That-Grows" System

If you are modeling an area where the predominant surface texture is grass or grass-like weeds, consider using this "Grass-That-Grows" system. The system begins as soon as you have finalized the shapes of the scenery using the Hydrocal-dipped paper towels or the Woodland Scenics Plaster Cloth or the shaped-Styrofoam in Chapter 10. The next step is to cover all the areas you wish to be grass (or mostly grass) with beige-colored felt from a fabric store. To apply the felt, simply drape a 4-by-4-foot sheet over the layout and mark where the track, bridges and buildings, dirt cuts and rock cliffs are located so you can cut the felt with heavy scissors to avoid these areas. You want to have plenty of felt for this method and it works well with hills and valleys. Test-fit the felt to be sure it covers all the areas you want, then lift the felt and spread on a thick layer of latex contact cement. Work quickly,

Figure 11-4. The Grass-That-Grows" system uses teased felt to simulate grass, with real dirt sifted through a tea strainer to "bury" the bottoms of the strands of felt fibers.

because you want to apply the felt before the contact cement dries. Press the felt firmly into the contact cement over every square inch of the layout and let it dry overnight. Next, use a utility knife to slice along the edges of the roadbed, along building sites and along roads, to remove any excess felt.

An alternate method of applying the felt works well for flat areas and for areas where there will be a lot of small areas of grass (felt). Lay the felt over the tracks, building sites and roads, and use a green felt pen to mark precisely where you wish to cut the felt. Use scissors to cut the felt to this shape, apply the contact cement, and then press the pre-fitted felt firmly into the still-wet contact cement. Cover all the areas of the layout with felt where you want grass or weeds, especially those narrow areas between the edges of the roadbed and the edges of the table. Even if you want mostly dirt, with just a few weeds, you can use the felt as the base. You can even cover it with narrow dirt roads.

Leave the larger areas of dirt around industries and roads bare. When you are satisfied with the coverage, spray the beige felt with green acrylic paint or artist's inks. I found that inks like Badger's "Air-Opaque" worked especially well and left little odor. Do work outside, however, because there is a lot of spray and it can get caught-up in the house's heater system to be spread everywhere (as I discovered for myself!). I mixed one-part Chrome Oxide Green with about 9-parts Green to make a Kelly Green. The idea is to color only the very top layer of the individual fibers of the felt so the beige is still very visible.

To make the grass appear to grow, spread a layer of dust-like dirt over the felt. Use a tea strainer with the small screen so mostly dust falls on the layout (Figure 11-4). Vary the amount of the dirt that you sift onto the layout, with the steeper slopes receiving more dirt and the flat areas receiving very little. Next, use a stiff steel-wire brush like those used to clean files, to work the dirt into the felt so that layer of green-painted fibers shows through the dirt. Look, closely and you'll see that it looks like those fibers really are "growing" up through the dirt. If you want a bit more dirt, sift on some more and brush it in. For dirt roads, trim the felt's fibers and apply enough dirt to completely bury the felt. Except for lawns and pastures, there are various types of weeds scattered through the grass fields. Use the various weed textures shown later in this chapter to add those effects to the felt.

When you're completely satisfied with the grass effects, spray the entire area with a mixture of three-parts water to one-part artists Matte Medium and a drop of dishwashing detergent to act as wetting agent or use Woodland Scenics Scenic Cement, or Champ's Decal Company's Resibond Spray to bond the dirt and textures to the felt. Use enough spray so the entire area turns a milky color. Use a pump sprayer from a hair salon supply store or Woodland Scenics' Scenic Sprayer to deliver just a mist so you don't disturb the loose dirt and texture materials. Let it dry for at least a week and the layout is ready for bridges, trees and bushes.

Ground Foam and Flocking Ground Cover

The most common ground cover on model railroads is ground foam. The material looks remarkably like leaves and is perfect for simulating leafy weeds as well as the foliage on bushes, vines and trees. Woodland Scenics, Accurail (Easy Scene), AMSI, Noch, Heki and others sell the ground foam in a variety of green and brown hues. To apply the ground foam, coat a 6-by-6-inch area with artist's Matte Medium and sprinkle the foam in place. Woodland Scenics, Scenic Express and others sell plastic bottles with holes in the lid or you can use an empty baby powder bottle. The foam is not very effective, however, in simulating blades of grass or grassy-type weeds. For that, the "Grass That Grows" system or flocking is a better choice. If you only want very small areas with grass, you can use the sheets of flocking sold by model railroad dealers and made by Noch, Heki, Kibri and others. Simply cut the sheet into random patches and cement it to the scenery (Figure 11-5), then cover the remaining area with sifted real dirt and ground foam. You can also apply individual strands of flocking with a squeeze bottle like that used to apply ground foam. Woodland Scenics, Scenic Express, Noch, Busch, Heki, Kibri,

Figure 11-5. The flocked papers can be used to apply grass or weeds to random areas. Cut the flocked paper to shape and cement it down with artist's Matte Medium.

and others offer flocking suitable for N scale. The 2-by-4-foot layout shown in the color section and in Chapter 2 (Figure 2-1 and 2-2) and in Chapter 12 (Figures 12-2, 12-3, 12-4 and 12-5) was textured with flocking.

Ballasting The Track

The process of adding various types of "earth" to your layout also includes surrounding the ties of the track with the crushed rock ballast that real railroads use to hold the track in place. The Kato Uni-Track, Bachmann E-Z Track and Life-Like Power-Loc track all include built-in ballast. The ballast on the Uni-Track is realistic enough to use as-is. If you want to hide the seams between the track sections, simply apply a dot of Chem Rex PL300 cement (the same stuff suggested for cementing Styrofoam in other chapters) or grey automobile body putty to the seams and spread it with your fingers so the joint disappears (Figure 11-6). Al Mack applied loose ballast to all of six scale miles of Kato Uni-Track on his 14-by-18-foot layout in Chapter 2 (Figure 11-7), but it's really not necessary. I would suggest, however, that you add loose ballast (later held firm with Matte Medium) for E-Z Track or Power-Loc track. You will, of course, want to use loose ballast with any of the different types of sectional track or flex track with cork roadbed or roadbed cut into Homasote or Styrofoam as described in Chapter 7.

The very first step when applying ballast to track laid on Homasote or cork roadbed is to seal the area beneath the track with a coat of latex paint. This is a job that's really best done when you first glue and nail the Homasote to the plywood, but it can also be done by using a small paint brush (Number 1 or 2 size) to apply the paint between the ties. It won't hurt if you get some of the paint on the ties; the ballast and the weathering you add later will disguise the paint smears. The paint seals the Homasote, so the Matte Medium won't soak into the Homasote before it has a chance to glue the ballast. If you are ballasting track laid on bare Styrofoam, you can skip this step because the Styrofoam does not absorb the Matte Medium.

I suggest that you wait until the scenery shaping is complete. You may find that you want to relocate the track or add additional turnouts during the interim, and those changes are a lot easier if you don't have to worry about the ballast and the track at the same time. Also, the real railroads add ballast last, so some of it spills over the surrounding terrain and you can capture that effect by applying ballast as one of the final steps in creating scenery.

You can use common dirt or sand for ballast or buy one of the many brands of prepared ballast. Pick a color that corresponds to the type of ballast used on your favorite real railroad. You can even pulverize chunks of real ballast by putting them in a thick cloth bag and hitting it with a hammer. Sift the "ballast" through a tea strainer. Use only the portion of the material that passes through the screen for your ballast or, if you buy ready-made ballast, buy a size that would sift through a tea strainer screen. You will want the smallest granules you can buy which may be marked "Fine" or "N scale" ballast. Some of the ballast marked "N scale" is not, however, fine enough to accurately simulate N scale-size ballast particles. For extra realism, use a gray or brown color for the mainline tracks' ballast and a beige color for the sidings. Later, in the weathering phase of track-laying, you can spray on a wash of black acrylic paint and water to give the ballast the dirty look it has on the real railroads. Always check for iron particles in any dirt you use by passing a small magnet over the loose dirt. If any particles cling to the magnet, find another source of dirt.

Buy a plastic mustard or ketchup dispenser with a pointed tip and use this to apply the artist's Matte Medium to bond the ballast. I prefer to use artist's Matte Medium to "glue" ballast and other loose scenic textures. The Matte Medium is used for mixing acrylic paints and it's available at any good artists supply store. It looks and feels almost exactly like plain white glue. However, it's just enough more flexible than white glue or carpenter's glue to keep the trackwork from amplifying sounds, and it's a bit easier to pry the trackwork loose when you want to relocate it or add a turnout to the layout. The Matte Medium also dries with little or no gloss.

Apply a drop of oil that is marked as being harmless to plastics to the moving switch tie bar and to any visible moving parts of the turnout. Cover the turnout's moving switch points with small strips of masking tape so the spray cannot reach

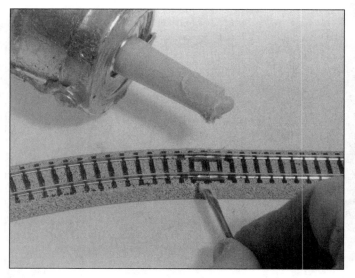

Figure 11-6. Kato Uni-Track has built-in ballast. To disguise the seams between track sections, just smear some grey cement or automobile body putty over the seams.

Figure 11-7. Al Mack applied loose ballast to his Kato Uni-Track, but kept the ballast well clear of the working levers and points of any turnout.

them to carry the diluted Matte Medium into the working parts of every turnout. Apply a bead of artist's Matte Medium along the edges of the ballast, just missing the ends of the ties. The ballast can now be sprinkled over the track. Cut a paper template for the inside (Figure 11-8) and outside (Figure 11-9) of the curves to help control the flow of the ballast as you apply it to the edges of the track. Use the diagrams in Chapter 7 (Figure 7-35) to determine the proper shape and size of the ballast shoulders on prototype track. Apply more than you feel you might need and spread it around with another a paint brush (Figure 11-10). Use the brush to carefully sweep away any ballast from around the switch points or between the second (guard) rail at every turnout frog and crossing frog (the places where the rails cross) so there will be no places where the ballast could hit the wheel flanges. Mix three-parts water with one-part Matte Medium and add a drop of dishwashing detergent to help reduce the surface extension so the mixture will not puddle so easily. You can also use Woodland Scenic's Scenic Cement or Champ Decal Company's Resinbond Spray fluid as described in Chapter 17. Next, spray the track and the ballast with a mist of the diluted Matte Medium from a plastic pump-type spray bottle or a plant atomizer. Finally, spray the ballasted track with water. This will allow the dilute Matte

Medium to work its way around each grain of ballast through a general diluting action. Let the ballast dry for at least a day and vacuum away the excess. Remove the masking tape from the turnout's moving switch points.

Be sure to keep both the ballast and the Matte Medium well away from the working parts of all the track turnouts, that is, the moving switch points. Simply paint the area around the switch points in a color to match the ballast. (No one will ever notice that there aren't any of those "loose-looking" rocks in that area.) The ballast itself can jam the switch points, and the Matte Medium will obviously render the switch worthless. I cannot provide a suitable method of removing glue-stuck turnout points, except to remove the turnout, try to free its mechanism from below and if that fails, replace the turnout.

No doubt some granules of the ballast will have been glued to the sides and the tops of the rails. Go over the track with an old hobby knife blade to scrape away both dried Matte Medium and ballast from the tops and the inside edges of the rails. Push a gondola or flat car over the track with a bit of downward pressure so you can feel if the wheels encounter any Matte Medium or ballast on the running surfaces of the rails, between the guard rails, or on the sides of the rails that you might have missed. The finished track will be far more realistic with ballast than without (Figure 11-11).

Figure 11-8. Cut a paper mask to match the diameter of the outside of the ties on curves to keep the ballast from spreading too far from the ties.

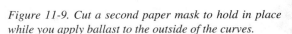
Figure 11-9. Cut a second paper mask to hold in place while you apply ballast to the outside of the curves.

Figure 11-10. *Use a soft 1/2-inch wide brush to gently brush the ballast from the tops of the ties and distribute it along the center of the track.*

Figure 11-12. *Use an airbrush to spray Boxcar Red paint on the inside and outside of the rails to simulate rust.*

Figure 11-11. *The Peco flex-track and turnouts on the lower three tracks of the Train Gang club's modular layout has been ballasted, but the upper tracks are still bare ties and rails.*

Weathering the Track

The track on a real railroad is constantly exposed to weather, and that is why the cars and locomotives look so well used. Few modelers realize that their layouts have this major "flaw": clean track simply doesn't look like the real thing.

In weathering track, first spray all the trackwork with a wash of 4 parts water to 1 part black acrylic paint, concentrating a bit more of the spray down the center of the track where oil and grease would drip from passing trains. The sides of the rails can then be painted reddish brown using model railroad Box Car Red paint with the air brush nozzle set on to supply a pencil-thin-line pattern (Figure 11-12). You can also paint the sides of the rails with a brush if you do not have an airbrush. A few dribbles of paint on the simulated plastic spikes or on the ties will probably look just like rusted ties or tie plates, so don't worry about them. Then, spray the entire area with a wash that matches the color of the "dirt" on the surrounding hills. This means everything, including the buildings. The entire layout should have a very light hint of that "earth" tint. Now you can scrape the rail tops and check for any paint or ballast that might stop the flow of electricity between the rails and wheels or cause a derailment. When all of the scenery textures are complete, including ballasting and weathering the track, clean the tops of the rails with one of the hard rubber track-cleaning erasers like Life-Like's Model Power or a Bright Boy (Figure 11-13).

Figure 11-13. Use a hard rubber eraser track cleaner like Life-Like's or a Bright Boy to remove all traces of paint or dried Matte Medium from the tops of the rails.

Trees and Bushes

The most critical part of most miniature trees and bushes are the tiny intermediate twigs that branch off from the main trunk to hold the leaves. There are some natural growths that have very delicate structures, including the Noch 5228-23800 Large and 528-23820 Medium "Natural Tree Forms." Similar tree forms are available in larger quantities from Scenic Express. These are a Scandinavian weed that makes incredibly realistic trees, especially when the weeds are covered with two or three layers of fine ground foam. These trees are more realistic if the "trunks" are painted a dark grey using automobile primer from a spray can. For variety, use both the rust-colored Oxide Primer and conventional gray primer. Work outdoors during this process and let the trees dry overnight.

To apply the foam, spray the tree with the cheapest hair spray you can find and sprinkle the foam onto the tree. Spray it again and sprinkle on more foam (Figure 11-14). Repeat the process a third time if you want a denser tree. An alternate method is to dip the trees in that mixture of three-parts water to one-part artist's Matte Medium and then sprinkle-on the foam. The Matte Medium helps to soften the relatively-brittle weeds and to preserve them. These are some of the trees that were used on the 6-by-6-foot Union Pacific layout. To add variety to the forest, about a dozen ready-made trees from Accurate Dimensionals were also used on this layout.

Realistic trees can also be made using natural weeds like sagebrush and some hedge trimmings for the main a trunk and major limbs. To simulate the "twigs" on these heftier weeds, use the hair-like plastic cloth (that is used for some types of packing insulation and for plastic scouring pads) and Woodland Scenics' Poly Fiber. Macramé shops sell bulk skeins of a coarse cotton-like material that some macramé rope is made from that can be substituted for the Woodland Scenics' Poly Fiber. The material is available in both a brown and a gray/beige. Do not be tempted by steel wool; the strands will certainly find their way into the magnets in the motors of the locomotives and will cause a short circuit.

Figure 11-14. Spray the Noch or Scenic Express "tree trunks" with cheap hairspray, then sprinkle-on fine ground foam to simulate leaves.

Tree Trunks

The trunks and major branches of trees and large bushes can be made from a wide variety of weeds and even the twigs of small bushes or trees. If you cannot find sizes and shapes that suit the types of trees in the geographic area of your model railroad, then make your own. Stranded steel clothesline can be cut into four to eight-inch lengths with diagonal cutters. Unwrap the individual strands for about half the length of the piece of wire and bend them into the shape of branches. Bend out all but two of the strands at the bottom of each piece to form roots. The two remaining strands will be pushed into the plaster or Styrofoam to support the tree. Use the putty-style two-part epoxy and catalyst to make the trunk texture for each tree, and paint the trunks with brown, gray, and beige acrylics to simulate bark.

The unwoven macramé fiber or Woodland Scenics' Poly Fiber can be applied in two different ways to simulate two different types of branch structures: the material can be cut and wrapped into a very loose ball or "cloud" and then glued to the tree-trunk structure, or the macramé material can be cut into short lengths and fanned out before being glued to the trunk structure.

The final step in making one of these trees is to spray the twig portion with a mixture of three-parts water to one-part artist's Matte Medium with a drop of dishwashing detergent to break the surface tension of the fluids or you can use Woodland Scenic's Scenic Cement or Champ Decal Company's Resibond Spray.

Let the glue dry until it is just becoming tacky, then dip the tree into a box of dyed ground foam rubber. This creates the individual leaves. Drill or punch a hole for the tree in the plaster or Styrofoam (Figure 11-15), push the tree into the hole and adjust it so it is perfectly vertical (Figure 11-16), and dab on a bit of grey-colored plaster, grey automobile body putty or the

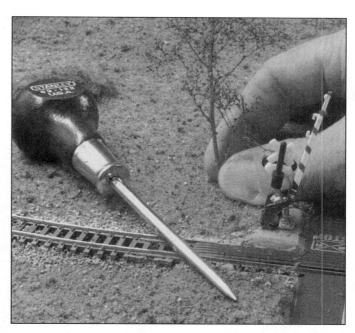

Figure 11-16. Dip the bottom of the tree in grey-colored plaster, grey automobile body putty or the Chem Rex PL300 cement before pushing the tree into the hole so the grey material forms a flared root structure around the base of the tree.

Figure 11-15. Use an awl to punch holes for the trees in the Styrofoam or plaster hills.

Figure 11-17. The final coat of ground foam "leaves" can be applied after the trees are in place.

Chem Rex PL300 cement to be worked in around the root system. Finally, glue a bit of ground cover around the base of the tree. Pay attention to nature's examples when you "plant" the trees on your model railroad. Most trees grow in small valleys or hollows, and they are often clustered in groups of three or more. When the trees were in place on the 6-by-6-foot Union Pacific layout, I sprayed the tops of each of them with another coat of hairspray and gently and carefully sprinkled-on another coat of fine ground foam so it would adhere only to the upward-facing limbs and so some of the foam would fall to the ground like fallen leaves (Figure 11-17). Use some of the gray-colored "twig" and "trunk" trees without the application of "leaves" to simulate an occasional dead tree in a small grove of living trees.

Woodland Scenics offers a Poly Fiber material with the ground foam already attached that can also be used to make trees, using Woodland Scenics, AMSI or Accurail (Easy Scene) tree trunks or sagebrush or other weeds for the trunks. Woodland Scenics has a similar material in their tree kits, but the ground foam is already glued to the mesh to save you a step in the construction of the tree or bush. Hobby shops also carry at least one brand of packaged, dyed and treated Norwegian lichen moss (usually called, simply, "lichen") that can be used in place of the Poly Fiber. Some modelers use the lichen as-is for trees and bushes and it is part of some of the ready-made trees from firms like Bachmann, Life-Like, and Model Power. The lichen looks far more realistic if it, too, is covered with a bit of ground foam to disguise the lichen tip texture.

Ready-Built Trees

Life-Like, Noch, Faller, Heki, Busch, Accurate Dimensionals, Model Power and others offer ready-built trees. There are about a dozen Accurate Dimensionals trees intermingled with about 40 hand-made trees on the 6-by-6-foot Union Pacific layout (Figure 11-18). Some of the ready-made trees have a wire core with bristle limbs similar to a baby bottle brush. These trees can be made more realistic by trimming their shapes with scissors to create a rougher, more natural form and by covering them with ground foam for a more random texture.

Figure 11-18. The trees on the 6-by-6-foot Union Pacific are mostly Noch or Scenic Express made as described in this chapter, with about 12 ready-built Accurate Dimensionals trees to add variety.

Chapter 12
Water and Bridges

Figure 12-1. This wide river on Gordon Bliss 14-by-40-foot N scale layout was made with clear casting resin. The waves were sliced into the resin during the curing process. The bridge is an Overland Models brass import.

The bridges on a real railroad serve a purpose that is somewhat similar to the benchwork on a model railroad. Both support the tracks that carry the trains. The benchwork has to come before the bridges on a model railroad, but the two supports for the model trackwork should be planned together for the best effect. A model of a bridge cannot look even remotely realistic unless the track that bridge carries is elevated above the surrounding terrain. I would also recommend that you finish all of the surface texturing including dirt, grass and weeds before adding water to the scenery. The bushes and trees can be the final step in the scenery process.

Over-and-Under Bridges

The over-and-under type of bridge and trestle or pier sets are fine for toy trains, but they add very little to a miniature's realism. In fact, uphill and downhill grades are far more difficult to accomplish successfully than merely allowing the scenery to fall away from the tracks, so the tracks appear to be going uphill. You must do some planning in order to build benchwork that allows the scenery to "fall away" from beneath the tracks, which makes a bridge just as necessary as it is on a real railroad. It is exciting to watch one train pass over or under another, but I would recommend that you save that complication for your second model railroad. If you do desire uphill and downhill grades, the techniques to build them are described in Chapter 6.

Bridges

It is essential that all locations for bridges be planned before finishing the scenery. It is possible to add a stream or lake to a finished layout, but the realistic slopes leading down to the lake are best planned during the scenery construction stages as described in Chapter 10. Small streams or lakes can be created by slicing through the Styrofoam or through a Homasote table-

Figure 12-2. This small stream is crossed twice on the 2-by-4-foot layout from Chapter 2.

top with a utility knife to lower the earth to the level of the plywood's surface. That's how the small streambed on the 2-by-4-foot layout in Chapter 2 (Figures 2-1 and 2-2) was formed (Figure 12-2). First, the areas between the tracks was carved away as shown in Chapter 10, then the area was painted an earth color and, for this layout, textured with flocking and ground-up tree bark. When the area was cut away, the cut was carefully planned to be the exact length of the Atlas 2548 Plate Girder Bridge, with enough depth for a 1/4-inch high bridge abutment from the Cal Scale 100 Trestle kit on each end of the bridge (Figure 12-3). The railroad crosses this small creek bed twice and the second crossing is supported by two Cal Scale plastic replicas of wood trestle bents from the 100 Trestle kit, These two trestle bents were cut to be force fit between the bottoms of the ties and the surface of the scenery. They were cemented to the ties with liquid cement for plastics (Figure 12-4).

Figure 12-3. The bridge abutments are from the Cal Scale 100 Trestle kit. The streambed has been shaped and textured and the bridge abutments fitted to the bridge.

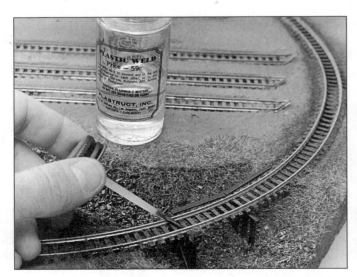

Figure 12-4. Two of the bents from the Cal Scale 1000 Trestle kit were cut to fit between the scenery and the bottoms of the ties, then cemented in place with liquid cement for plastics.

Building Bridges

Remember, it is best to make all the preparations, including building and test-fitting the bridge in place, before the scenery is textured. It is also best to have the bridge abutments in place so they can be "buried" realistically in the scenery texturing. If no part of the "water" will touch the bridge, it's even best to pour the "water" before installing the bridge (Figure 12-5). If you've fitted the bridge carefully, it will virtually snap into place and can be held there with a dab of Liquid Nails "Projects and Foamboard" cement or Chem Rex PL300 "Foam on the 6-by-6-foot layout Board Adhesive."

I wanted a steel viaduct over the valleyon the 6-by-6-foot layout so I used the Micro Engineering 518 Tall Steel Viaduct kits. The initial bridge construction really must begin while you are still in the scenery-shaping stage of construction as shown in Chapter 10 (Figure 10-20). Hold one of the bents for the bridge against the track (Figure 12-6) to see how much of the bent can be used. I needed only the top section of each bent.

Deck girder bridges are good choices for use as bridges on relatively tight 11-inch or even 19-inch radius curves because nothing protrudes above the rails to foul overhanging cars or locomotives. These bridges can be cemented directly to the bottom of the ties with clear Liquid Nails "Projects and Foamboard" cement or Chem Rex PL300 "Foam Board Adhesive." Make bridge abutments that will appear to support the ends of the girder bridges from .125-by-.125-inch Evergreen styrene or 1/8-inch square balsa wood. The girder bridges included in the Micro Engineering viaduct kit were used beneath the viaduct and beneath the second curved track on the 6-by-6-foot Union Pacific layout.

I made a cardboard template the length of the deck girders in the Micro Engineering 518 Tall Steel Viaduct kit to be sure that the two deck girders for each tower would be square. I then cut the remaining deck girders with a razor saw to lengths that

Figure 12-5. The artist's Gloss Medium for the "pond" area of the stream on the 2-by-4-foot layout was poured with the bridge and its built-in track removed.

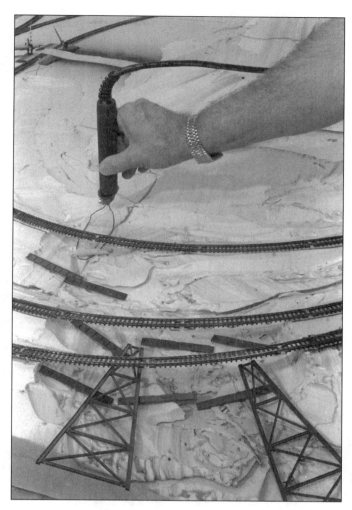

would fill in the spaces between the towers and attached all the girders to the bottom of the roadbed (Figure 12-9) with clear silicone bathtub caulking compound.

Paint the bridge abutments a concrete grey and cement them to the bottoms of the bridge girders and to the blue Styrofoam. Finish all the scenery beneath the bridge as described in Chapter 11.

"Build" the bridge right on the layout to fit that distance between the bottom of the bridge girders and the surface of the scenery. The bents were short enough so none of the cross-bracing between the bents that is supplied with the kit was necessary. Just install the two girders by gluing them to the bottom of the ties, and then glue the abutments to the bottoms of the girders. I used two leftover girders from the viaduct for the bridge with 1/8-inch square abutments beneath the second curve track (Figure 12-7).

"Wet" Water

The ideal material for the most realistic water with the least effort is artist's Gloss Medium. This is essentially a clear latex paint that dries to a high shine. It looks and acts like plain white glue but it does not dry as hard so there's little chance it would crack. Unfortunately, it can remain milky if you try to pour it over about 3/8-inch deep. You can minimize the cloudy effect by pouring only 1/8-inch layers and let each dry for a week (Figure 12-8). The technique is also illustrated in the color section of this book.

Steeper streams can be poured by tilting the entire layout so that the stream itself is level. The artist's Gloss Medium for the "pond area of the stream on the 2-by-4-foot layout (Figure 12-2) was poured first and allowed to dry, then the 2-by-4-foot layout was tilted upward so the rest of the streambed was level and the artist's Gloss Medium was poured into the temporarily-level streambed. If you cannot do that, then build up the thickness of the water using artist's Gloss Gel, a clear acrylic with the consistency of grease. The fast water and rapids areas can be created by making wavy streaks of the Gloss Gel (Figure 12-10). When the Gloss Medium and Gloss Gel dry completely, the

Figure 12-6. The Avalon Concepts Detail Wand hot wire cutter was used to shape the streambed area on the 6-by-6-foot Union Pacific layout as shown in Chapter 10. The steel trestle bents and girder bridges are part of the Micro Engineering 518 Tall Steel Viaduct kit.

Figure 12-7. Two of the girder bridges from the Micro Engineering 518 Tall Steel Viaduct were cemented beneath the rails to span the stream on the inner curve of the Union Pacific layout.

Figure12-8. The artist's Gloss Medium is poured into the highest level of the streambed (the pond area on the Union Pacific layout) and allowed to move through the streambed by gravity. The second layer of artist's Gloss Medium was poured into any areas of the stream that needed to be wider.

Figure 12-9. A "dam" of duct tape was placed across the edge of the layout until the artist's Gloss Medium had dried completely.

Figure 12-10. The steeper slopes of the stream were filled-in with artist's Gloss Gel, formed into wavy streaks.

bridge can be installed (Figure 12-11). It may take as long as a week, but eventually the milky appearance will disappear and the material will be clear and shiny (Figure 12-12). If milky areas do remain, poke a few holes in that area with an ice pick, let it rest for a week until the milky appearance disappears, then apply another thin coat of Gloss Medium to hide the holes and smooth the surface.

For deeper water and for more realistic rapids and faster water, use the epoxy sold by craft shops for use in decoupage. This material differs from the resin sold to repair fiberglass boats in that the epoxy requires only a few drops of the catalyst per cup of resin, while the fiberglass material demands a nearly equal mix of resin and catalyst. The two look the same when cured, but the decoupage epoxies do not produce the horrible odors of fiberglass resins while they cure. Both run like water (as does the artist's Gloss Medium) until they cure or harden, so the bottom of any lake, river, or streambed must be sealed and perfectly water-tight where you intend to pour the resin. If the river runs right to the edge of the table, you can build a "dam" by sealing the end with cloth silver-colored air-conditioner duct tape (Figure 12-9). If the stream is deep, back up the duct-tape dam with a temporary sheet of plywood or Masonite.

Before pouring either the artist's Gloss Medium or the epoxy resin, add any sunken boats, old tires, weeds, or logs that you want to see submerged. Spray the entire submerged portion of the river or stream with several coats of Testors DullCote to seal any loose dirt or debris so that trapped air cannot form bubbles in the bottom of the epoxy-resin water. Let the DullCote dry for at least two days before pouring the epoxy resin. Mix the resin and the catalyst exactly as shown on the side of the can. Mix several small batches so you can build up deeper water in layers that are no more than 1/16-inch thick. If you try to pour too much of the resin, it will crack as it cures. You can add another "pour" to help disguise the crack, but it will never look quite right. You should be ready to insert a few weeds cut from hemp rope and a bit of ground foam rubber dyed green into the edges of the last layers of the resin while the resin is still wet. Wiggle a wooden stick around on the last layers, just as they are becom-

ing hard, to simulate ripples on the water's surface. If you pick at the resin right through the hardening stage, you can even simulate rapids and white caps. Touch a few of the hardened tips with a wash of white oil paint and turpentine to give a white-water effect.

Figure 12-12. The artist's Gloss Medium and Gloss Gel will dry to a high shine that effectively simulates "wet" water.

Figure 12-11. It is best to install the steel trestle bents after the "water" has been poured and allowed to dry.

Chapter 13
Steam and Diesel Locomotives

Every model railroader claims to love trains. Truth be known, it's often the locomotives that are the first love with the rest of the train merely being something for the locomotive to pull, the track something for the locomotive to run on and the structures and scenery backdrops to the locomotive with an environment that is, at least, something like the real world that is the habitat of the full-size locomotives. The growing popularity of N scale model railroading means that more and more manufacturers are producing more and more products and that includes an ever-increasing number of locomotives.

Steam Locomotives

There is a wide choice of locomotives in N scale, virtually all of them ready-to-run right out of the box. Starting with the smallest steam locomotives, you can choose from an 1860-era 4-4-0 produced by Bachmann (Figure 13-1) or 1900-1950 era 2-8-0 and 2-6-0 locomotives produced by MDC. The prototypes for MDC's 2-8-0 and 2-6-0 lasted until the mid-fifties, especially on branchlines and smaller railroads (called "shortlines"). Most of the other steam locomotives available in N scale are

Figure 13-1. Bachmann offers several different paint schemes on their 1865-era 4-4-0 steam locomotives.

Figure13-2. The Kato USRA 'Heavy' 2-8-2 is a replica of a locomotive that was used by nearly a dozen prototype railroads.

also replicas of locomotives that were built in the thirties or forties and many of them lasted until the mid-fifties. Bachmann offers a replica of the common USRA-design 0-6-0 switcher (and a 2-6-2 version of the 0-6-0) and Life-Like offers a 0-4-0 and a 0-6-0T switcher and Minitrix has a 0-6-0 replica of Pennsylvania Railroad switcher. Medium-size steam locomotives include a replica of the Indiana Harbor Belt's 0-8-0 switcher from Rivarossi, very nice 2-8-0 from the Spectrum division of Bachmann, a Reading Railroad 2-8-0 (and a 2-8-2 version) from Bachmann, a Pennsylvania Railroad 2-10-0 and 4-6-2 from Minitrix, a common USRA-prototype 'Heavy' 4-6-2 and a replica of the New York Central 4-6-4 (as well as several streamlined versions of the 4-6-4) from Con-Cor, and a USRA 'Heavy' 2-8-2 from Kato (Figure 13-2). Large steam locomotives include a Santa Fe-prototype 4-8-4 and a streamlined Norfolk and Western-prototype 4-8-4 from Bachmann, a Norfolk & Western-prototype 2-8-8-2 articulated and a Union Pacific-prototype 4-8-8-4 articulated from Con-Cor and Rivarossi. In addition to these locomotives, there is a steady flow of hand-crafted steam locomotives made from brass in Korea being imported by Key Imports (Figure13-3), Hallmark Models and others.

Those numbers used to identify steam locomotives are part of the Whyte Classification system, which designate that the first number is the number of small "pilot" wheels that help guide the locomotive into curves, the next number is the number of large-diameter driving wheels that power the locomotive and the third number is the number of trailing wheels that also help guide the locomotive around curves. The "T" at the end of any number series indicates that the fuel and water tanks are mounted on the locomotive so there is no separate tender. The articulated locomotives have two complete sets of cylinders beneath a single boiler. Therefore, they use a four-digit numbering system, with the second and third numbers being the number of driving wheels.

Nearly every railroad had it's own assortment of switchers (locomotives with neither pilot wheels nor trailing wheels, like a 0-6-0), freight locomotives (usually with a single pair of pilot wheels, like a 2-8-2) or passenger locomotives (usually with four pilot wheels, like a 4-6-4). In addition, most real railroads also had light, medium and heavy versions of these locomotives. The particular appearance of these locomotives varied considerably from railroad to railroad. GHQ offers some cast-metal conversion kits with new superstructures and/or tenders to

Figure 13-3. Key Imports offers a variety of brass locomotives, produced in Korea, that are exact replicas of prototype steam locomotives including this Southern Pacific railroad cab-forward 2-8-8-2 articulated.

Figure 13-4. GHQ produces cast-metal superstructures and tenders to convert the Kato 2-8-2 into replicas of Burlington, Southern, or Northern Pacific (shown) locomotives.

convert some of the more popular N scale locomotives into specific Pennsylvania Railroad and Northern Pacific Railroad prototypes (Figure 13-4). Most of the N scale steam locomotives are, however, available painted and lettered for all the popular prototype railroads, even if each specific railroad did not actually operate a steam locomotive with those exact details, cab shape and tender type. If you are particular about the exact details of your steam locomotives, look very carefully at the available N scale steam locomotives before you decide to build an N scale layout set in the steam era. Hobby dealers and ads in the model railroad magazines can help you locate currently-available brass locomotives as well as out-of-production models. If steam locomotives are your first love, you may want to consider HO scale, because exact replicas of the majority of all the prototype steam locomotives have been produced in HO scale as brass imports over the past four decades and, eventually, you can find even the out-of-production models at flea markets or through classified ads in the hobby magazines.

You will discover that the smaller the locomotive is, the more difficult it is to keep it running smoothly, without stalling or derailing. Steam locomotives, regardless of their size, present the most problems in stalling and derailing. You can, of course, eliminate some of these problems with perfect track alignment and by keeping the track pristinely clean. The steam locomotives, however, are lighter than most diesel models so they will stall on the least amount of dust or lint that finds its way onto the tracks. Whenever possible, experienced N scale modelers operate steam locomotives (and, for that matter diesel locomotives) in pairs so that, if one locomotive stalls, the other will push or pull it. The lighter weight of N scale steam locomotives and their longer rigid wheelbases (the drivers don't pivot like those on a diesel) make them prone to derailments if the track is not perfect. The larger steam locomotives usually operate more smoothly and with fewer derailments than the smaller steam locomotives.

Diesel Locomotives

The selection of diesel locomotives is far greater than the selection of steam locomotives. First, there are many more locomotives and, further, those locomotives are all factory-painted and lettered to match specific prototype diesels so there are literally hundreds of N scale diesels. Fortunately, for modelers, the real railroads purchased standard diesels without the differences in cabs, tenders and fittings that were common to each railroad's steam locomotives. Most real railroads did add a few small details like snowplows, special horns or other fine details, but the basic shapes and most of the details on one road's GP9, for example, are the same as those for any other road's GP9. Most of the small detail parts are available from firms like Detail Associates, Athabasca, Gold Medal Models, JnJ Trains, Miniatures by Eric, and Sunrise. There are several excellent books about full-size diesel locomotives. If you want to be able to spot the differences between diesels and identify when they were produced I would recommend *The Diesel Spotters Guide* by Jerry Pinkepank and the *Contemporary Diesel Spotters Guide*, by Louis A. Marre.

Diesel locomotives, like steam locomotives, were also designed for specific applications. The "First Generation" diesels often had fully-enclosed bodies that matched the shape of streamlined passenger cars, on both passenger and freight locomotives. These cab-style diesels include the most popular model diesel of all time, the ElectroMotive Division (of General Motors) F7A that is most commonly painted in the silver with red nose and yellow stripe Santa Fe Railway "Warbonnet" paint scheme. The F7A and the very similar F3A are available from Kato, Con-Cor, Life-Like, Mini-Trix, Model Power and Bachmann. These eight-wheeled diesels were used on both freight and passenger service. The majority of early cab-style passenger diesels had twelve wheels like the EMD E8A made by Kato, Life-Like and Con-Cor. The cab-style diesels made for the prototype railroads by Alco are considered to be the most pleasing industrial designs of the forties and are also available in N scale including the 8-wheeled FA2 from Model Power and Life-Like and the PA1 that is available from Life-Like, Kato and Con-Cor.

EMD and Alco realized the railroads would want to run several locomotives at once to provide the power for longer trains so they offered cab-style locomotives without cabs as "B" units. The EMD F3B is available from Kato, the EMD F7B from Bachmann, EMD E8B models are available from Kato and Con-Cor, and Alco PB1 B units are available from Life-Like, Kato and Con-Cor. Most of the prototypes for these models were built in the forties to replace steam locomotives and they lasted into the mid-sixties. The modern-era cab-style passenger diesels are the EMD F40PH that is available from Life-Like and Model Power, the General Electric U39CG that is available for Model Power, and a replica of the current Amtrak locomotive, the EMD P-40 (AMD-103) that is available as an imported brass model, painted and lettered, from Overland Models, Incorporated. Overland Models, Key Imports and Hallmark Models have imported a variety of N scale brass diesels.

Models of the smaller 4-axle locomotives used for yard switching were built with full-width cabs, but the hood was only wide enough to clear the engine and radiators. The large windows in the cabs and the narrow hoods made it easier for the engineer to see the train when he was performing switching moves. Diesel switchers are available in N scale including "First Generation" EMD SW9 and SW1200 diesel yard switchers from Life-Like, Alco S2 yard switchers from Atlas, and Fairbanks-Morse H-44-10 yard switchers from Mini-Trix and Model Power. The "Second Generation" EMD SW1500 switchers are available from Con-Cor and Rivarossi.

The real railroads discovered that the improved visibility of the yard switchers, with their narrow hoods and large cabs, was also useful for freight locomotives that might, even if just occasionally, be required to switch cars in and out of trains. Electro-Motive built the "First Generation" four-axle GP7, GP9 and GP18 and GP30 and the six-axle SD7 and SD9, and Alco produced the four-axle RS1, RS3 and RS11 and the six-axle RSD15 and C420. The "Second Generation" diesel locomotives appeared in the mid-sixties and include the four-axle EMD GP35, GP38-2, GP40 and GP50 and the six-axle SD40, SD40-2, SD45, SD60, SD60M and the massive 8-axle DD40AX, and General Electric produced the four-axle U36B and the six-axle U28C, C30-7, Dash 8-40CW and C44-9W diesels. Atlas offers GP7, GP9, GP30, GP35, GP40, GP40-2, SD60, SD60M, RS11 and RS11 diesels. Life-Like produces the EMD transition-era BL2 and the SD7. Kato offers SD40, SD40-2, C30-7 and C44-0W models. Bachmann produces GP50, DD40AX, U36B, SD40-2 and Dash 8-40CW. Model Power offers GP40 and Model Power and Mini-Trix offer RSD15, C420 and U28C N scale models. Overland Models and Hallmark also import a variety of modern era brass N scale diesels painted and lettered.

The real railroads operated dozens of additional diesel locomotives built by EMD, Alco, General Electric, Fairbanks-Morse and others but the diesels listed above are the most common diesels and they are available as N scale models. If you do not see your favorite diesel listed here, it may have been imported at some time in the past, by Overland Models, Hallmark or some other brass importer. The manufacturers of the mass-produced locomotives add six or more new diesels to this list every year, so check with your dealer to see what is currently available. Not all of the diesels I have listed are available at any given time, but they are often put back into production and the out-of-production models can usually be located at flea markets, through classified ads or through dealers if you are willing to shop.

Locomotive Maintenance

The major factor in the performance of any model locomotive is the electrical contact or pickup and return through the drivers or wheels. The metal rails and metal wheels oxidize and even the most minute layer of oxidation can serve as an electrical insulator. Slightly dirty track or wheels can promote electri-

Figure 13-5. Use one of the hard rubber track-cleaning erasers to remove the residue from locomotive wheels and drivers.

Figure 13-6. The chassis of this Atlas SD60 fills most of the interior of the model. The round shiny objects on each end of the motor are brass flywheels to help provide smoother performance.

Figure 13-7. Use a jeweler's screwdriver or your fingernail to pry one corner of the body from its internal mounting clips and insert a metal ruler to keep the body free, then pry the opposite side of the body from its retaining clip.

cal sparks or arcing which often results in an even thicker deposit of oxidation. Then there is the oil and air-borne grunge that collects on any metallic surface. The relative light weight of N scale locomotives makes it especially important that there be no dirt or oxidation because there just is not enough weight to break through the coating to complete the electrical circuit from rails to motor and back again. HO scale and larger locomotives are heavy enough so the dirt problem is not as critical. You should clean the track and wheels after every 20 hours of operation or, if more than a month has passed between operating sessions, the track and wheels should be cleaned before operations begin. Clean track and clean drivers or wheels are equally important. Use one of the special hard rubber track-cleaning erasers like those sold by Atlas, Model Power, Life-Like or Bright Boy (Figure13-5). You can prolong the effect of clean wheels or drivers by rubbing the treads that contact the rails with a slightly-oiled rag. Use only the specially electrical-conductive oils sold by Bachmann and Atlas or Wahl Hair Clipper oil. Barely dampen the rag and wipe away any excess. The goal is to leave just enough to prevent oxidation, but not so much as to attract extra dust and lint.

The next most-important factor in locomotive performance is weight. There is virtually nothing you can do about that with N scale locomotives because the interior of the body is almost always packed as full as possible with metal (Figure 13-6). What you can do is operate two or more locomotives at once. This is a trick that the operators of NTRAK modular layouts have learned. With two locomotives you have twice the number of drivers or wheels in contact with the track and, of course, twice the power. The major benefit, however, is that, if one locomotive stalls briefly over a turnout or a piece of lint, the second locomotive will push or pull the other locomotives. Real railroads often double-headed steam locomotives or, in today's terms, operated diesels in multiple-unit or "mu" sets. The first diesels were sold in sets of a cab (called the "A" unit) and a booster (called a "B" unit), and often they were coupled back to back in four locomotive ABBA sets. It is not uncommon to see even two small yard switchers operating in multiple-unit, like Life-Like's SW9 and SW1200 and the SW1500 "cow and calf" pair of diesel switchers, one a conventional switcher with a cab and the other the "calf" with no cab sold by Rivarossi and Con-Cor.

The only part of your locomotive that is likely to wear might be the brushes on the motor, but they should last for hundreds of hours of operation. Most of the damage that occurs to model locomotives is the result of an inexperienced modeler trying to repair something that wasn't broken in the first place. The second most frequent causes of damage are, of course, accidental trips from table to floor.

The only maintenance or repairs you should make are to see that the wheels (and the track rails) are kept spotlessly clean, that the motor and gears are cleaned occasionally, and that only a small amount of grease or oil is added to replace what you wipe off in the process of cleaning the mechanism with a lint-free rag or pipe cleaner (Figure 13-7). If you have a perfectly clean engine, and if you have gone through all the troubleshooting steps in this chapter, and your locomotive still does not run, then you should take it to your hobby dealer to determine if he, one of his customers, or even the factory itself, offers repair service. At worst, you can remove the motor so the locomotive will roll, then use it as a "dummy."

Disassembling Diesel Locomotives

The relatively tiny size of N scale locomotives has served to limit the choices the designers have in placing the motor and gears. The designers' goals are to provide the lowest possible gearing for those tiny wheels, with the smoothest-operating motor and a chassis that fills as much space inside the body as possible for maximum weight. The result is that nearly all N scale diesels appear to be identical once the body is removed.

The locomotive body can remain on the model when you clean the wheels. When it is time (about once a year) to clean and lubricate the motor and the worm gears, the body must be removed. Most brands of diesel bodies can be removed by spreading the body apart with your fingertips or the blade of a jeweler's screwdriver so you can pull the chassis down from beneath the body. It's a good idea to have someone help, so one of you can spread the body while the other tries to wiggle the chassis free. In some cases, it may be necessary to insert a very thin steel ruler or, better, a .010-inch thick automobile mechanic's steel-strip feeler gauge, between the body and the side of the chassis on the side you have just pried lose before prying out the opposite side (Figure 13-7). It can be helpful to have two of these thin steel rulers or two feeler gauges so you can keep at least the front half of the body spread apart while you pull the chassis a mere fraction of an inch to disengage the clips. Hold that end firmly while you insert the rulers or feeler gauges between the body and chassis on the opposite end to free those clips. Yes, it's a fiddly operation but it becomes easier with practice. If you do break the retaining clips from inside the body, you can hold the body in place with a couple of small dots of rubber cement (it's sold by stationery stores). When you want to remove the body, simply slice through the dots of rubber cement with a hobby knife and apply another dab when you reassemble the body to the chassis.

The bodies on a very few N scale diesels, including the Bachmann Spectrum Dash 8-40CW, are held in place by screws. Two of those screws are hidden by the fuel tank on the Bachmann Dash 80-40-CW, so the additional two screws that hold the fuel tank must be removed before you can gain access to the body-mounting screws (Figure 13-8).

Most of the model locomotives operate very nicely as shipped by the factory. Often, the models will actually run more smoothly and more quietly after they are broken in with 20 or 30 hours of operation in one- or two-hour sessions. If the locomotive is running erratically, or if you simply like to fiddle with mechanical objects, the chassis can be disassembled for cleaning and inspection. Each brand of locomotive, however, has a different method of attaching the trucks and motor to the frame.

Cleaning and Inspection

N scale diesel and steam locomotives have some type of metal wiper that contacts the backs of the wheels or drivers or a metal strip that rubs on the axles to carry the electrical current from the rails to the motor through the wheels or drivers. Most N scale diesels have a small copper strip that contacts the back of each wheel. Remove the wheels and notice how far the copper strip moves. That strip should move about 1/32-inch so that the wheel forces that copper strip inward 1/32-inch. Thus, the strip provides pressure on the back of the wheel when the wheel moves from side to side in the truck. If necessary, bend the clips in or out to achieve that contact. The backs of the wheels and the contacting portion of the copper strip also must be clean.

Use a hard rubber eraser like those sold by Atlas, Life-Like, Model Power or Bright Boy to clean the wheels and the strips. If there is black grease inside the trucks, remove the wheels and gears and clean them in model railroad track cleaning fluid.

Cleaning The Motor

The only parts of the motor that should require attention are the commutator and the motor brushes that rub on the revolving commutator. I do not, however, recommend that you attempt to replace the brushes or clean the commutator in the motors used by most N scale locomotive manufacturers because the motors are enclosed (and dirt is unlikely to enter). It is difficult to disassemble these motors without breaking the holding tabs. If the motor does not run, even with the wires from the power pack touched directly to the frame contact strips on the motor, replace the motor.

Figure 13-8. To remove the body from the Bachmann Spectrum Dash 8-40CW diesel, remove the two screws that retain the fuel tank, then remove the screws that retain the body.

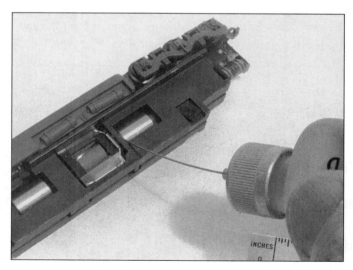

Figure 13-9. You can apply oil to the motor bearings with a needle applicator as shown, but it's easier to control the amount by applying oil to a toothpick, so just a drop hangs from the toothpick, then touching the single drop of oil to the bearing.

Cleaning the Parts

Use a tissue soaked in the track cleaner fluids sold for model railroads to remove the grease and grit from the wheels and the gears. Work outdoors, away from fire or flame and away from any electricity that could cause a spark interacting with those volatile and poisonous fluids. Wear rubber gloves to protect your hands and goggles or safety glasses to protect your eyes. Wood toothpicks can be dipped in one of the fluids to reach the tight areas. Small wood sticks can be used to scrape away the worst dirt from wheels. Never scrape wheels with metal objects. You might scratch them, and the scratches will collect even more dirt more quickly. Never use steel wool on any of your model railroad equipment; the tiny strands will be attracted to the motor magnets and can lodge in the rails of the turnouts to cause short circuits. You should only need to do a thorough cleaning job once a year or so unless you're running your trains on the floor.

Many N scale locomotives are equipped with rubber-like black traction tires on some of the wheels or drivers. Carefully inspect these tires for any signs of cracks. If they are cracked, order replacement tires direct from the manufacturer of the model. You can pry the tires from the wheels or drivers with a jeweler's screwdriver. The track cleaners sold for model locomotives are usually formulated to be harmless to the traction tires. If you have difficulty seating the new tires, apply a small amount of track cleaner to act as a lubricant, then wipe off any excess amount.

Lubricating the Chassis

Use the special model locomotive oil sold by LaBelle, Atlas, Bachmann, Woodland Scenics Hob-E-Lube, and others. Be sure to select oils and grease that are identified on the label as being harmless to plastics. Use a toothpick to apply just a single drop of oil to the motor (Figure 13-9) and driver bearings. Most grease is non-conductive, so you want to keep it away from the wheels, drivers and the copper strips that contact them. Apply just enough grease to fill in the bottom of the worm teeth (Figure 13-10) and the worm gear teeth in the trucks (Figure 13-11), then wipe across the teeth with a lint-free rag to remove any excess.

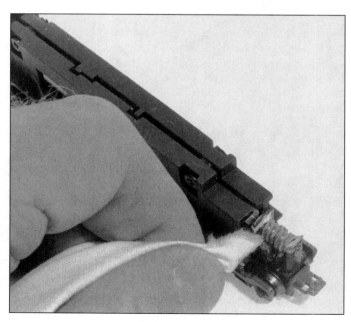

Figure 13-10. Apply just enough grease to fill in the bottoms of each of the gear teeth on the worm.

Disassembling Steam Locomotives

A combination of screws and clips holds the body of most N scale steam locomotives to the superstructure. These screws must be removed to gain access to the motor and gears. You can determine the correct screws by examining the underside of the model. A screw often leads up from the bottom of the chassis toward the smokestack, and it must be removed, in addition to one or two screws or clips between body and chassis toward the rear of the locomotive. Be extremely careful when you remove the body so you don't break any of the wires leading to the motor or light bulbs. If you do, the wire will have to be resoldered. You may be able to find someone in an electronics hobby store or in a television repair shop to do the soldering for you if you do accidentally break a wire. Clean the chassis and the motor area just as described for maintaining diesels and apply light oil to the bearings and grease to the gears. Apply a single drop of oil, with a toothpick, to the places where the links (called "rods) between each driver pivot and at any pivot points on metal linkage near the cylinder (those links are called the "valve gear").

Figure 13-11. Turn the motor with one hand, while you touch the worm gear teeth with the grease, to spread the grease around the entire circumference of each of the worm gears.

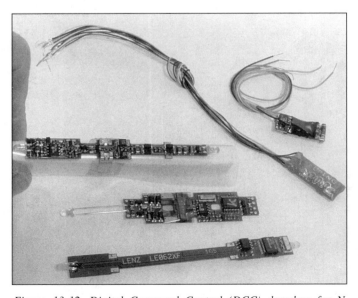

Figure 13-12. Digital Command Control (DCC) decoders for N scale locomotives include solder-in decoders like MRC's (upper right) and Digitrax (right), and replacement circuit board decoders like Digitrax for the Atlas SD60 and Kato PA1 (upper and center left) and the Lenz unit for the Atlas SD60 (bottom right).

Assembling the Locomotive

The assembly of the locomotive is the reverse of the disassembly. If you have removed the wheels or drivers (not recommended, if you can avoid it), you must be particularly careful about the wheels. One wheel of each diesel wheel pair, one driver of each steam locomotive driver pair, and one wheel of each steam locomotive tender wheel pair is insulated so the wheels will not create a short circuit. The insulated wheel will have a plastic washer in its hub or, with some steam locomotive drivers, a thin band of white or red fiber or plastic near the rim. All the insulated wheels must be on the same side on the front truck and on the opposite side of the other truck on diesels. On steam locomotives, the insulated drivers must be on the opposite side (or contact the opposite rail) from the insulated wheels on both tender trucks.

If you discover that a locomotive travels in the opposite direction from all the others, that problem can be corrected by removing the wheels or drivers, turning them end-for-end and then replacing them.

Digital Command Control Locomotives

The Digital Command Control or DCC system of operating two or more trains on the same track is explained in Chapter 8. The decoders (receivers) that allow the locomotives to respond to the signals sent through the rail must be mounted in the locomotives. The newest N scale models are usually available with a removable circuit board that can be replaced with a circuit board containing a DCC decoder. For older locomotives or those without this design, decoders are available that can be wired into the locomotive (Figure 13-12). Dealers who sell DCC systems usually have someone who will install these decoders for you for a reasonable fee. If you cannot locate a dealer, contact one of the DCC manufacturers for the name of the nearest dealer. Many dealers will even handle the installation on a mail order basis or install the decoder for you when you order a new locomotive. Some of the new Atlas N scale diesels (Figure 13-13) are offered with decoders already installed when the diesel is first introduced.

Replacement circuit boards with DCC decoders are available to fit specific N scale diesel models from many of the firms that manufacture DCC products including Digitrax and Lenz. Separate decoders with connector wires are available from Digitrax, Lenz, MRC, Wangrow and others to fit any N scale locomotive,

Figure 13-13. Most of the Atlas locomotives are available, at the time of their introduction, with built-in DCC decoders.

including the older diesels and steam locomotives that are not designed to use a replacement printed circuit board. Many of the older diesel locomotive models have no space for a decoder, so a small portion of the metal frame must be cut away to leave space for the decoders. Some firms, including Aztec, offer replacement frames already cut away to clear a DCC decoder. You must, of course, completely disassemble the locomotive to replace the frame. Decoders small enough to fit inside the cab of an N scale diesel switcher are available from Digitrax and Lenz, but the wire connections must be soldered to install these decoders.

If your N scale diesel is fitted with a printed circuit board, chances are you can locate a replacement board with the decoder built in. To install these decoders, it is only necessary to remove the screws that hold the two halves of the chassis together so you can spread the halves just enough, allowing the printed circuit board to be pulled from the shallow retaining slot (Figure13-14). Install the replacement board with the new decoder in exactly the same position as the original circuit board, replace the screws and test-run the locomotive before installing the body.

If there is no replacement printed circuit board with built-in decoder available for your particular locomotive, you will have to purchase one of the solder-in types of decoders and attach the wires with solder. The wiring varies slightly with each locomotive, but the manufacturers of the decoders can usually supply instructions for your particular locomotive. Digitrax offers an instructional video for installing solder-in decoders in N scale locomotives. For most steam locomotives, the decoder must be mounted in the tender and the wire connections run near the drawbar that connects the locomotive to the tender.

Troubleshooting

The Locomotive and Electrical Troubleshooting chart in Chapter 8 (Figure 8-13) includes the probable causes of trouble that can occur in the track and the power pack as well as in the locomotive. All three components are part of the same electrical circuit. I suggest that you use a 12 volt model railroad light bulb as a troubleshooting "test lamp."

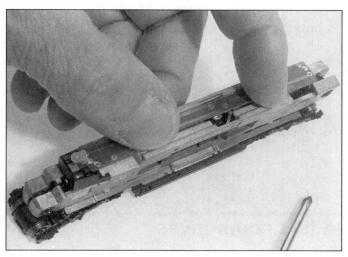

Figure 13-14. To replace a printed circuit board with a decoder in most N scale diesels, simply remove the screws that hold the two halves of the frame together. Pry the frame halves apart just enough to slip the printed circuit board from its retaining clips.

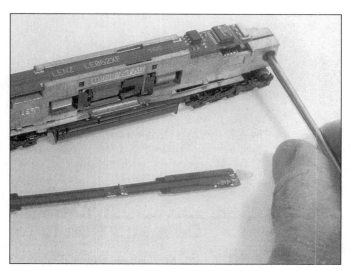

Figure 13-16. Like many N scale diesels, this Kato PA1 chassis completely fills the body.

Figure 13-15. Snap the decoder into the retaining clips in the chassis and replace the screws. Check the trucks to be sure they pivot freely and that all the copper electrical contact strips are in their proper places.

Figure 13-17. The DCC decoders that are offered on printed circuit boards to replace the factory circuit board and, hence, require virtually no space. This is the Kato PA1 with the Digitrax decoder mounted in place of the Kato printed circuit board.

Figure 13-19. This Life-Like PA1 has heavy lead weights mounted on the chassis but no printed circuit board for the lighting circuit. Any of the solder-in DCC decoders could be installed in this model, but a small portion of one of the weights would have to be removed with a hacksaw.

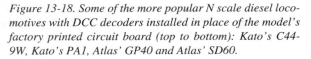

Figure 13-18. Some of the more popular N scale diesel locomotives with DCC decoders installed in place of the model's factory printed circuit board (top to bottom): Kato's C44-9W, Kato's PA1, Atlas' GP40 and Atlas' SD60.

Do's and Don'ts for Model Locomotives

- Do clean the locomotive wheels and polish them with an ink eraser or the track cleaning erasers sold by Atlas, Life-Like, Model Power and Bright Boy.

- Don't allow dirt to accumulate on locomotive wheels since it can cause erratic electrical pickup and unreliable speed control.

- Do clean the bearings, axles and gears of the locomotives to remove any dirt, lint or excess oil or grease.

- Don't apply oil or grease to any plastic bearings. Use plastic-compatible oil on metal bearings and grease plastic-compatible on plastic or metal gears.

- Do remove or mark any locomotives or cars that derail regularly for later inspection so the fault can be found before the next operating session.

- Don't just hope that a derailment-prone locomotive or car will eventually fix itself.

- Do inspect the couplers on all locomotives to be sure they are at the proper height for coupling and that the uncoupling pin does not hang down so far that it can cause a derailment over turnouts or crossings.

- Don't continue to operate locomotives or cars with faulty couplers since they may derail or catch on the turnouts to cause damage and derailments.

- Do use the Troubleshooting Chart in Chapter 8 (Figure 8-13) and check each step, in the order presented, to pinpoint the cause of derailments or poor locomotive performance.

- Don't assume you know the cause of a problem without checking the alternatives on the Troubleshooting Charts.

Chapter 14
Rolling Stock

Today, freight cars provide the means for real railroads to make a profit. Even at the height of passenger travel in the twenties and thirties, freight revenues made up the majority of most real railroads' income. Chapters 17 and 18 will show you how to duplicate the operating patterns of real railroad freight cars. First, though, you'll need a few freight cars. It isn't possible to duplicate the thousands of freight cars that move in and through each town on a real railroad. Only a club layout is large enough to recreate the hundred-car trains of the prototype. But part of the art of model railroading is making just a relatively few freight cars look like many, and to make them at least appear to be carrying something to somewhere.

Your Freight Car Fleet

Real railroads have hundreds, even thousands, of freight cars that look alike except for the car numbers and the degree of weathering. You can increase the realism of your freight car fleet by simply selecting cars that are a close match for those on your favorite real railroad during the era or eras you wish to model. Model railroaders tend to pick as many different kinds and colors of cars as possible. Next time you buy a freight car, particularly one lettered for your favorite real railroad, buy as many of the same style, same color freight cars as you can afford. N scale modelers have a wide choice of freight cars from virtually every era of railroading. The Walthers N scale catalog usually devotes about 40-pages to freight cars alone, and it doesn't show them all! You can certainly pick any car that you like.

If you are going to operate your model railroad using the "Waybill" system in Chapter 17, you will want to collect enough cars to serve the industries you have selected. You will not likely need auto rack cars, for example, because there's nowhere to even simulate unloading them. You can certainly operate auto racks (and any other cars that have no matching industries on your railroad) on "through" freights that are traveling from imaginary points on either end of your railroad.

Rolling Stock Reliability

Real railroads are generally operated on nearly endless stretches of straight track with curves that would reduce to about a 76-inch radius in N scale. The real railroads, then, don't have the problems with tight curves that plague model railroaders. Almost any of the N scale plastic cars or locomotives will make it around the 9-3/4-inch or 11-inch radius curves that are standard in most train sets. Many of the longer freight and pas-

Figure 14-2. The DeLuxe Innovations model (left) of a 40-foot steel boxcar and Micro-Trains model have different roofs, ends and doors that exactly match specific prototype cars.

Figure 14-1. You can buy N scale freight cars from any prototype era including (clockwise, from lower right) Micro-Trains 1890-era truss rod reefer, InterMountain's 1945-era steel reefer, Red Caboose's 60-foot insulated reefer, and Atlas 1960-era mechanical reefer.

senger cars and locomotives will, however, derail on the turnouts as they lurch from straight to curve and pick and click over the turnout points and rattle through the frogs of the smaller-radius turnouts. That's why all of the plans in this book utilize turnouts with at least a 19-inch radius and many have the even larger number 6-size turnouts. You can operate even the longest N scale cars and locomotives on a layout built with any of the plans in this book.

If your space is so limited that you feel you must build a layout using 9-3/4-inch or 11-inch radius curves and matching turnouts, I would recommend that you limit the length of your freight cars to an N scale 50 or 60-feet and passenger cars to an N scale 72-feet. I would also suggest that you avoid passenger and freight cars with 6-wheel trucks because they, too, tend to derail on the smaller turnouts.

Time, Place, and Your Railroad

Before you begin buying a fleet of passenger or freight cars, consider what you want your model railroad to represent. There is enough equipment available in N scale so you can make your layout a moving museum of just about anything that's rolled on a real railroad from 1860 to the present. The vast majority of N scale modelers choose to buy whatever appeals to them, regardless of prototype or era.

You may, however, want to discriminate a bit and just select equipment from your favorite real railroad, or railroads. A few N scale model railroaders go one step further and limit the equipment they buy to just one or two eras and, often, to just a single real railroad. You can easily assemble a 100-car train of freight cars that were common in the thirties, a similar train of fifties-era cars, or cars from the sixties, or from the modern era. But there is another option, especially if you have a limited layout space: buy cars from two or more eras and only operate those from a single era at any given time. You can, of course, match your locomotive choices to the eras of the rolling stock.

Some modelers even pick a specific town or section of their favorite real railroad and era so they are creating an accurate representation of a real time and real place. If you take that approach, be willing to scratch build many of your buildings and you may need to paint and decal many of your locomotives. You may also need to build some of your cars from cast resin or plastic kits and apply the paint and decals to match your favorite real railroad.

There are no car-by-car guides to help you determine which cars are appropriate for which eras. You'll have to do some research, which means you'll have to look at lots of pictures of trains. That's probably what you like to do anyway, but now you have a reason to invest in those real railroad books you crave. Briefly, wood freight cars were virtually the standard until about 1915, when steel cars began to take over. Similarly, 40-foot cars were common from the teens through the forties, when 50-foot cars began to take over. Each era also had its own particular paint schemes, as both railroads and private owners changed heralds and colors on their cars and the traffic patterns shifted on the railroads. Refrigerator cars (reefers) were rare until the twenties and they are rare today. Reefers were, however, a large part of the prototype freight cars fleet from about 1925 until 1955.

Selecting Freight Cars

N scale modelers also have a wide choice of freight cars from nearly every era. Bachmann has some 32-foot cars from the 1860 era including a boxcar, gondola, flat and vat car and a four-wheel caboose. MDC offers kits to build 1890 era 36-foot boxcars, reefers and cabooses. Micro-Trains offers 1900 era boxcars and reefers. Fine N Scale offers tank cars, gondolas, reefers and boxcars from the 1890 era as cast-resin kits that must be assembled, holes drilled for the grabirons and other parts and the models painted and decaled. These Bachmann, MDC, Micro-Trains and Fine N Scale cars are replicas of prototypes with wooden underframes and steel truss rods. Micro-Trains has some very well-detailed replicas of wood-sided boxcars, reefers, hoppers and a caboose and flat car from the twenties and thirties pre-dieselization eras. On the real railroads, many of these wood freight cars lasted in revenue service through the fifties.

There are dozens of ready-to-run plastic replicas of the steel boxcars, reefers, tank cars, gondolas, stock cars, flat cars, hoppers, covered hoppers and cabooses of the forties and fifties. N scale modelers also have a broad selection of equipment from the sixties and later including the usual boxcars, reefers, tank cars, gondolas, stock cars, flat cars, hoppers, covered hoppers and cabooses, as well as modern intermodal cars to carry trailers and containers, articulated intermodal cars and intermodal cars that allow double-stacks of containers, stacked one on top of the other. Usually, the N scale rolling stock from InterMountain, Red Caboose, DeLuxe Innovations, Micro-

Figure 14-3. The DeLuxe Innovations 40-foot boxcar (left) is a replica of a prototype car that was a scale foot taller than InterMountain's model (right). The InterMountain car has separate ladders and grabirons.

Trains, Dimi-Trains, Roundhouse and Walthers has finer details, but is somewhat more expensive than the rolling stock from Bachmann, Model Power, E-R Models, Con-Cor and Rivarossi. The Atlas or Life-Like freight cars produced from newer manufacturing tooling are a match for the better models and are somewhat higher priced than the Atlas or Life-Like cars made from older tooling.

It would take dozens of pages to illustrate all of these cars, and the list is growing each month. The cabooses in Figure 14-4 are one example. The cars on the left are "extended vision" cabooses from Bachmann, Con-Cor and Atlas and a Life-Like replica of a common East Coast railroad steel car. The cars on the right are a replica of a Santa Fe steel caboose from Bachmann, a Micro-Trains replica of a Union Pacific wood car, a Micro-Trains replica of a Missouri Pacific steel car and an E-R Models bay window caboose. All of these cars are available painted for dozens of different roads than those shown.

Maintenance of way equipment is also available from many manufacturers in N scale. Modelers often refer to this equipment simply as "work cars." Some manufacturers offer freight cars painted and lettered for maintenance of way service. Bachmann, Dimi-Trains and Con-Cor offer wrecking cranes and Bachmann and Dimi-Trains offers crane boom cars, Dimi-Trains also has fine models of work cars and a rotary snowplow. Walthers offers a wedge-style snowplow.

Freight Car Loads

I suggest that you add some type of load to all of your flat cars, but you should load only half of your fleet of hoppers or gondolas. Ways to simulate loads for hoppers and gondolas appear in the "Loads-In/Empties-Out" section of Chapter 17. Real coal ground to the size of N scale coal is available in several sizes or grains from hobby stores, or you can powder real coal by putting it in a cloth bag and hitting it with a hammer. Cut a piece of cardboard to fill the car interior so only about 1/8-inch of coal is needed to fill it. Pour in the coal so the peaks of the piles are level with the car sides, but no higher. Spray the loads with water from a plant atomizer or one of the lever-style plastic hairspray bottles. Mix three-parts water to one-part artist's Matte Medium and apply it to the water-wetted load with an eyedropper. You may need to add a few drops of liquid detergent to the Matte Medium and water to keep it from sitting on top of the coal loads.

Flat cars are more realistic in operation if they are partially loaded. This way, if you leave a flatcar at an unloading dock for a scale "day," you can pick the "unloaded" car up again without anyone wondering much about it. A completely empty flatcar is far too obvious to serve as a "loaded" car.

Be sure to simulate the tie-downs on any loads of lumber or other loose commodities. You can use 7-pound test nylon fish-

Figure 14-4. These eight cabooses are all accurate replicas of eight different prototype cabooses. Each is available in a variety of real railroad paint and lettering schemes.

ing line dyed black with common Rit dye. The nylon line can be woven through the various stake pockets along the sides of the flat cars and tied at just one place out of sight on the bottom of the car. Thread is too coarse and has too many hair-like strands to be realistic rope or cable in N scale.

Picking Passenger Cars

MDC and Bachmann both offer passenger cars from the era when cars were wood and steel truss rods were used to support the wooden underframe. The Bachmann cars are replicas of 1860 era cars and the MDC cars are replicas of 1890 era cars that continued in use, on some branchlines and shortlines until the forties. Bachmann, Con-Cor, Rivarossi and Model Power offer replicas of the riveted steel "heavyweight" baggage, combine, coach, Pullman, diner and observation cars. The Bachmann models are 72-scale feet long, slightly-shortened versions of longer cars. The Model Power models are about 76-foot long replicas of Pennsylvania Railroad cars that were used on a few other roads. The Rivarossi and Con-Cor models are usually replicas of full-length 80-foot cars. Con-Cor, Kato and Model Power have full-length replicas of both smooth-side and corrugated-side streamlined passenger cars that began operations in the thirties and continued into early Amtrak operations in the seventies. Model Power offers some shortened 72-foot versions of the corrugated side coach, dome and observation cars. Con-Cor offers replicas of most of the modern era hi-level Amtrak cars and Bachmann has the low-level Amfleet cars and the early Santa Fe hi-level car used on early Amtrak trains. Con-Cor also offers the Amtrak Material Handling Car that is seen at the head end of many cross-country trains. Brass Car Sides and Ameri-can Model Builders offer sides to match specific real railroad smooth-side streamlined passenger cars. The sides fit American Limited Models roof, end, and floor kits so you can build cars that are not available as kits. Microscale offers decals for most railroads' streamlined passenger cars that can be used with these kit components.

Superdetailing N Scale Cars

Very few of the N scale freight or passenger cars can match the level of detail of the best HO scale models. A few N scale manufacturers, including DeLuxe Innovations, Red Caboose and InterMountain, offer kits and ready-built models with separate detail parts that might include ladders, see-through or etched-metal roofwalks and scale-size stirrup steps. If you want the level of detail on other brands of rolling stock to be that high, you will have to add your own detail pats. Gold Medal Models and Plano offer etched-metal roofwalks and Gold Medal and Micro-Trains offer steps and brake wheels that are much finer than those on most N scale cars.

You can improve the appearance of any scale freight car by removing the couplers and pockets from the trucks and mounting them on the body as described in Chapter 16. Only the least expensive HO scale toy trains have truck-mounted couplers. The truck-mounted couplers force the manufacturer to raise the body so it will clear the moving coupler.

To replace the roofwalk on most N scale models, simply pry the original plastic roofwalk from the model. Use a hobby knife to trim-off the mounting pegs and glue the pegs back in the hole with liquid cement for plastics. Use a sharp hobby knife or small flush-cut diagonal cutters to remove the Gold

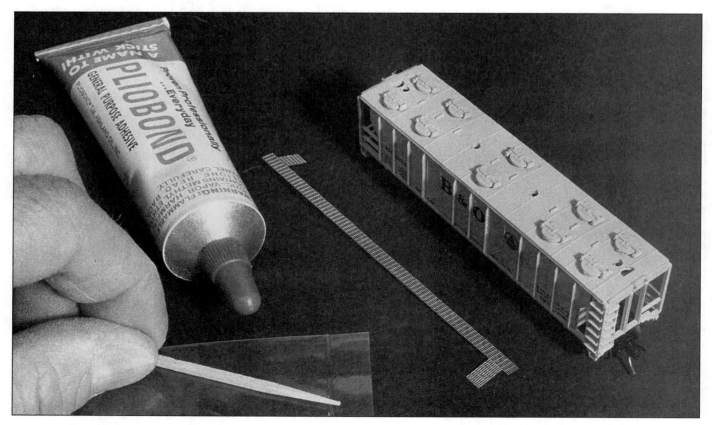

Figure 14-5. Use five-minute epoxy, Walthers Goo or Goodyear Pliobond to attach the Plano etched-metal roofwalk to this DeLuxe Innovations covered hopper.

Figure 14-6. The etched metal roofwalk provides a far more correctly-scaled detail than the plastic roofwalk.

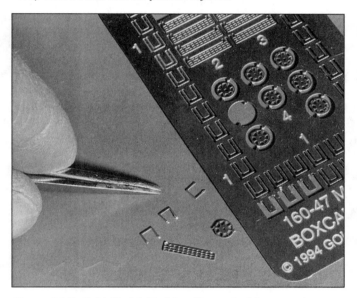

Figure 14-7. Gold Medal Models offers etched brass replacement steps, brake wheels and end platforms (for modern cars) to replace the oversize details on most N scale models.

Medal Models or Plano etched brass roof walks from the fret of scrap metal that surrounds the part. File the edges smooth and gently bend the end ramps down to match the slope on the roof of the car. You can paint the roofwalk as a separate piece and let it dry. Cement the roofwalk to the car with a flexible cement like Walthers Goo or Goodyear Pliobond, or with a five-minute epoxy. Apply just a tiny drop of the cement to the tops of each roof rib (Figure 14-5), then position the roofwalk and hold it down tight with a steel ruler weighted down with some jars of paint.

You can replace the overly-thick stirrup steps on each corner of the car with the etched brass steps from Gold Medal Models (Figure 14-7) or the plastic steps from Micro-Trains. The Micro-Trains steps require a notch in the metal underframe that can be difficult to file. Micro-Trains also offers 40-foot and 50-foot underframes that can be fitted in place of the original underframe although, they, too, may require some filing to fit. Cement the steps in place with Goo or Pliobond and paint them with a brush.

Gold Medal Models also offers etched brake wheels and etched replicas of the small platforms that appear on the ends of modern cars. Micro-Trains offers replacement brake wheels. These smaller parts can be substituted for the kits parts, glued in place, then painted with a brush.

The most effective "superdetailing" you can do with an N scale freight car, however, is to apply a bit of "weathering" as described in Chapter 15.

Rolling Stock Maintenance

Rolling stock must be free-rolling, not wobbling as it rolls down the track, with trucks that are free to swivel so the cars don't derail on curves or turnouts. All couplers must be the same height, with no low-hanging uncoupling pins. In addition, all rolling stock must be able to travel anywhere on the layout without derailing. The "Derailment and Track Troubleshooting Chart" in Chapter 7 (Figure 7-43) describes the problems that cause derailments. Most often, the problem will lie with the track rather than the rolling stock. Still, if a single car derails and no other cars have problems, inspect that car carefully for possible causes of derailments. The most frequent cause of derailments on rolling stock is coupler pins that hang down so far that they snag at turnouts or crossings. Chapter 15 includes information on how to be sure the couplers are mounted properly.

The second most common cause of derailments by freight or passenger cars is dirt, which usually is attracted to the car wheels and bearings by oil. Virtually all of the N scale freight car models and kits include plastic trucks made of a slippery plastic that should never require lubrication. Oil in the ends of the axles on freight cars merely attracts dust and dirt and turns it into a sticky substance. Excessive oil or grease on locomotives can also dribble onto the rails to be picked up by the wheels of the rolling stock. You can, then, avoid most dirt by simply not lubricating anything but the metal bearings and gears of the locomotives with the least amount of oil or grease possible.

Most N scale freight and passenger car's trucks also have plastic wheelsets. Many N scale modelers find that they have fewer derailments if they replace all the wheelsets with metal wheels.

Figure 14-8. Use five-minute epoxy, Walthers Goo or Goodyear Pliobond to attach the Gold Medal Models brake wheel, end platform and corner stirrup steps.

InterMountain, NorthWest Short Line and others offer metal wheelsets for N scale freight and passenger cars. The metal wheels may or may not attract more dirt than the plastic wheels, but it's just as easy to clean the metal wheels as the plastic wheels.

If you find a sticky residue on the wheels, scrape it off very gently with a hobby knife or the blade of a small screwdriver.

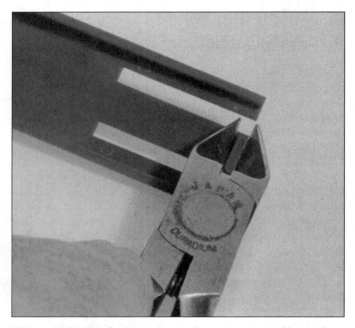

Figure 14-9. Use flush-cut diagonal cutters or a hobby knife to remove the tab from the Con-Cor (shown) or Kato rerailers so the rerailer no longer needs to fit between the ties.

The wheels can be removed from most model railroad trucks by simply spreading the plastic sideframes apart between your fingers so the axle and wheel set fall out. With the wheels removed, the bearings for the pinpoint axle ends can be cleaned with a toothpick dipped in paint thinner. Work outdoors and avoid any fire or sparks when using any flammable fluids. Do not use a knife to scrape the bearings clean or you may scratch the bearings and reduce the free-rolling qualities of the trucks.

If you find that the cars rock from side to side as they roll down the tracks, one of the truck pivots must be tightened. Nearly all N scale models have trucks mounted with a separate press-in pin. On some cars the underframe often can be modified at the truck pivot (bolster) on the underframe. Use a hobby knife to slice about 1/64 inch from the truck pivot. With this material removed, the pin for that truck can be pushed in enough so the truck will be free enough to pivot but too tight to allow the car to rock from side to side. Leave the opposite truck alone so it can wobble from side-to-side as well as pivot. The single pivoting (but not rocking) truck will keep the car level and the rocking truck will allow the trucks to follow uneven or rough trackwork without derailing the car.

Some of the least expensive cars may have thin wisps of plastic around the extreme outer edges (the flanges) of the wheels. This plastic is called "flash" and occurs during the manufacturing process. You can remove it with a sharp hobby knife.

I would suggest you invest a few dollars in a rerailing tool like those sold by Kato, Rix and Con-Cor. If the rerailer has a web of plastic designed to slide between the ties, I would suggest you remove it with a hobby knife or with flush-cut diagonal cutters (Figure 14-9) so the tool will work when ballast fills the area between the ties.

Chapter 15

Painting, Lettering, and Weathering

There is an ever-increasing selection of ready-to-run locomotives, freight cars, and passenger cars in paint schemes to duplicate equipment owned by both real railroads and private owners. There is enough of a choice that you may not ever need to repaint and decal a model. You may, however, want to change the number on a car, especially if you have two or more identical cars. And you may discover a particular prototype that you wish to match with your model and the only way to do it is to paint and letter the model. Painting and lettering allows you to match the unique character of real railroad equipment. I would suggest that you paint all the plastic buildings, if just to remove that slightly translucent look of the plastic.

The details and paint and lettering on most N scale models are usually a precise duplicate of the real thing. Still, there's something not quite as realistic as it could be about any N scale model. The flaw in the appearance of the models lies in the fact that all of them look like they just came out of the paint shop. On a real railroad, that out-of-the-shop shine lasts about a day or until the first rainstorm or tunnel. About 999 freight cars out of a 1000 are dirty. If you really want a realistic model railroad, you will want to duplicate the effects of weather and dirt on your models. Modelers call this process "weathering."

Painting Railroad Models

Most paints for model railroads are sold in bottles. You can apply these paints with a brush and achieve very good results because most of the visible brush strokes will be hidden by the final clear coat that protects the decals and, if you choose, the weathering colors. You can buy a bottle of any real railroad color from Floquil, Polly Scale, Modelflex, SMP, or Scalecoat and apply it with a paint brush, but it's a lot easier and quicker to use spray paint. Floquil and Scalecoat make some aerosol railroad colors, but the selection is limited.

You can apply any of these paints with an airbrush, a miniature version of the spray guns used to paint automobiles (Figure 15-1). Hobby shops sell airbrushes and the cans of propellant or air compressor you will need to provide the air for the airbrush. The cans of propellant are very similar to conventional aerosol cans of paint, except the cans of propellant contain no paint. If you only paint occasionally, the propellant cans might work, but they lack any means of adjusting the air pressure, so you really are working with a spray can. The lowest-priced air compressors also have no air pressure control. If you do buy an air compressor, pick one that has air pressure control so you can adjust

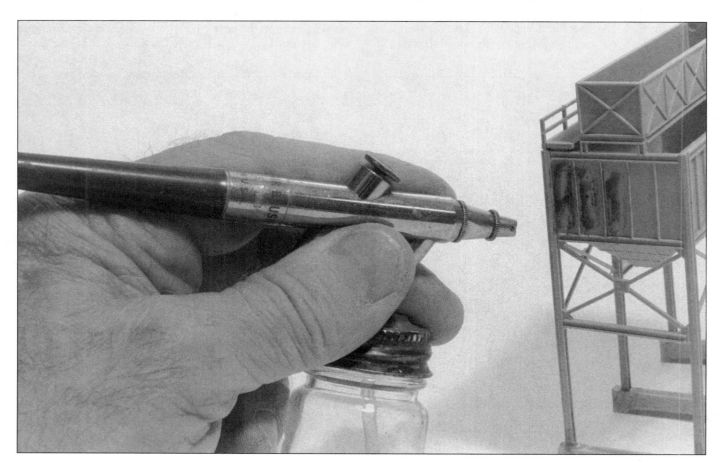

Figure 15-1. An airbrush can be used to apply any color of model railroad paint to cars, locomotives and structures.

the pressure to between 20 and 40 pounds per square inch (psi). The airbrush can be used to spray Floquil, Polly Scale, Modelflex, SMP, or Scalecoat bottled paints that are available in colors matched to real railroad paint chips.

Removing the Original Paint

Repainting a model freight car or locomotive means that you must also apply new letters, heralds, and numbers to the model after the paint dries. You should also remove the original letters, heralds and numbers, however, because they will show through the paint in the form of a raised outline all around the markings. Common rubbing alcohol and a cotton swab or tissue will remove most markings. Dip the swab or tissue in the alcohol and rub the lettering or numbers on the side of the car with it for a moment until the marking is "erased." The inks used on most models are alcohol-based and can be removed quite easily with this technique. However, some inks may have to be removed with an abrasive like number 600 sandpaper.

The original paint on model railroad cars is very difficult to remove. You can try an oven cleaner, such as Easy-Off, or automobile brake fluid, but you could ruin the model rather than removing the paint. Several types of plastic are used on model railroad cars and on the locomotive bodies, so a paint remover that doesn't dissolve one body might melt another.

You must apply a coat of primer to give the surface some "tooth" so you can keep the applications of that final color coat as thin as possible. I have found that the Magic brand of primer sold by Standard Brands and the Tempo primers sold by some hardware and automobile parts stores work quite well. Some primers will attack paint or plastic, and most are so thick that they obscure most of the rivets and other fine details. You'll have to experiment with the primer you want to use (even if it's one of the two I've had good luck with) to be certain it won't attack the paint on your particular model. Test spraying on the inside of the body or near the bottom of one of the car ends will reveal whether or not the primer will cause the paint beneath it to curl or crinkle. If you have an airbrush, you can apply a primer made by the same firm that made the color you selected for the model.

Spray Painting

There's a bit of an art to spray painting with either an aerosol can or an airbrush. First, wash the models in detergent before any painting, rinse them, and allow them to air dry to remove all traces of grease and fingerprints. Then, you will need some sort of a handle to hold the model so you don't touch the paint. I use a wire coat hanger straightened and rebent to a small "e" shape so the inside of the car body is held under a spring tension by the two tips of the wire. For smaller parts I attach masking tape, looped inside out so the sticky side is up, to a scrap of wood. The smaller parts can be placed on the tape, spray painted, and left there until the paint dries (Figure 15-2). The wood serves as a handle so you can hold the parts while painting. I wear a disposable plastic work glove on one hand for holding the coat hanger or the scrap of wood, and I spray the car or parts with the airbrush in my other hand.

Begin the spray just off the model and pass it evenly over the model before releasing the button. Starting or stopping the spray directly on the model can produce splatters and runs. It's best to apply as many as a dozen very light coats rather than trying to do the job with just one. You'll almost always produce runs in the paint if you try to cover with just one or two coats. If you're using an aerosol can of paint, invert the can when you are finished painting so the nozzle is down and press in on the nozzle until just gas but no paint flows from the nozzle. The paint-

Figure 15-2. Hold the parts to be spray painted to a scrap of wood with masking tape folded sticky side out.

pickup tube will be above the paint, with the can inverted, so this technique allows the can's own pressure to clean both the nozzle and the spray tube inside the can. Gloss paint makes a much better surface for the application of decals but you can achieve a glossy finish over flat-finish paints by spraying a final coat of clear gloss.

Decals

A decal is nothing more than a number, name, herald, or other marking that is printed or painted on a piece of glue-covered paper. The colored portion of the decal is then sprayed with several coats of clear paint. When you soak the glue-covered paper in water, the glue dissolves and allows the decal to be pushed from the paper and onto the model. Because the decal is too thick to snuggle in tightly around rivets, seams, and other details, decal manufacturers, such as Microscale and Walthers, make decal-softening fluids that can be applied like so many drops of water. These fluids almost dissolve the decal back to its original "paint" state, so it really does look as though it's painted on.

The major decal manufacturers can handle direct-mail orders, and Microscale and Northeast offer catalogs for $6.00 each. Walthers includes theirs with the 400-plus page catalog, *N Scale Model Railroad Reference Book*, (the catalog price varies from year to year so send a stamped, self-addressed envelope to Walthers for the current price of the catalog or ask your local hobby dealer to order a copy of the catalog). I suggest you obtain all the decal makers' catalogs so you'll know what choices you have for relettering rolling stock and locomotives. A few decals are made for station and industrial signs as well as names, and these can be used if you want to make up your own railroad names. Contact the decal firms directly.

How to Apply Decals

The decal must first be cut close to the printed portion with scissors or a hobby knife to remove as much of the clear border as possible from Northeast and Walthers decals. Microscale decals have a tapered edge to most of the clear decal films. This can be seen if you hold the decal so that light reflects off the shiny clear part. Cut the Microscale decals apart near the outer edges of the clear portions. From this point on, the decal cannot be touched with a bare finger until the final protective coat of clear flat paint has dried. Use pointed tweezers to pick up the decal and dip it into warm water for just a moment. Set the decal on a blotter or on a paper towel for a few minutes while the glue dissolves (Figure 15-3).

When the decal can be moved on its paper backing, it is ready to be applied to the model. Hold both the decal and its paper backing exactly where you want the decal. Keep just the decal in place with the tip of the hobby-knife blade while you pull the paper backing from beneath it (Figure 15-4). If the area that is beneath the decal is textured with rivets or other details, it's wise to wet the area with the decal-softening fluid; it's best to apply a first coat of decal-softening fluid to the model before applying the decal.

Apply a thin coat of the decal-softening fluid to the surface of the decal with a number O-size paint brush. Allow the fluid about 15 minutes to dry, and, if necessary, dab at the decal lightly with a finger wrapped with a dampened tissue to force the decal down over the surface. Don't push too hard or the decal will grab the tissue; just dab at it (Figure 15-5). It might take as many as six applications of the decal-softening fluid, applied over a period of an hour or more, to get some decals to

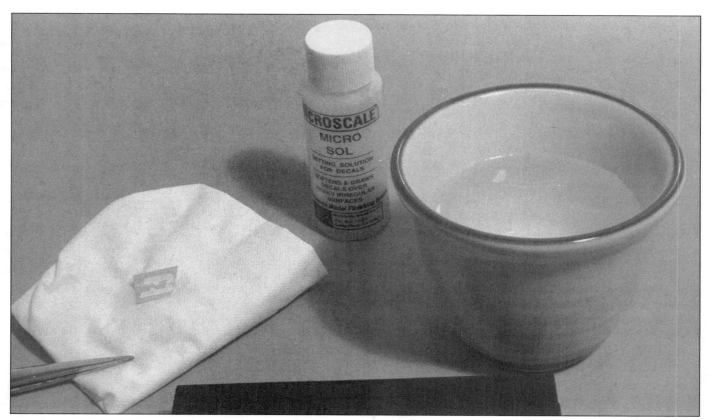

Figure 15-3. Cut the decals apart and dip them briefly in water before resting them on a tissue to soak.

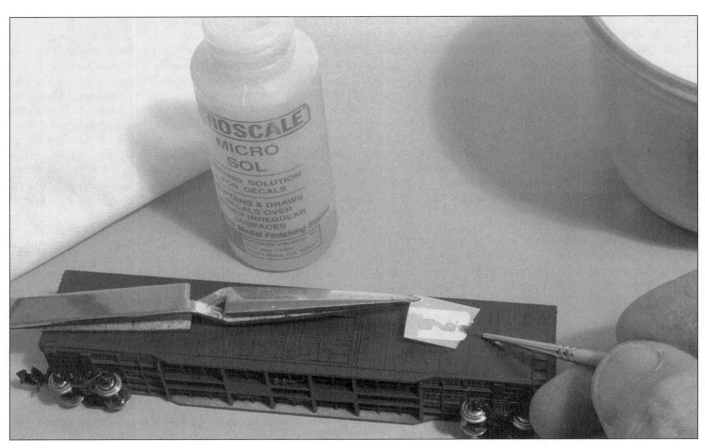

Figure 15-4. Hold the decal in place with the tip of a paintbrush while you pull the paper backing from beneath it with tweezers.

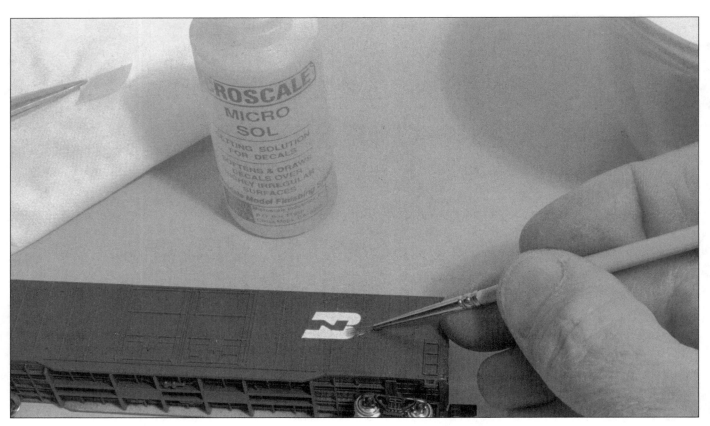

Figure 15-5. Position the decal carefully with the paintbrush, then apply a coat of decal-softening fluid.

snuggle tightly around curved or highly detailed surfaces. When the decal-softening fluid has dried overnight, scrub the surface of the decal lightly with a cotton swab dipped in water to remove any traces of the decal-softening fluid or the decal glue. Let the model dry overnight again and apply a protective spray-on coat of Testors "DullCote," Model Master "Clear Flat," or some other spray-on flat finish clear paint that you have pre-tested to be sure it will not attack either the paint or the decals. The final coat of paint will match the finish or gloss (or lack of gloss) of the decal to the rest of the model, and it will help to disguise those clear edges of the decal so only an expert could tell it was a decal rather than painted on lettering.

Dry Transfer Markings

CDS, Clover House and Woodland Scenics offer dry transfers. Dry transfers are somewhat easier to apply than decals but you must have the dry transfer in precisely the right spot because there is no way to move it like you can with a decal. Cut each marking from the sheet, position the marking precisely where you want it, and tape its top to the model to act as hinge. Rub over the dry transfer firmly with a number 2 pencil or one of the special decal burnishers sold by art supply stores. Gently lift the transfer on its hinge to see if all the transfer is stuck, If not, hinge the transfer back into perfect alignment and repeat the process. If you have trouble applying dry transfers directly to the model, you can apply the dry transfers to clear decal film, then apply them as a decal as described earlier. Microscale and Walthers offer blank decal film that can be used for this purpose.

Masking and Painting Two Colors

The same techniques described for painting rolling stock will work equally well on locomotives. On most diesel locomotives, however, the painting might become slightly more complicated because you may want to use a two-color paint scheme to match a particular prototype or for your own railroad.

Use Scotch "Magic Transparent Tape" for masking. It's thin-ner than regular masking tape, and you can tell whether or not it's stuck by just looking to see if the part shows through the tape. Paint the lighter color first on most two-color paint schemes.

You can use dark gray acrylic primer in back of flat black on color schemes that are predominantly black. This is a short-cut that saves the detail-hiding thickness of another coat of paint. You might be able to find a primer in a light gray or a light brown or even in white for the "second" color on other railroad paint schemes. Apply a strip of Scotch "Magic" tape all around the model, with one edge of the tape forming the color separation line between the existing color and the one you are about to spray on. If the color separation line has V or Z shapes, you may want to cover the whole area with the tape and cut through it to make the design; then you can remove the excess tape along the cut lines. You might also want to remove the end and side railings to make masking easier. I removed just the last posts from the side railings and the complete end railings to mask the end platforms.

Spray on the second color and let it dry for at least a day. Use a new number 11 blade in your X-Acto knife to slice carefully along the edge of the "Magic" tape so the second color won't stick to the tape. Do not rely on just the tape to make a clean color separation edge because it will leave a ragged and rough line when it is removed. When you do pull the tape away, dou-ble it back over itself to minimize the chances of lifting the orig-inal color. If there are some zigs and zags in the paint separation line, touch them up with either (or both) colors applied with a number O paint brush. When the paint is dry, the model can be decorated with decals. It will be necessary to use plenty of decal-softening fluid to get those decals to snuggle tightly around the louvers and rivets on any diesel body.

Weathering and Aging Tips

Weathering is a term used to describe a final coat of very thin paint that is applied to the model to simulate the effects of sun, wind, dirt, and rain. The only way you'll learn how to weather a model is to study and practice the techniques. You'll want to go out into the real world to study how weathering really looks, and you'll have to practice the techniques I offer to learn how to use them properly. The "weathering paint" can be just about anything from artist's water-base acrylics to artist's oil colors to artist's pastel chalks powdered on sandpaper and brushed onto the model. You can produce some of the rust stains and other rain water-borne streaks using a felt-tipped pen. The corrugated iron buildings and roofs at the Corning Mine (Figure 15-6) and the Consolidated Edison coal bunker on the 6-by-6-foot Union Pacific layout were applied with a felt-tip pen. If you have access to an airbrush, you can use the incredible range of bot-

Figure 15-6. Felt-tip markers can be used to apply sim-ulated rust streaks and stains to structure models.

Figure 15-7. Use a wide brush to apply a "wash" of diluted grey paint to accent mortar lines, then apply a wash of diluted black paint to produce the weathering effects of air-born soot and smoke.

tled model railroad paints. Excellent weathering effects can be achieved with oils, acrylics, or pastel chalks applied with a paint brush (Figure 15-7) or a fine-pore sponge in a dabbing technique. The paint, however, must be thinned with about five parts water (for acrylics) or turpentine (for oil colors) to one-part paint, so that the color will be barely visible.

Weathering With Powdered Pastel Chalks

Most of the weathering effects you will want to apply to cars, locomotives, and structures can be created using powdered pastel chalk. Art supply stores sell both oil-base and chalk-base pastels. Buy the chalk-base type in ochre, burnt sienna, burnt umber, light

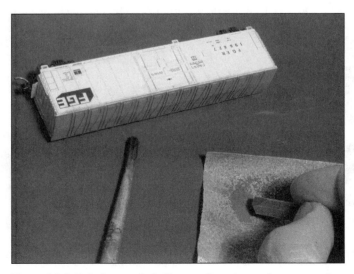

Figure 15-8. Rub the pastel chalks over fine-girt sandpaper to reduce the pastels to powder to be used for weathering effects.

grey and black. Rub each stick on piece of fine sandpaper (Figure 15-8) to reduce it to a powder and store each of the powders in its own empty paint jar. The powdered pastels produce realistic weathering effects with a minimum effort because you are, in effect, applying "dirt" very much like it is applied to the prototype. Brush the powdered pastels onto the model with paint brush. If you want a darker effect, wet the sides of the model before you apply the powdered pastels. When you are satisfied with the effect, protect the model with light application of Testors DullCote. You will find that the DullCote reduces the intensity and color of the weathering by about half, so you may want to apply another layer of weathering colors. With practice, you'll be able to estimate how much darker to make the initial weathering so it produces the desired effect after the application of DullCote.

Sand and Dust

There are really only two secrets to the art of weathering a railroad miniature with paint. First, keep the paint thin enough so that you can apply two or three coats without obscuring the lettering and numbers on the car or locomotive. Second, use photographs or very recent memories of the real thing as your guide to where and how much of the weathering colors to apply. You'll find that light beige or gray will be useful in simulating the sun-bleached effects of nature on any color car, locomotive, or structure. Those lighter shades can also be used on darker cars to simulate dust from desert areas, such as the Southwest. Many Southern Pacific cars, for instance, have a beige tint to their surfaces from traveling through the desert dust and from the effects of the hot Southwestern sun. Black or dark brown are the colors to use to simulate steam locomotive soot, diesel locomotive exhaust stains, and coal dust on your models. Mix your weathering colors with about five-parts thinner to one-part paint.

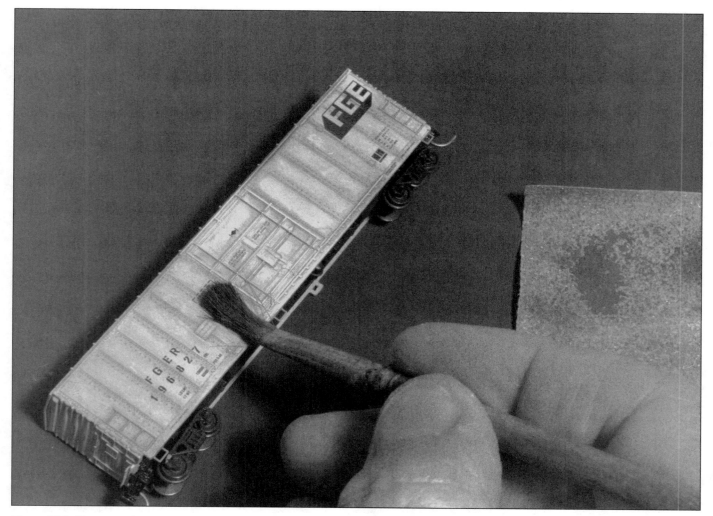

Figure 15-9. Use a paintbrush to apply the powdered pastels to duplicate the streaked and blotched weathering patterns you see on real railroad equipment.

You should try to simulate as many different types of weathering as you can on your models, about half of them should have weathering patterns common to the area you are modeling. Most of the cars you'll see in the coal-mining regions, for example, are stained with coal dust, and most of the cars that serve in areas where most of the rocks and soil are limestone streaked with gray, and the Southwestern cars are beige-tinted. Vary the degree of the weathering, from the barest trace that might collect on a new car, to the years of grime that collect on an older car. If you apply too much weathering to a car or two, do as the real railroads do and paint over the number in the original car color and add a fresh decal number.

Wood and Rust Effects

The weathering techniques can be used to weather track and to simulate wood flat-car floors or industrial loading platforms. Paint the "wood" surface a very light shade of beige, and then apply a wash of dark brown with a sponge, streaking the wash in the direction of the grain. Make every other board or tie or so a darker shade and just touch a few of them to leave mostly the faded-wood look of the light beige.

Paint the track rails with dark red-brown to simulate rust, and add drops of "rust" to flat-car floors or loading docks to simu-late rusted nails. Scrape just the tops of the rails gently with a knife blade to remove any paint from the electrical pickup surfaces, and do keep the rust-colored paint away from the moving parts of the switches. You can make Uni-Track, E-Z Track, Power-Loc Track and sectional track look like it was laid on real wood ties with individual spikes by using these weathering techniques.

Weathering Model Locomotives

Virtually all the three-dimensional details that appear on the real thing appear on the model. There are several ways, however, that you can make these locomotives seem even more like the real thing. A wash of ninety-five-parts water and five-parts black acrylic can be used to fill in the hollows of louvers and grills. This will make it appear as though there really could be engines inside the diesel bodies. You can also use the powdered pastels, as described earlier, to weather both steam and diesel locomotives (Figure 15-10).

Every steam and diesel locomotive, even those at the head ends of passenger trains, have some degree of weathering such as that described in this chapter. Locomotives are even more likely to become dirty than rolling stock, but the patterns of the dirt will be different indeed. Again, photographs from railroad

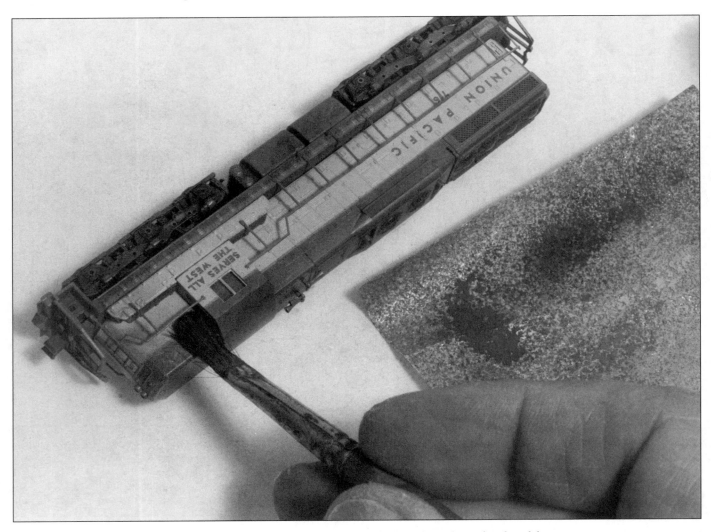

Figure 15-10. Powdered pastel chalks can also be used to apply the smoke stains and streaks on diesel models.

books and visits to real railroad yards will show you just where and how the real locomotives collect their dirt.

That black acrylic wash can also be applied to the trucks, ends and lower areas of the locomotives to simulate dirt and grime. You'll see an example of the light gray "wash" applied to one steam locomotive and three or four varieties of diesel weathering on the models in this book, but there are hundreds of other variations on the full-size locomotives.

Weathering Structures

The last step in finishing any structure model (or in preparing a ready-built model for use on your layout) is the most important. The building must be weathered by spraying it lightly and from a distance of about two feet with flat paint that comes close to matching the surrounding scenery. Spray a bit more of the paint near the edges of the roof to simulate rain-washed dirt that accumulates near the rain gutters, and spray a bit more near the base of the building to simulate where rain

would have splattered mud around the base of the building. Practice this weathering technique on an old shoe box until you can determine just how far away you can hold the spray can to get the effect of dust. If you have an air brush, mix about five-parts thinner to one-part paint and apply the weathering effects with the air brush. You can also use the powdered pastel technique as described earlier, with the pastel colors matched to the surrounding earth.

The entire town or industrial area should receive this roof and foundation treatment. You might want to select a different "weathering" shade for different towns. The town of "Alliance" on the 6-by-6-foot Union Pacific layout has an overall touch of beige to match the nearby dirt. The areas around the "Corning Mining Company" have been weathered with a very light touch of black to simulate rain-washed coal dust. The buildings in the town of "Emmett" were given a weathering tint of dark brown. This overall weathering is the single most important step in making your layout look real.

Chapter 16
Automatic Coupling and Switching

You can recreate all of the actions of real trains with N scale models. You can just run trains—even run two or more trains on the same track—and you make-up and breakdown trains one car at a time. The process of picking up cars for a train or leaving one at a siding is called "switching". It is exciting to watch any train weave its way around a model railroad layout, especially if the layout has some structures and scenery for that train to pass, so it really seems to be going somewhere. If you tire of just watching the train run, you can stop it—or start a second train while the first one continues its travels—and perform some real railroad-like switching operations.

If you are one of the many model railroaders who consider "switching" to be nothing more than simply running a train forward, backward, and forward again, I think you are missing one of the more fascinating aspects of the hobby. The real excitement of switching comes from the duplication of all the movements of the real trains, and for precisely the same reasons. If you want your model railroad to be authentic, you will want to learn how to perform the switching moves used by the real railroads.

The "Hands-Near" Approach

One of the many differences between a toy-train operator and one who is running a real railroad in miniature is a "hands-off" approach. That's why those endless laps around the layout with the same old trains become boring. There's a thrill in sitting or standing at a control panel while you flip levers to switch trains in and out of sidings or stop one train while you start another. The towerman's job is always going to be a part of both real and model railroading. Please don't let that be the only part of the hobby you practice. Step down from that tower (here is where the walk-around control from Chapter 8 is a big help) and try the engineer's or brakeman's jobs for a while. You still won't have to destroy the illusion that yours is a real railroad by actually touching the miniature trains. The true model railroader is the person who practices a hands-near approach, which means that he or she remains close enough to the moving train to be a participant, rather than being only a spectator at a control panel.

Figure 16-1. Some of the better quality N scale freight cars, like this DeLuxe Innovations model, are fitted with dummy knuckle couplers.

Rapido Couplers

The majority of N scale cars and locomotives are fitted with a large square-shaped coupler. These couplers first appeared on some of the Arnold-Rapido cars and locomotives in the mid-sixties. They are often listed as "Rapido" couplers. Gradually, they became the standard coupler for N scale models. They are designed to be uncoupled with a ramp placed between the ties and raised when you want to uncouple a car. Roco offers a remote controlled uncoupling ramp that can be used to uncouple the Rapido couplers. These couplers can be coupled anywhere, but it requires so much force that it is seldom possible to just couple onto a single car unless that car is against an end-of-track bumper or it is part of a five- or six-car train. The Rapido couplers are fine if you simply want to run trains, without any coupling or uncoupling. You can always fit one of the knuckle-style couplers to the front of the locomotive and the end of the caboose for more realism. The Rapido couplers do have one advantage over the old HO scale "horn hook" couplers; it is easy enough to couple or uncouple cars or a car and locomotive if you use your hands to simply lift one car up from a train without snagging the couplers and derailing the rest of the train. The unrealistic and oversize appearance of these couplers is certainly not as apparent when they are on the ends of cars that are coupled in a train. If the Rapido couplers work for you, keep them because they are far less likely to uncouple than the knuckle-style couplers.

Knuckle Couplers

Real railroads use a standard coupler design that is referred to as a "knuckle" coupler because of its similarity to a human hand held in a loose fist position. The "thumb" of a knuckle coupler is rigid, while the "fingers" are pivoted so the coupler can open to couple with another coupler. Keith and Dale Edwards designed and patented an operating HO scale knuckle coupler in the fifties. This coupler was eventually redesigned so

it could be uncoupled with a magnet placed between the rails. The design was further modified in the seventies, so it could be produced in N scale. About that time, the firm was reorganized and Dale Edwards continued to produce HO and large scale products at Kadee. Keith Edwards assumed production and control of the N scale rolling stock and the N scale automatic magnetic couplers under the Micro-Trains name. In 2000, Atlas introduced a knuckle coupler that can be coupled anywhere and uncoupled automatically with between-the rails magnets, and it will couple with the Micro-Trains couplers. Several firms also offer non-operating "dummy" knuckle couplers (Figure 16-2).

The Micro-Trains automatic knuckle coupler has been the "standard" coupler choice for N scale modelers who want to perform switching operations and for those who prefer a more realistic-looking coupler. The Micro-Trains coupler will couple anywhere. It can be uncoupled manually by inserting a small screwdriver and gently twisting the knuckles apart. The Micro-Trains coupler can also be uncoupled by remote control over a hidden magnetic ramp or the uncoupling delayed after pausing at the hidden ramp to uncouple on down the track (Figure 16-3).

These couplers look like real railroad couplers, although they are about 25 percent larger than they should be for truly accurate N scale couplers. The coupler knuckle actually opens similar to a real coupler, too. The real magic of these couplers, however, is that they really will couple with a gentle force. The couplers will uncouple without derailing the train by using a magnetic ramp that is buried beneath the track or placed between the rails so it looks like a highway crossing. Just stop the car and locomotive with the couplers over the 2-inch long ramp and the two couplers open to disengage. That leaves a lot of room for error, and the train doesn't have to be spotted very carefully to catch part of the ramp.

The Micro-Trains and Atlas knuckle-style couplers have a small bent wire that hangs below the coupler. This uncoupling pin is repelled by the magnetic ramp and that action is what pivots the coupler knuckle open to uncouple. The wires vaguely

Figure 16-2. There are several choices of N scale couplers including (left to right): Micro-Trains operating magnetic couplers, and dummy knuckle couplers from DeLuxe Innovations, Red Caboose, InterMountain, Kato and the common Rapido coupler.

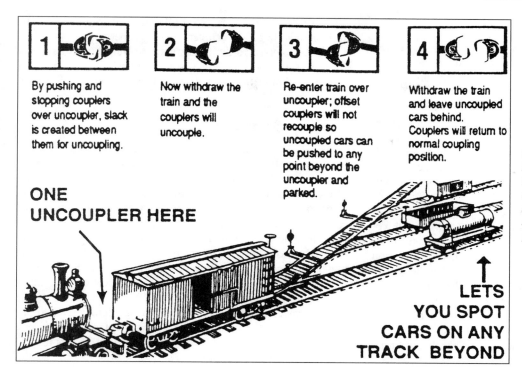

1 By pushing and stopping couplers over uncoupler, slack is created between them for uncoupling.

2 Now withdraw the train and the couplers will uncouple.

3 Re-enter train over uncoupler; offset couplers will not recouple so uncoupled cars can be pushed to any point beyond the uncoupler and parked.

4 Withdraw the train and leave uncoupled cars behind. Couplers will return to normal coupling position.

ONE UNCOUPLER HERE

LETS YOU SPOT CARS ON ANY TRACK BEYOND

Figure 16-3. This illustrates how the Micro-Trains N scale couplers (and Kadee HO scale couplers) operate over the ramp (1 and 2) and how the delayed-action principle functions (3, 4, and the lower drawing). –Courtesy Kadee Quality Products

resemble the air hoses that hang beside the couplers on real trains, but honestly, the uncoupling pin does not look realistic when a single car is seen from the end. Still, the appearance is vastly more realistic than that of the Rapido-style couplers.

The Micro-Trains and Atlas knuckle-style couplers on your N scale cars and locomotives will couple together just about anywhere, except on a curve or a downgrade. Coupling, then, can be a hands-off operation as long as the couplers are working properly and the car or locomotive being coupled are on a straight section of track. Uncoupling is a bit tricky to do from a distant control panel because you have to be able to judge exactly where the couplers and the cars are on the track. The couplers on your N scale models will only uncouple by remote control when they are directly over the magnetic uncoupling ramps. The magnet repels the steel wires that hang below the couplers (somewhat like air hoses on real couplers) to open the coupler. When you pull the train away, the uncoupled car or that portion of the train will stay at the uncoupling ramp. You must perform a quick succession of moves for reliable uncoupling. Stop at the ramp, back up just a fraction of an inch, then pull forward immediately. You can put the magnetic ramps on any six-inch or longer piece of straight track. Most of these couplers have a delayed action that allows you to "cock" the coupler open over the ramp and shove (but not pull) the car to any location on the railroad (Figure 16-3). When you stop the train and reverse it, the coupler will uncouple.

Figure 16-4. Use a jeweler's screwdriver or a Rix or Accurail uncoupling tool to gently pry the knuckles of Micro-Trains or Atlas couplers apart so cars can be uncoupled anywhere on the layout without lifting the car from the track.

Manual Uncoupling

There's a better way of uncoupling that will let you get even more involved with the operation of your trains. Simply use a small screwdriver to operate the couplers (Figure 16-4). Accurail and Rix also make special uncoupling picks that work very well for manual uncoupling. You're still not actually touching the models but you are performing the function of the brakeman, in addition to your other duties as towerman (or dispatcher) and engineer. This may sound simple, but don't laugh until you've tried it for several operating sessions to get a sense of the greater feeling of realism you get using hands-on coupling and uncoupling operations.

You don't have to put your miniature railroad equipment through those toy train gyrations of lurching backward and forward to get the couplers to open, and you don't have to try to figure out how to place an uncoupling ramp every place you want or need one. You really should use the uncoupling tool in conjunction with the walk-around throttle (in Chapter 8), so you can use the throttle to set the locomotive in motion when you have the couplers open. It will take some practice to determine the best ways to use the screwdriver or pick. The trick is to push the point straight down to get it just into the gap between the couplers, then twist or lean the tool slightly to pry the couplers apart. The movement should be very delicate.

Coupler Maintenance

The couplers are the most vulnerable parts of your models, and it's easy for them to be knocked out of alignment. You should check every coupler on every piece of equipment you own, and make it a habit to check the couplers whenever you put a new piece of equipment into operation. Be sure the coupler is free to pivot from side to side without any binds or jerks. Try coupling it to a coupler on another car by pushing the two cars together on the track, by hand, so you can feel if it takes too much pressure to get the two to couple. Sometimes small wisps of plastic or small ridges of "flash" must be sliced off cleanly with a sharp hobby knife in order to get the coupler to work properly.

The couplers, like the trucks beneath freight and passenger cars, are self-lubricating, so if someone has applied any oil or grease, it should be cleaned away before it has a chance to attract dust and lint.

Dummy Couplers

Many N scale locomotives and cars are now fitted with couplers that look like the Micro-Trains couplers but do not pivot open or closed (Figure 16-5). These couplers will couple with Micro-Trains couplers or with the Atlas coupler and they will, of course couple with each other, but you must lift one of the cars far enough to disengage or engage the coupler. Because the knuckle-style couplers don't actually operate, they are usually referred to as "dummy" couplers. If you don't care about the magnetic uncoupling feature, you can replace the Rapido couplers with dummy knuckle couplers from Red Caboose, Inter-Mountain, Kato, Con-Cor and others.

To replace the couplers, use a jeweler's screwdriver to pry the trucks from the car (Figure 16-6). To replace the couplers, use your fingertips or a small pair of needle-nose pliers to hold the Rapido coupler (Figure 16-7). Gently twist the coupler 90 degrees and the tee-shaped shank should snap from a horizontal to a vertical position in the coupler pocket. You can then wiggle the coupler out and down to remove it. To replace the coupler with a dummy, insert the dummy coupler with the operating end twisted 90 degrees to the side so one leg of the tee-shaped shank will slip into the notch in the coupler pocket. Engage the coil spring on the small peg on the rear of the coupler as you insert the coupler (Figure 16-7). Move the coupler up and down to be sure it is seated properly and use the Micro-Trains 1055 Coupler Height Gauge (Figure 16-13) to be sure the height is correct. If you need to adjust the height up or down, simply bend the coupler pocket up or down.

Figure 16-5. The most common N scale truck-mounted couplers (top to bottom): Micro-Trains, Rapido and dummy knuckle-style.

An aerial view of Buzz Lenander's 2-by-8-foot NTRAK refinery module. Note that the three NTRAK "standard" tracks can be routed so there are only parallel for the last four-inches from the extreme ends of the module.

Bill Denton uses Micro-Engineering flex track with code 55 rail for his trackwork. He cuts, files, and solders nickel silver code 55 rail to build his own turnouts.

The members of the Tulsa, Oklahoma NTRAK modular group assembled this 4-by-4-foot corner module. The pueblo was assembled from 1/16-inch thick balsa wood sheets, with the edge sanded smooth and coated with wall sizing.

An aerial view of the Tulsa, Oklahoma NTRAK club's corner module. On the module, that inner track is modeled as an abandoned line with a new track (with red ballast) leading away from the remaining two tracks. The module is usually interfaced with a 2-by-4-foot module that brings the inner of the three main tracks back into the NTRAK standard alignment.

Rich Romando built this 7-by-11-foot N scale layout from 1-by-4 lumber. The entire layout is rigged so it can be lifted by an electric wench to be stored against the ceiling of his two-car garage. There are more photos of the layout and the rigging in Chapter 2.

Rich Romando modified an Atlas plan for a 4-by-8-foot layout to fit his 7-by-11-foot area. His layout has the broader 19-inch or larger radius curves that are suggested for the more realistic N scale layouts.

Wayne and Bill Reid have recreated the Cumberland Valley, in Maryland, on their N scale layout. There are more photographs and a track plan of the layout in Chapter 3. Most of the foliage, including the rows of cabbages, is made from Woodland Scenics ground foam.

The town in the distance is Winchester, an NTRAK module that is part of Wayne and Bill Reid's Cumberland Valley System.

The Pennsylvania Railroad's tracks are in the foreground, with the Western Maryland's in the background as both lines cross Rush Run on Wayne and Bill Reid's Cumberland Valley System.

Wayne and Bill Reid's model of Shippensburg captures the atmosphere of towns along the real Cumberland Valley. Most of the structures are modified plastic or resin kits.

Bob Carrey used 1/16-inch dowels and HO scale 1-by-2 stripwood from Northeastern to scratchbuild this tall trestle on his N scale shelf-style layout. The river is casting resin.

Robert Mohr used a variety of injection-modeled plastic and resin structure kits to build a city on a 2-by-4-foot module. He added another 2-by-4-foot module on each end to allow the passenger terminal that is below the city to sweep back into the three-track NTRAK standard. There's another photo of his layout in Chapter 4.

Al Mack's much-reduced N scale recreation of the Southern Pacific railroad's Tehachapi Loop in N scale. There's more on his layout in Chapter 3.

Al Mack uses Kato Unit-Track for the entire 6 scale miles of trackwork on his 14-by-18-foot Southern Pacific layout. Al decided to cement loose ballast to the track, but the newer Kato track has more realistic ballast that can be left as-is. There's more information on track with built-in ballast, like Kato, in Chapter 7.

The single street in the real town of Thurmond, West Virginia fronts the railroad tracks. Paul Fulks has recreated that scene, along with a model of the C & O coaling tower he scratch-built from Evergreen Scale Models and Plastruct styrene plastic shapes and sheet, on his NTRAK multi-module set. There's a plan of his module and some of the other club modules in Chapter 4.

Paul Fulks included all the major structures that stand in Thurmond, West Virginia on the Chesapeake and Ohio Railroad on two 2-by-6-foot NTRAK modules joined to make a 2-by-12-foot "multi-module set." His layout is part of the New River Subdivision NTRAK modular club.

The array of the New River Subdivision club's NTRAK multi-module sets as seen from looking down the New River on Matt Schaeffer's recreation of Hawk's Nest, West Virginia multi-module set. Paul Fulk's Thurmond scene is just out of sight to the left.

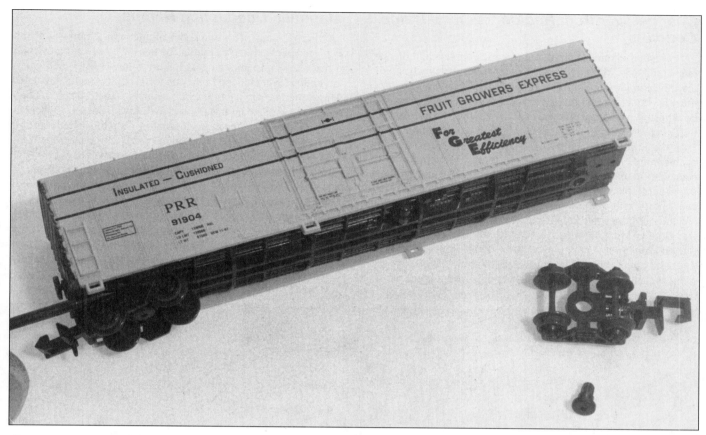

Figure 16-6. Pry the trucks from the car to replace truck-mounted couplers.

Figure 16-7. Twist the Rapido coupler 90-degrees and pull its tee-shaped shank from the coupler pocket.

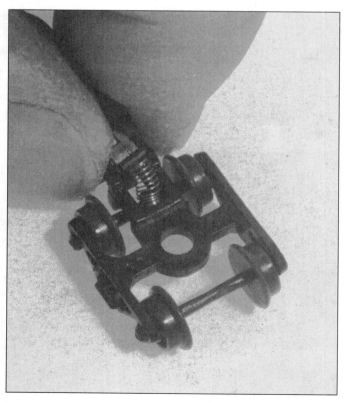

Figure 16-8. Insert the knuckle-style coupler and twist it 90-degrees until the tee-shaped shank snaps into place. Be sure the coil spring is in its proper place.

Change-over from Rapido to Micro-Trains Couplers

The Micro-Trains and Atlas automatic couplers and the various brands of "dummy" knuckle couplers are much smaller than the Rapido coupler. The smaller size means that the track must be smoother and more even and that the couplers must all be adjusted so they are the exact same heights. Some modelers find it's more trouble than they are willing to face and just stick with the Rapido couplers. You can test a few pairs of Micro-Trains couplers by simply buying a few Micro-Trains freight cars. Buy a pair of Micro-Trains trucks with truck-mounted couplers. Replace one of the trucks on just one end of one of the cars fitted with Rapido couplers. That car will serve as an "adapter" car so you can make up trains with cars that have both Rapido and Micro-Trains couplers. Mount the second truck on one end of another car equipped with Rapido couplers and have a second adapter car. Run trains with this mix of car and couplers and decide for yourself which coupler you prefer.

Magnetic Uncoupling Ramps

Micro-Trains offers two styles of uncoupling ramps: one that is placed between the rails after the ties have been cut away with a razor saw, and another that is buried in a 3-by-3-inch cavity cut about 1/8-inch deep in the roadbed (before the track is laid). These ramps are permanent magnets. The ramps include instructions on their installation and suggestions on where to place them. Atlas and Kato also offer standard-length straight track sections with built-in magnetic ramps (Figure 16-9). There will be places, like between two turnouts, where you do not have room for a track section with built-in magnetic ramp. To install the Micro-Trains 1310 Between-the-Ties ramps use a razor saw to slice through the ties to leave a gap the width of the ramp (Figure 16-10). Test-fit the ramp to be sure the height is that described in the instructions. You may need to cut a few cardboard shims to raise the ramp slightly. When the height is correct, cement the ramp (and shims) in place with artist's Matte Medium (Figure 16-11).

Figure 16-9. Atlas and Kato (shown on Al Mack's layout) offer straight track sections with built-in magnetic ramps to actuate Micro-Trains or Atlas couplers.

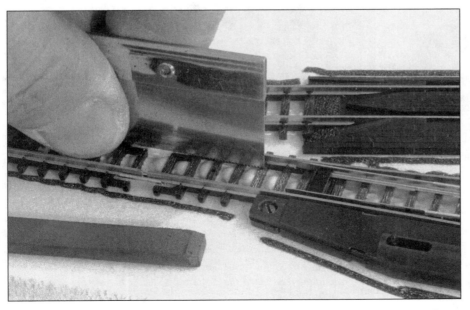

Figure 16-10. Use a razor saw to remove the center of the ties to install a Micro-Trains magnetic uncoupling ramp.

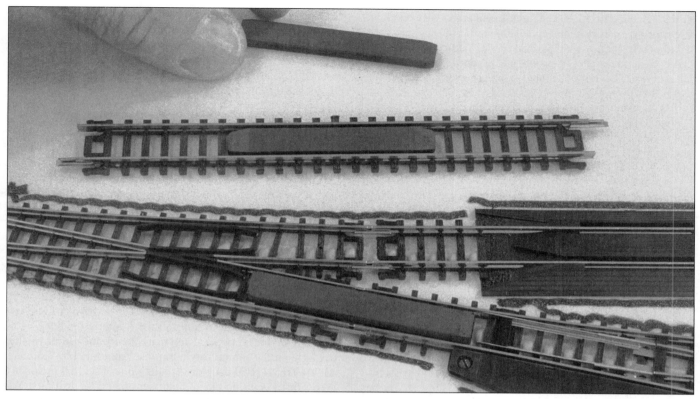

Figure 16-11. Position the ramp exactly as described in the instructions, then cement it in place with artists Matte Medium.

Installing Automatic Knuckle Couplers

Micro-Trains manufactures three different lengths of replacement couplers for passenger and freight cars, each with the "standard" tee-shaped shank. The couplers may require some slight trimming on the stock trucks for some applications and they are furnished with complete instructions. I suggest you buy all three so you'll have a proper coupler for any truck-mounted coupler pocket design. The installation procedure is exactly the same as that for replacing Rapido couplers with dummy knuckle couplers. It is important, however, that the height of both the Micro-Trains couplers and the coupler's metal actuating hose be precisely correct. Use the Micro-Trains 1055 Coupler Height Gauge to check each coupler. If the couplers are too high or low, you can usually bend the coupler pocket near the bolster to raise or lower the coupler. If the coupler height is okay but the hose is too high or to low, bend the hose to the correct position with needle-nose pliers. Micro-Trains also makes offset couplers that can be used to raise the coupler about 1/16-inch for some applications. Micro-Trains includes lubrication and installation instructions with each package of couplers.

Micro-Trains makes several dozen coupler and pilot end kits to fit their couplers to nearly every N scale steam or diesel locomotive ever made. Some of the Micro-Trains installation kits for older N scale locomotives (with a huge hole in the pilot or end beam) include a fill-in piece to reduce the size of the hole and provide mounting for the couplers. The Micro-Trains catalog lists all of the applications and, as new locomotives are introduced, Micro-Trains either produces a new coupler-mounting kit or can suggest which of the existing kits will fit the locomotive. In some of the newer locomotives, the coupler can merely be replaced with one of the tee-shank Micro-Trains couplers as described earlier.

Micro-Trains sells a number 1055 coupler height gauge (Figure 18-12) that is an essential tool for reliable coupler operation. The gauge is a cast metal device that holds a coupler and rests on the track. Some modelers glue a 12-inch-long piece of track to a board and mount the Micro-Trains Number 1055 gauge permanently to the track as a test track. Place the car or locomotive with the new Micro-Trains couplers installed on the track and roll the coupler up to the gauge. The height of the coupler and the height of the uncoupling pin must match the gauge. If the pin or coupler is too high, the couplers won't operate properly. If the pin is too low it can catch on the turnouts and cause derailments.

Body-Mounting Micro-Trains Couplers

All of the N scale freight cars and passenger cars are furnished with couplers and pockets attached to the trucks. Modelers call these Talgo-style trucks. The truck-mounted coupler system dates back to Lionel toy trains in the thirties and was needed to allow cars to negotiate very small-radius curves without derailing. If you must use 9-3/4-inch and 11-inch radius N scale curves, then you may need to retain the truck-mounted couplers. If, however, you are building a layout with 19-inch or larger curves or if your operations are primarily on NTRAK modules, you may want to consider removing the couplers and pockets from the trucks and mounting them on the bodies.

Truck-mounted couplers impart a toy-like appearance because the car must be raised at least an N scale foot and the lower edges of both ends of the car are cutaway to clear the swinging coupler pocket. The truck-mounted couplers work just fine when a train is being pulled forward, but they can cause derailments when a train is backed up, particularly over ess bends or through sets of turnouts that produce sudden right and left curves. The body-mounted couplers cause fewer derailments, however, if a train is being backed up.

The technique for providing body-mount couplers begins with the purchase a new pair of Micro-Trains 1025 assembled couplers and pockets. The couplers include mounting screws and they are also available unassembled as part number 1023. Micro-Trains offers five other styles of body-mount couplers that can be useful on cars that have a very small mounting area like hoppers, covered hoppers and tank cars. Try installing the couplers on a boxcar or reefer first to understand what to do. You must also have a Micro-Trains 1055 Coupler Height Gauge.

Use a jeweler's screwdriver to gently pry between the lower sides of the body and the frame, to lever the frame from the body. Use the jeweler's screwdriver to pry the trucks from the underframe. Spread the truck sideframes and remove the wheelsets. You can use small flush-cut diagonal cutters to remove the coupler pockets from the trucks, but keep the cutters as far from the edges of the truck-mounting hole as possible so you do not damage the hole. If you'd prefer, you can simply replace the trucks. Micro-Trains offers six different styles of freight car trucks and both 4-wheel and 6-wheel passenger trucks without coupler pockets. I would also suggest you buy new Micro-Trains truck-mounting pins to be sure the pins fit the trucks properly. Reinstall the wheelsets (or better, replace the wheelsets with NorthWest Short Line or InterMountain metal wheelsets) and mount the trucks (now without coupler pockets) on the frame.

Use a pair of tweezers to hold the assembled Micro-Trains 1025 coupler and pocket in position on one end of the car while you place the underframe and trucks on the track. Hold the Micro-Trains 1055 Coupler Height Gauge near the coupler to see if the coupler must be raised or lowered. Usually, the cou-

pler will be about 1/16-inch too high. Look at the distance between the wheel flanges and the bottom of the frame to see how much you could remove from the underframe's bolster without the wheels touching the underframe. Remove the trucks. Use a flat file to remove as much of that excess-height dimension from the underframe bolster (the flat area on the frame where the trucks contact the frame) so you are lowering the car as much as possible as well as the coupler. Be careful when you file to keep the bolster perfectly flat so the car will not lean. Also, test-fit the trucks after you have removed just a bit of material from the bolster to be certain the wheels do not touch the frame. Remove the same amount of material from both bolsters. Reassemble the trucks and hold the coupler in place to recheck its height with the 1055 Gauge. You might also have to insert a spacer or shim between the top of the coupler pocket and the bottom of the frame to lower the coupler a bit further. If so, you can cut the shim from a strip of Evergreen .010-by-.125-inch plastic. Insert the shim between the coupler pocket and the frame and check the coupler height again. One shim will probably be enough, particularly if it was possible to remove a significant amount from the bolster, but you can use two or more.

Remove the trucks and install the frame in the body. Hold the coupler pocket in place and mark the location of its mounting hole on the frame. Buy a pin vise from a hobby store and Micro-Trains 1059 coupler-installation tool set that includes a 00-90 thread-cutting tap and number 56 and 62 drill bits. You can buy the tap and drill bits separately. I would suggest you buy at least four of the number 62 drill bits because you will break some learning the technique. The number 56 drill bit is only needed if you need to clean-out the hole in the coupler pocket that might have become clogged with cement. Chuck the number 62 drill bit in the pin vise and drill through the hole you have marked. Then, thread the 00-90 tap through the hole. Finally, use the 00-90 screw supplied with the 1025 couplers to mount the coupler pocket (Figure 16-12). Repeat the process on the opposite end of the car. In some cases, you will

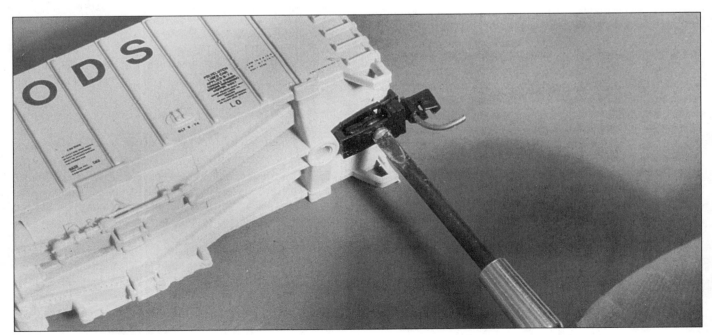

Figure 16-12. Install Micro-Trains number 1025 couplers and pockets on the frame of the car with the 00-90 screw provided with the couplers.

discover that the hole is located right at the end of the frame. For those rare instances, use a triangular jeweler's file to file a notch to just clear the 00-90 screw and attach the screw and the coupler pocket with Walthers Goo or Goodyear Pliobond (so you can pry them free if you need to replace the coupler). Be careful to keep the Goo or Pliobond from the moving parts of the coupler.

Check the height of the coupler and the metal trip pin with the 1055 gauge once again (Figure 16-13), and test-run the car with others to be sure the coupler is functioning properly. Each body-mount coupler installation is different. Most of the installations are described and illustrated, step-by-step in *The Journal Of N Scale Modeling*, published by *Railmodel Journal*.

Micro-Trains does not offer body-mounted couplers on any of their freight cars. Micro-Trains (and some other manufacturers) usually does however, provide a small dimple in the frame to indicate where to drill the hole for body-mount couplers. If you want to body-mount couplers on Micro-Trains cars, you must still cut-off the coupler pockets. It is seldom possible, however, to simply attach the Micro-Trains couplers you just cut from the trucks onto the body. The truck-mounted coupler pockets are so thick they interfere with the wheels and axles on the trucks. You can, however, modify those leftover Micro-Trains couplers and coupler pockets. The coupler pockets have an unusual cover with a tab that does not appear on the Micro-Trains coupler pockets (like the numbers 1023 or 1025) intended for mounting on the body or frame of the car. The tabs interfere with the axles when you try to install the pockets on the floor of the car.

To eliminate the problem, try flattening the coupler pocket tabs into the corners of the pocket with a hot soldering iron (a woodburning tool will also work). This is a delicate procedure because too much heat, held for too long, will fuse the coupler to the inside of the pocket and too little heat or time will not remove enough material. You want to push the tab down flush with the bottom of the coupler pocket (so the tab won't hit the axle) and still allow it to retain the other half of the coupler pocket. Work outdoors because the melting plastic gives off fumes that are definitely hazardous to your health. Be careful, too, of the hot plastic.

Figure 16-13. Check the height of any Micro-Trains coupler and actuating wire with the Micro-Trains 1055 Coupler Height Gauge (right).

Chapter 17

Real Railroad Action

Your model railroad is most like the real thing when the trains are moving. You have nothing more than a three-dimensional sculpture until you add the action of the trains. That's what this chapter is all about; how to move your fleet of freight and passenger cars around the layout in the same manner the real railroads do, but without any of the paperwork.

There's also an "almost-magic" method of installing four switches and some track so you can switch open-top cars (like hopper cars loaded with coal) into an industry and pull unloaded cars out (or vice versa). This is called "Loads-in/Empties-out" operations and I'll explain it in detail later.

All of these operations can, of course, be performed with a temporary layout on a tabletop. You really do not even need the actual industry buildings, just small cards with the name of the industry beside the siding will do for now. You may even want to try operating for a while before you decide which industries you might actually want to build for your layout and exactly where you want to locate industrial sidings.

Achieving Authenticity

One of the problems that a model railroader must face is a lack of credibility. We have to keep reminding ourselves that our miniatures often aren't real enough, and we don't need some glaring toy-like sight to make it more difficult for our imaginations to work. The switching suggestions you'll find here in the "Waybill" system will allow you to move freight cars into and out of industrial sidings almost exactly as though those cars were indeed carrying freight. That scene will be silly, though, if you try to imagine that an empty flatcar really does have a load after it leaves the factory that was supposed to have "loaded" it. The "Loads-in/Empties-out" system is one way around the problem because it will really put "loads" in those cars.

There are other easy ways of tricking even your own imagination. First, try to include as many industries as you can that would ship and receive something in the same kind of car. A furniture factory might receive fine hardwood in a boxcar and ship furniture out in the same car. An electricity-generating power plant might receive hopper carloads of coal and ship almost identical-appearing carloads of coke. An intermodal terminal is just as likely to receive flat carloads of full trailers or containers as it is to ship similar loads. Second, try to "load" flat cars and gondolas with only a partial load, so they can be considered either "empty" or "full." Load a few of those intermodal "Piggyback"-style flat cars with just one trailer. Both methods will add to the "power of suggestion."

The Waybill System

Each shipment made by a real railroad is the result of dozens of papers that order the shipment and the car that will hold it and route that car to the customer. Paperwork is seldom enjoyable enough to become a hobby, and we certainly don't need it to operate a model railroad. But you should have some system of directing the flow of each and every car over your railroad, so that your line will have the appearance of really moving goods, not just freight cars.

The waybill system will make every car have a definite purpose as it moves empty or loaded with a specific commodity bound for a specific destination. The system requires only a 2-by-3-inch clear plastic envelope (billfold photo-carriers will do)

Figure 17-1. The vacant space beside the intermodal yard at Alliance (on the Union Pacific layout) is used, here, to hold the box of waybills and car envelopes.

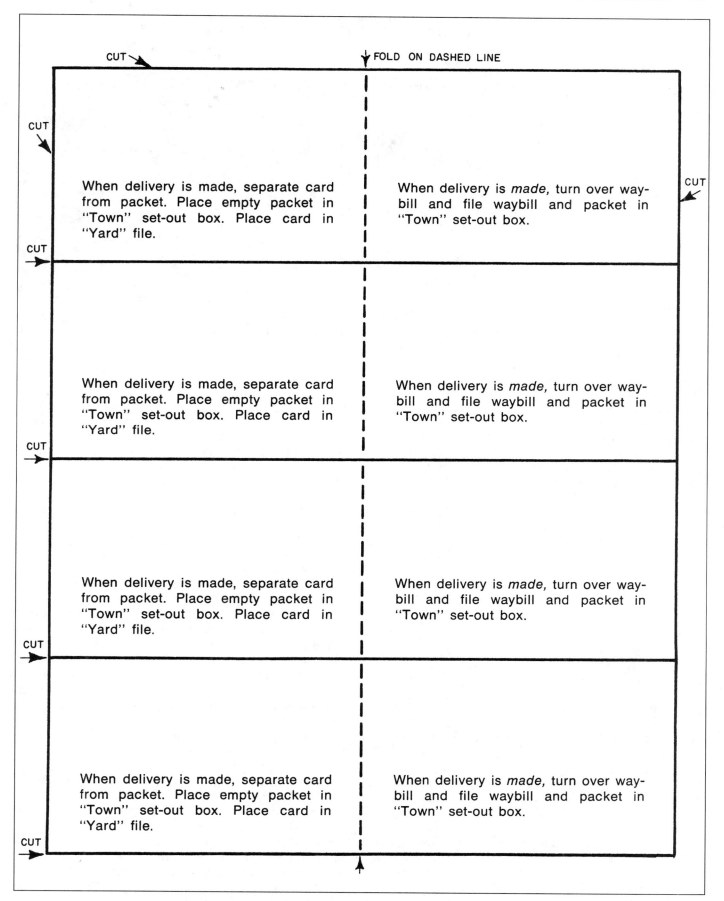

Figure 17-2. Four waybills that can be photocopied and cut apart.

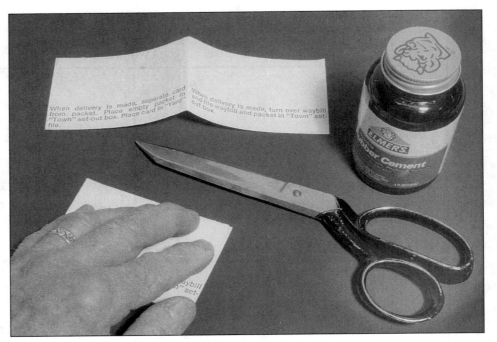

Figure 17-3. Cut out the waybills, fold them, and cement the halves together with rubber cement.

for each and every freight car you operate. A self-adhesive white sticker is applied to the upper-left corner of each clear plastic envelope and the label is marked to show the car's railroad initials and the car number. The envelope then "follows" that car wherever it goes on your layout. A small box can be glued to the side of the table near every town to hold the envelopes for any cars that may be sitting in that town. The envelopes for cars in trains are simply carried by the engineer (that's you) along with the walk-around throttle.

Place a larger file box near whatever area you consider to be your main yard, like Alliance on the 6-by-6-foot Union Pacific layout to hold the cars stored there (Figure 17-1). Put some dividers in the box for stock, refrigerator (reefer), tank, flat, box, gondola, hopper, and covered hopper cars to make it easier to find them when you need a specific car and its matching card. That main yard may well be the shelf or box where you store the cars that you don't have room for on the layout!

Waybills

The second part of the system is the waybills themselves. These are patterned after the waybills the real railroads use with most shipments, but they are somewhat simpler and are much more "powerful" and versatile in directing the railroad crew's actions. Four blank waybills are included in Figure 17-2. Make photocopies of that page so you will have about four times as many waybills as you do freight cars. Because waybills are supposed to be folded in half, you need only one-sided copies. You can then cut the waybills apart, apply some rubber cement to the backside, and fold them to give a two-ply piece of paper that is about as stiff as cardboard (Figure 17-3). You might want to spray them with clear paint (the same kind you use on your models after decal applications) so they will last "forever" without any fingerprint-grease smudges. Save the clear coat, though, until you've used the waybills for a week or so and you know the information on them is the information you need. Each of the waybills must be filled out to indicate how its particular commodity should be transported.

Shipping and Receiving

You will use the waybills to decide which cars to move and where to move them. The first consideration, when creating the waybills, however, will be the industries and other "sources" of freight on your own railroad. On a pad of paper, list each of the industries you plan to locate on the sidings of your layout. The industries don't have to be there yet, but the sidings must be, so you'll have a place to spot that freight car. The copy-and-cutout station and industrial signs in Chapter 9 will give you an idea of the different types of industry you might choose, and there are others indicated on the key to the 6-by-6-foot Union Pacific layout in Chapter 3 (Figure 3-4).

Write down the goods or commodities that might be received by each industry under an "IN" column and the goods or commodities it might ship under an "OUT" column. There is no reason why any industry would ship or receive everything by rail, however. A power plant, for instance, would receive coal, but it would "ship" electrical power over wires rather than over rails. And some firms, like warehouses, would ship small boxes of manufactured products by truck, or a concrete plant might receive raw materials like coal or ore by barge or conveyor. You'll need to do this paperwork only once; when it and the waybills are completed, operations will only involve placing cards in the clear plastic "car" envelopes. You can also add additional goods or commodities to the list to make more waybills after you have used the system for a few months and you are more familiar with the kind of freight traffic your railroad needs.

Add two more columns beside each of those industries for "TO" and "FROM." List all of the places that each industry might ship those commodities to in the "OUT" column and the places where it might get the stuff from in the "IN" column. Those places can be other industries on your own railroad. A fuel dealer for instance, might receive its coal from the coal mine on your layout. About half of the places should be "off" your layout because that's a bit more like real life; few railroads are lucky enough to have both the shipper and the receiver.

Filling Out the Waybill

You can now use your list of industries and their shipments to fill in both sides of the waybills. Begin on the side of each waybill that ends with the sentence "Place card in 'Yard' file." Then, follow these steps:

1. Write "TO:" and list the name of the town where the industry is located, followed by the name of the industry.

2. List the type of car that would be used for the commodity that that industry "receives." (This is the "IN" commodity from your list.) Then write "Empty—For Loading."

3. Turn the card over, and write "TO:" and the destination for that industry's products. The destination can be a bit tricky, but it's logical if you think it out: List the name of any city (say, Chicago) as the destination, write "VIA" (meaning "through"), the name of the town on your layout, and the interchange track in that town (write "Interchange").

4. Note the type of car, just as you did on the opposite side of the waybill, but here add the words "Carload" (or "Loaded") and the commodity the car will actually carry.

That completes the standard waybill. A variation would be simply to list the town and industry name for a "receiver" industry that is actually on your layout. Make about four cards, each with a different destination, for each industry on your layout.

You will also want to make some variations on those "standard" cards to suit particular industries and track situations. If the car is a flat car or a gondola, try to list a "load" on both sides of the waybill so there will be no "Empty—For Loading," just two different loads. You can do the same thing for any type of car that might appear on both the "IN" and "OUT" lists for a specific industry.

Interchanges

It is most common for a shipment to be loaded on one railroad and transferred (railroads use the word "interchanged") with three or four or more other railroads before it reaches its final destination. For our purposes, the "off-line" places can be marked simply "interchange," and one end of a stub-end siding can be designated as the "industry interchange."

I suggest that you put a rerailer track section at the end of that siding so your "interchange" area can be the box or shelf where you store extra cars. That way, cars destined for interchange really do travel off the layout—you pick them up by hand and place them on the storage shelf or box and select new cars to be replaced on the layout at that same "interchange" track. The interchange track may also be a simple tunnel, such as track "IBN" (the interchange with the Burlington Northern Railroad) on the Union Pacific layout in Chapter 3 (Figure 3-4).

You can also use a passing siding (such as the track "ISF," the AT&SF RR interchange) on the Union Pacific layout as an interchange track. Designate one end as "IN"—it's at "Bedford" on the Union Pacific layout—so you can just keep adding cars until they appear for "pickup" at the other end of the siding—at "Duncan" on the Union Pacific layout.

"Empty—For Loading"

If you do add a pair of passing sidings for the "Loads-In/Empties-Out" operations, you'll need a special card for the cars that are always empty. It should read: "Empty—For Loading" on both sides. That lists the town the "empty" is picked up from in place of the preprinted word "Yard" on both sides of the card. Cross out the sentence "Place card in Yard file" because the car (and the card) will never get back to the yard.

Make another type of card for the cars that are always loaded, which reads: "Carload of Coal" (or whatever the commodity) on both sides of the card. Cross out the word "Yard" on both sides of this card and list the name of the town that ships that load. Cross out the sentence "Place card in Yard file" on these cards too. The cars that have these special cards will be cycled back and forth through "their" industry until you decide to pull the cards and insert them in some other cars' clear plastic envelopes. The cards in Figure 17-4 that read "TO: Corning..." on both sides and "TO: Alliance..." on both sides are examples of the "Loads-In/Empties-Out" cards.

The "Yard" File

The waybill system of operation begins when you pick some of the waybills at random that match the types of cars in your "yard" area. On the Union Pacific layout (Figure 3-4), the" yard" would be the trackage at Alliance. Follow the directions on those cards to switch the now-loaded cars onto the appropriate sidings. From that point on the system is self-perpetuating, so long as you follow the instructions on the waybills. Keep the extra waybills in that "yard" file and return the "used" waybills to the rear of the pack of waybills. Draw fresh ones each time you're ready to operate a train. Figure 17-5 shows how the car (and its clear plastic envelope) originates in the "yard" where the waybill is inserted. The waybill is then turned over (according to its own printed instructions), and that car is ready to be picked up by the next train through town. In some cases, the car may go directly back to the yard, or, in the case of "Loads-in/Empties-out," operations, the car may never go back to the yard. If you want the car to sit on the siding for awhile, add another "hold" card with a note stating it is to be picked up after one or more passes ("days" or "weeks") by the freight trains through town.

Find a box large enough to hold 40 or so of the clear plastic envelopes and use it to store your Waybills and empty car envelopes. Make dividers for each type of car like "Boxcar", Caboose", "Covered Hopper", "Flatcar", "Gondola" and "Tank-car". You can purchase pocket protector envelopes large enough to hold a dozen "car" envelopes and that can be your "train" or you can simply use a large paper clip to hold the pile of envelopes together that make up each "train" (Figure 17-6).

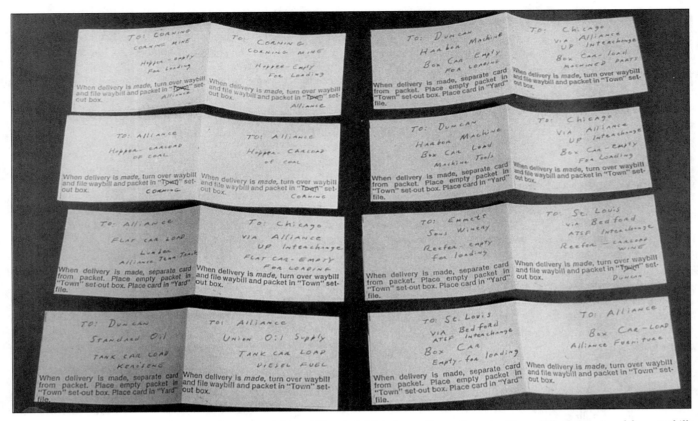

Figure 17-4. Eight sample waybills, including (upper left) two "Loads-in/Empties-out", two "standard" waybills (bottom) and four waybills with cars routed to the interchange tracks.

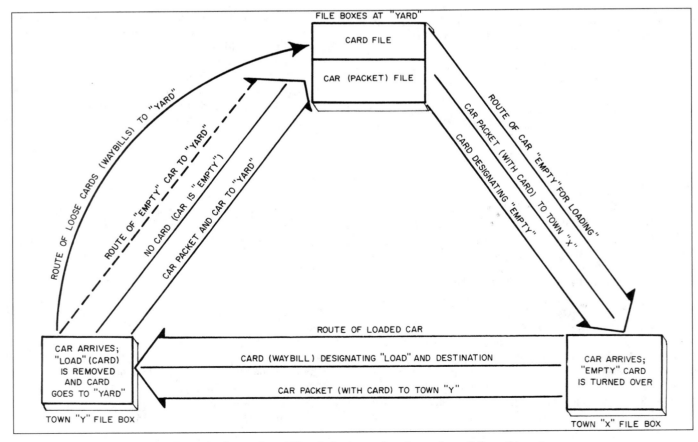

Figure 17-5. The "cycle" for each standard type of waybill and plastic envelope for each car follows this pattern.

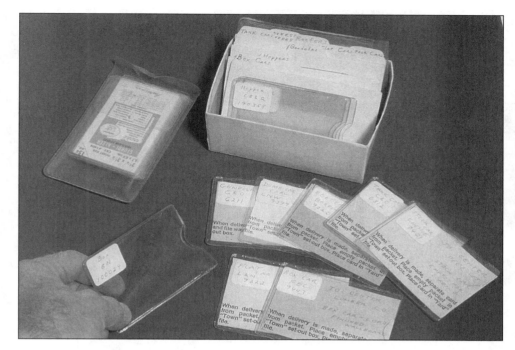

Figure 17-6. Make an empty plastic envelope for every car. The waybill "loads" are inserted into the envelopes. "Trains" of car envelopes can be collected in clear plastic pocket protectors (upper, left). The waybills can be stored in the file box.

Loads-In/Empties-Out

Most of the commodities that are loaded into hoppers or gondolas are raw materials that are used by another industry, so the flow of traffic is mostly a repetitive pattern of loaded cars traveling to the industry and empty cars traveling back to the commodity source for reloading. Hoppers loaded with coal for a power plant or to be dumped into ships, gravel traveling from a quarry to a cement plant, iron ore traveling to a steel mill or to be dumped into ships, and logs traveling from the mountains to the sawmill are other examples of heavy traffic flow that are popular prototypes for model railroaders.

All of these involve the use of cars that are most obviously loaded in one direction and unloaded in the opposite direction—a difficult challenge for the modeler, because it would be too time consuming to load these tiny N scale cars. The answer to this is the concept known as "Loads-in/Empties-out."

"Loads-in/Empties-out" concept requires a model of both the shipping industry (a coal mine, for example) and the primary receiving industry (say, a power plant). Either industry may also use cars from or to other sources, but the majority of the traffic is between the two. The "unit trains" that carry a hundred carloads of coal, and that never uncouple as they cycle from Colorado mines to Illinois power plants, are a modern example of such traffic. The modern era trains of nothing but hoppers or coal-carrying gondolas are often operated as a single set of cars called "Unit" trains. Unit trains are a variation on the "Loads-in/Empties-out" system where the entire train, not just a few cars, is run right into the coal mine and the power plant. On a model railroad, you can have one N scale hopper be the equivalent of 10 prototype cars so your 10-car "unit" coal train represents a 100-car train on the prototype.

Each industry must have two tracks of its own, and the two must be located near each other on your layout. They could be separated visually by a mountain like the Union Pacific layout (layout), a tall and thick forest, or by a painted sky backdrop, or some other feature that breaks any visual connection between the two industries. The two sidings appear to be stub-ended at each industry, but, in fact, they connect inside a tun-

Figure 17-7. Loaded cars of coal are picked up from the Corning Mining Company on the track to the left beneath the coal bunker. Empties are delivered to the track to the right of the coal bunker.

At the Corning Mining Company , loaded cars are picked up on the track beneath the coal bunker and empty cars are left on the track to the right of the coal bunker.

nel between the two industries. The two tracks that lead into the "Corning Mine" (Figure 17-7) on the 6-by-6-foot Union Pacific layout (layout) in Chapter 3 are actually the same two tracks that lead into the "Consolidated Edison Company" coal bunker (Figure 17-9) at Alliance.

You can see the two tracks in the "satellite" view in Chapter 3 (Figure 3-4), but the mountain effectively blocks any connection between the Alliance and Corning from normal viewing angles. It helps the illusion if the tracks enter each industry from slightly different directions. The right-hand track into the mine receives only empty hoppers; and loaded hoppers are picked up only on the left-hand track at the mine. At the power plant, the left-hand track into the coal bunker receives only empty hoppers; and loaded hoppers are picked up only on the right-hand track at the power plant. Those "loaded" cars are actually shoved through the mountain by other loaded cars being delivered to the power plant. The empty hoppers that are pushed into the mine will eventually be pushed out from the power plant as empties. It takes about six cars to fill each track, on this model railroad, so the seventh car into the mine will always push the first car out the power plant's end. The system provides an endless supply of loaded hoppers at the mine and an endless supply of empty hoppers at the power plant.

The "Loads-in/Empties-out" system does exactly what its name implies. It allows you to have extremely realistic operations, which include empty cars traveling toward a mine and carloads of coal traveling toward the power plant. Notice that no locomotive actually travels through the tunnel that connects the mine and the power plant. The cars alone are pushed, by other cars, through the tunnel.

If you want to simulate the operation of modern unit coal trains, you can operate a single complete train of loaded hoppers with a permanently coupled locomotive and caboose. You will need matching trains with identical car numbers and identical weathering, however. One set of cars would be filled with coal and the other set would be empty. When the train of empty hoppers entered the mine on the right track, you would hold it there and wait a moment before flipping the block switch, which would allow the second train of loaded cars to exit on the left track, thus simulating the loading cycle. The process would be repeated when the loaded train reached the power plant, except that the train of empties would appear after the train of loaded cars disappeared. I prefer the individual-car method over the "unit-train" operation, but you can take your choice with the same trackwork and industries. You would alter only the shape of the industries to duplicate the "Loads-in/Empties-out" coal-hauling operations with gravel, ore, or logs.

Timetable Operations

You can establish a timetable just like the real railroads when you establish a point-to-point run, such as that for the layouts in Chapters 2, 3 and 4. Time the amount of seconds it takes for a train to travel from one "town" (siding) to the next and call the seconds "minutes." Duplicate the general format of any real railroad timetable. There is, I feel, a better way to run a railroad in miniature than to spend your leisure hours "watching the clock." Timetable operations really are necessary on some of the gigantic club layouts, where there may be as many as twenty trains on the tracks at the same time. The timetable that helps to keep the real trains from running into each other works on these club layouts as well. Most home layouts, however, are operated by just one person for most of their sessions, and, at most, there may be three operators.

The 6-by-6-foot Union Pacific layout plans in Chapter 3 (Figures 3-5 and 3-6), the 8-by-11-foot plan in Chapter 3 (Figure 3-13) and the 6-by-6-foot "Double-Track Mainline" plan in Chapter 4 (Figure 4-5) are large enough to keep three people busy on an operating night. One person is in the "yards" making up trains, while the other two are operating trains out on the main line. Another blocking switch must be added to allow the yard areas to be operated by a third power pack unless you are using the Digital Command Control System described in Chapter 8.

The "Sequence" Timetable

If you have as many as six trains waiting on the holding tracks or passing sidings, no more than two ever need to be running at one time. With that thought in mind, you can stage what I call "sequence" timetable operations. The sequence timetable merely means that you establish an operating pattern for your trains, such as that on the 6-by-6-foot Union Pacific layout (layout). Those trains originate in "Alliance" and travel over the route described in Chapter 3 (Figure 3-12), to arrive at Emmett as shown in the schematic diagram (Figure 17-8).

Two additional patterns can be applied to this particular layout. Every fourth or fifth train can be routed through the innermost curve at "ISF" (between Bedford and Duncan) which leads to an imaginary interchange with the Santa Fe. The operator in the "Alliance" yard then makes up a new train on that curved siding by hand-carrying cars to and from storage shelves. (The single track qualifies as what model railroaders call a "fiddle" yard, for just that reason cars are "fiddled" on and off the layout.) There is also a second stub-ended "interchange" siding at Alliance marked "IBN" for an imaginary interchange with the Burlington Northern Railroad. The two alternate routes allow you to use locomotives from different railroads to break up the pattern of running just Union Pacific trains from "Alliance" to "Points East" and return. You can choose to run one or more Burlington Northern trains that originate and the "IBN" track and, perhaps, are routed "off-line" via the Santa Fe Interchange at "ISF." Or, Santa Fe trains can originate at "ISF and, perhaps, go off-line via the Burlington Northern interchange track at Alliance. The once-a-day Amtrak passenger train can also originate or terminate at either the Burlington Northern or the Santa Fe interchange tracks for even greater variety.

A Typical Day

By stipulating that it takes one hour for a train to travel from "Alliance" to "Points East," you can create your own 24-hour day on the Union Pacific layout by completing 24 train movements over the railroad. The arrows in Figure 17-8 indicate the direction of travel of trains 5, 6, 7, 8, and 9 at eight random hours during a "typical" day. When any arrow changes direction, that train has been reversed at the "Alliance" wye.

Train 5 would be the best one to pick as that Amtrak streamliner. Train 5 makes an imaginary trip "off" on your layout and onto the Santa Fe interchange at 2:00 P.M., to reappear about 7:00 P.M., before heading back to the Burlington Northern interchange. Train 8 has a similar route and "timetable." Train 6 is a "through freight" going cross-country over our railroad. Cars would be added or taken off this train only at "Alliance." Train 7 is a "peddler freight," or "way freight," which means that it makes switching moves at almost every town (where there's a car ready to be picked up or scheduled to be dropped off all through the "waybill" process). Train 9 can be another peddler freight. There's more information on operations on the Union Pacific layout, particularly at Alliance in Chapter 3.

Staging Yard Operations

The staging yards are the places where trains are made up, usually by moving cars and locomotives by hand, before the operating session begins. The trains are then released onto the mainline to match the sequence shown on the timetable. Trains leaving the layout fill the vacated tracks as the operating session evolves. When the session is over, the trains are rearranged by hand to be ready for the next session. This is a technique that allows you to see a number of trains operating over a layout without seeing the same train making lap after lap of the layout. Staging yards are a feature of nearly every model railroad that is based on the appearance and the operations of a specific prototype railroad. Wayne and Bill Reid's Cumberland Valley System in Chapter 3 (Figure 3-22) uses hidden stub-ended staging yards. Al Mack's 14-by-18-foot Southern Pacific layout in Chapter 3 (Figure 3-18) uses the visible yards at Bakersfield and Mojave as staging yards where the trains are setup as required just before an operating session begins.

It is helpful to have three or even thirty staging tracks, but you can accomplish the same thing on a small layout by designating just one track near the edge of the benchwork as a "staging" track so you can remove each train as it completes its one path around the layout. Conversely, you "feed" new trains onto the layout, one locomotive and one car at a time on the staging yard track. It's certainly helpful to have a rerailer track or two at the stub end of the staging track to make it easier to place the locomotives and cars on the tracks. The "IBN" track on the 6-by-6-layout in Chapter 3 (Figure 3-5) and the Seaboard Railroad interchange track "ISB" and the Santa Fe Interchange track "ISF" on the 8-by-11-foot layout in Chapter 3 (Figure 3-13) can be used for this type of "hands-on" staging.

From Imaginary to Real

The waybill system, as well as every operating and construction idea on these pages, is based on the actual operations of the prototype. None of this was created for "toy trains." When you operate with the quick "through freight" system of endless oval operations to simulate cross-country trains, when you make up trains using a switch engine in the yards, when you move every freight car with the waybill system, and when you operate with a sequence timetable, you are running a real railroad in miniature. Combine all these types of operation with, perhaps, one of those Santa Fe interchange freight trains or an Amtrak passenger train added to the sequence timetable, and you can plan to keep yourself busy for years before you even think about building another railroad.

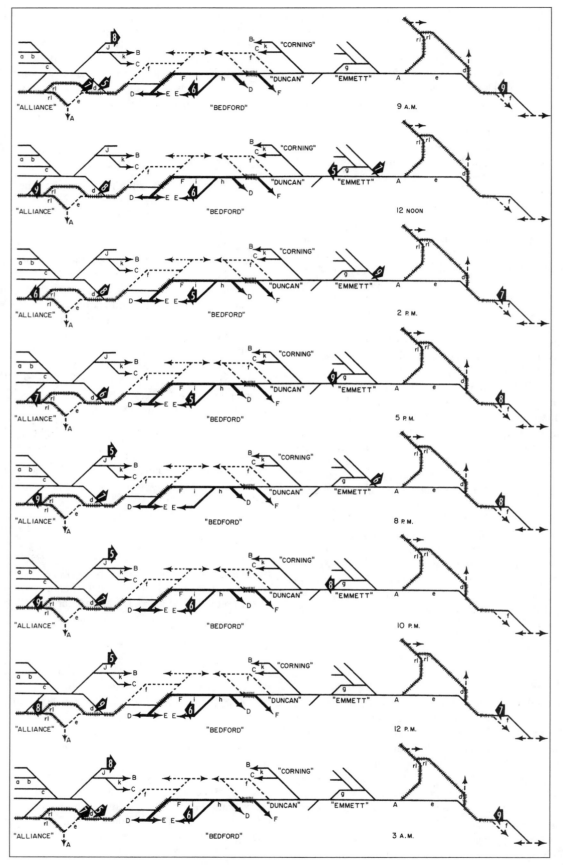

Figure 17-8. A, B, C, D, E, F, G, and H. Examples of where Trains 5, 6, 7, 8, and 9 might be at some specific "times" during a "24-hour" operating period with the use of the "sequence" timetable. This is similar to playing musical chairs but with trains.

Chapter 18

Switching Operations

Real railroads exist to deliver single carloads of commodities from one customer to another. The railroads are the most efficient means of transporting goods because those individual carloads can be consolidated into trains. A model railroader can recreate both types of railroad action; operations of full trains as described in Chapter 17, and the movement of individual cars as they are made-up into trains or as those trains are broken-down into individual cars as described in this chapter.

In truth, the real railroads often keep groups of 2 to 20 cars that frequently travel between the same customers in sets called "blocks". On a model railroad, you can designate a single car to represent a "block" of, say, 10 cars to make up for the fact that our trains are seldom the 100-car long freights of the prototype railroads.

Here are the most common real railroad switching movements. You can duplicate them precisely on your model railroad. In fact, some model railroaders even provide pauses to allow the brakeman time to disconnect or to reconnect the brake hoses and time for a brakeman that may have been dropped off to open or close a switch, to get back on the train.

Trailing Switch Maneuvers

Once you understand how to perform switching maneuvers, you'll discover why those freight trains make so many back and forth movements. And once you know the reasons for them,

you'll realize that it can be an important part of your model railroad operations. When you've learned how to perform switching movements, you may find you like that kind of action far more than just running trains. When you learn how to operate the "Waybill" switching system (discussed in Chapter 17), you may want to spend most of the time at any operating session just switching cars in and out of trains. Even without the "Waybill" system, though, you'll need to learn the basic switching moves. Then you can make-up trains and break them down, using a locomotive, rather than your hands, as a switch engine.

There are really only three basic switching moves, the "trailing-point" move, the "facing point" or "run-around" move, and the "reverse" move, which reverses a train through a wye. Since most track plans include these three, there are endless combinations. These are the only ways to move railroad cars on railroad track by pushing or pulling them with locomotives.

"Trailing-Point" Moves

The "trailing point" simply describes the direction of the turnout's points of the siding relative to the direction of the train on the main line. If the siding trails off behind the train as the train passes, it is considered a "trailing-point" siding. The direction of the train (from left to right in Figures 18-1 through 18-3) determines the type of maneuver; if the train were traveling in the opposite direction (right to left in Figures

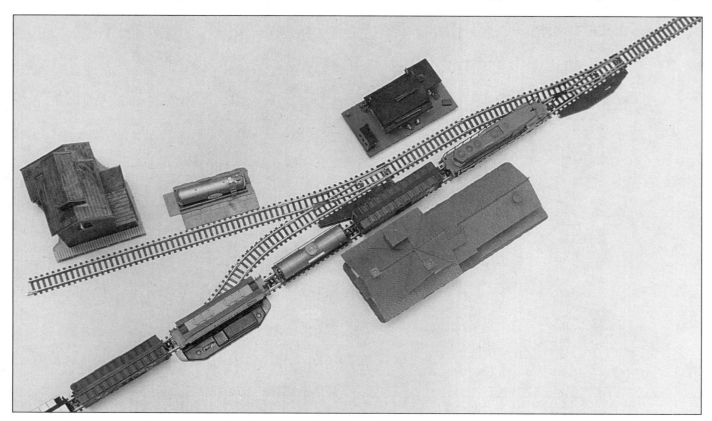

Figure 18-1. The "trailing point" switching move begins when the train crew uncouples the covered hopper and the tank car from the boxcar.

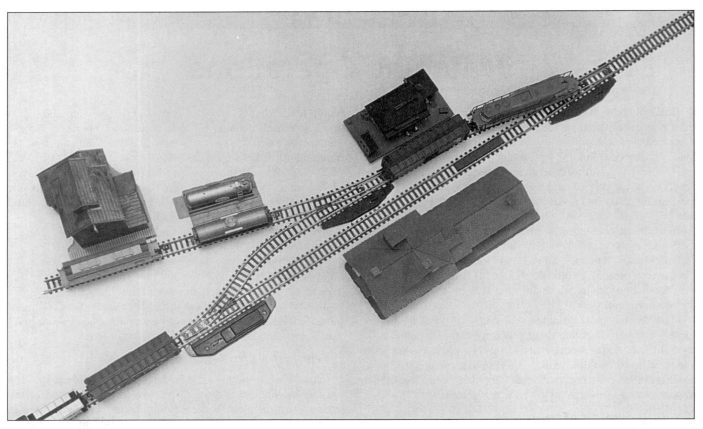

Figure 18-2. The locomotive has moved forward through the right turnout, then reversed to leave the covered hopper, then tank car, on the stub-end siding. The locomotive remains coupled to the boxcar through all these moves.

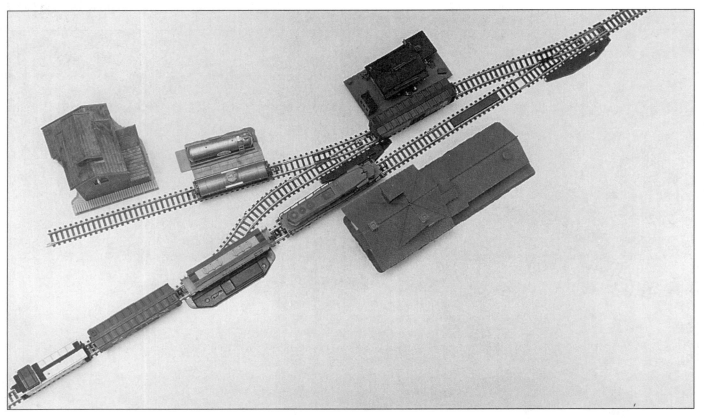

Figure 18-3. The locomotive pulls forward to the right to clear the switch points, then reverses to couple onto the train and proceeds forward on the mainline to the next town.

18-1 through 18-3), the siding and the turnout points would be facing the train. This would become a "facing-point" turnout. However, the moves necessary to get a car in or out of a siding that is a "facing point" are much more complicated than the moves needed to switch a car in or out of a "trailing-point" siding as you can see later in this chapter.

The locomotive stops its train so it can uncouple however much of the train is behind the car that is to go onto the trailing-point siding (Figure 18-1). This time, the crew has orders (Way-bills) to leave the covered hopper, and the tank car at their respective industries on the stub-ended siding. The two cars happen to be next to each other in the illustrations, but there could just as well be one or two or more cars (like the boxcar) between the locomotive and the car that is to be switched or "spotted" on the siding. The fact that the two cars are coupled together should be no accident; the yard crew that assembled the train should have put cars for the same town together in what is (also) called a "block". The locomotive then moves forward with the three cars until the wheels of the covered hopper clear the points of the turnout. The locomotive stops while the brakeman throws the turnout from the main line to the siding. The locomotive then reverses to shove the cars into the siding and stops while the covered hopper is uncoupled, then moves forward with the tank car and waits while the tank car is uncoupled, then proceeds forward with the boxcar past the freight station (Figure 18-2). The locomotive pulls forward again until it (or the boxcar) clears the turnout points at the right, where it will stop, while the brakeman moves the turnout from the siding position to the main-line alignment. The locomotive reverses

until it gently couples back to the remainder of the train (Figure 18-3). Then it stops while the brakeman sets the couplers and connects the air hoses. The train then moves forward to its next destination. Each time the train starts and stops is counted as a "move"; the fewer the moves in a complex switching situation, the quicker the time.

Most of the sequence for switching the car into the siding would, of course, be reversed if a car was already on the siding waiting to be added to the train. When you become proficient at switching maneuvers, you may want to set up situations where two or three cars need to be moved in or out of any given siding. The long industrial siding at Alliance on the 6-by-6-foot Union Pacific layout in Chapter 3, with the four industries marked AB, AC, AD and AX (Figure 3-4), has only room at the entrance siding (AE) for a single car and locomotive. That means that if an empty hopper is consigned to the Consolidated Edison generating plant (at AX) to be loaded with coke, all the cars along that siding must be pulled, one at a time, before the hopper can be positioned. The moves are even more complicated if there are freight cars sitting at the industries marked AA and AE that must be moved just to gain access to the siding with AB, AC, AD an AX. To make the operations a bit more efficient, it would be best to wait until there is more than one car consigned to some industry on that siding or that one or more cars are waiting to be shipped.

"Run-Around" or "Facing-Point" Moves

The switching moves are more complex when the siding is facing the direction in which the train is traveling. In the old days, the train crews would make such a move with a "flying

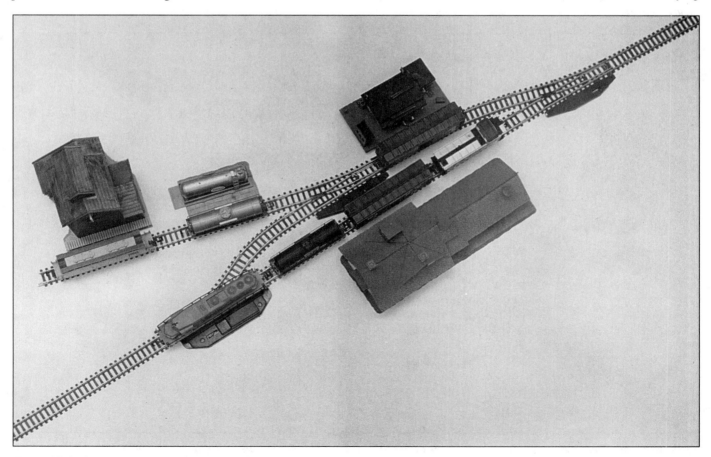

Figure 18-4. The train is now traveling from right to left, so switching the stub-ended siding requires "facing point" switching moves.

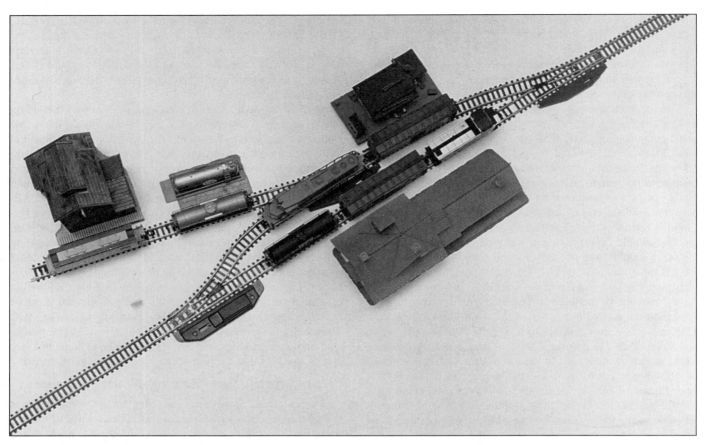

Figure 18-5. The locomotive backs up, couples onto the boxcar, then continues until it clears the switch points to the siding on the far right.

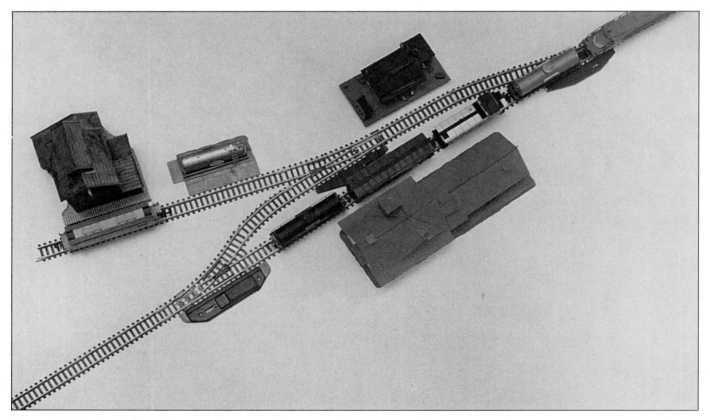

Figure 18-6. The locomotive picks up the aluminum tank car, reverses to clear the switch points on the right, then couples the tank car onto the caboose.

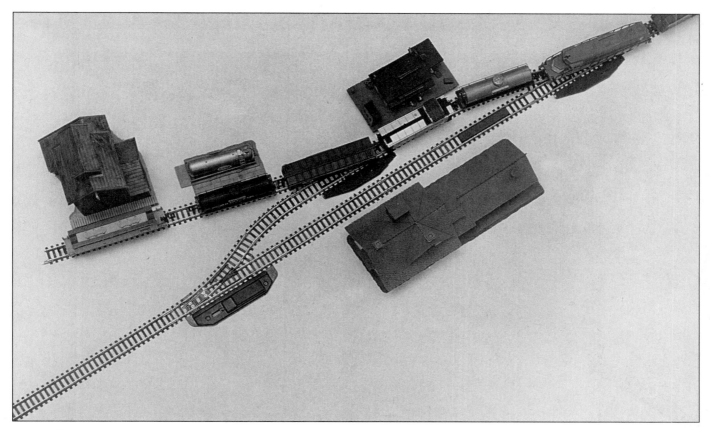

Figure 18-7. *The locomotive reverses with the entire train until the black tank car clears the switch points at the right, then it pushes the train forward to spot the tank car at the oil dealer.*

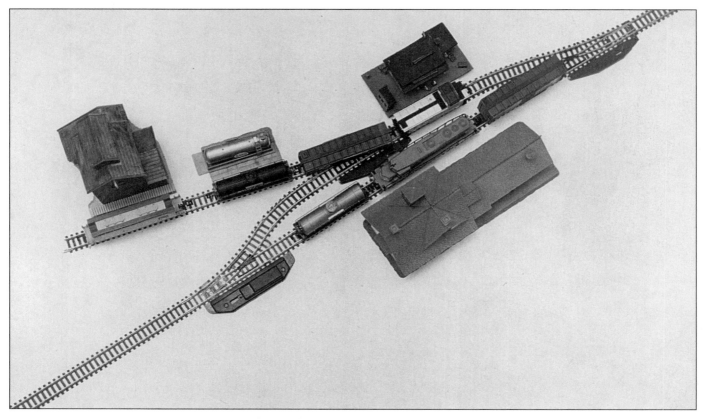

Figure 18-8. *The caboose and the second boxcar are left on the siding while the locomotive reverses, then pulls forward to leave the aluminum tank car on the mainline.*

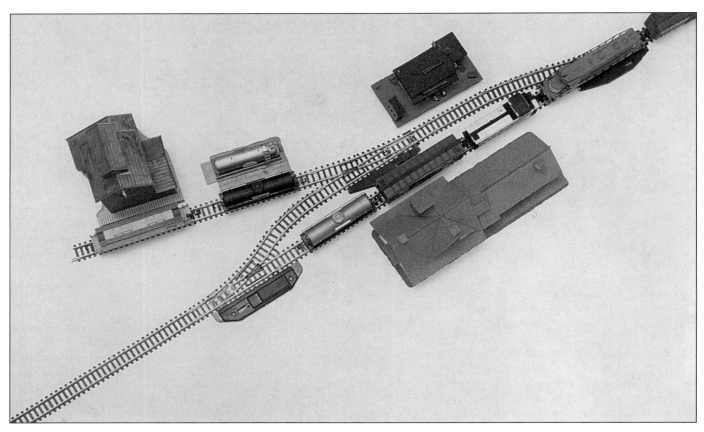

Figure 18-9. The locomotive reverses, then pulls forward to pick up the caboose and the second boxcar to pull them back through the right turnout and push them onto the mainline to couple the second boxcar to the aluminum tank car.

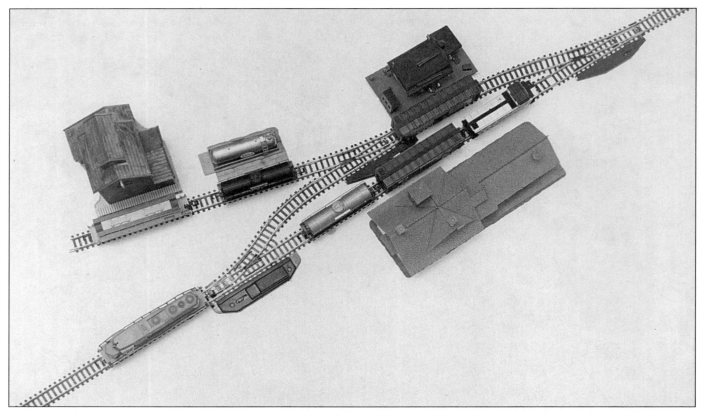

Figure 18-10. The locomotive reverses, then pulls the first boxcar back into its spot at the freight house, uncouples, and proceeds forward to clear the left turnout. It then backs up to couple onto the train and proceeds, from right to left, to the next town.

switch." This means running the locomotive forward past the switch, throwing the switch just as the locomotive clears it (but while the train is still moving), and uncoupling the car so it will roll on into the siding. That's no longer "legal" on real railroads, and it's impossible to do on a model railroad because there's no way to uncouple while the train is still in motion. The only way to get that car into or out of a "facing-point siding" is to "run around" the car at the nearest passing siding. A passing siding is generally considered to be a siding that has a switch at both ends, although a train can back into a stub-ended siding (and they often do) to wait while another train passes by. The siding with a switch at both ends is needed so the locomotive can literally run around its train to couple onto the back of it.

The sequence of the "run-around" moves in Figures 18-4 through 18-10 shows the essential train movements that are used to pick up the empty aluminum-colored tank car and replace it with the loaded black tank car that is in the train. The moves are complicated by the fact that a boxcar is resting on the passing siding that must be used for the locomotive to "run-around" the train. The illustrations skip one or two of the obvious start-stop moves.

First, the locomotive stops and uncouples from the train (Figure 18-4). The locomotive pulls forward to clear the points of the turnout, then backs up, and couples to the boxcar (Figure 18-5) being loaded at the freight house. It then proceeds backward, pushing the boxcar through the opposite end of the siding, and stops when the locomotive clears the turnout points on the siding. The locomotive then moves forward to couple onto the silver tank to pull it backwards through the far right turnout. The locomotive then pushes the tank car forward to couple to the caboose at the rear of the train (Figure 18-6), and pulls the entire string of cars backward until the black tank car clears the switch points to the right. The locomotive then pushes the train into the siding to position the black tank car at the oil dealer (Figure 18-7). The locomotive uncouples the boxcar

from the black tank car, then leaves the caboose and the boxcar on the siding and backs up to clear the turnout's points to the right. It then pulls forward to leave the aluminum tank car on the main line (Figure 18-8). The locomotive uncouples from the aluminum tank car, then reverses to clear the turnout points to the right and moves forward to pickup the caboose and boxcar. It pulls them back until the boxcar clears the turnout points and pushes them forward to couple boxcar with the aluminum tank car (Figure 18-9). The locomotive uncouples from the caboose, backs up to clear the turnout points, then pulls through the siding, stopping long enough to leave the first boxcar at its original position in front of the freight station. The locomotive then proceeds forward to clear the turnout points to the left (Figure 18-10). Finally the locomotive backs up to couple onto the aluminum tank car and proceeds on down the mainline to the left. You can understand, from studying these moves and from trying them on a section of your own railroad, how complicated even this basic switching situation can be.

You will notice that there is at least one passing siding (which, when switching, serves as a "runaround track") on nearly every layout plan in this book, as well as one or two stub-ended sidings. Both types of track configurations are needed if you want to operate your layout like the real thing. Even the simplest of layouts should have at least four turnouts to provide a passing siding and two stub-end sidings. Position those turnouts for the stub-end sidings so that one will be a "facing point" when the other is a "trailing point." This will provide the maximum amount of operating action.

Wye-Switching Operations

The wye that is shared by switch crews in "Alliance" and for reversing trains for holdover at "Points East" on the 6-by-6-foot Union Pacific layout (Figures 3-5 and 3-6) and the 8-by-11 version (Figure 3-13) are examples of the type of double-duty that track-

Figure 18-11. A stub-ended wye with the locomotive on the mainline leg of the wye, the boxcar on the "reversing" leg of the wye and the curved "branchline" leg of the wye open.

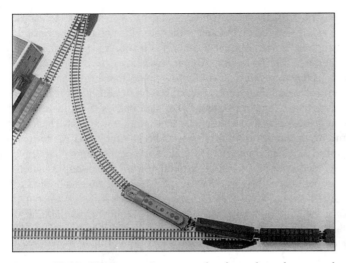

Figure 18-12. The locomotive uncouples from the caboose and proceeds up the "branchline" leg of the wye.

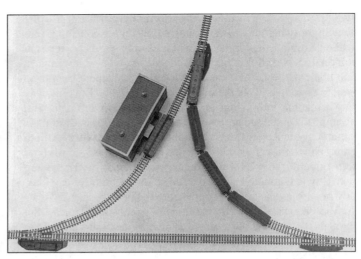

Figure 18-13. The locomotive uncouples from the three cars and proceeds up the stub end of the wye.

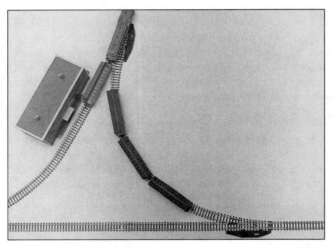

Figure 18-14. The locomotive backs down the "reversing" leg of the wye and couples onto the boxcar.

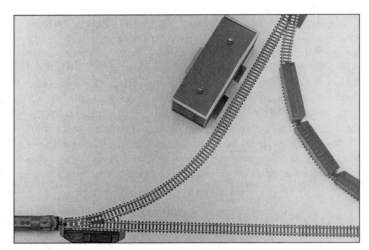

Figure 18-15. The locomotive backs on down the reversing leg of the wye and onto the mainline with the boxcar.

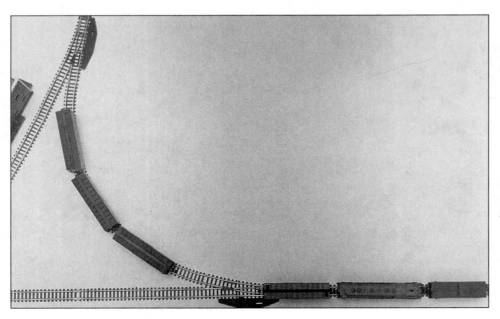

Figure 18-16. The locomotive and boxcar pull forward on the mainline to couple onto the caboose.

work must do on a typical model railroad. The situation is often seen in the tight trackage in older industrial areas and yards on the real railroads, so the problems are as real as any you'll duplicate on your model railroad. The reversing sequence for turning trains (or just for turning locomotives or cabooses, when the stub end of the wye is short) is simple enough. Use the track in front of the Alliance Station ("SA" in Figure 3-4) as the wye track, on any of the three layouts in Chapter 3, leaving the track at the freight station clear for serving the freight station or for run-around moves. The leg of the wye occupied by the boxcar in the following sequence of photographs is the same leg of the wye occupied by the intermodal yard "PT" in Figure 3-4.

The reversing operation through the wye begins as the train moves forward from right to left along the "branch" leg of the wye (Figure 18-12), leaving the caboose behind. Only the locomotive is to be reversed in this series of moves, but the series is complicated by the boxcar on the reversing leg of the wye that is supposed to be picked up and added to the train. The locomotive continues forward with three cars, then stops to uncouple from the first car (Figure 18-13). The locomotive then proceeds on into the stub end of the wye until it clears the switch points. The locomotive now reverses and proceeds down the reversing leg of the wye to couple onto the boxcar (Figure 18-14). The locomotive backs the boxcar out onto the mainline (Figure 18-15) until the locomotive clears the switch points to the left. The locomotive now proceeds forward in the opposite direction it started (Figure 18-16). The locomotive couples to the caboose and backs down the mainline, through the turnout to the left, then pushes the caboose up the "reversing" leg of the wye and uncouples from the caboose, leaving the caboose on the stub end of the wye. The locomotive and box car back down the reversing leg of the wye and out onto the mainline, then the locomotive proceeds forward (from left to right) with the boxcar (Figure 18-17) until the boxcar clears the switch points at the right. The locomotive and boxcar then reverse to, first, couple onto the three cars, then to couple onto the caboose. Finally, the complete train now proceeds forward (Figure 18-18) and out onto the mainline in the opposite direction (this time, with one more car in the train) from when it began this series of reversing moves.

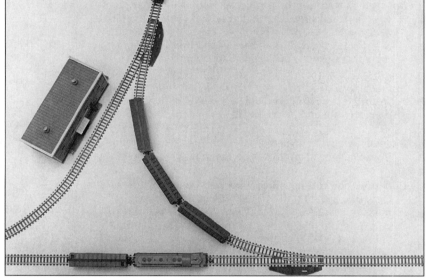

Figure 18-17. The caboose is pulled backwards along the mainline, then pushed forward up the reversing leg of the wye and spotted (barely visible) on the stub end of the wye.

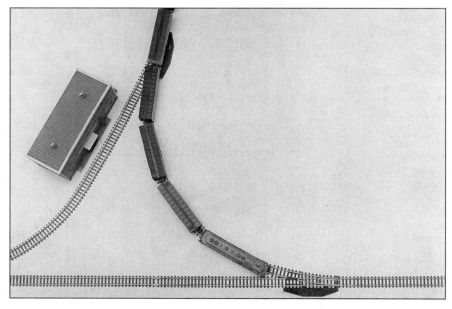

Figure 18-18. The locomotive and boxcar back down the reversing leg of the wye, proceed forward along the mainline, then reverse again to couple first to the three cars, then to the caboose. The train now proceeds forward, traveling in the opposite direction (from left to right) that it started in Figure 18-12.

Glossary

AAR: The full-size railroads' trade group, the Association of American Railroads, that establishes their standards for equipment and safety.

Articulated: A steam locomotive with two separate sets of drivers, rods, and cylinders beneath a single boiler. Usually one set of drivers, rods, and cylinders is pivoted so it can swing from side-to-side around curves while the boiler remains rigidly attached to the rear set of drivers, rods, and cylinders.

Bad order: The term the real railroads use to describe a malfunctioning part.

Big Hook: The wrecking crane.

Block: A section of track that is electrically isolated from the adjoining sections for multiple-train operation or to prevent short circuits.

Bolster: The portion of a railroad freight or passenger car that runs across the underbody of the car to connect the trucks' pivot points to the body of the car. Sometimes used to describe all the cross members, including the ends, of a car's underframe.

Branch: A portion of a real railroad that branches off from the main line to reach a town or industry or to connect with another railroad.

Bumper: A device placed at the stub end of a track siding so cars or locomotives do not derail.

Caboose: The rolling office and living quarters for the crew of a freight train. Usually identifiable by a small box with windows on the roof (called a cupola) or one on each side (called bay windows) so the crew can see the length of the train from inside. Sometimes called crummy, bobber, or way car.

Catenary: Overhead trolley wires, usually used by prototype interurbans (electric-powered locomotives and self-propelled cars) with diamond-shaped current pick up devices on the roofs called pantographs.

Coaling station: Any building where coal for steam locomotives is stored and shoveled or dumped through chutes into the locomotives' tenders. When the storage bins are elevated and the coal hoisted by conveyor belts or buckets, the structure is usually called a coaling tower. When the elevated storage bins are reached by a trestle so the coal can be dumped from the cars or shoveled right into the storage bins, the structure is usually called a coaling trestle.

Crossing: When two tracks cross each other, as in the center of a one-level figure-eight-style model railroad.

Crossover: The pair of turnouts that allows trains to travel from one parallel track to the adjacent one on double-track systems.

Cut: When the railroad has to dig or blast through a hill or mountain to maintain a level roadbed. Also, a few cars coupled together.

DCC: Short for Digital Command Control. A system for controlling model locomotives that sends a signal through the track to a decoder in the locomotive to instruct the locomotive to go forward or backward, to change its speed or to stop or go. With the least-expensive systems, a non-equipped standard locomotive and up to nine more locomotives (each equipped with a decoder) can be controlled independently on the same track. More expensive systems can control over 200 locomotives as well as activate sound systems and operate turnouts.

D.P.D.T.: An electrical slide or toggle-type switch that is used for reversing the flow of current to the tracks by wiring across the back of the switch. Some types have an "off" position midway in their throw and these "Center-off D.P.D.T." switches are often used for wiring model railroads to allow two-train and two-throttle operation.

Draft gear: The box under the ends of a prototype car or locomotive (and on most models) where the coupler is spring-mounted to center it and to help absorb shocks and bumps.

Fiddle yard: A hidden track or series of tracks used by modelers to make up or break down trains, lifting the equipment by hand.

Fill: When the prototype railroad has to haul dirt to fill in a valley with an embankment to bring the roadbed level up to that of the nearest trackage.

Flange: The portion of any railroad wheel that guides that wheel down the rails. The flange extends around the circumference of each railroad wheel as its largest diameter.

Frog: The point where the track rails actually cross at every turnout and rail/rail crossing.

Gap: A break in the rails to electrically isolate some portion of the track from another to prevent short circuits or to allow for multiple-train operation on the same stretch of track.

Gauge: The spacing of the rails as measured from the inside of one railhead to the next. The "standard gauge" for most American railroads is 4 feet 8-1/2 inches; this distance was also once the standard center-to-center spacing for horse-drawn wagon wheels.

Grade: The angled rise or fall of the track so it can pass over another track or so it can follow the rising or falling contour of the land.

Grab iron: The steel hand rails on the sides, ends, and roofs of rolling stock.

Head-end cars: The cars that are normally coupled to the front of a passenger train, including express refrigerator, baggage, and mail cars.

Helper: The locomotive that is added to a train to supply extra power that may be needed to surmount a steep grade.

Hostler: Men who service and sometimes move locomotives from one servicing facility to another to prepare the locomotive for the engineer.

Hotbox: A bearing that has become overheated from lack of lubrication.

Interchange: A section of track or several tracks where one railroad connects with another so trains or individual cars can move from one railroad to the next.

Interlocking: A system of mechanical or electrical controls so only one train at a time can move through a junction of two or more tracks like a crossing or yard throat.

Intermodal: The transportation concept of using railroads, trucks and/or ships to carry the same container or trailer from its shipper to its destination without having to unload and reload along the way. If the railroads are carrying just trailers, some refer to it as "piggyback" service.

Interurban: Prototype railroads and railroad cars that were self-propelled with electrical power pick-up from an overhead wire, catenary, or from a third rail suspended alongside the track. The cars ran from city-to-city as well as inside the city limits and hence the name. (See also trolley and traction.)

Journal: The bearing that supports the load on the end of a railroad car or locomotive axle.

Kingpin: The pivot point for a freight or passenger car truck where it connects to the bolster.

Kit-bash: To combine parts from two or more kits to produce a model different from both. Sometimes called cross-kitting, customizing, or converting. The process is also a kit-conversion.

LCL: Less-than-carload lot; freight shipments that are too small to require an entire car.

Main line: The most heavily trafficked routes of the railroad.

Maintenance-of-way: The rolling stock or structures that are directly associated with maintaining the railroad or with repairing and righting wrecked trains.

Narrow gauge: Railroads that were built with their rails spaced closer than the 4-feet 8 1/2-inch standard gauge. Two-foot and three-foot spacings between the railheads were the most common in this country, particularly in the 1880-1900 period.

Pedlar freight: A freight train that switches cars at most towns along its route from terminal to terminal. Also called a way freight.

Piggyback: The modern railroads' special flatcar service to transport highway trailers. Sometimes called TOFC. Also see "intermodal."

Points: The portions of a turnout that move to change the track's route from the main line to a siding. The point where the rails actually cross is called the "frog" part of the switch.

Prototype: The term used to describe the full-size version that any model is supposed to duplicate.

Pullman: The passenger cars that were owned and operated by the Pullman company, usually sleeping cars, diners, or parlor cars. Sometimes used to describe any sleeping car.

Rail joiner: The pieces of metal that join two lengths of rail together. They slide onto the ends of the rail on a model railroad; they are bolted to the rails on the prototype.

Reefer: The insulated cars, cooled by either ice in bunkers fed through hatches on the roof or, in modern times, by mechanical refrigeration units.

Right of way: The property and the track owned by the railroad.

r-t-r: Abbreviation for ready-to-run that also includes the simple snap-together and glue-together plastic kits. Some of the brands included are: Accurail, Athearn, Atlas, Bachmann, Con-Cor, E & C Shops, IHC, Life-Like, Model Die Casting, Model Power, Rivarossi and Walthers. Some of the more complex InterMountain kits are also available assembled or r-t-r.

Snowshed: The protective buildings that cover the track, usually in mountain areas, so deep snow and drifts won' t cover the tracks themselves.

Spot: The switching maneuver whereby a freight or passenger car is moved to the desired position on the track, usually beside some industry's loading platform.

Superelevation: Banking the tracks in a curve so the trains can travel at some designated speed with a minimum of load on the outer wheels and rails and with a minimum of sway.

Switch: Usually used to refer to the portion of the railroad track that allows the trains to change routes, but also used for electrical switches on model railroads, such as D.P.D.T. or S.P.S.T. switches. Track switches are often called "turnouts" to avoid this confusion.

Switch machine: The electrical solenoid-type devices that move the track switch from one route to another to allow remote-controlled operation of trains over diverging trackage.

Switch points: The moving portion of a turnout that changes the route. Also called turnout points.

Talgo: Model railroad trucks with the couplers mounted to them so the couplers swivel with the trucks to allow operation of longer cars on tighter radius curves. Talgo trucks can, however, cause derailments when pushing or backing a long train.

Tangent: Straight sections of trackage.

Tank engine: A steam locomotive without a tender where the coal or fuel oil is carried in a bunker behind the cab and the water in a tank over the top of the boiler. Often used for switching on the prototype and on model railroads.

Tender: The car just behind most steam locomotives that carries the water, coal, wood, or fuel oil.

Throat: The point where the yard trackage begins to diverge into the multiple tracks for storage and switching.

Timetable: A schedule, usually printed, to tell railroad employees and customers when trains are scheduled to be at certain stations or points on the railroad.

Traction: The term used to describe all prototype locomotives and self-powered cars like trolleys and interurbans that operate by electrical power.

Transistor throttle: An electrical speed control for model railroad layouts that is used in place of the older wire-wound rheostat to provide infinitely better and smoother slow speed and starting control for locomotives.

Transition curve: A length of track where any curve joins a tangent with gradually diminishing radius to ease the sudden transition of straight-to-curve for smoother operation and to help prevent derailments of extra-length cars that are caused by coupler bind in such areas of trackage. Also called an easement.

Turnout: Where two diverging tracks join; also called a switch. The moving parts that divert the trains from the straight to the curved-path are called "turnout points" or "switch points."

Trolley: Self-propelled, electric-powered cars that ran almost exclusively in city streets as opposed to the interurbans that ran through the country between cities and towns.

Truck: The sprung frame and four (or more) wheels under each end of most railroad freight and passenger cars.

Turntable: A rotating steel or wooden bridge to turn locomotives or cars and/or to position them to align with the tracks in the engine house or round house.

Vestibule: The enclosed area, usually in both ends of a passenger car, where patrons enter the car from the station platform and where they walk to move from one car to the next.

Way freight: See Pedlar freight.

Wye: A track switch where both diverging routes curve away in opposite directions from the single straight track. Also, the triangular-shaped track (in plain view) where trains can be reversed.

Sources Of Supply

The majority of the manufacturers of toy trains and accessories sell only through hobby dealers. The best use for this list, then, is to provide your hobby dealer with an address to contact to order the items you need. Some of the manufacturers and importers offer catalogs but there is usually a charge. If you do contact any of these importers or manufacturers, always include a stamped, self-addressed envelope if you expect a reply. You can ask for the price and availability of catalogs or price sheets, but expect to pay from $3.00 to $15.00 for each catalog.

AMI
Box 11861
Clayton, MO 63105

AMSI (Architectural Model Supplies, Inc.)
P.O. Box 750638
Petaluma, CA 94975

Accurail
Box 278
Ellburn, IL 60119-1202

Accurate Dimensionals
4185 So. Fox St.
Englewood, CO 80110-4564

American Limited Models
P.O. Box 7803
Fremont, CA 94537-7803

American Model Builders
1408 Hanley Industrial Court
Saint Louis, MO 63144

Aristo-Craft
346 Bergen Avenue
Jersey City, NJ 07034

Athabasca Scale Models
771 Wilkinson Way
Sassskatoon, SK S7N 3L8
Canada

Atlas
603 Sweetland Ave.
Hillside, NJ 07205

Avalon Concepts
1055 Leisz's Bridge Rd.
Leesport, PA 19533

Aztec
2701 Conestoga Dr.
Carson City, NV 89706

Bachmann Industries
1400 E. Erie Ave.
Philadelphia, PA 19124

Badger Air-Brush Co.
9128 Belmont Ave.
Franklin Park, IL 60131

Blair Line
P.O. Box 2291
Lee's Summit, MO 64063

Bowser Manufacturing Co.
Box 322
Montoursville, PA 17754

Builders in Scale (Switchmaster)
Box 460025
Aurora, CO 80046-0025

CDS Lettering Limited
P.O. Box 2003, Station "D"
Ottawa, Ontario KIP 5W3
Canada

C in C
8090 University Dr. NE
Firdley, MN 55432

Caboose Industries
1861 Ridge Dr.
Freeport, IL 61032-3637

Cal Scale (see Bowser)

Centerline Products
18409 Harmony Rd.
Maraengo, IL 601152

Centralia Car Shops
1468 Lee St.
Des Plaines, IL 60018

Champ Decals
Division Champion Decal Co.
P.O. Box 1178
Minot, ND 58702

Chooch Enterprises
Box 217
Redmond, WA 98052

Circuitron
211 RocBaar Drive
Romeoville, IL 60446

Clover House
P.O. Box 62
Sebastopol, CA 95473

Con-Cor International
8101 E. Research Court
Tucson, AZ 85710

DeLuxe Innovations
P.O. Box 4213
Burbank, CA 91503-4213

Detail Associates
Box 5537
San Luis Obispo, CA 93403

Digitrax, Inc.
450 Cemetery St., #206
Norcross, GA 30071

Dimi-Trains
P.O. Box 70310
Reno, NV 89570-0310

E-R Model Importers, Inc.
1000 So. Main St.
Newark, NY 14513

Easy Scene (see Accurail)

Earl Eshleman (see Ye Olde Huff n' Puff)

Evergreen Scale Models
18620-F 141st Ave. NE
Woodinville, WA 98072

F & H Enterprises
2562 Silver State parkway
Building C, Suite 3
Minden, NV 89423

Fine N-Scale Products
Box 287
San Pedro, CA 90731

Floquil-Polly S (see Testors)

GHQ
28100 Woodside Road
Shorewood, MN 55331

Gloorcraft (see Walthers)

Gold Medal Models
Route 2, Box 3104
Lopez, WA 98261

Grandt Line Products, Inc.
1040 B Shary Court
Concord, CA 94518

Hallmark Models
4822 Bryan
Dallas, TX 75204

Heiki (see E-R Models, Portman, or
Walthers)

InterMountain Railway
Box 839
Longmont, CO 80501

JnJ Trains
P.O. Nox 1535
Ottumwa, IA 52501

Kadee Quality Products
673 Avenue C
White City, OR 97503-1078

Kato USA
100 Remington Rd.
Schaumberg, IL 60173

Key Imports
P.O. Box 1848
Rogue River, OR 97537

Kibri (see E-R Models, Portman, or
Walthers)

Lenz Agency of North America
Box 143
Chelmsford, MA 01824

Life-Like Products
1600 Union Ave.
Baltimore, MD 21211-1998

MRC (Model Rectifier Corp.)
Box 6312
Edison, NJ 08818-6312

Micro Engineering Company
1120 Eagle Road
Fenton, MO 63026

Microscale Industries
18435 Bandilier Cr.
Fountain Valley, CA 92708

Micro-Trains
Box 1200
Talent, OR 97540-1200

Miniatures by Eric
RR #1
Busby, Alberta T0G 0H0
Canada

Model Die Casting (MDC)(see
Roundhouse)

Model Power
180 Smith St.
Farmingdale, NY 11735

Modelflex (see Badger)

Mountains-In-Minutes
I.S.L.E. Laboratories
Box 663
Sylvania, OH 43560

NJ International
230 W. Old Country Rd.
Hicksville, NY 11801

Noch (see E-R Models, Portman, or
Walthers)

Model Expo
Box 221220
Hollywood, FL 33022

Model Rectifier Corp. (MRC)
80 Newfield Ave.
Edison, NJ 08818-6312

Northeastern Scale Models, Inc.
P.O. Box 727
Methuen, MA 01844

Northeast Decals
P.O. box 324
Deerfield, MA 01342

North West Short Line
P.O. Box 423
Seattle, WA 98111

Overland Models, Inc.
3808 W. Kilgore Ave.
Muncie, IN 47304

NJ International
Box 99
East Norwich, NY 11732

P-B-L
Box 769
Ukiah, CA 95482

PSI (Dynatrol)
56 Bellis Cr.
Cambridge, MA 02140-3296

Peco (see F & H or Walthers)

Period Miniatures
Box 1421
Golden, CO 80402-1421

Plastruct
1020 So. Wallace Dr.
City of Industry, CA 91748

Plano Model Products
2701 W. 15th St.
Plano, TX 75075

Polly Scale (see Testors)

Pola GmbH
Am Bahndamm 59
D-8734 Rothhausen
West Germany

Portman Hobby Distributors
851 Washington St., Box 2551
Peeksill, NY 10566

Precision Scale
3961 Highway 93 North
Stevensville, MT 59870

Precision Masters (see Red Caboose)

Preiser (see E-R Models or Walthers)

PSI (Power Systems, Inc.)
56 Bellis Circle
Cambridge, MA 02140

Red Caboose
Box 250
Mead, CO 80542

Rapido (see E-R Models or Walthers)

Rivarossi (see Model Expo and Con-
Cor)

Rix Products
3747 Hogue Rd.
Evansville, IN 47712

Roco (see E-R Models or Walthers)

Roundhouse (MDC)
5070 Sigstrom Dr.
Carson City, NV 89706

SMP Industries
Box 72
Bolton, MA 01740

Scalecoat
Box 231
Northumberland, PA 17857

Scenic Express
1001 Lowry Ave.
Jeannette, PA 15644-2671

Shinohara (see Walthers)

Showcase Miniatures

P.O. Box 753
Cherry Valley, CA 92223

Signs Galore
109 Saligugi Way
Loudon, TN 37774

Sunrise Enterprises
P.O. Box 172
Doyle, CA 96109

Switchmaster (see Builders in Scale)

Testor Corporation
620 Buckbee St.
Rockford, IL 61104

Tortoise (see Circuitron)

Wm. K. Walthers, Inc.
5601 W. Florist Ave.
Milwaukee, WI 53201-0770

Wiking (see E-R Models or Walthers)

Woodland Scenics
101 E. Valley Dr., Box 98
Linn Creek, MO 65052

Ye Olde Huf n' Puff
Rear 606 Knepp Ave.
Lewistown, PA 17044-1651

Clubs

NTRAK, Inc
1150 Wine Country Pl.
Templeton, CA 93465

National Model Railroad Association
4121 Cromwell Rd.
Chatanooga, TN 37421

Publications

Model Railroader
P.O. Box 1612
Waukesha, WI 53187-1612
Largest model railroad magazine with
some N scale and many ads. Sample
copy $4.50

NTRAK
1150 Wine Country Place
Templeton, CA 93465
Bimonthly Newsletter $8.00 per year,
and booklets on N scale

N Scale
13100 Beverly Park Rd.
Mukilteo, WA 98275
Bi-Monthly magazine featuring typical layouts and techniques. Sample
copy $4.95

Railmodel Journal
2403 Champa St.
Denver, CO 80205
Monthly magazine with regular N
scale articles, focuses on accurate and
realistic models and layouts. Sample
copy $4.95.

Figure 3-14. Al Mack is modeling the Southern Pacific railroad's operations from Mojave to Bakersfield, California. This is his much-reduced recreation of the famous Tehachapi Loop.

Index

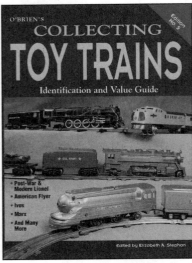
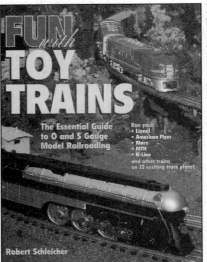
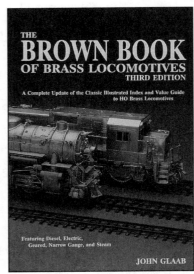